Rethinking the Soviet Collapse

'An important and intriguing collection of essays by some of the finest scholars working in the field. Always lively, often provocative, this book provides contrasting explanations for the demise of the Soviet system and the success or failure of Western academics to predict it. Quite simply, the best collection so far produced on the end of the Soviet Union and the fate of Sovietology.'

Caroline Kennedy-Pipe, University of Durham

———

'This richly diverse collection of essays by Soviet Studies luminaries from both sides of the Atlantic should be studied by all social scientists, foreign policy practitioners and economic advisers (including those employed by the international financial institutions). Apart from offering a series of honest, thoughtful and serious critical analyses of the failures – and the oft-forgotten successes – of past Soviet Studies, it warns against the naïve fallacy that post-socialist Russia can be moulded by advisers and crusaders into their own ideological image of a democratic neo-liberal economy. Statutory reading.'

Margot Light, The London School of Economics

———

'Why did the experts in the field of Soviet Studies fail to anticipate the death of Soviet communism? Now, at long last, a study that confronts and seeks to answer this difficult and still sensitive question. In this superb new book Michael Cox has brought together leading specialists from both sides of the Atlantic. Together they provide the most comprehensive analysis to date of the evolution and final demise of Sovietology as a complex academic discipline. Its ideological assumptions, its links (at times close) with the world of policy-making and its relationship with the irregular rhythms of the Cold War are all laid bare. This most important book is certain to provoke a debate – one that should have taken place a long time ago – about Soviet Studies as an intellectual endeavour. Essential reading for specialist and student alike.'

Dr Peter Shearman, University of Melbourne

Rethinking the Soviet Collapse

Sovietology, the Death of Communism and the New Russia

Edited by

Michael Cox

London and New York

Pinter
A Cassell imprint
Wellington House, 125 Strand, London WC2R 0BB
370 Lexington Avenue, New York, NY 10017-6550

First published 1998

© Michael Cox and the contributors 1998

British Library Cataloguing-in-Publication Data
A catalogue record for this book is available from the British Library.

ISBN 1-85567-321-5 (hardback)
1-85567-322-3 (paperback)

Library of Congress Cataloguing-in-Publication Data
Rethinking the Soviet collapse: Sovietology, the death of communism and
the new Russia / edited by Michael Cox.
    p. cm.
Includes bibliographical references and index.
ISBN 1-85567-321-5. — ISBN 1-85567-322-3 (pbk.)
1. Soviet Union—Historiography.   2. Soviet Union—Study and
teaching.   3. Soviet Union—Politics and government.   4. Russia
(Federation)—Politics and government—1991-   I. Cox, Michael.
DK266.A33R48   1999
947'.0072—dc21   98-30260
                                                            CIP

Typeset by BookEns Ltd., Royston, Herts.
Printed and bound in Great Britain by Biddles Ltd, Guildford and King's Lynn.

Contents

The Contributors

Michael Cox is Professor in International Politics at the University of Wales, Aberystwyth, Associate Research Fellow at the Royal Institute of International Affairs and editor of the *Review of International Studies*. His books include *Superpowers at the Crossroads? US Foreign Policy after the Cold War: Superpower Without a Mission?* (with Hillel Ticktin) (eds), *The Ideas of Leon Trotsky,* and *E.H. Carr: A Critical Reassessment.* He is currently completing a study on theories of the Cold War for Cambridge University Press.

Robert Arnot is Principal Lecturer in Economics at the Caledonian University, Glasgow and has written extensively on labour in the former USSR and in Russia. His most important study to date, *Controlling Soviet Labour,* was published in 1988. He is currently writing a volume on the Soviet system in disintegration from 1985 to 1998, to be published by Macmillan.

Stephen F. Cohen is Professor of Russian Studies and History at New York University and Professor of Politics Emeritus at Princeton University. His books include *Rethinking the Soviet Experience, Sovieticus: American Perceptions and Soviet Realities,* and most recently *Rethinking Russia: The Soviet Experience and its Aftermath.* Cohen also writes and broadcasts widely for the American media.

Robert V. Daniels is Professor Emeritus of History at the University of Vermont. He is author or editor of many books on Soviet history and politics, including *A Documentary History of Communism, The End of the Communist Revolution,* and most recently *Russia's Transformation: Snapshots of a Crumbling System.*

M. Steven Fish is Associate Professor of Political Science at the University of California, Berkeley. He is the author of *Democracy from Scratch: Opposition and Regime in the New Russian Revolution* as well as of articles on regime change, civil society, social movements, elections and economic transformation in the post-communist world.

Ron Hill is Professor of Political Science and Fellow of Trinity College, Dublin. The founding editor of *Irish Slavonic Studies*, his books include *Soviet Politics, Political Science and Reform*, *The Soviet Union: Politics, Economics and Society*, and (with J.A. Dellebrant) *Gorbachev and Perestroika*.

Carl G. Jacobsen is Director of Eurasian Security Studies in the Department of Political Science at Carleton University, Ottawa. The author and editor of many volumes, his most recent publications include *The Soviet Defence Enigma*, *Soviet Foreign Policy: New Dynamics, New Themes*, *Strategic Power: USA/USSR*, and *World Security: the New Challenge*.

David Lane is a Fellow of Emmanuel College, Cambridge. He is author of many books on the USSR, socialism, stratification and political power, including *Politics and Society in the USSR*, *The End of Inequality? Soviet Labour and the Ethics of Communism*, *Soviet Society Under Perestroika*, and *The Rise and Fall of State Socialism*.

Terry McNeill teaches in the Department of Politics at the University of Hull. A regular writer on Soviet and post-Soviet affairs and major contributor to many volumes including *The Soviet Union and the Challenge of the Future: The Soviet System – Stasis and Change*, and *The Cost of Peace: Assessing Europe's Security Options*.

Peter Rutland is Professor of Politics in the Department of Government at Wesleyan University, Connecticut. He has written two studies on Soviet political economy: *The Myth of the Plan* and *The Politics of Economic Stagnation*. Between 1995 and 1997 he worked as Head of the Russian section at the Radio Free Europe/Radio Liberty Research Institute in Prague. Currently he edits an annual survey of political events in the former socialist countries and is now writing on the Soviet oil industry.

Richard Sakwa is Professor of Russian and European Politics at the University of Kent at Canterbury. His books include *Soviet Communists in Power: A Study of Moscow During the Civil War – 1918–1921*, *Soviet Politics*, *Gorbachev and his Reforms: 1985–90*, and *Russian Politics and Society*.

Vladimir Shlapentokh is Professor in the Department of Sociology at Michigan State University and specializes in the study of public opinion, ideology, values and politics in the former socialist countries.

Hillel Ticktin teaches political economy in the University of Glasgow where he is also Head of the Centre for the Study of Socialist Theories and Movements. Founding editor of the journal *Critique*, he is also author, editor and co-editor of many books including *Il Compromesso Sovietico: Planlose Wirtschaft, Origins of the Crisis in the USSR, The Politics of Race Discrimination in South Africa*, and (with Bertell Ollman *et al.*) *Market Socialism: the Debate among Socialists*.

Mike Urban is Professor of Politics at the University of California, Santa Cruz. His research has focused on issues of identity, power and culture in Russian politics. Amongst his published works are *The Rebirth of Politics in Russia, More Power to the Soviets*, and *An Algebra of Soviet Power*.

Stephen White is Professor of Politics at the University of Glasgow. A former President of the British Association for Slavic and East European Studies, he is the author and editor of several books including *After Gorbachev, Russia Goes Dry, The Politics of Transition, Developments in Russian and Post-Soviet Politics*, and (with Richard Rose and Ian McAllister) *How Russia Votes*.

Acknowledgements

This book has been a long time in the making and over the past three years or so I have accumulated numerous debts: to John Gaddis for having raised the difficult and yet unanswered question about why the experts failed to predict the end of the Cold War; to Michael Ellman for hosting a seminar in Amsterdam where I first raised some of the issues outlined here; to Stephen White, who published my first assault on the Sovietological profession; to those many members of the profession who responded so generously and intelligently to my critique; to the UK Political Studies Association for hosting two round tables on the subject of this book; and last but not least to the contributors to this volume who have been patient beyond the call of duty. I hope the wait was worthwhile. On a less embarrassing note, I would also like to thank Steve Smith, head of the Department of International Politics in Aberystwyth. His vision has helped establish a truly exciting department in west Wales where work on this book was completed. Within the department I would also like to thank Pauline Ewan, Elaine Lowe and Elizabeth Weber. Together they helped turn a set of essays into a polished manuscript. My gratitude as well goes out to Nikola Vinnikka and Petra Recter, both previously at Pinter and Cassell; what they began has now been steered home to port with great skill by Sarah Bragginton. Finally, a very special thank you to Fiona Stephen who quite literally managed the manuscript from beginning to end. Without her encouragement and patience, the project might not have been completed. The book is dedicated to her in gratitude and love.

Michael Cox
Aberystwyth, Wales

Introduction

Academic disciplines, it has been observed, 'go through regular bouts of soul-searching', and no discipline has been as subject to as much intellectual dissection over the past few years as Soviet Studies.[1] Indeed, all those connected in one way or another with the analysis of the former Soviet Union have probably experienced some degree of intellectual anguish or doubt since the last remaining European empire came tumbling down in late 1991. Variously accused by their numerous critics before the collapse of the USSR as being either unreconstructed cold warriors who exaggerated the nature of the Soviet threat, or liberal fellow-travellers who turned a blind eye to the system's less pleasant features, they have since the Soviet Union's demise been tried and found guilty of possibly the biggest intellectual sin of all: of actually not understanding the contradictions of communism and thus failing to anticipate the USSR's subsequent disintegration. As one historian of the late Soviet period asked rather plaintively, 'how could we have been so wrong?'[2] Certainly, there has been no shortage of post-mortems on the subject; and in the main the one-time experts have not fared particularly well, in spite of valiant attempts by some of its practitioners to prove that they were not quite as short-sighted as their critics suggest. There are few today, it seems, who would defend the academic record of Soviet Studies, and even fewer perhaps who would respond robustly to the charge recently levelled at them by a famous American editor of an equally famous foreign policy journal, that in spite of its prodigious labours, in the end Sovietology failed to get Russia right.[3]

The charge that Soviet Studies failed to anticipate the collapse of the USSR is one which many academics would dispute, including a number of contributors to this volume. Unfortunately, the response by many practitioners has not been to look back but to avoid any serious discussion of the topic whatsoever. Indeed, amongst most former Sovietologists (though not all) there was and remains a marked reluctance to engage in serious retrospective analysis: partly one suspects out of a desire to protect the historical reputation of the discipline, partly because such a self-examination raises some difficult and embarrassing questions, and partly because many seem to feel that the issue is not an important one.[4] Many scholars, in fact, have simply brushed the whole problem aside, arguing that they cannot be attacked for having failed to foresee the end of the Soviet Union because prediction in a complex world, where we only have imperfect knowledge, is an almost impossible task. Moreover, in their view, to criticize practising academics for not anticipating what happened in the USSR implies there was something inevitable about what happened. But this was not the case. According to many writers indeed other outcomes than Soviet disintegration were just as likely; and if Gorbachev had not emerged when he did – and did what he did – the system could have limped along for a good deal longer.[5] But who, they ask, could have anticipated a Gorbachev or the decisions he took? And if one could foresee neither, then how can students of the former USSR be accused of failing to predict something that need not necessarily have occurred? As Mark Almond has pithily observed, 'what happened' to the Soviet Union 'did not have to be'.[6]

Without doubt, the issue of prediction is a complex one, and it would be a foolish person who suggested otherwise. But to assert that social science should not at least attempt to anticipate future trends is intellectually myopic, not to say disingenuous. After all, we all engage in some form of futurology, even if we don't call it that. However, in the case of Soviet Studies, one gets the distinct impression that far too many academics have tried to hide behind the issue of 'prediction' and its problems as a way of not exploring their own intellectual past. This is neither acceptable nor wise. It is also naïve, and certainly other commentators have not exercised the same intellectual restraint. In fact, and almost as soon as the Soviet system began to unravel in the late 1980s, critical questions started to be asked of those whose job it had been to understand the Soviet Union. The CIA, for instance, became involved very quickly in a heated, and as yet unresolved discussion about its analytical skills.[7] Having for years been accused of exaggerating the Soviet threat, the Agency now came under early fire for having overestimated the size and efficiency of the Soviet economy and hence understating the extent to which the USSR was in trouble.[8] The question has also provoked much political comment, especially from those on the right who since 1991 have used the issue of Soviet collapse to mount a full-scale attack on what they see as the intellectual shortcomings of left-leaning academics. One whole issue of the neo-conservative magazine *The National Interest* was even devoted to uncovering what it termed the 'sins' of the 'scholars'. Though it was nowhere clearly defined what these sins were, the clear implication was that in their rush to move beyond Cold War stereotyping of the Soviet Union, a generation of progressive analysts had failed to expose the basic flaws of the Soviet system. Consequently, they had been unable to predict its later implosion.[9]

The idea that progressives alone might have failed to detect the underlying weaknesses of the Soviet system is obviously absurd. In reality, most conservatives said little or nothing about Soviet frailties either, and instead talked throughout the Cold War about the very real danger which a powerful Soviet Union continued to pose to the 'free world'. But their attack does at least point to the fact that there is more involved in this little spat than just individual reputation. It also illuminates the very real connection that exists between the controversy surrounding Soviet Studies and the ongoing debate about the fall of Soviet communism. Thus far this second discussion has been both intense and vibrant. It also remains unresolved, and after almost ten years the academic jury is still out: with some claiming that Soviet collapse so-called was no collapse at all but simply the unintended consequence of Gorbachev's bungled reforms, others that it was the result of Western pressure, a few that it was the consequence of Soviet imperial overstretch, and still more that it was the inevitable result of a failed economic system.[10] The issue is not just an academic one, of course, but takes us right to the heart of the problem which this book tries to deal with – namely did Soviet Studies get it wrong? After all, if the end of the USSR was not the result of profound flaws in the Soviet system, but the consequence of Gorbachev's failed reforms of the system, the experts can hardly be accused of failing in their intellectual duties. If, on the other hand, it was, then it is perfectly legitimate to ask them why they were unable to detect these flaws and anticipate where they might ultimately lead.

Finally, the issue of how well, or badly, the experts did in anticipating the demise of the Soviet system is related to the discussion about post-Soviet Russia. For scholars of the former Soviet Union, the new times are certainly very exciting ones, and there must be a tendency amongst many of them to just get on with the job. Amongst many of the more brash, one even detects an attitude bordering on the intellectually contemptuous towards those who went before them.[11] But this attempt to draw a line in the sand is questionable to say the least. First, if the experts before 1989 could not fully grasp the nature of the old Soviet system, why should we assume that the new generation will fare any better – especially as many of the new scholars bear more than a passing family resemblance to the old ones!? There is also the important issue of assumptions. A large number of contemporary Western analysts originally assumed that Russia was in transition to something better and higher. But if the history of the former USSR teaches us anything, it is that unquestioned notions about the direction in which societies are supposed to be going can often lead (and have, in the case of Russia, led) to the most fundamental of errors. There is, in addition, the question of 'lessons'. Though one can well understand scholarly impatience, it is hardly unreasonable to ask the new cohort to look once again (and for some for the first time) at the history of Sovietology as a discipline: not just because it is interesting in its own right, or might even have something to teach them, but because genuine intellectual progress only takes place in the context of a critical interaction with the past. Certainly, if the latest batch of 'transitionolgists' do not want to make the same errors as their predecessors, they might well be advised to see where their predecessors went wrong. Many would even insist that until they do, they are doomed to fail again.

The belief that we cannot make sense of the present without first studying our intellectual past, was at least one of the reasons why I became interested in the history of Sovietology: and the discussion here opens with an updated version of a paper I penned some years ago about what I saw then as some of the problems inherent in the discipline. When the piece was originally written and finally published it provoked a good deal of comment.[12] Most of this was friendly and agreed with what I had to say. But a good deal, to be blunt, was quite critical. Clearly, I had touched a very raw nerve. A number of colleagues were dubious about the possibility of ever 'knowing' the nature of a closed system like the Soviet Union. Some suggested my piece smacked of determinism; others that I was far too tough on Gorbachev. A few pointed out that some scholars had got it right. More implied this was not even a legitimate question and that to expect social scientists to predict the future was methodologically unsound. I was even accused by one critic of oversimplifying the character of the discipline, when in fact my whole purpose had been to show the opposite. That said, I was heartened rather than dismayed by the response. It also led me to the not illogical conclusion that if my rather short provocation could evoke such a lively and mixed response, there was a need for a more developed and genuinely international (that is not just American) discussion on the subject.[13]

My early efforts to 'deconstruct' Soviet Studies were hardly unique. Others were trying to do much the same after 1991. One such writer was Peter Rutland, a British scholar working in the United States. At about the same time, he had arrived at broadly the same conclusions as myself. However, in his view (as well as mine) the picture was not a simple one. Some had anticipated the demise of the Soviet system. Moreover, as he points out here, it would be both wrong and foolish to ignore the role of accident and unintended consequence in explaining the end of Soviet rule. But in the end something went wrong, and Rutland sets himself the difficult task of explaining why the Soviet Studies community believed the USSR was either more stable or more reformable than it turned out to be. He also casts a critical glance at the structure of knowledge in the West and asks why it might have been difficult for students of the former USSR to ask big questions about the nature of the Soviet system. His conclusions are as revealing as they are useful, and he is surely right to remind us that if we train people in 'group think' to be narrow empirical specialists (as post-Soviet Studies also seems to be doing) we should hardly be surprised when they fail to come up with genuine insights. Small-scale thinking about small-scale problems is unlikely to come up with large-scale theories about the way systems in general function and malfunction.

One of those who managed to break free from the constraints of the academy, according to Rutland, were a number of émigré scholars and a group of like-minded Western conservative analysts – including Terry McNeill. McNeill had already written a typically controversial piece before 1989 in which he concluded that whilst it might be wise to 'prepare contingency obituaries for Soviet communism, it would be premature to publish them'![14] In his contribution here he takes the discussion forward considerably and concludes that if Soviet Studies failed, which in his view it did, it was largely because it asked the wrong questions. Indeed, in his opinion, there were too many in the discipline who were afraid of thinking the unthinkable, and who continued to parrot the old cliché that the Soviet elite would be able to muddle along. McNeill tellingly cites the work of one particularly well-known American Sovietologist who rather too easily dismissed those who predicted the system's decline. McNeill takes him to task and suggests that if he (and others like him) had not been so dismissive of what he terms the 'right-wing realists', they too might have anticipated the disintegration of the Soviet system.

If McNeill lays great stress on the contribution made by conservative theorists to our understanding of the Soviet crisis, Hillel Ticktin – without doubt the most dissident voice in Soviet Studies over the past 25 years – is keen to expose what he sees as the limits of orthodoxy.[15] Dividing the different schools of thought into loosely composed camps ranging from the crude apologetics of the communist parties to the work of the totalitarians, he argues that the main problem with most approaches was their failure to develop a mature sociology based upon a developed political economy of the USSR. To this he adds the problem of empiricism whereby those so afflicted assumed that simply by accumulating more and more facts, or just reading the original Russian sources, one could arrive at an understanding of the contradictions of the Soviet system. This turned out not to be the case. Ticktin is also highly critical of those various professional gate-keepers who until 1991 had denied the possibility of Soviet collapse, and since have refused to engage in a critical discussion of why Soviet Studies might have failed. This is neither a legitimate response nor does it bode well for the future. Ticktin indeed suggests that the new cohort of post-Soviet scholars is faring no better in explaining the aborted transition to the market in Russia than their predecessors were in anticipating the demise of Soviet power. Guided by the same flawed methodology they are arriving, inevitably, at the same incorrect conclusions. The lessons of history, it would seem, have not been learned.

The charge that academic Sovietology failed in a most fundamental way is restated at length by Vladimir Shlapentokh in his panoramic discussion of Soviet Studies in the United States. Shlapentokh had already set the cat amongst the proverbial academic pigeons in 1993 by accusing what he termed the 'Sovietological guild' of failing to see the signs of decay when they were visible to all.[16] In his chapter here, he does not dismiss the contribution made by generations of American writers. Rather he seeks to explain why, with few exceptions, they seemed unable to detect the Soviet Union's later tendency to stagnation. Shlapentokh, however, does much more than simply critique American Sovietology. He also seeks to theorize the relationship between the American intellectual community and the Soviet experiment. He concludes that the real problem had less to do with a lack of information, than with the inclination of many in the USA to oscillate between praising the Soviet Union and demonizing it. However, he saves his sharpest barbs for what he sees as those American scholars who attempted to move beyond the Cold War in the 1960s and 1970s and 'revise' our understanding of the Soviet system. According to Shlapentokh, this new generation of left-liberal writers not only managed to soften the image of the Soviet Union – even to the extent of 'proving' that Stalin might not have been personally responsible for so many deaths in the 1930s – but in their efforts to paint a more 'normal', less repugnant picture of the system, made a number of very basic mistakes. The most important by far, he concludes, was to assume that this most abnormal of societies would endure.

Though Robert Daniels could hardly be described as a 'revisionist', he is certainly less critical of his American colleagues than Shlapentokh is. A former President of the American Association for Advancement of Slavic Studies, Daniels' chapter is a useful (some would argue, essential) counterweight to Shlapentokh's. His defence of Sovietology had already been prefigured in an earlier discussion where he not only warned against the dangers of what he termed 'irresponsible and potentially destructive' criticism, but also suggested that scholars of the former Soviet Union had gone 'as far as any in anticipating the crisis of the Soviet system'.[17] Here he mounts the same spirited defence of the discipline. In the process, he makes the important observation that Sovietology was never a monolithic subject. Hence, attacks against 'it' for getting the USSR wrong are really besides the point. Daniels makes the point ever more forcefully by painting a complex picture of a diverse subject in constant evolution from the end of the Second World War until the late 1980s. Those looking for a guide to the history of Soviet Studies in the United States, as well as a sophisticated discussion about what actually happened in 1991, could do a lot worse than studying his contribution with care.

If Daniels has important things to say about the nature of American Sovietology, Stephen White has equally vital things to say about the events of 1991 and what followed. One of the most productive scholars of the last 25 years, White correctly reminds us that we should always be careful in our use of language, especially in our use of words like 'collapse' and 'transition'. In White's view, the great upheavals after 1989 left much of the old order untouched. For this reason the new system which began to take shape under Yeltsin bore more than passing resemblance to the old one. White admits that there were some in the wider Sovietological profession who failed to anticipate the events which finally led to the break-up of the Soviet Union. In his view, however, there were many voices within the discipline, and quite a few of these did anticipate major change. Furthermore, according to White, it was not only those concerned with the detailed study of the USSR who foresaw the potential for evolution within the Soviet system. Important social theorists such as Talcott Parsons, Robert Dahl, Karl Deutsch and Gabriel Almond also anticipated change. Though coming at the problem from different theoretical directions, all of them seemed to agree that a modernizing system was quite literally 'bound to pluralism'; though what form this would ultimately take in the former Soviet Union, and when this would happen, remained to be seen.

If White raises some really quite profound questions about the complex nature of the 'transition' in the former USSR, David Lane examines the ways in which classical sociology theorized the Soviet Union. Lane insists that far from being unaware of the dynamics inherent in communism, a number of social theorists believed that change was more or less inevitable. It was Talcott Parsons no less who foresaw that if certain necessary 'functions' were not performed by the Soviet system then its 'structures' were likely to stagnate and regress. This leads Lane to the startling but arresting conclusion that Gorbachev was only trying to deal with the type of problems already anticipated in the work of the influential American sociologist. But what of the future? Lane makes no absolute predictions. However, like White, he wonders just how far the 'transition' to a new order has gone, and, moreover, can go given the legacy of the past 70 years. Certainly, those who naïvely predict a rosy liberal capitalist future are bound to be disappointed, according to Lane. A people brought up to expect full employment and universal welfare are unlikely to give their wholehearted support to the sort of neo-liberal economic model now being pushed on the former USSR by Western advisers.

Whilst Lane anticipates a different future for the former USSR from that naïvely predicted by advocates of Western capitalism, Urban and Fish, two American political scientists, ask whether or not a new generation of post-Soviet scholars can do any better than their Sovietological predecessors.

About the latter, Urban and Fish are strongly critical, and even suggest that their theorizing was little more than a reflection of the needs of the American state at different times. Thus the early totalitarians provided a useful enemy image in the early days of the Cold War; the later revisionists a less grim picture of Soviet reality which helped sell détente to a sceptical American public. But are things any better now? In some ways yes, for as Urban and Fish point out, the sheer amount of information on tap and the ability of Western scholars to immerse themselves in post-Soviet society clearly makes for a much better scholarly environment. However, having access to the 'facts' alone will not solve all intellectual problems. For one thing, the very complexity and novelty of post-communist societies makes the task of the modern social scientist very difficult. Moreover, one always has to ask why do we privilege certain facts over others and who in the end pays for them? These are not frivolous epistemological issues but go to the very heart of the new research agenda. Objectivity might be a noble dream, but there remains a complex yet real relationship between the knowledge we produce and the power it serves: and the questions of for whom are we producing knowledge about the new Russia, and for what political purpose, are as much problems now as they were in the days of the Cold War when Western elites needed to know the Soviet enemy in order to contain it more effectively.

If Urban and Fish are right to warn students against the dangers of naïve 'fact-grubbing', Richard Sakwa attempts to situate the fall of the USSR and the emergence of the new Russia in a longer historical and larger theoretical perspective. This leads him to make the important observation that whilst actually existing communism in the former USSR did, in its way, establish itself as an 'alternative', it never really constituted itself as a 'successor' to capitalism. Consequently, it was rarely if ever able to create the conditions for its own stable reproduction over time. From this perspective, the period between 1917 and 1991 represented not so much a failed transition to socialism, but a historical detour or what Sakwa calls a '74-year long regime of crisis management'. Gorbachev, it is true, tried to adapt the old regime but with disastrous consequences for its stability. Yeltsin has attempted to transform the country, but in the process has unleashed an enormously destructive storm which still shows no signs of abating. Certainly, to describe this highly contradictory process as being a 'transition' from one nodal point to another is extraordinarily naïve. Post-Soviet reality is simply too complex to be so neatly pigeon-holed.

If, according to Sakwa, we almost need entirely new categories to explain the Soviet past and Russia's future, Ron Hill in his measured contribution argues that scholars of the new post-Soviet Union still have a good deal to learn from traditional Sovietologists. The contribution of this now much-derided and somewhat demoralized group should not be overlooked or merely set aside because they failed to anticipate the collapse of the USSR. If nothing else, the skills they acquired are ones which every student of the new order must have before doing serious work. Hill is especially critical of those who have recently parachuted into the former USSR, equipped with text-book guides on how to build market democracies but very little else. He is equally concerned about what he sees as the new orthodoxy, which almost seems to demand of researchers that they accept the underlying premises of Western policy. This he feels can only limit the value of the work they do by structuring the sort of 'legitimate' questions they are allowed to ask. But this is not all. It also means that ordinary citizens in the former Soviet Union are likely to provide Western analysts with the type of answers they think they want to hear. In the new post-communist order, researchers might be able to ask questions they never could before: it does not follow they will always get an honest response.

Whilst Hill is keen to explore the possibilities of constructing a new intellectual partnership between area specialists and social scientists, in his contribution Bob Arnot seeks to expose the limits of Western economics. In a wide-ranging survey and critique he first explains why orthodox economists interested in the former USSR could not, in the end, comprehend its underlying dynamics. This was not a function of stupidity, a lack of empirical material or apologetics. Rather it was the result of a flawed methodology which in Arnot's view was 'partial, static and ahistoric'. It was hardly surprising therefore that the overwhelming majority of economists were unable to anticipate the demise of the USSR. Unfortunately, those who employed a dubious technique to misunderstand the nature of the old Soviet economic system are now using the same flawed method to explain the transition, with the same imperfect results. Equipped with a hit-list of market reforms deemed necessary to transform the old moribund planning system, Western economists and Western advisers have weighed into the debate about the shape of the new post-Soviet economic order. But all has not gone according to 'plan', and the impact of their neo-liberal programme has been little short of catastrophic. Industrial production has declined precipitately. The position of most ordinary Russians has got worse. Food consumption has declined and the public sector has gone into free-fall. However, according to Arnot, there is no easy Keynesian solution to Russia's problems either, and those who suggest that there is neither understand Russia, nor for that matter Western capitalism in the post-war period. In the end, other, more radical solutions are called for if Russia is not going to continue along its current downward path.

Arnot's clinical dissection of the pretensions of Western economics is mirror-imaged in Stephen Cohen's equally scathing attack upon US foreign policy. An effective and informed critic of the impact of the Cold War upon traditional Sovietology,[18] since the early 1990s Cohen has been an equally forceful opponent of the way in which Washington in particular has tried to deal with post-communist Russia. More sceptical than most about Washington's ability to shape Russia's future (in 1992 he coined the phrase 'cold peace' to characterize the likely shape of US-Russian relations after the Cold War), his advice to policy-makers has always been unambiguously clear: Russia can find its way only within the limits of its own traditions and possibilities, not America's.[19] Unfortunately, US policy-makers have neither been so sensitive nor so wise. Indeed, US policy since 1991 has in his view been based on a number of false assumptions: the three most egregious being that the events of 1991 constituted a genuine revolution that removed most of the obstacles to fundamental economic reform, that Russia could quickly make the transition to the market through the application of radical shock therapy policies, and finally that the West had little choice but to back Yeltsin. The consequences of what Cohen has referred to as 'America's failed crusade in Russia' have been as unfortunate as they were predictable, with Washington ending up acting as cheerleader for Yeltsin, but without there being very much movement towards a genuine market or a flourishing democracy. In fact, far from there being a transition towards something new or better, there has, in effect, been an endless collapse of everything essential to a decent existence. According to Cohen, this is the brute reality underlying the reforms that most US commentators still extol and seem to think are the only desirable kind.[20]

Whilst Cohen remains sceptical about talk of a transition which only serves to mask the extent of Russia's downward economic slide, Jacobsen in his highly suggestive essay takes us back to basics and asks what was it exactly that 'collapsed' in 1991? For Jacobsen the issue of whether or not Soviet Studies got it right or wrong is less important than a proper characterization of the Soviet regime itself. The USSR, he maintains, was neither totalitarian nor Communist when it disintegrated in 1991: Gorbachev had undone Stalinism long before the Soviet Union fell apart, and Stalin had destroyed the revolutionary aspirations of the Bolshevik party in the 1920s and 1930s. Jacobsen also questions the neo-conservative view which claims that the ultimate responsibility for what happened in the USSR can be laid at the door of one Karl Marx. Nothing could be further from the truth, he argues, and to blame Marx for what subsequently came to pass is just about as logical as placing the responsibility for the Spanish Inquisition at the feet of Jesus Christ! Yet there was always something of a tragic dilemma inherent in the Russian revolution. Premature by definition and acknowledged to be so by both Lenin and Trotsky, the revolution had only a limited chance of success in a backward country. Moreover, like all revolutions it faced the classic problem of being motivated by utopian aspirations that could not easily be realized. Yet though the vision was perverted by Soviet practice, the ideals which animated the revolution in the first place have not died: in fact cannot die, because they embody some of our noblest aspirations. The Soviet Union may have disappeared as an entity, but this does not mean that the programme which originally inspired its founders has died too. In this very important sense, History has not come to an end.

Professor Michael Cox
Department of International Politics
University of Wales
Aberystwyth

July 1998

Notes

1 George Breslauer, 'In Defense of Sovietology', *Post-Soviet Affairs*, Vol. 8, No. 3, July–September 1992, p. 197.
2 Quote from David Remnick in his 'Getting Russia Right', *New York Review of Books*, 22 September 1994, p. 20.
3 See Moises Naim, 'Editor's Note', *Foreign Policy*, No. 110, Spring 1998, p. 9.
4 In March 1990, the US-based Social Science Research Council and the American Council of Learned Societies recommended that a panel be set up to 'clarify the future challenges and opportunities ... in the field of Soviet Studies over the next five to 10 years'. The panel accepted that 'Soviet Studies' was in 'much disarray', but at no point did it even hint – let alone recommend – that academics might benefit from a period of reflection on their intellectual past before engaging in new tasks such as 'reconceptualizing modernity', 'bringing culture back in' and (inevitably) studying the 'transition to the market'. See Robert T. Huber and Susan Bronson, 'The August Revolution and Soviet Studies', *Items*, Vol. 45, No. 4, December 1991, pp. 69–75.
5 According to one writer, 'we must give serious weight to the proposition that the much touted 'collapse of "communism"' was perhaps not nearly as inevitable and surely not necessarily so imminent as it has been made out to be'. See Alexander Dallin, 'Causes of Soviet Collapse', *Post-Soviet Affairs*, Vol. 8, No. 4, October–December 1992, p. 296.
6 See Mark Almond, '1989 Without Gorbachev', in Niall Ferguson (ed.), *Virtual History: Alternatives and Counterfactuals* (London, Papermac, 1997), p. 392.
7 See Michael Wines, 'C.I.A. Accused of Overestimating Soviet Economy', *The New York Times*, 23 July 1990; 'The Once and Future C.I.A.' (Editorial), *The New York Times*, 18 October 1990; and 'C.I.A.'s Track Record Stands Up to Scrutiny' (Letter) from Richard J. Kerr, Acting Director of Central Intelligence, *The New York Times*, 24 October 1991.
8 The debate about the role of the CIA and its assessments of the former USSR rumbled on through the 1990s. See, for example, Bruce D. Berkowitz and Jeffrey

T. Richelson, 'The CIA Vindicated: The Soviet Collapse Was Predicted', *The National Interest*, No. 41, Fall 1995, pp. 36–47; Melvin Goodman, 'Ending the CIA's Cold War Legacy', *Foreign Policy*, No. 106, Spring 1997, pp. 128–43; and Robert M. Gates, *From the Shadows: the Ultimate Insider's Story of Five Presidents and How They Won the Cold War* (New York, Touchstone, 1996), especially pp. 562–6.

9   See *The National Interest*, No. 31, Spring 1993, pp. 67–122.

10 For a brief useful guide to the debate see Vladimir Treml, 'Two Schools of Thought' and Michael Ellman, 'The Many Causes of the Collapse' in *RFE/RL Research Report*, Vol. 2, No. 23, 4 June 1993, pp. 53–8.

11 As one of the new generation of American 'Young Turks' observed, 'if you look at the names of people in journals from the 1970s who were studying the Soviet Union, probably only 10 per cent would turn up in journals now'. Quoted in Christopher Shea, 'New Faces and New Methodologies Invigorate Russian Studies', *The Chronicle of Higher Education*, 20 February 1998, p. A18.

12 See Michael Cox, 'The End of the USSR and the Collapse of Soviet Studies', *Coexistence*, Vol. 31, No. 2, June 1994, pp. 89–104.

13 Here I would like to thank all those who responded to my initial intervention: Mike Bowker, Archie Brown, Robert Conquest, Bob Daniels, Michael Ellman, Matthew Evangelista, Lawrie Freedman, Fred Halliday, Neil Harding, Ron Hill, Geoffrey Hosking, George F. Kennan, David Lane, Paul Lewis, Mary McAuley, Martin McCauley, Mike Pugh, Richard Sakwa, Peter Shearman, Rachel Walker, Michael Waller and Stephen White.

14 See Terry McNeill, 'Images of the Soviet Future: the Western Scholarly Debate', in Alexander Shtromas and Morton A. Kaplan (eds), *The Soviet Union and the Challenge of the Future* (New York, Paragon House Publishers, 1988), p. 348.

15 Hillel Ticktin was founder of the journal *Critique* in 1973, and author of several articles and numerous monographs on Soviet political economy. His view had always been that the Soviet economic system existed at such a high level of contradiction that it could not be considered historically viable. This view is systematically laid out in his *Origins of the Crisis in USSR: Essays on the Political Economy of a Disintegrating System* (Armonk, Myron Sharpe, 1992).

16 See his 'The American Vision of the World: The Tendency to Find Nice Things', *AAASS Newsletter*, Vol. 33, No. 3, May 1993, pp. 5, 7.

17 Robert Daniels, 'The State of the Field and its Future', *AAASS Newsletter*, January 1995, p. 11.

18 See Stephen Cohen, 'Scholarly Missions: Sovietology as Vocation', in his *Rethinking the Soviet Experience* (New York, Oxford University Press, 1985).

19 See his essay 'The Election's Missing Issue', *The Nation*, 22 November 1992, pp. 622–4.

20 See Stephen Cohen, 'American Policy and Russia's Future', *The Nation*, 12 April 1993, pp. 476–85; 'America's Failed Crusade in Russia', *The Nation*, 28 February 1994, pp. 261–3; 'Clinton's Yeltsin and Yeltsin's Russia', *The Nation*, 10 October 1994; and 'Transition or Tragedy?', *The Nation*, 30 December 1996.

1

Whatever Happened to the USSR?
Critical Reflections on Soviet Studies

MICHAEL COX

Introduction

Between 1989 and 1991 the Soviet Union disappeared in at least four senses: as a functioning 'planned' economy, as the actually existing alternative to capitalism in the world, as a perceived or real threat to the West, and finally as an Empire. The consequences of this collapse have been, and will no doubt continue to be, profound – for the former USSR, for Central and Eastern Europe, and for the West as a whole where the impact of the end of the Cold War continues to reverberate. Of one thing we can be sure. The consequences of a disintegrating Soviet Union upon the world will be enormous; certainly there is no guarantee it will make the world a more stable place. The international system may indeed be more integrated and, at one level at least, less dangerous. The United States may have even realized its historic dream of creating a truly open world economy where all players are now prepared to read from the same economic song-sheet printed in Washington. But there is another story to be told, and the descent into barbarism in a number of African countries, the genocide in Bosnia, and the current turmoil in global markets (even some fairly orthodox economists now predict a major recession by the turn of the century) would suggest that the world is no more orderly now than it was before 1989. The manic logic of what Greider has called one-world capitalism may have superseded the dangerous logic of bipolarity and nuclearism, but that hardly makes our collective future any more secure. No wonder the USA no longer thinks, or talks, about building a 'new world order' on the rubble left behind by the Soviet experiment.[1]

Because the Soviet Union was a political cause as much as a very large country with a serious military capability, the impact of its collapse upon intellectual life in the West has been profound – and certainly in the short term, its passing has effectively destroyed the credibility of the socialist left and created the impression that there really is no alternative to the market.

Indeed, the fall of the USSR, and with it the notion that history had been moving in a certain direction for the past few decades, has even compromised the very idea of 'progress'. It is thus hardly surprising to discover an extraordinary interest now in subjectivist theories such as post-modernism which not only question the idea of science and scientific objectivity, but are strongly opposed to any attempt either to understand the world 'out there' or to move it in a certain direction. Even to suggest the possibility that we can actually know something and alter it, or that some 'narratives' may in fact be superior to others, is only likely to invite scorn and ridicule in many departments of social science today. Intellectual pessimism sustained by a self-obsessed individualism have in effect become the ideology of a new generation living in what is now termed the post-socialist world.

But spare a thought, if you will, for one particular academic discourse: Soviet Studies. The fall of the USSR has not so much challenged its assumptions, but to all intents and purposes buried it as a discipline. The results thus far have been calamitous, and for some at least, personally traumatic as well. In effect, the subject has ceased to exist and those once trained to read between the lines of Soviet and East European newspapers now find their skills are no longer in much demand. Many who once counted tanks, analysed Soviet foreign policy, or tried through various means to detect significant changes at the top of the Communist Party apparatus have found themselves facing a stark choice over the past few years: of either retooling and learning something about markets and democracies, and how to facilitate the transition to both in the former communist countries, or quickly learning about another, more important country (usually China) or region (invariably, the Pacific Rim). Symptomatically, the amount of money going into post-Soviet Studies has declined dramatically since 1990 for the simple reason that governments no longer need 'to know the enemy'. Why should they? The enemy no longer exists.[2]

Those who remain in what is left of Soviet Studies have a few options, though not many. They can, as implied, move into entirely new areas. They could return to the safer haven provided by history, quite a reasonable move now that there is more information issuing forth from Soviet archives. Or they could try and understand what is now going on in the land mass once referred to as the Soviet empire: try in other words to analyse the highly contradictory processes now taking place in a disintegrating system – a system whose disintegration was neither expected nor foreseen. This brings us to the heart of the matter and my basic thesis, which is that few practising Sovietologists actually foresaw the possibility of a specifically 'Soviet' history coming to an end. In this sense, the collapse of the USSR not only came as something of a shock to those who either supported, vilified or were neutral about the Soviet system but also to those whose job it was to analyse it.[3]

The scale of the failure should not be underestimated. First, most experts did not foresee the possibility of someone like Gorbachev coming to power. Many were then slow in recognizing the significance of his radically new agenda. A large number assumed – incorrectly – that he would soon be overthrown and the old order restored. Others believed, equally erroneously, that he would succeed in his endeavours and actually revitalize the USSR. Nobody expected the USSR to withdraw from Eastern Europe in 1989; fewer foretold of the 1991 coup; and following its collapse, only a handful predicted the rapid disintegration of what Mary McAuley once described as 'probably the most powerful empire' the world had ever known.[4] Exceptions there were to this general rule. But in the main, those who had earlier suggested that the USSR might be unviable, as opposed to being just plain inefficient or morally repugnant, tended to be peripheral figures in the profession; outsiders rather than insiders; marginal to the mainstream; unwelcome at the conferences; and often laughed out of court by those who thought they knew better.[5]

Now admittedly, many experts did detect signs of a mounting crisis in the USSR in the late 1970s; in fact, certain social theorists with little detailed knowledge of the society even posited the likelihood of some evolution taking place over time.[6] A few on what might be termed the far right of Soviet Studies also looked forward to the system's demise, and some tried to accelerate the process by actively encouraging the United States to pile on the pressure in the 1980s. But they did not expect the Soviet system to go under completely. Moreover, few of them provided anything more than just a general statement about why the Soviet Union was unlikely to remain in being. And most argued (and many predicted) that when political push came to shove, the old Soviet elite would do what it did best: sack the reformers, terrorize its people into submission and turn against the West.

What I intend to do in this chapter therefore is try to understand what can best and only be described as the collective failure of a discipline to anticipate the implosion of an entity whose structures, leaders and policies it had been studying in minute detail for over 40 years. As I will show, there is not one answer to this question but many. By the same measure, there is not just one ex-Sovietologist with egg on his or her face but several. However, I want to begin my discussion not with Soviet Studies, but with the position of the academic in the modern university. It is here that the deeper cause of Sovietological failure has to be sought.

The Academic Dilemma

Let us begin, then, with an observation about the structure of knowledge in the West. It can be argued (and I would certainly want to argue the point here) that academics teaching in highly specialized discipline areas in Western universities are either discouraged, or not inclined, to ask big questions. They are deterred from doing so in all sorts of ways: by a doctoral system which emphasizes the footnote over the idea; by the subdivision of knowledge which finds its organized expression in the departmental system; and finally by career opportunities. Those who stray outside the narrow channel do so at some professional risk to themselves. Universities are, after all, like business organizations and reward their members for their ability to publish detailed monographs in increasingly specialized journals. Indeed, there are few journals (except the less prestigious ones on the margins of academia) which actually publish material of a non-specialist nature.

Modern academics, including those within Soviet Studies, are thus caught (and have been for a long time) on the horns of a dilemma. To succeed he or she has to specialize and do 'useful, or 'practical' research. However, once involved in what is effectively a web of professional dependency, it becomes increasingly difficult to examine large issues. In fact, it looks decidedly odd if one does. In this way large-scale problems about the dynamics or contradictions of this or that social system (including, I would submit, the former USSR's) are simply pushed off the agenda. Far easier and almost certainly more rewarding to research very specific topics such as interest groups, party structures, electoral systems and the like.

This leads to a second general observation – not about the structural constraints imposed upon the academic in the modern university, but the intellectual ones. To put it bluntly, the very nature of conventional social sciences would have made it extraordinarily difficult for the student of the USSR (or of any country for that matter) to have foreseen the country's decline and final break-up. There were three reasons why. All are connected.

The first reason has to do with the dominance of empiricism in the academy. The results of this were profound, but the most important consequence from our perspective was that those so influenced simply avoided theorizing about systems. In fact, they were literally invoked not to, with the result that most academics were almost incapable of examining the large picture historically. Indeed, in terms of their own training, the large picture was precisely what they were not supposed to look at. The proper object of study was the very specific and the highly detailed; parts of the whole but not the whole itself. Small-scale problems could be looked at. Large issues such as why systems – including the Soviet system – might rise, mature and finally wither away were ignored. These were best left to the speculator or the journalist; or it might be added, to the Toynbee or the Marx, neither of whom would have felt very much at home in an academic department in the post-war period.

The second inhibiting factor has to do with academic resistance to the very idea of prediction. Though no serious scholar should attempt to make a precise guess at what exactly lies round the historical corner, or when something might happen and under what circumstances, they should at least have some idea of where current tendencies and trends might lead. Unfortunately, the average academic in the West was (and still is) taught from an early age to eschew such 'futurology' on the grounds that it is either too difficult or likely to lead to mere guesswork. It is quite extraordinary, in fact, how much effort seems to have gone into educating otherwise intelligent people into believing that prediction was for fools and crystal-ball gazers and not serious intellectuals – least of all those engaged in important (sometimes policy relevant) work studying the 'other superpower'. Admittedly, few Sovietologists showed very much interest in philosophy. Indeed, as a general rule, those in Soviet Studies were a decidedly pragmatic bunch. Perhaps for this reason, they more than most were unlikely to be diverted away from 'real research' by spending time on a mad venture like trying to look ahead. Anyway, why should they? Accurate prediction, it was argued, could only take place under conditions of perfect knowledge: and because that was impossible to achieve, prediction in any form was clearly a waste of time.

Thirdly, even if prediction had not been such a dirty word in the normal academic vocabulary, it is unlikely the end of the USSR could have been foreseen because most social scientists (amongst whom we should include Sovietologists) were – and presumably remain – much better equipped at dealing with stable political patterns than with radical shifts in structure. As even one of Soviet Studies' more sophisticated defenders has pointed out, social science has always been better at predicting continuity than discontinuity: 'turbulent fields' simply do not play to its strengths, according to George Breslauer.[7] Nor it would seem do they play to those of the CIA. They also failed to anticipate the end of Soviet power – possibly for the same reasons. Significantly, it has been noted that CIA analysts utilized what is known as 'single-outcome forecasting'. This assumed that they (like most of their colleagues in Soviet Studies) could and should count on historical trends remaining the same. Conversely, they could (and should) disregard the possibility of sharp changes or discontinuities. Armed with such a conservative methodology it was hardly surprising that the Agency and their various friends and advisers in American universities in particular, were so surprised by 1991![8]

The final dilemma worth mentioning here is perhaps less methodological in nature than institutional and professional. For over 40 years careers had been made, journals produced, books written, budgets justified and international conferences organized on the assumption that something would continue to exist: that something, of course, was the Soviet Union. It would be no exaggeration to say that the USSR became a way of life for a very large number of people; and not just for academics in universities. Western intelligence services, military establishments, important industries, diplomatic missions and alliances abroad were all in a very obvious and direct sense dependent upon the Soviet Union. The object of their distrust had, ironically, become the reason for their being. The idea that one day it may no longer be there was virtually inconceivable – as one academic discovered when he asked a group of leading American officials in 1985 whether or not we should be 'looking ahead to the possibility that the Cold War might someday end?' According to the academic in question, 'an embarrassed silence ensued'. This was finally broken by an observation from a highly respected senior diplomat: 'Oh it hadn't occurred to any of us that it ever would end.'[9]

Soviet Studies and the Cold War

This brings us to Soviet Studies itself. Here we need to ask a simple but important question: Why was the Soviet Union a subject of Western interest? For what purpose was it studied? And to what end? There is no one answer to this. Yet it would be somewhat disingenuous to abstract the discipline of Soviet Studies from its context. And that context was the Cold War. This, I would argue, profoundly influenced the assumptions of many Sovietologists. To understand how, we must briefly look at the development of the subject after the war.

The serious study of the USSR clearly pre-dated the Cold War. But its exponential growth as a subject was very much the result of the collapse of the wartime alliance and the West's need to understand the dynamics of Soviet policy. This, of necessity, required a reasonably objective under-standing of the Soviet Union's capabilities and intentions. The problem was that as the Cold War unfolded this more or less balanced approach was replaced by one which increasingly emphasized the worst. The reasons for this happening were complex. In part it had to do with Soviet actions themselves. These only seemed to confirm its threatening and monstrous character. But it also had a great deal to do with developments in the West itself: anti-communist hysteria in the United States, the Korean War, the requirements of military planning for the long term, and above all the need to mobilize domestic support for what was turning into a costly and lengthy struggle. Whether policy-makers believed their own propaganda is an open question. The fact remains, however, that in public at least they invariably emphasized Soviet power and understated its known weaknesses. Even talking about the latter was almost discouraged on the assumption this would undermine the consensus which supported and justified Western policies towards the USSR.

The official tendency to exaggerate Soviet strengths and underestimate its flaws was at least one reason why many were so taken aback by the fall of the USSR in the late 1980s. Another was the equally important Cold War assumption that the USSR was bound by its very nature to expand but not to retreat. The thesis was not an entirely unreasonable one. After all, before 1941 the Soviet Union had attacked a number of bordering countries, and at an earlier date, fomented revolution abroad. Then after 1945 (and until the late 1970s at least) it tried, with varying degrees of success, to increase its weight within the wider international system. The problem was that those who talked reasonably enough about Soviet 'expansion' – there was to this degree some form of a Soviet threat – seemed almost completely oblivious to other things: that Soviet influence was limited to the most backward parts of the world; that Moscow frequently exercised great caution, in fact on many occasions refused to take on new commitments; that it probably lost as much influence as it gained in the 40-year period after the war; that it sometimes retreated voluntarily, as it did in Austria in 1954; and most importantly of all perhaps, that expansion for a system as inefficient and uncompetitive as the Soviet Union's was an extraordinary burden and that this burden was likely to increase as the economy began to slow down. However, none of this seemed to lead commentators to the conclusion that the USSR might one day do what all other imperial powers have had to do: decolonize.[10]

The assumption that the USSR could never withdraw from entrenched positions also helps us explain why Soviet Studies failed to predict the most important strategic development of the post-war period: Soviet disengagement from Eastern Europe in 1989. In fact, on this particular issue, all strands of Sovietological opinion – from the most conservative to the most pro-Soviet – assumed the USSR would stay where it was. Even those who were reasonably sensitive to the impact of perestroika upon Soviet-East European relations felt the USSR could not withdraw from the region; and for apparently good reasons.[11]

First, according to the common view, the USSR would remain where it was because this both placed pressure on the West whilst reducing Western pressure on itself. It also limited German ambitions by guaranteeing Germany's continued division. Indeed, if there were no other reason for the USSR remaining in Eastern Europe, the desire to keep Germany divided would have been enough. But there was more. The USSR needed Eastern Europe (or so we were informed) for economic purposes. It required it too for the conduct of its foreign policy, for without the support of its Warsaw Pact allies abroad it would not have been able to project its influence so effectively. And lastly, it could not withdraw from the region for the very important reason that to have done so would have threatened the integrity of the USSR itself. For all these reasons the USSR could not possibly do what it finally did in 1989: disengage and return home to base.[12]

Finally, if we are considering the impact of the Cold War upon Soviet Studies we have to look at the dominant paradigm of the Cold War: totalitarianism. First used as a term to describe Fascist Italy in the 1920s and then by dissident socialists to understand the Stalinist system of the 1930s, after the war it became increasingly popular as a means of characterizing the USSR. The post-war popularity of the concept can be explained in several ways. Most obviously, it seemed to describe the peculiarities of the Soviet system rather well. It was simple. It was politically correct by the conservative standards of the time. And it provided a moral justification for Western policy in the Cold War by equating the Soviet Union with Nazi Germany. In fact, precisely because it looked like an ideological device designed to legitimize (and perpetuate) the Cold War, the idea of totalitarianism soon came to be opposed by many within the Soviet Studies profession.[13]

Yet in spite of the backlash against the totalitarian thesis, it continued to exert a tremendous influence on Soviet Studies. This had a number of consequences, but perhaps the most important was that those who supported the idea (and there were many) tended to assume the Soviet regime would persist; not because it was legitimate, but because it could deploy an enormous battery of controls to prevent latent discontent becoming overt. These controls, it was pointed out, had guaranteed the system after the Bolsheviks seized power in 1917. They had then been perfected under Stalin. And in spite of certain modifications after his death, still remained in being. The people might mutter, the intellectuals may moan; but given the power of the secret police and the atomized character of the population, there was no possibility of society's contradictions ever expressing themselves. In fact, according to émigré writer Alexander Zinoviev (whose work exercised a great deal of influence in the West following the publication of *The Yawning Heights* in 1976), 'Homo Sovieticus' was so traumatized, that he (and presumably she) preferred the order guaranteed by Soviet communism to the likely disorder that would follow its demise. The system therefore was secure. Not only was it strong in its own right, but by so shaping the individual actually implicated the ordinary Soviet citizen in his or her own subordination to this perfected form of the Leviathan state.[14]

The Social Sciences

The Cold War shaped the contours of Soviet Studies for nearly two decades. Yet it was not a self-contained subject, and in the 1960s and 1970s there was what can only be described as a serious and determined drive to both modernize the subject and integrate it more completely with the broader social sciences.[15] This drive proved very effective and by the early 1980s the discipline had been changed beyond recognition by the grafting of modern 'scientific methods' on to the original body of Kremlinology. But in spite of this methodological invasion of what had once been a rather isolated academic preserve inhabited by the émigré, the government official and the conservative, the new wave proved no more successful in predicting the upheavals of the late 1980s than their more orthodox predecessors. Carrying neither the intellectual nor the political baggage of the 'totalitarians', the second generation of Sovietologists nevertheless failed as completely as their less liberal opponents in anticipating the collapse of the Soviet system. The question is why?

One part of the answer, ironically, has to be sought in the new cohort's rejection of the original totalitarian model.[16] Supporters of the latter, we should recall, believed the USSR would remain in being, not because the system was popular or inherently stable, but because the Soviet state was extraordinarily repressive.[17] According to a number of social scientists who rose to intellectual prominence in the 1970s and 1980s, this view was profoundly misleading; not only because it overemphasized the role of force in maintaining the Soviet regime, but underestimated the reserves upon which the regime could draw to reproduce itself. The system may not have been legitimate in the Western sense. However, this did not mean it was without support. On the contrary, it had deep roots in the Soviet population. Some even spoke of a 'social contract' existing between rulers and the ruled in which the former fulfilled their part of the bargain by guaranteeing the latter full employment and minimal welfare. But this was not all. The Soviet people, it was argued, were proud of their country's achievements. They were very patriotic too. And they had far more educational opportunities than their parents or grandparents. Moreover, their children, crucially, had the chance of a better life than they.[18]

But it was not merely social factors that challenged the totalitarian myth of a system without a base. Political developments in the post-Stalin period also suggested the regime had some support. The Communist Party clearly remained dominant in a single-party state. Nevertheless, the elite did permit a degree of group involvement and popular participation in the political process. In fact, according to one leading American political scientist, the Soviet system was nearly as open (if not more so) than the liberal democracies of the West.[19] Moreover, whilst elections may have been a façade, it would be wrong to conclude the Soviets meant nothing. If nothing else they allowed yet one more access point for the ordinary citizen to be involved in, or at least bring pressure to bear upon, the deliberations of government. Further proof, if proof were needed, that the USSR was a long way away from the totalitarian nightmare portrayed in the popular literature by Orwell and in the academic field by such notables as Friedrich and Brzezinski.[20]

The consequence of all this new writing was twofold: it made the Soviet system look decidedly more pleasant than had previously been assumed; and, by implication, led those who analysed the USSR in this way to the not illogical conclusion that the system was relatively stable. Indeed how could such an order - which guaranteed jobs for life to an upwardly mobile, patriotic people who were not excluded from the political process - be on the verge of disintegration? It was just beyond the bounds of possibility. A mere fantasy entertained by extremists, but not supported by the facts.

This conclusion was endorsed (in part) by another innovation introduced by modern social scientists to understand the Soviet system: that of political culture.[21] Once again trying to move beyond the limits of a totalitarian model whose residual influence it was argued had less to do with its scholarly merits than its ideological usefulness, a number of leading scholars (political scientists in particular) sought to use the concept of culture as a way of allowing a greater degree of attention to be paid to the historical and national specificity of Soviet politics. The results were not devoid of value or merit. Nevertheless, one of the consequences was to reinforce the view that the USSR was a good deal more stable than it probably was. That may not have been the intention. But that was the consequence of using an approach which stressed the deeply rooted character of many values; and which tended to emphasize the success of most (if not all) Soviet socialization programmes in shaping the beliefs and attitudes of the ordinary people. Moreover, according to those who favoured the notion, the regime itself had to be regarded as legitimate - not because it was elected - but rather because it did certain things, especially in the socioeconomic sphere, which fulfilled popular needs and demands. As one noted sociologist pointed out in the late 1970s, the study of Soviet political culture was especially useful, for not only did it reveal a previously unknown degree of congruity between the attitudes of the political elite and the people, but it showed that the political system itself was perceived positively because it was 'carrying out many desirable policies'. It was reasonable to conclude therefore that the elite (or more precisely 'political elites') had 'some level of support among the population' as a whole.[22]

The argument that the regime may have been more successful than the totalitarians assumed was implicit too in much (though not all) of the new writing on the national question.[23] Here, once again, traditional views came under attack from a group of social scientists who neither sympathized with nationalist aspirations, nor believed that nationalism was as potentially dangerous to the system as had hitherto been supposed. Implicitly, and in some cases explicitly, attacking the thesis that the USSR was 'a prison house of nations', a modern generation of analysts arrived at some rather interesting conclusions about the ethnic question in the former USSR.

The first, and perhaps the least controversial, was that in spite of the great historical wrongs done to many nationalities, since Stalin's death the policy of the centre had been culturally more tolerant, politically less oppressive, and, by and large, economically more equitable too. Thus there was little reason to assume the so-called 'captive nations' were straining at the leash to escape from their now relatively benign captors. Nor did it follow that there was an inherent conflict between being a member of one of the various nations and a citizen of the wider Soviet republic. As one writer put it, ethnic consciousness 'did not necessarily signify a lack of loyalty to the Soviet regime'.[24] In fact, according to another analyst, it could be so channelled as to make it 'integrative' rather than disintegrative of the state.[25] There was, in other words, no *prima facie* case to think that nationalism presented the system 'with an impossible or even a potentially disturbing future'.[26] Indeed, as one commentator noted in a popular and widely used text-book published in the second half of the 1980s, 'for the foreseeable future, most communist states, certainly the more legitimate ones' (like the Soviet Union) 'should be able to cope with, though not fully solve the problems of nationalism and ethnic conflict'.[27]

A final, and particularly important reason why social scientists might have assumed the USSR would persist was economic. Whilst most accepted that the problems facing the country in the 1980s were great (and growing), few felt they would actually lead to the end of the system.[28] The consensus, basically, was that the economy had enough reserves to get by. This was certainly the view of the CIA, which in a well-publicized report of 1984 concluded the leadership could muddle along almost indefinitely.[29] It was also the opinion of influential American economist Ed Hewett. Hewett, who later became adviser on Soviet affairs to the Bush White House, in fact warned the West in 1989 not to overestimate Soviet economic weakness. The Soviet economy he insisted was not 'teetering on the brink of collapse'.[30]

So why did so many Western experts fail to detect the fact that the Soviet economy was in terminal decline? One reason was technical. Using Soviet figures (which most had to) it was almost inevitable that economists would arrive at overly optimistic conclusions about the USSR's potential: partly because these figures hid the depth of the Soviet crisis, and partly because they seriously overestimated the actual size of the economy.[31] There was also a more specifically political reason why some might have underestimated the Soviet malaise. Opposed as they were to the Reagan policy of squeezing the USSR, many liberal (and not-so-liberal) economists were inclined to find arguments with which to undercut the neo-conservatives in the White House. The simplest, and most effective way of doing this was to pour cold water on the argument that the USSR was in dire trouble and could be forced on to what Reagan termed the 'trashheap' of history.[32] In this way, the fight over foreign policy within the United States led to some interesting results when it came to estimating Soviet weaknesses and strengths in the 1980s.

Lastly, although there was diverse range of economists studying the USSR, most were reformist at heart, and believed, for both intellectual and political reasons, that there had to be a pragmatic and moderate solution to Soviet economic problems. That there were profound obstacles standing in the way of reform was obvious. But there was no reason to conclude that improvements could not be made; even possibly that some 'third way' might not be found between the Scylla of the command system and the Charybdis of the free market. This is where Gorbachev enters the picture. Assuming, or at least hoping, that he would directly address some of the difficulties facing the USSR, economists helped reinforce the belief (very widespread before the Gorbachev strategy began to implode) that the system would persist: not because the economy was working particularly well - it obviously wasn't - but because it was susceptible to improvement from above.[33]

The Gorbachev Factor

This leads us logically to Gorbachev himself. From the perspective of the late 1990s, Gorbachev now looks like a transitional, quasi-tragic figure who failed in nearly everything he attempted to do. In 1985 he set out to revitalize the Soviet economy but in the end only managed to accelerate - some would insist cause - its collapse. He also sought to turn the USSR into a more dynamic and attractive superpower. However, by the time he was forced from office in 1991, the country was no longer a major force in world politics. Finally, he tried to construct a new relationship between the peoples of the Soviet Union, but his ambiguous policies in this vital area only led to the empire's fragmentation. History will not deal kindly with Gorbachev, one suspects.

Yet at the time, this was not how things appeared. In fact, to most professional students of the USSR, the early Gorbachev years were a golden age dominated by an energetic reformist leader; the modern equivalent of 'Peter the Great and Stalin' according to one noted commentator.[34] Moreover, here was someone who actually courted the intelligentsia and who spoke openly about the nation's problems. How could one not be impressed by the man, especially as he was providing Soviet Studies with the biggest boost it had received in over 20 years? Herein perhaps was the key to understanding the 'Gorbymania' which swept Soviet Studies for a short while. For the first time in nearly a generation, the world as a whole was actually interested in the Soviet Union; and who was on hand to provide instant, in-depth analysis about the latest developments in the Kremlin? None other than the long-ignored experts from the Sovietological profession. Many an academic career was given a sudden shot-in-the-arm by Mikhail Gorbachev.

Other than boosting the sales of text-books on the USSR, the temporary cult of Gorbachev had a number of consequences for Soviet Studies. One was to make some well-known liberal scholars virtual cheerleaders for perestroika abroad. The other was to obscure from view what was actually taking place. The common wisdom was that Gorbachev was renovating the Soviet system whilst redefining the meaning of international security. Globally, there is little doubt about the benign impact of his policies (at least as far as the West was concerned). On the home front however, the combination of changes taking place under his leadership did not merely change the face of the USSR, but actually accelerated its more rapid decline and fragmentation. Yet few seemed to appreciate the fact at the time: certainly few talked about it – and when they did finally, it was too late. Momentarily buoyed up by the new man in the Kremlin, most seemed to feel (until it became clear in 1990 that the system was imploding) that Gorbachev was not only breathing new life into Soviet Studies, but into the Soviet Union as well. Consequently, they ignored or failed to see what was really happening. It took the coup of August 1991 for many to find out just how far the process of decomposition had gone.

Socialists and the Soviet Experience

It would be easy to leave the discussion at this juncture; to point the finger (so-to-speak) only at those within the academy. However, this would be both intellectually one-sided and politically misleading. The fact remains that the so-called 'Russian question' had been as much a subject of controversy amongst political activists as it had been amongst academics. It is also a fact that those on the left who were preoccupied with the Soviet Union – and that meant nearly all of them – seemed no more capable of understanding the dynamics of the system than their more mainstream colleagues. Consequently, they were as surprised as nearly everybody else when the country collapsed in the late 1980s. The interesting question is why?[35]

One reason, clearly, is that many on the left either identified with, were sympathetic to, or had residual hopes in the Soviet project. Accordingly they believed (or hoped) that the USSR would survive, possibly even prosper. How could it be otherwise? The Soviet Union, after all, still retained its socialist character and remained therefore economically and socially superior to Western capitalism. Naturally, it had its problems. But these had to be set against the USSR's many past achievements and its continuing deep reservoir of support amongst the Soviet people. Moreover, under Gorbachev's leadership there was every reason to believe its problems could be resolved; either through a process of economic adaptation or political reform, or a combination of the two. Anyway, the USSR had confronted hard times before and won through. It would do so again. Soviet socialism had been created against the odds. There was no reason to assume it could not be re-created in the 1980s.[36]

Trotskyists, not surprisingly, took a somewhat more critical approach to the problem. The USSR, they accepted, was not a form of socialism, but rather a degenerated workers' state which could only be regenerated after the workers themselves had regained political power. But even the most critical of Trotskyists did not believe the system would disintegrate. How could it? For according to their own theory, the USSR remained a planned economy with a superior mode of production to that found in the West. Thus in spite of its deformed nature, it would continue to function, albeit not very well.[37] This was also the view of those who endorsed the politically virtuous but theoretically idiosyncratic view that the Soviet system was a species of state capitalism. The adherents to this particular school of thought travelled a different theoretical route from their rivals on the left. Yet in the end, they arrived at the same destination. The reason they did so was implicit in their original argument. For if, as they maintained, the Soviet Union was another form of capitalism, then it followed that it was no more – or less – likely to grind to a halt than the economies of the West. And as those economies were not on the verge of breakdown, it seemed reasonable to conclude that the Soviet system would not break down either. Indeed, one exponent of the state capitalist theory went to some length in 1987 to remonstrate with those who conjectured about Soviet collapse. The Soviet economy was extraordinarily wasteful, he agreed. On the other hand, the level of waste – and by implication the degree of contradiction in the system – was no greater than existed in the West. It was all a question of degree, not fundamental difference.[38]

Crying Wolf – and Beyond

Let us conclude this chapter with a brief story about a 'wolf' called Soviet collapse. After 1917, the end of Soviet power was announced on a number of occasions: just after the revolution itself; then under the New Economic Policy (NEP) in the 1920s; later during the early years of the Second World War; and finally in the high years of the Cold War by 'liberationists' on the American right. Even Trotsky at one stage suggested the USSR would not survive alone. But the pessimists were proved wrong. The revolution did survive. NEP did not lead to the restoration of capitalism. Hitler was defeated. The USSR successfully recovered from the war – and survived the 1950s. There was ample reason therefore to be sceptical of claims that the USSR was on its last legs. 'Wolf!' had been cried before; many times in fact. But there had been no beast at the door then. So why assume it was there now in the 1980s?

It is important to make this point, not by way of a defence of Soviet Studies, but to understand the context within which those in the discipline operated and continued to operate until the last years of Soviet power. Basically, the old hands had heard the bad news before. It had always turned out to be wrong. So why conclude it was not wrong again? Moreover, by training and inclination, Sovietologists (like all reasonable academics) were sceptics. As such, they had to be able to distinguish between fantasy and fact; and the fact of the matter was that it was just too fantastic to suppose that the USSR, with its vast apparatus of controls, huge arsenal of weapons, extensive welfare system, and economy that had transformed the country into an industrial giant, could simply fall apart. It might go to war with China, impose or reimpose its brutal control over one or more of the East European countries, even kill thousands of its own citizens. But collapse? That was just out of the question.

But why was it out of the question? Why did the USSR have to survive? And why did those working in Soviet Studies think that it would? As I hope I have shown, Sovietologists thought the USSR would endure in one form or another not because they were foolish or ill-informed, but rather because the intellectual tools at their disposal did not, perhaps could not, incline them to the conclusion that the USSR had a finite life-span. Some might have got it right. But few did. We could of course ignore the issue or argue that what happened was not ordained by history. We could even try to hide behind the defensive argument that because we can never know the future, it is unfair to accuse Sovietology for failing to anticipate the end of Soviet power. But that would be pointless; and it would be disingenuous. It would also mean that we will have learned nothing. For if the fate of Soviet Studies teaches us anything it is that we ignore the unlikely, the impossible, the absurd even, at our peril. Yet we should not be too harsh. After all, the failure to foresee what later seemed inevitable has made fools of even wiser men and women than those who dissected the USSR before its unexpected disintegration. That said, those who did the dissecting should at least own up and accept that all was not well in the house called Soviet Studies. A shrug of the shoulders is no defence against critics.

Notes

1 See William Greider, *One World, Ready or Not: The Manic Logic of One World Capitalism* (Harmondsworth, Penguin Books, 1997). For an official exposition of what the Bush administration meant by the term 'New World Order', see *The New World Order: An Analysis and Document Collection* (London, United States Information Service, July 1991). The Foreign Secretary, Douglas Hurd, made clear what he thought of the idea in a lecture to Chatham House on 27 January 1993. 'Talk of a New World Order', he observed, 'was not helpful.' Why? Because it 'promised more than we could perform'. The text of his speech can be found in *Arms Control and Disarmament Quarterly* Review (London, Arms Control and Disarmament Research Unit, No. 28, January 1993).

2 As Professor Edward L. Keenan of Harvard observed: 'since the dangers are supposed to be less, the chance to tap the public purse for those activities is also less'. Cited in Felicity Barringer, 'Sovietology Loses Academic Glamour in Cold War Wake', *The International Herald Tribune*, 1 April 1993. Barringer noted that like the now-defunct empire it sought to understand, the field once known as Sovietology was 'undergoing a painful transition in the United States. Once heavily subsidized and often first among equals in the academic world, it is now a discipline in turmoil.'

3 The inability of Sovietologists to foresee the demise of the Soviet system was paralleled by an equally notable (and related) failure on the part of those in international relations to predict the end of the Cold War. This issue is explored very thoroughly by John Lewis Gaddis in 'International Relations Theory and the End of the Cold War', *International Security*, Winter 1992/93, Vol. 17, No. 3, pp. 5–58. Gaddis has correctly observed that the inability of those in international relations to see the end of the Cold War coming must raise big questions about the 'methods' it previously employed to understand world politics (p. 6).

4 Mary McAuley, *Soviet Politics: 1917–1991* (Oxford University Press, 1992), p. 9.

5 The outsiders I have in mind here are a number of émigrés whose insights were often disregarded, and the work of the critical Marxist, Hillel Ticktin. See his later collection of essays collected in *Origins of the Crisis in the USSR: Essays on the Political Economy of a Disintegrating System* (Armonk, NY, Myron E. Sharpe, 1992).

6 On the crisis see, for example, Marshall Goldman, *The USSR in Crisis* (New York, Norton,1983). On the predictive capacities of social theory, see Talcott Parsons, *Societies: Evolutionary and Comparative Perspectives* (Englewood Cliffs, New Jersey, Prentice Hall, 1966). See also Randall Collins and David Waller, 'What Theories Predicted the State Breakdown and Revolutions of the Soviet Bloc?', in *Research in Social Movements, Conflict and Change*, Vol. 14 (Greenwich, JAI Press, 1992), pp. 31–47.

7 See George W. Breslauer, 'Reflections on the Anniversary of the August 1991 Coup', *Soviet Economy*, Vol. 8, No. 2, April-June 1992, p. 164.

8   Theodore Draper, 'Is the CIA Necessary?', *The New York Review of Books*, 14 August 1997, p. 20.

9   Quote from John Lewis Gaddis, *The United States and the End of the Cold War: Implications, Reconsiderations, Provocations* (New York, Oxford University Press, 1992), p. vi.

10 Interestingly, one of the few serious commentators to suggest the USSR might be impelled to retreat from empire because of relative economic decline was not a Sovietologist at all, but a historian of comparative civilizations, Paul Kennedy. See his *The Rise and Fall of the Great Powers: Economic Change and Military Conflict from 1500 to 2000* (London, Fontana Press, 1989).

11 Most commentators assumed perestroika in the USSR would bring about what one called 'fundamental changes in the ways' East European societies were organized and run. What they did not foresee, indeed almost precluded, was that the Soviet Union would finally disengage from the region. See David S. Mason, 'Glasnost, Perestroika and Eastern Europe', *International Affairs*, Vol. 64, No. 3, Summer 1988, pp. 431–48.

12 To give a few (typical) examples of the views expressed on Soviet-East European relations before Soviet disengagement in 1989: In early 1986, one noted writer believed that in Eastern Europe, Gorbachev 'recognized' there were 'limits that he himself cannot overstep'. See Vladimir V. Kusin. 'Gorbachev and Eastern Europe', *Problems of Communism*, Vol. 35, No. 1, January-February 1986, p. 53. The following summer another commentator emphasized that 'no one can doubt that the region continues to provide a vital security guarantee that Moscow is unlikely to abandon'. See A. James McAdams, 'New Deal for Eastern Europe', *The Nation*, 13 June 1987, p. 800. In an important discussion of the Soviet bloc at about the same time, Charles Gati speculated that the most likely outcome of change in Eastern Europe would be to undermine glasnost in the USSR itself. See his 'Gorbachev and Eastern Europe', *Foreign Affairs*, Vol. 67, No. 3, Summer 1987, pp. 958–75. As late as June 1989, another expert could still write that the states of Eastern Europe would 'survive, albeit greatly changed'. See Valerie Bunce, 'Eastern Europe: Is the Party Over?', *Political Science & Politics*, June 1989, pp. 238–9.

13 One of the most influential early critiques of the totalitarian model was H. Gordon Skilling, 'Interest Groups and Communist Politics', *World Politics*, Vol. XVIII, No. 3, April 1966, pp. 435–51. For a useful, and less critical discussion of the concept see Archie Brown, *Soviet Politics and Political Science* (London, Macmillan, 1974), especially pp. 30–41. Absurdly, once the applicability of the concept of totalitarianism to the post-Stalin period had been questioned, a number of so-called revisionist writers began to challenge its relevance to our understanding the 1930s as well. This attempt to 'rethink' Stalinism (some would argue provide an apologia for it) was led by Arch Getty in his *Origins of the Great Purges: The Soviet Communist Party Reconsidered: 1933-1938* (Cambridge University Press, 1985).

14 See Alexander Zinoviev, *The Reality of Communism* (London, Paladin Books, 1984).

15 One writer saw the problems facing Soviet Studies in the late 1960s as stemming from its isolation from the best of systematic and comparative political science. Because of this, it had 'grown up methodologically impoverished'. See Robert S. Sharlet, 'Concept Formation in Political Science and Communist Studies:

Conceptualizing Political Participation', *Canadian Slavic Studies*, Vol. 1, No. 4, Winter 1967, p. 641.

16 For a brief, but fairly scathing attack on the notion of totalitarianism by one of the new cohort of social science scholars, see David Lane's highly influential *Politics and Society in the USSR* (London, Weidenfeld & Nicholson, 1970), pp. 188–90.

17 See Leonard Schapiro, *Totalitarianism* (London, Macmillan, 1972).

18 Although as David Lane pointed out in the early 1970s, as a result of 'greater economic maturity and political stability' in the USSR, one might expect the pattern of social stratification to become more stable and the amount of upward mobility to decline. The statement is as interesting for what it tells us about the author's views on the durability of the USSR as it is upon the Soviet social structure. See his *The End of Inequality? Stratification under State Socialism* (Harmondsworth, Penguin Books, 1971), p. 119.

19 This is certainly implied by Jerry Hough in his odd and controversial rewrite of Merle Fainsod's classic which effectively turned the original (*How Russia is Ruled*) into its opposite – *How the Soviet Union is Governed* (Harvard University Press, 1979). Hough's benign picture of Soviet politics is also conveyed in his *Soviet Leadership in Transition* (Washington, Brookings, 1980).

20 For an early attempt to demonstrate how certain groups exploited their access to the policy-making process, see Joel J. Schwartz and William R. Keech, 'Group Influence and the Policy Process in the Soviet Union', *American Political Science Review*, Vol. LXII, No. 3, September 1968, pp. 840–51.

21 For the best study using the concept, see Stephen White, *Political Culture and Soviet Politics* (London, Macmillan, 1979).

22 See David Lane, *The Socialist Industrial State: Towards a Political Sociology of State Socialism* (London, George Allen & Unwin, 1976), p. 91.

23 For a more 'traditional' (some believed at the time apocalyptic) treatment of the national question in the USSR, see Helene Carrere d'Encausse, *Decline of an Empire: The Soviet Socialist Republics in Revolt* (New York, Newsweek Books, 1979).

24 Brian Silver, 'Social Mobilization and the Russification of Soviet Nationalities', *American Political Science Review*, Vol. 68, 1974, p. 66.

25 Peter Rutland, *Nationalism and the Soviet State: A Functionalist Account*, Paper presented to the Annual Conference of the National Association of Soviet and East European Studies, Cambridge, March 1982, p. 1. (Rutland at least now admits he was wrong.)

26 Mary McAuley, *In Search of Nationalism in the USSR*, Paper presented to the National Association of Soviet and East European Studies, Cambridge, March 1982, p. 2.

27 Leslie Holmes, *Politics in the Communist World* (Oxford, Clarendon Press, 1986), p. 353.

28 Marshall I. Goldman expressed the dominant Western view about the Soviet economy in 1987. Though well aware of Soviet difficulties, he concluded that 'short of some unexpected catastrophe, the Soviet economy is unlikely to come close to collapse. … In the end, Gorbachev, like his predecessors, will probably have to settle for an economy that has to rely more on its natural riches than on its creative potential.' See his *Gorbachev's Challenge: Economic Reform in the Age of High Technology* (New York, W.W. Norton, 1987), pp. 26–7.

29 The CIA concluded that although there had been a marked 'slowdown' in Soviet growth since the 1970s, 'the Soviet economy' was 'not going to collapse'. Indeed, the Agency expected 'GNP to continue to grow, although slowly'. For the full text see Henry Rowen, 'Central Intelligence Briefing on the Soviet Economy', reprinted in Erik P. Hoffmann and Robbin F. Laird (eds), *The Soviet Polity in the Modern Era* (New York, Aldine Publishing, 1984), pp. 417-46.

30 Hewett warned against overestimating Soviet weakness, 'something' he said we had 'done in the past'. There were, in his view, still strengths and reserves left in the system. These included 'a huge defense industry producing many world-class products, a formidable, hitherto underutilized scientific establishment, enormously rich natural reserves, a modest international debt, and a well-educated workforce'. See Ed A. Hewett, 'An Idle U.S. Debate About Gorbachev', *The New York Times*, 30 March 1989.

31 Conventional Western analyses of the Soviet economy in the 1980s were hardly glowing, of course. However, even these seemingly unfavourable assessments were too optimistic: the true economic situation was much worse. According to officials from the ex-USSR, the 'real' Soviet economy was barely a third of the size of the American economy, and Soviet per capita output about a quarter. See Michael Wines, 'C.I.A. Accused of Overestimating Soviet Economy', *The New York Times*, 23 July 1990, and Colin Hughes, 'CIA is Accused of Crying Wolf on Soviet Economy', *The Independent*, 25 July 1990. For a defence of the CIA's record, see Richard J. Kerr (Acting Director of the CIA), 'C.I.A.'s Track Record Stands Up to Scrutiny', *The New York Times*, 24 October 1991.

32 President Reagan's views on the 'crisis' of Soviet 'totalitarianism' were unambiguously expressed in a speech he gave to the British Parliament on 8 June 1982. See 'Promoting Democracy and Peace', in *Realism, Strength, Negotiation: Key Foreign Policy Statements of the Reagan Administration* (Washington, United States Department of State, May 1984), pp. 77-81.

33 The best account of Gorbachev's economic reforms remains Anders Aslund, *Gorbachev's Struggle for Economic Reform* (London, Pinter, 1989).

34 Quote from Phillip Hanson, 'The Soviet Twelfth Five-Year Plan', in *The Soviet Economy: A New Course?* (Brussels, NATO, 1-3 April 1987), p. 10.

35 One of the few Marxists (apart from Ticktin) who assumed the USSR tended towards absolute stagnation was Pavel Campeneau in his *The Syncretic Society* (Armonk, NY, Myron E. Sharpe, 1980). This was published under a pseudonym, 'Felipe Garcia Casals'.

36 This was certainly the message conveyed in Jon Bloomfield (ed.), *The Soviet Revolution: Perestroika and the Remaking of Socialism*, (London, Lawrence & Wishart, 1989).

37 For an orthodox Trotskyist assessment of the USSR under Gorbachev, see Ernest Mandel, *Beyond Perestroika: The Future of Gorbachev's USSR* (London, Verso, 1989). For a less orthodox Trotskyist perspective on the Soviet Union in the late 1980s, see Tariq Ali, *Revolution From Above - Where is the Soviet Union Going?* (London, Hutchinson, 1988). One of the two people to whom Tariq Ali dedicated his book (the other being Boris Kagarlitsky) was Boris Yeltsin!

38 See Mike Haynes, 'Understanding the Soviet Crisis', *International Socialism*, No. 34, 1987, pp. 4-5.

2

Sovietology: Who Got It Right and Who Got It Wrong? And Why?

PETER RUTLAND[1]

Introduction

The fall of the mercurial Khrushchev in 1964, followed in the 1970s by a period of relative calm in the superpower relationship, conditioned Western scholars to assume that nothing very much was ever likely to happen in the USSR. The Soviet Union it seemed had become a stable system embedded in a stable set of relations with the outside world. This all changed, quite remarkably, with the ascension to power of Mikhail Gorbachev; and after 1985 not only did the pace of the Western debate about the Soviet Union change considerably, but so too did the nature of the discussion itself – and a considerable effort now went into predicting the Soviet future. The discussion also assumed an increasingly public form and moved out from the narrower confines of academia and into the life-blood of everyday discussion. Pundits, politicians and undergraduates who could not locate the Volga river on a map now happily wrote essays or delivered speeches about Gorbachev's real intentions. Professional conferences also responded to the new-found interest in Soviet affairs and were increasingly devoted to round-table discussions of Gorbachev's next move, rather than to the presentation of research findings.

Yet in spite of all this frenetic effort, most commentators – as Michael Cox has suggested in the opening chapter – got it totally wrong. One might conclude from all this that social scientists should not be enticed into futurology. It may also be that prediction can work if one is dealing with a large number of human events, as in Durkheim's classic study of suicide. But there was only one Soviet Union, and the unexpected and quite unpredicted collective suicide of its ruling elite (which has few historical parallels) clearly took the 'experts' by surprise.

In my contribution to this volume, I want to explore the issue in some detail, and though I accept that some did indeed get it right (and to this extent at least I concur with the conclusions of my fellow authors, Robert

Daniels, Stephen White and David Lane) the fact remains that most got it wrong. The serious question, then, is why? As I will attempt to show, the problem was not one of left-wing political bias – as some conservatives have suggested – or a defective methodology (as others in this study claim). The flaws lay elsewhere: firstly in what I identify as a tendency by analysts to assume that because the Soviet Union was an established system it was bound to persist; and secondly, in what I see as an equally debilitating form of 'group think' which not only stifled creative thinking but made it difficult if not impossible for many to think the impossible.

However, before going on to discuss these problems, it might be useful in the first section to say a bit about something which most social theorists have great problems in dealing with: the role of accident in history.

Accidents Happen

One of the principal arguments of historians that social scientists will have to accept concerns the role of accident in history. In the Soviet context, acknowledging this role is usually a prelude to a discussion of the strengths and weaknesses of Mikhail Gorbachev; his courage in launching perestroika; and his foolishness in failing to see that democratization would undermine the very institutions which sustained him in power.

This concentration on interpreting and reinterpreting Gorbachev's actions has been overdone, on occasion to the point of absurdity – as, for example, in Gail Sheehy's biography, *The Man who Changed the World,* where the transformation of the USSR seems to hinge on Gorbachev's reaction to male menopause. This is not to deny Gorbachev his place in history. But Gorbachev was not a Lincoln or an Ataturk, a Lenin or a Hitler; he was merely an above-average product of the *nomenclature* system. It is hard to find anybody fluent in Russian who has heard Gorbachev speak and come away in awe of his intellectual abilities. And despite all the talk of factionalism within the Politburo there is little evidence that he faced serious opposition in the upper reaches of the party until 1988–9 – by which time the die was cast.

There are at least two other serious candidates for the role of the critical accident in the demise of the USSR, though they have been neglected because of the obsession with Gorbachev. One is the Afghan War.

At the time the war in Afghanistan was not taken particularly seriously by Sovietologists, who dismissed the notion that it was the Soviet Union's 'Vietnam'. Instead, it was portrayed as an embarrassing vestige of the Brezhnev era, a minor impediment to perestroika. Thus Ernest Gellner, arguing that the USSR was not likely to collapse in the near future, mentions by way of contrast that the Hapsburg and Ottoman empires only fell after defeat in foreign wars. But he does so without referring to the Soviet defeat in Afghanistan (Ernest Gellner, in Alexander Motyl (ed.), 1992). Afghanistan, though, was a humbling reversal for the Soviet Army, and raised serious doubts in the minds of the military about the relevance of 'socialist internationalism' and the competence of the established political elite. It also caused no little anguish amongst thousands of ordinary Soviet families whose brothers, sons and fathers had been killed or injured fighting in this pointless, bloody and clearly unwinnable war. No surprise, then, that when in 1991 the Party needed the army, it deserted them. (Perhaps the main contribution Ronald Reagan made to the fall of communism was sending Stinger missiles to the *mujaheddin*.)

Second, there was Chernobyl, literally and figuratively an accident of the first magnitude. It is amazing how many contemporary accounts of 'the Gorbachev era' only dealt with Chernobyl in a sentence or two. Yet Chernobyl played a crucial role in transforming glasnost from a sterile political campaign into a genuine movement for change. The so-called 'pluralist' school of Sovietologists was in the habit of proudly noting that under Brezhnev the environment was one of the few topics of legitimate public debate (albeit within carefully defined limits). However, Chernobyl changed the character of that debate, from a tolerated discourse amongst specialists to a massive outpouring of public concern by ordinary citizens worried about the physical survival of themselves and their children. In many ways, the most important political result of Chernobyl was to displace lingering fear of the KGB with fear of ecological catastrophe. This popular 'radiaphobia' was not without foundation, of course. In subsequent years, for example, high-radiation meat was spread around the USSR, in order to limit dosage accumulation in Ukraine and Belarus. Thanks to glasnost, moreover, local newspapers in Siberia were actually able to warn readers when 'Chernobyl beef' was due to arrive. Chernobyl also stimulated protest movements around nuclear plants and chemical factories in the Baltic and Armenia – and frightened the Russian intelligentsia into challenging the bureaucratic state responsible for the disaster and the way its consequences were mishandled.

So accidents matter. But how to put these contingencies into some sort of intelligible context? What approaches are available to social scientists who do not want merely to catalogue the accidents of history? To be more specific, what approaches permitted some students of the Soviet Union to foresee, not particular accidents, but the vulnerability of the regime to accident? Before trying to deal with that question, however, it might useful to mention some who got it right; who effectively challenged the conventional wisdom that the Soviet Union (in spite of its many problems) was bound to endure.

Some Got It Right

Given our scepticism as to the possibility of predicting historical events, the real issue is not who provided the answers as to the USSR's longevity, but who was asking the right questions? Some apparently were – including a number of French authors who were more prone to see the fragility of the Soviet system. For example, Emmanuel Todd (not himself a Russian specialist) wrote a popular book in 1976 *(La Chute Finale)* underlining the instability of the Soviet system by pointing to the precariousness of its internal and external empire and its economic and political stagnation. In the United States, however, one commentator – and one volume of essays – may be singled out as showing extraordinary prescience about the Soviet political system. The commentator, of course, was Zbigniew Brzezinski.

Brzezinski was one of the founders of the much-criticized school of totalitarianism and a later advocate of human rights as at least one way of putting pressure on the Soviet Union. Brzezinski was, without doubt, one of the most prolific and influential American writers on Communist affairs in the post-war period. Though in his early work he argued that the USSR could not survive without repeated purges (Brzezinski, 1956), after 1962 he never wavered from the view that ideology and power were the key categories to understanding Soviet politics. This led him to conclude that the system was incapable of incremental reform (Brzezinski, January 1962; 1966). He repeated much the same point in 1976 – the year in which he assumed the mantle of National Security Adviser to the Carter administration. A breakdown of the Soviet system, he noted, was much more likely than reform; amongst other things, the 'national question' in the USSR created 'a major block to gradual evolution' (Brzezinski, in Paul Cocks *et al.* (eds), 1976). Thirteen years on he was arguing that we could easily witness another 'Spring of Nations' as in 1848 (in George Urban (ed.), 1989). And, in his magisterial *The Grand Failure* (1989), he saw turmoil in the Soviet Union as being far more likely than either reform, stagnation, fragmentation or a coup. He also rejected the then conventional view that the Politburo was split between advocates and enemies of reform. The main obstacle to change was the intrinsically unreformable nature of the system, and not some sort of reactionary opposition to Gorbachev inside the Communist Party. Brzezinski recognized the historical importance of Gorbachev, though less as reformer and more as someone who had unleashed forces he could not control. As he noted at the time, quite 'unintentionally, Gorbachev's policies [were] contributing to the build-up of a potentially revolutionary situation' by 'reducing the level of political fear, even as they [were] raising the level of social frustration'. 'Such a combination', he concluded, was 'inherently explosive.'

If Brzezinski got it right by swimming against the current of the

Sovietological mainstream, then so too did a group of writers whose contribution to the debate was a 1987 conference published in 1988 under the editorship of Alexander Shtromas - a Lithuanian émigré - and Morton Kaplan. One of the contributors to that volume was Terry McNeill whose piece in this book reasonably reflects the working assumptions and arguments of at least some of the participants at the original gathering in Geneva (billed later as 'the largest and intellectually most systematic conference ever held on the Soviet Union'). Though the conference was a product of the 'Professors' World Peace Academy' - an organization funded by the Reverend Myung Sun Moon's Unification Church - the authors themselves were not Moonies! And even though some might find it hard to believe that a gathering supported by the 'Moonies' got it right when the CIA, Brookings, the RAND Corporation, Harvard, Columbia and the rest got it wrong, the book still deserves to be read for its detailed examination of the Soviet crisis which Shtromas believed could 'shake and eventually lead to [a] change of ... regime'.

In his contribution, for example, Richard Burks concluded that 'the chances for system breakdown in the next 5-10 years are probably better than even, since all these problems have to be dealt with by a government that is no longer working as it was designed to do'. This erosion of authority was a result of the veto power accumulated by bureaucrats and the succession struggles which turned the general secretary into a 'walking corpse'. Burks warned of 'the danger of a political landslide [where] total control has ended by producing total dissent'. Similarly, Shtromas argued that 'the new technocratic elite, with Gorbachev at its helm, would certainly not hesitate to introduce the long overdue radical system reforms that, being incompatible with totalitarian communist rule, would surely lead to its dismantlement'. He also anticipated a split in the elite and the emergence of what he termed a 'second pivot', as a rival to the Communist Party. Shtromas did not predict that an elected Congress would emerge in such a role (his favoured candidate was the military), but the concept of a 'second pivot' was a useful insight into the mechanism of perestroika's demise - before the event. Shtromas, moreover, correctly perceived that the Soviet ideological state had fatally weakened the immobilizing power of Russian nationalism.

The contribution to the volume by Fedoseyev, a radio engineer, was perhaps the most perspicacious of all, however. Chaos loomed, he maintained, because of the 'gradual collapse of state planning'. He also observed that 'not one decree of the Politburo' was 'now being fulfilled'. A popular revolution was unlikely, but some sort of coup could be expected by the military or KGB, or of the 'palace' variety. Another contributor was equally forthright and speculated at some length about the prospects for the reception of Soviet law 'after the collapse of the Soviet system'; and whilst

Terry McNeill was a little more guarded in his conclusion, he held out little hope for the Soviet Union. The 'ice' had only begun to 'shift a little' perhaps. Nonetheless, the system was now living on what he called 'borrowed time'. (All quotes from Alexander Shtromas and Morton Kaplan (eds), 1988.)

What Went Wrong with Sovietology?

But if some got it right, why then did so many get it wrong? There is already a conventional wisdom about where Sovietology went wrong - built around the following seven explanations:

1. Academic objectivity was obscured by political bias, either of the left (who were keen not to seem hostile to the USSR) or of the right (who were too hostile).
2. Soviet area studies was methodologically feeble because of its isolation from the core social science disciplines (Frederick J. Fleron Jr and Erik P. Hoffman, September 1991).
3. Specialists lacked a rigorous grounding in the languages and histories of the region - particularly of the non-Russian peoples of the USSR.
4. Those who tried to conduct research inside the USSR faced insuperable hurdles: unreliable or non-existent data, problems of access, deliberate misinformation by Soviet officials and academics, etc.
5. Professional, personal and political rivalry left most émigré scholars 'out in the cold', and so prevented Sovietology from benefiting from their insights.
6. The seduction of leading academics into the role of media pundits and soothsayers meant that they had few incentives to engage in either careful empirical research or close supervision of doctoral dissertations.
7. Excessive dependence on government funding led to a situation where the intelligence agencies or the military were able to set the academic agenda.

All these arguments - with the exception of the last one - contain a degree of truth. However, they only take us some of the way in explaining why Sovietology failed. Let us deal first with the contentious issue of 'political bias'.

Since the 'fall', each side has accused the other of misunderstanding the nature of the USSR because they manipulated Soviet Studies for their own narrow ends. The left, for example, have attacked the right for being ethnocentric, of projecting their own values on to a society that was (and is) not ready for them, and of course for holding to the outmoded and static Cold War formula that the Soviet Union was a species of totalitarianism. The right in turn have argued that many liberal Sovietologists were driven as much, if not more, by their distaste for the Cold War and fear of the Bomb than by a real desire to analyse the USSR - warts and all. As a result, they tended to portray the USSR in as favourable a light as possible, to prove that they were 'just like us'.

The liberal case against conservative 'totalitarians' is as unconvincing as the conservative case is against the left. Indeed, the argument that there was serious left-wing bias in the study of Soviet politics does not stand up to close examination (the same was not true for Soviet history). There were in fact very few Marxists engaged in the detailed study of the USSR. Moreover, if writers such as Seweryn Bialer and Jerry Hough exaggerated the stability of the Soviet state, it was not because of closet sympathies for the Brezhnev regime, or out of a desire to demean the achievements of the American political system. Their fault (and that of many others like them) was not that they displayed too much political bias, but that they showed too little, and tried to analyse the USSR in as 'non-judgemental' a fashion as possible. This distracted them from the glaring inefficiencies of the Soviet system - flaws which both conservatives on the one hand, and critical Western Marxists on the other, found it much easier to recognize (see Mandel, 1989 and Arnot and Ticktin in this volume for a Marxist perspective).

On the question of the role (or marginalized role) of émigrés, it is true that Sovietologists tended to disparage the potential contribution of émigré scholars. However, whilst having a profound understanding of the internal contradictions of the Soviet system, émigrés and dissidents did not do much better than Sovietologists at foreseeing its demise in 1991 (Vladimir Krasnov, in Shtromas and Kaplan (eds), 1988). Three decades ago, the dissident historian Andrei Amalrik boldly stated: 'I have no doubt that this great Eastern Slav empire, created by Germans, Byzantines and Mongols, has entered the last decades of its existence' (Andrei Amalrik, 1970). But Amalrik thought the USSR would inevitably be drawn into a war with China, which would serve as the *deux ex machina*. About 20 years later, Vladimir Bukovsky was arguing that the system was in terminal crisis, and that reforms would eventually fail, though they could prolong the life of the system in the short term (Vladimir Bukovsky, in Henry S. Rowen and Charles Wolf (eds), 1987; and in Urban (ed.), 1989). Bukovsky, however, did not try to estimate how long the death throes would last, nor precisely how the system would come to an end.

If a greater sensitivity to the views of émigrés would have made little difference to Sovietology's predictive capacities, would the subject have been helped by an injection of 'hard' methodologies? I see no evidence to support this view. Content analysis of speeches, for example, and statistical analysis of career data, did not bring greater understanding of the Soviet political system than did 'softer' methodologies. In fact, one can quite plausibly argue the opposite. Most of the best-funded research projects were indeed those that adopted quantitative techniques, such as the Soviet Interview Project (SIP), a survey of 4500 émigrés. This focused on the routines of daily life in the USSR. This was useful enough. There was nothing especially wrong with the findings. It was just that when it was completed there seemed to be little to show for the $8 million the project allegedly cost. Nor did the report tell us much about the future of the Soviet system itself (James R. Millar (ed.), 1987). In addition, when comparativists from other fields were brought in to discuss Soviet affairs, far from changing our ways of thinking, in the end they tended to accept, rather than challenge or reject, the prevailing assumptions of Sovietology. Thus, only one of the ethnicity specialists assembled by Alexander Motyl in 1990 raised the break-up of the USSR as a serious possibility (N. Eisenstadt, in Motyl (ed.), 1992). The others all saw the incentives for the elites of the republics as lying within the existing state structure. David Laitin *et al.* even concluded that 'language claims by nationality groups' would not be 'the spark' that would ignite 'the ethnic time bomb' (Peter Rutland, in Neil Harding (ed.), 1984).

American PhDs: 'Nonsense on Stilts'?

But this is not to say that there were not genuine problems with the methodology of Soviet Studies. Some of these were vividly evident in the type of doctoral dissertations undertaken in the USA before 1989.

The PhD is typically the most serious research project an academic will undertake in his or her entire career. Thus they should provide the most reliable guide to the prevailing intellectual framework and the quality of the basic research in the field. It was with this in mind that I obtained a small grant in 1988 to read all 87 dissertations written between 1976 and 1987 on Soviet domestic politics (Kennan Institute, October 1990). Whilst several of the theses made for excellent reading, the overall effect was to remind one of Bismarck's comment that there are certain things, such as sausages and legislation, whose creation should not be studied too closely.

The sample amounted to a mere 4 per cent of the total number of comparative politics theses written during the decade. Graduate student interest in the USSR slumped in the 1970s, and only slowly started to recover in the 1980s - thanks in part to large injections of taxpayers' money. Five universities produced an average of six theses each on Soviet domestic politics during the decade, whilst a quarter of the theses were written in universities that produced only one or two over the period. This implies that most students were working in relative isolation, despite the concentration of resources in research centres.

Incredibly, only 17 of the 87 thesis writers had actually studied in the USSR - this at a time when organizations such as IREX (International

Research and Exchanges Board) were sending dozens of scholars to Russia each year (presumably all historians and literature specialists). Thus the charge that Sovietologists were ill-prepared as area specialists has some justification. One quarter of the theses relied exclusively on English-language sources, and only six showed proficiency in non-Russian languages. Those who did visit the USSR typically relied upon library work and interviews with academics. Only a handful were able to conduct anything resembling fieldwork (such as interviewing officials).

The present author knows from personal experience how difficult it was to do serious research in Brezhnevite Russia. I went to the Plekhanov Economics Institute in 1982 to study labour relations. My visit began with my 'scientific supervisor' handing me a ten-page reading list on 'socialist competition', the first four pages consisting of works by Marx, Lenin and Brezhnev. He told me to come back when I had read them all. Another lecturer who happened to be present took pity on me, and explained in the corridor that socialist competition was 'bullshit'. He gave me the names of some journalists and ministry officials to talk to (but was too scared to invite me to his home). In the end I learned something about industrial management – but never did see the inside of a Soviet factory.

Given the quality of the primary material being fed into the base of the Sovietological discipline, it is hardly surprising that much of its high theorizing turned out to be 'nonsense on stilts'. As far as subject matter was concerned, dissertation topics seem to have been selected on the basis of the availability of sources. A great deal of effort went into poring over the brief published biographies of Central Committee members, and into content analysis of newspaper articles. In the late 1970s several theses were generated by the CIA-funded Soviet Elite Perceptions project at Ohio State University, which involved an exhaustive content analysis of Politburo speeches. (No less than five distinct factions were identified among the 11 full Politburo members!) Few authors dallied over the question of how much interpretative weight such source material could bear. (In what sense, for example, did Politburo members express their own views in their formal speeches?) The simple fact was that the texts printed in *Pravda* were all that analysts had to go on.

And whilst all this attention was being devoted to Politburo speeches and the career background of Central Committee members, little was being given to the core institutions of political power in the USSR: the Communist Party and government ministries. Moreover, although there were four theses on women, two on students, and several on professional groups such as journalists, no doctoral research was conducted on the basic groups which made up Soviet society: the workers, peasants and intelligentsia. There was, however, a good deal of interest shown in the nationalities and ten of the theses addressed the problem; and most have stood the test of time fairly well. However, whilst Ukraine and Uzbekistan were well covered, there was nothing done on the Baltic, the Caucasus, Belarus, or Moldova, and very little on the Russian provinces.

In terms of the framework adopted, the most 'popular' was straightforward historical narrative. Significantly, few of the theses utilized a model, such as pluralism or corporatism. The most frequently cited works in the obligatory introductory literature review were Jerry Hough's *The Soviet Prefects* and George Breslauer's *Khrushchev and Brezhnev as Leaders*; whilst the most common approach was a case study of a policy decision, with the influence of Brzezinski and Huntington's 1965 text-book still visible (Zbigniew Brzezinski and Samuel P. Huntington, 1965).

Not surprisingly, in view of the paucity of empirical material, many authors retreated into the realm of theory – but unfortunately some sought to fill the vacuum by adopting Soviet categories. Thus one in four of the theses started off with a discussion of the thoughts of Marx, Engels and Lenin on the subject in question (be it nationalism, the environment, military policy, industrial management, or whatever). The result was that a number of works were not so much about the subject itself, but about Soviet views of the subject. It was not as if these writers were convinced Marxists. It was simply that they assumed that Marxism-Leninism shaped Soviet reality, so that was the logical place to begin. In this way, much of the Sovietological community 'went native' (at a distance) with the result that entire books were devoted to such Soviet-defined subjects as 'the scientific-technological revolution' and 'developed socialism' (Terry L. Thompson, 1988; Donald R. Kelley, 1986).

Group Think and Soviet Stability

I now want to turn to the issue of 'disciplinary group think'. In my view this stifled creative thinking and controversial ideas – the most controversial, of course, being that the USSR might one day disappear as an entity! There were, however, good reasons why Sovietologists found it difficult to contemplate this as a possibility. One is very specifically methodological and relates to a mode of thinking which assumed that if there was such a thing as the Soviet system, then our collective task was to explain how it functioned. Such an approach not only encouraged closed thinking, but led those who were so trapped to the not illogical conclusion that if the USSR was 'real' then in some grand Hegelain sense it was 'rational' too.

Sovietologists who accepted the description of the Soviet Union as a functioning, coherent 'system' then had to address two further questions: How well did the system work? And what were the prospects for systemic reform? The answer to the second question depended, in large part, on one's answer to the first.

Two general answers were given to the question of how the Soviet system worked: well and badly. Optimists - mostly political liberals - thought the system was held together by more or less the same mixture of habit, consent and coercion that applied in most developed countries. The system had flaws, but those flaws were amenable to reform and would diminish over time. On the other hand, most conservatives saw the USSR as a totalitarian regime in a class of its own, fundamentally illegitimate and irrational, and only held together by force. Let us examine the liberal argument first and then the conservative perspective.

Liberals

The liberal consensus on how the system worked revolved around the themes of stability, convergence, pluralism and leadership. Back in the 1960s Samuel P. Huntington argued that Leninism, for all its flaws, represented an alternative path to modernity, with the Communist Party as an institution capable of aggregating social interests (Samuel P. Huntington, 1968). Bialer picked up the theme, making the concept of stability the centrepiece of his analysis. In 1986, he maintained that the USSR was facing 'a crisis of effectiveness' but not 'a crisis of survival'. 'The economy is not going bankrupt', he asserted, and 'the Soviet state is certainly in no immediate danger of disintegration' (Seweryn Bialer, 1986). The book barely addressed the national question, commenting that there was 'no evidence that' it would 'become the focus of social instability'. Bialer's respect for the system's permanence led him to conclude in an article in 1983 that 'I do not believe that even such a threat as the loss of the East European empire might spark an attempt by the military to take over the reins of government [because] the Soviet leadership itself will command the armed forces to crush such a danger' (Seweryn Bialer, in Robert F. Byrnes (ed.), 1983). Bialer himself did not, however, believe that liberal reforms would succeed, since the political forces arrayed against them were too powerful. But his arguments as to the USSR's stability were eagerly accepted by those credulous of perestroika.

What was the foundation of this system stability, given the absence of mass terror? Bialer and others argued that the regime had made the transition from totalitarianism to one based on popular legitimacy. This was established through the mechanism of what became known in the Sovietological profession as a 'social contract'. Under its terms, the people in general and the workers in particular were (it was argued) guaranteed a basic standard of living in return for their political quiescence (Seweryn Bialer and Peter Hauslohner, in Ferenc Feher and Andrew Arato (eds), 1989;

George W. Breslauer, in Karl W. Ryavec (ed.), 1978). However, the coalminers' strikes of 1989 seemed to disprove this thesis. After all, if there had been such a contract, this (relatively privileged) section of the proletariat would not have done what they did. Indeed, it was clear from their demands that they had been ignored for years (their soap ration had not even changed since 1923!) (Peter Rutland, Winter 1990).

The social contract aside, most scholars believed that the industrialization unleashed by Stalin would eventually produce a society comparable to that in the developed West. The logic of modernization was supposedly reinforced by forces of socioeconomic competition on a global scale (Walter C. Clemens, 1978). Jerry Hough was the most sophisticated and prolific exponent of these views (Jerry F. Hough, 1988). Hough also urged that the transition to a Western-type society would accelerate once leaders who matured after the death of Stalin rose to power. Hough was right in stressing the importance of the arrival of the first post-Stalin generation (with Gorbachev at their head), but wrong in believing that the new generation would be able to salvage the system.

Although most Sovietologists balked at describing the Soviet system as pluralist, few challenged the idea that interest groups were actively lobbying behind the façade of the one-party state (Susan G. Solomon (ed.), 1983; H. Gordon Skilling and Franklyn Griffiths (eds), 1971). For liberals, politics in the USSR, as elsewhere, was of the 'who gets what, when and how' variety. As perestroika gathered pace, however, it became common to argue that elements of a civil society were emerging from below, in the form of myriad informal groups, and that this would guarantee the irreversibility of Gorbachev's reforms (Gail W. Lapidus, in Seweryn Bialer (ed.), 1989; S. Frederick Starr, in Seweryn Bialer and Michael Mandelbaum (eds), 1988). This was hopelessly wrong, and no amount of wishful thinking could alter the basic fact that the political system had been constructed along totalitarian lines, and its institutions could not be retooled to serve pluralist goals. In fact, it was particularly misleading to suggest that a civil society was present in the USSR. Indeed, the idea that a 'civil society' could grow up under a tyranny which denied private property and the rule of law, would have struck Adam Smith and Adam Ferguson as absurd.

The aspect of Soviet politics which attracted the lion's share of attention was the question of leadership. Much effort was expended on scrutinizing Politburo politics and second-guessing the moves of the General Secretary. This stress on the importance of leadership was congruent with the idea that the system was essentially stable – it is only worth studying the captain's orders if the crew is going to carry them out. But the assumption that power was still concentrated in the Kremlin contradicted the idea that the USSR possessed a Western-style political system. Liberal Sovietologists apparently saw no incongruity between their obsession with Gorbachev and their assertion that the system was essentially pluralist.

Rather than seeing perestroika as the harbinger of a profound social crisis, most authors preferred to slot it into their comfortable paradigm of leadership struggle. For them perestroika was just the latest example of what one of them described as the 'familiar cycle' which had repeated itself throughout Soviet and Russian history (Herbert Ellison, in Lawrence W. Lerner and Donald Treadgold (eds), 1988). In the post-Stalin era this played out as a contest between the General Secretary and his conservative colleagues. Analysts argued back and forth over whether the leader's power was greatest at the beginning of his period in office (the honeymoon effect) or whether it increased over time (thanks to patronage) (Archibald H. Brown, in Lerner and Treadgold (eds), 1988; Breslauer; Valerie Bunce, 1981). Unfortunately, these debates distracted attention from the question of the Kremlin's ability to influence events in the country at large. In the 1980s the Politburo's power and authority were haemorrhaging at an accelerating rate, and by 1989 Gorbachev was far from being the omnipotent leader portrayed in the West.

Conservatives

Writers of a conservative bent regarded the USSR as an unnatural creation that would sooner or later go the way of all empires. However, most of them thought it would be later rather than sooner, and so were stuck with having to explain the obstinate presence of what George Urban described as a 'ramshackle but functioning empire'. Writing in 1989, Urban went on to argue that 'one cannot see any Soviet leader's experimentation with reform carrying him to a point where the self-questioning of the system would drive it to self-destruction'.

In his 1984 work, *Survival is not Enough,* Richard Pipes saw the USSR as entering a revolutionary situation – but lacking a group capable of making a revolution (Richard Pipes, 1984; Fall 1984). Because of Russia's innate conservatism, reform would only result from a profound crisis. But Pipes was ambiguous as to whether such reforms would lead to transformation or collapse. For Jeane Kirkpatrick the main question in her 1990 collection of essays was the reversibility of the reforms rather than the collapse of the system (Jeane J. Kirkpatrick, 1990). Contemplating the disturbances in the Baltic in November 1988, she commented that 'none of this means that the Soviet Union is falling apart'. She was correct in arguing that totalitarian regimes, unlike their authoritarian counterparts, do not cycle in and out of power. But she did not go one step further and discuss the possibility that such a system could collapse.

For a glimpse of thinking that received serious attention in the US government, we can turn to a book entitled *The Future of the Soviet Empire*, put together by RAND Corporation specialists in 1987 (Rowen and Wolf). The authors could not bring themselves to imagine that the Soviet elite would voluntarily relinquish its control over the coercive apparatus. The empire in the book's title is the external one: there was no specific chapter on nationalism, and the editors considered that 'increased alienation and disaffection [among non-Russians], rather than substantially increased active dissidence, seems in store'.

The dominant analytical framework in the RAND collection was that of the 'guns vs butter' trade-off. As economic crisis deepened and the burden of empire mounted, the USSR would be forced to divert resources from its military budget. This is undoubtedly part of the story, but 1991 showed that it was not the decisive factor. Although the guns vs butter metaphor has intuitive appeal (even though the phrase was coined by Nazi propagandist, Joseph Goebbels), it was quite misleading. There was more to Soviet budgetary planning than a divide-the-dollar game. Moreover, there is no econometric evidence that states anywhere actually make such a trade-off. Countries have more guns and butter if the economy is growing, and less of both if the economy is declining. It is very difficult (in either market or command economies) to transfer resources from one sector to the other.

Five Scenarios in Search of the Soviet Future

Over the years many conferences and monographs were devoted to predicting the Soviet future (George W. Breslauer, 1978; Rowen and Wolf (eds), 1987; Robert Conquest (ed.), 1986; Shtromas and Kaplan 1988; Barrington Moore Jr, 1954). The most important question which analysts had to confront was the reformability of the USSR. Was the system capable of adaptation? And would reforms make the system more stable or less so? Alternative scenarios produced five possible outcomes. We shall look at each in descending order of popularity. Significantly, the least popular option turned out to be the most accurate!

(a) *Systemic change in a liberal direction (perestroika)*. This was the ruling paradigm, accounting for at least 60 per cent of the Sovietological output. It flowed directly from the mind-set of mainstream Sovietology. The paradigm's dominance was a result of many factors, not least wishful thinking and a lingering belief in 'History as Progress'. It helped that perestroika was also the official Soviet interpretation of what was going on, energetically spread by the Moscow-based academics who were the main source of information for most Western journalists and Sovietologists.

(b) *The system muddles through without major reform.* This was the second most popular scenario, favoured by perhaps 25 per cent of authors (including the present one) on both the left and right wings of the discipline (Timothy J. Colton, 1987). Extrapolation of past trends into the future is the reflex response of social scientists, *faut de mieux*. If the system had lasted for 74 years, it seemed safe to infer that it would survive.

(c) *The system slowly collapses due to chronic problems.* Many authors argued that the system's chronic problems would eventually cause its downfall, although they rarely laid out a timetable, or suggested precisely how such a collapse would come about. Chronic ailments, after all, are not necessarily fatal. The weakness of the economy was obviously a prime candidate in explaining the collapse. However, although the economy experienced a declining rate of growth in the 1970s, it was still growing. The real breakdown only began after 1988, and this was as much a product of political processes as their cause. It is true that Russia suffered from rising rates of morbidity and mortality, crime, pollution, alcoholism, and so forth. But exactly how these social problems would translate into the overthrow of the political system was something of a mystery. Alcoholics do not make good revolutionaries (and August 1991 showed that they make lousy putschists).

(d) *Systemic change in a reactionary direction.* This option had a few subscribers among Western scholars, but was popular among émigrés, who saw Russian nationalism as the most likely candidate to fill the vacuum caused by the erosion of Marxism. Alexander Yanov, one of the leading exponents of this view, criticized both liberal and conservative Sovietologists for failing to give due weight to the possibility of a nationalist take-over (Alexander Yanov, in Robert O. Crummey (ed.), 1989). Solzhenitsyn may also be included in this category, since he was waiting for some sort of moral revolt by the Russian people. Events showed, however, that Russian national consciousness was even more debilitated by 74 years of communism than these writers imagined.

(e) *The system collapses quickly due to failed reforms.* Virtually no one explored this possibility. However, it was this – the least expected of all academic scenarios – which turned out to be what actually transpired. Amongst the first to spell out the imminence of the apocalypse was Martin Malia (alias 'Z') ('Z', Winter 1990). Also in spring 1990 Charles Fairbanks wrote that 'the end of the rule in Moscow by people who identify themselves as communists … will probably come by 1995. It could conceivably happen as early as this summer' (Charles H. Fairbanks Jr, Spring 1990).

Nationalism

Many specialists, naturally enough, saw the multinational character of the Soviet state as being its Achilles' heel, but in spite of this, few thought that a break-up of the USSR was imminent (Teresa Rakowska Harmstone, in 1986). Alexander Motyl concluded that the 'non-Russians will not rebel, because they cannot rebel', given the power of the security apparatus, which even economic decline would not diminish (Alexander J. Motyl, 1987). For Motyl, republican elites were too dependent on Moscow to risk playing the nationalist card.

Most writers on nationality issues specialized in individual republics and avoided discussion of systemic stability. Perhaps the most widely used text on nationality policy was the volume *Nationalities and Reform in Soviet Politics* by Lubomyr Hajda and Mark Beissinger (1990). In their conclusion Hajda and Beissinger focused on Gorbachev's agenda, and rather than regard the USSR as doomed they looked ahead to a new 'non-imperial formula for legitimacy'.

Those nationality specialists who did predict the collapse of the USSR, such as Helene Carrere D'Encausse, saw the demographic time-bomb of Central Asia as the decisive factor (Helene Carrere D'Encausse, 1982; Michael Rywkin, 1990). Extrapolation of Muslim birth rates implied the Islamicization of the army and thus the erosion of one of the central pillars of Soviet power. Population pressure would also force the Central Asian leaders to demand more resources from Moscow and an end to the region's colonial dependence on cotton.

In the event, however, Muslim demographics were irrelevant to the collapse of the USSR, and the Central Asian leaders were amongst the last and most ardent defenders of the Union. It was the Western nationalisms which pried open the cracks in the Soviet empire. Whilst Sovietologists recognized the strength of national feeling in these peripheral Western regions, no one foresaw the role they would play in bringing down the USSR.

Learning from Failure?

The conclusion of this chapter is that Sovietology utterly failed to foresee the speed and scope of the fall of the USSR. It did so not because it lacked a sound methodology, or as a result of a sinister political conspiracy, but because of a basic inability to contemplate the end of the Soviet Union. To this extent, Sovietology failed because of a failure of imagination. More specifically, Soviet Studies got two things very badly wrong: it exaggerated the Soviet system's stability and it seriously overstated the scope for reform. Even amongst those few writers who tried to sketch alternative futures for the USSR, only a handful even raised the possibility of system collapse.

This 'grand falsification' will have served a purpose only if the profession shows itself willing to face up to the magnitude of its failure. Unfortunately, there is as yet little sign of this happening. It is true that the major research centres have run some 'what went wrong?' seminars. Yet, contrary to what one might have expected, at such gatherings *mea culpas* were rather thin on the ground. Indeed, having attended half a dozen such meetings, I have yet to hear a single contributor stand up and explain how his or her own approach was flawed. (See the results of these reflections in Fleron and Hoffman, 1991; William E. Odom, October 1992; Thomas F. Remington, October 1992.) On the contrary, many people seemed to be convincing themselves that they had really foreseen the collapse all along! Indeed, it would appear that the true purpose of these early meetings was not to engage in a serious discussion of past intellectual flaws but to protect budgets and guard against falling student enrolments.

No doubt Sovietologists (like historians of the Cold War) will make great strides forward in the next few years, as more memoirs are published and documents are slowly released. The last major surge in our knowledge of the Soviet system came in the mid-1950s, with the publication from the Harvard interview project. This time around, however, scholars will be able to interview not displaced persons and ex-POWs, but former members of the Politburo and Central Committee. These new opportunities should help to fill the gaps in our knowledge. Whether or not it will help us explain why the Soviet Union collapsed when it did remains uncertain however: possibly as uncertain as the legacy of Sovietology itself.

---

1   This is a slightly revised version of an article which first appeared in *The National Interest*, No. 31, Spring 1993. It appears here with their permission and the written permission of the author.

References

Amalrik, A., *Will the Soviet Union Survive until 1984?* (New York: Harper & Row, 1970).

Bialer, S., *The Soviet Paradox* (New York: Knopf, 1986).

——'The Political System', in R. F. Byrnes (ed.), *After Brezhnev* (New York: Pinter, 1983).

——and Hauslohner, P., 'Gorbachev's Social Contract', in F. Feher and A. Arato (eds), *Gorbachev: The Debate* (Atlantic Highlands, NJ: Humanities Press, 1989).

Breslauer, G.W., 'On the Adaptability of Soviet Welfare-State Authoritarianism', in K.W. Ryavec (ed.), *Soviet Society and the Communist Party* (Amherst: University of Massachussetts Press, 1978).

——*Five Images of the Soviet Future* (Berkeley: University of California Press, 1978).

——*Krushchev and Brezhnev as Leaders* (London, Allen & Unwin, 1982).

Brown, A.H., 'The Era of Gorbachev?', in Lerner and Treadgold (eds), *op. cit.*

Brzezinski, Z., *Ideology and Power in Soviet Politics* (New York: Praeger, 1962).

—— 'The Soviet System: Transformation or Degeneration?', *Problems of Communism* (January 1966).

——(ed.), *Dilemmas of Change in Soviet Politics* (New York: Columbia University Press, 1969).

——'Soviet Politics', in Cocks *et al.* (eds), *op. cit.*

——and Huntington, S.P., *Political Power: USA/USSR* (New York: Viking Press, 1965).

Bukovsky, V., 'The Political Condition of the Soviet Union', in Rowen and Wolf (eds), *op. cit.*

——in Urban (ed.), *op. cit.*

Bunce, V., *Do New Leaders make a Difference?* (Princeton: Princeton University Press, 1981).

Clemens, W.C., *The USSR and Global Interdependence* (Washington: American Enterprise Institute Press, 1978).

Cocks, P. *et al.* (eds), *The Dynamics of Soviet Politics* (Cambridge, Harvard University Press, 1976).

Colton, T.J., *The Dilemma of Reform in the Soviet Union* (New York: Council on Foreign Affairs, 1987).

Conquest, R. (ed.), *The Last Empire* (Palo Alto: Hoover Institution Press, 1986).

D'Encausse, H.C., *Confused Power* (New York: Harper & Row, 1982).

Djilas, M., 'New Utopias for Old', in Urban (ed.), *op. cit.*

Eisenstadt, S.N., 'Center-Periphery Relations', in Motyl, (ed.), *op. cit.*

Ellison, H., introduction in Lerner and Treadgold (eds), *op. cit.*

Fairbanks Jr, C.H., 'The Suicide of Soviet Communism', *Journal of Democracy* (Spring 1990).

Fleron Jr, F.J. and Hoffman, E.P., *Sovietology and Perestroika: Methodology and Lessons from the Past*, Paper given at Harriman Institute Forum (September 1991).

Gellner, E., 'Nationalism in the Vacuum', in Motyl, (ed.), *op. cit.*

Goldman, M., *USSR in Crisis: The Failure of an Economic System* (New York: Norton, 1983).

Hajda, L. and Beissinger, M., *Nationalities and Reform in Soviet Politics* (Boulder: Westview Press, 1990).

Harding, N. (ed.), *The State in Socialist Society* (New York: Macmillan, 1984).

Harmstone, T.R., 'Minority Nationalisms', in Conquest (ed.), *op. cit.*

Hough, J., *The Soviet Prefects* (Cambridge: Harvard University Press, 1969).

——*Russia and the West* (New York: Simon & Schuster, 1988).

Huntington, S.P., *Political Order in Changing Societies* (New Haven: Yale University Press, 1968).

Kelley, D.R., *The Politics of Developed Socialism* (Westport, CT: Greenwood Press, 1986).

Kirkpatrick, J.J., *The Withering Away of the Soviet State* (Washington: American Enterprise Institute Press, 1990).

Krasnov, V., 'Images of the Soviet Future: The Emigre and Samizdat Debate', in Shtromas and Kaplan (eds), *op. cit.*

Lapidus, G.W., 'State and Society: Toward the Emergence of Civil Society in the Soviet Union', in Seweryn Bialer (ed.), *Politics, Society and Nationality Inside Gorbachev's Russia* (Boulder: Westview Press, 1989).

Lerner, L.W. and Treadgold, D. (eds), *Gorbachev and the Soviet Future* (Boulder: Westview, 1988).

Mandel, E., *Beyond Perestroika* (New York: Verso, 1989).

McNeill, T., 'Images of the Soviet Future: The Western Scholarly Debate', in Shtromas and Kaplan (eds), *op. cit.*

Millar, J.R. (ed.), *Politics, Work and Daily Life in the Soviet Union* (New York: Cambridge University Press, 1987).

Moore Jr, B., *Terror and Progress: USSR* (Cambridge: Harvard University Press, 1954).

Motyl, A.J., *Will the Non-Russians Rebel?* (Ithaca: Cornell University Press, 1987).

—(ed.), *Thinking Theoretically About Soviet Nationalities* (New York, Columbia University Press, 1992).

Odom, W.E., 'Soviet Politics and After', *World Politics* (October 1992).

Pipes, R., *Survival is not Enough* (New York: Simon & Schuster, 1984).

—'Can the Soviet Union Reform?', *Foreign Affairs* (Fall 1984).

Remington, T.F., *Common Knowledge: Soviet Political Studies and the Problem of System Stability*, Paper delivered at Kennan Institute (October 1992).

Rowen, H.S. and Wolf C. (eds), *The Future of the Soviet Empire* (New York: St Martin's Press, 1987).

Rutland, P., 'The Nationality Problem and the Soviet State', in Harding (ed.), *op. cit.*

—'Labour Movements and Unrest 1989-1990', *Soviet Economy* (Winter 1990).

—LBJ School of Public Affairs, University of Texas at Austin, *Sovietology: From Stagnation to Perestroika? A Decade of Doctoral Research in Soviet Politics.* Kennan Institute, Occasional Paper No. 241 (October 1990).

Rywkin, M., *Moscow's Muslim Challenge* (Armonk, NY: Myron E. Sharpe,1990).

Sheehy, G. *The Man who Changed the World* (New York, Perennial Library, 1990).

Shtromas, A. and Kaplan, M. (eds), *The Soviet Union and the Challenge of the Future* (New York: Paragon House, 1988).

Simon, G., *Nationalism and Policy Toward the Nationalities in the Soviet Union* (Boulder: Westview Press, 1991).

Skilling, H.G. and Griffiths, F. (eds), *Interest Groups in Soviet Politics* (Princeton: Princeton University Press, 1971).

Solomon, S.G. (ed.), *Pluralism in the Soviet Union* (New York: Macmillan, 1983).

Starr, S.F., 'The Changing Nature of Change in the USSR', in Seweryn Bialer and Michael Mandelbaum (eds), *Gorbachev's Russia and American Foreign Policy* (Boulder: Westview Press, 1988).

Thompson, T.L., *Soviet Ideology from Khrushchev to Gorbachev: Developed Socialism under Brezhnev* (Denver: Westview Press, 1988).

Todd, E., *La Chute Finale* (Robert Lafont, 1990 [1976]).

Urban, G. (ed.), *Can the Soviet System Survive?* (New York: Pinter, 1989).

Von Wright, G.H., *Explanation and Understanding* (Ithaca: Cornell University Press, 1971).

Yanov, A., 'Is Sovietology Reformable?', in R.O. Crummey (ed.), *Reform in Russia and the USSR* (Champaign: University of Illinois, 1989).

'Z', 'To the Stalin Mausoleum', *Daedalus* (Winter 1990).

3

Soviet Studies and the Collapse of the USSR: in Defence of Realism

TERRY McNEILL

Introduction

At every turn the historian encounters the unpredictable: contingency; historical accident; biological accident intruding itself into history, as when the death of a history-making person brings a change of direction; changes of mood; emergence of new situations; sudden leaps that seem to turn an accretion of little events into a big one; the complicated interaction of multiple determinants on every event; the unintended consequences of intended actions.[1]

It would be a foolish social scientist who denied the unpredictable, the contingent and the role of accident in history. This is why anticipating the future in any accurate way is such a difficult undertaking, a point well made by Robert Jervis amongst others.[2] In this respect, forecasting the fate of the Soviet Union proved no exception to this general rule – and those specialists who apparently failed to predict the demise of the Soviet system may derive some comfort at least from the fact that such a hazardous undertaking would inevitably produce some theoretical casualties along the way. Ultimately, they may console themselves with the knowledge that had it not been for the 'biological accident' that was Gorbachev and the 'unintended consequences' arising from his 'intended actions', their particular prediction that the USSR (in spite of its problems) would endure might well have proved to be correct.[3]

The approach adopted here does not seek to blame but rather suggests that the Soviet system was seriously and fundamentally flawed by a basic contradiction between its repressive political system on the one hand, and the degree of liberalization and rationalization of the economy and society needed to maintain the country's long-term economic viability on the other. As the years passed – and this conflict became more severe – the possibility of a resolution of the problem within the existing political framework diminished. The likelihood of a profound crisis in the Soviet system thus increased the longer the Soviet leadership delayed implementing economic reforms. Seen from this perspective, some form of unravelling of the Soviet order was most likely - at some time. Gorbachev's policies undoubtedly hastened the process. Indeed, as many analysts have pointed out, it was his actions more than anything else which led to the speedy disintegration of the USSR. Yet we should not forget that Gorbachev himself was responding to a pre-existing malaise which made the system extremely fragile. In this sense, he did not cause the decline of the USSR, but rather accelerated it by exposing and seeking to resolve its underlying problems. He, or some other leader, might have pursued another agenda; but in my view this would only have delayed what I think was its almost inevitable decay.

The thesis of this chapter is that those who focused predominantly on the core contradiction at the heart of the Soviet system were more likely to anticipate the system's implosion than those which did not: and by and large the theorists who did this tended - in the main - to be either 'realists' on the political right or theorists of a critical Marxist persuasion, on the political left. By the same token, those who failed to anticipate the possibility of the Soviet system disintegrating, did so in large part because they concentrated on issues, concepts or processes that were either marginal to, or ignored, this central problem.

To make good my claim, it is necessary to examine the different schools of Sovietological thought, of which there were many of course. Amongst the most important and influential I look at here in detail are the totalitarian school, the different shades of Marxism, elite analyses and what I term 'ideological perspectives'. I will then examine the overall contribution made to the study of the former USSR by the social and political sciences, before turning to assess the relevance of different realist theorists. Finally, I will conclude with a brief discussion of why Soviet Studies 'failed'.

Totalitarianism

Totalitarian theory evolved in the 1930s and 1940s, in an attempt by several Western political theorists to explain the apparently modern form of autocratic regimes that had arisen under Stalin in Russia, Hitler in Germany, and to a lesser extent Mussolini in Italy.[4] The chief characteristics of such regimes which - it was argued - distinguished them from all others, past or present, included: a totalist ideology; a single party committed to this ideology and usually led by one man; a fully developed secret police; and three kinds of monopoly or, more precisely, monopolistic control of mass communications, operational weapons and all organizations - including economic ones.[5]

Though there was little opposition to this view of the Soviet Union whilst Stalin remained its leader (even certain socialists critical of the USSR used the term), after 1953 the idea came under sustained attack. Certainly, amongst a number of Western analysts there was a very strong reaction indeed to a theory which in their view seemed to be more concerned to celebrate the West than to explain the peculiar features of the USSR. Some in fact rejected the notion on straightforward political grounds, insisting that the concept was merely an ideological justification for the policies of the Cold War. Marcuse even went so far as to suggest that the characteristics the model purported to describe in the Soviet Union were not much different to those found in the United States. Others also wondered whether totalitarianism was so new, whilst a few argued that the concept had little useful meaning, since most of the requisites of mass democracy were also requisites of totalitarianism. Finally, many doubted the value of a concept which sought to identify the very different systems of Fascist Italy and Nazi Germany with the Soviet Union. This was not merely clumsy, they believed, but was bound to lead to confusion, bearing in mind that Fascist and Communist ideologies and economic systems were quite distinct.

The more general critique of totalitarianism was linked to a more specific series of questions being asked about it by more liberal writers keen to lead Sovietology out of the intellectual ghetto into which it had purportedly been trapped by the exigencies of the Cold War. This in part was stimulated by several changes in the USSR itself which led to a number of limited reforms within the party, the termination of mass terror and the development of some form of collective leadership. Sovietologists also attacked the concept for being incapable of explaining change, of being unable to understand the policy-making process and of ignoring the existence of a vibrant social structure with its usual share of social problems. One of the doyens of American Sovietology – George Breslauer – even proposed an alternative characterization of the Soviet Union ('welfare-state authoritarianism') on the grounds that far too much had changed in the USSR since Stalin's death to still label the system as 'totalitarian'. His argument was not without some merit. Political organization, he noted, had shifted towards institutional pluralism at the top. Terror had been abandoned and mass mobilization had ceased to be employed as a means of control. There had also been a depoliticization of political and social life, an extension of privacy for loyal citizens and an increased commitment by the elite to minimal welfare and educational provision for all citizens. Thus what was the point of using a term which did not, and could not, take account of these various changes?[6]

The attempt to replace old ways of thinking about the Soviet Union with new concepts which more adequately and accurately described the country's complex character in the post-Stalin years was entirely reasonable. But in the process the very real strengths of the totalitarian model were almost ignored altogether. No doubt all theories have their weaknesses. But the demands placed upon this particular ideal type by its various critics seemed unreasonable, a point well made by Seton Watson who pointed out that if the Soviet regime continued to make total claims on its subjects' lives, it was perfectly legitimate to call it totalitarian. This view was also endorsed by Leonard Schapiro. One of the originators of the concept, Carl Friedrich, also urged retention, though he felt that totalitarianism should be kept and treated as a relative rather than an absolute category. Meissner argued that the concept should not be discarded either, because the Soviet system – unlike despotism, autocracy and absolutism in the past – was intent not only upon undivided power, but also all-embracing control. Moreover, the critics, in his view, had paid insufficient attention to those features of the Soviet system that were distinct and unique. Indeed, as others pointed out, the term totalitarianism did at least capture something about the special character of Soviet political life. And whilst it could not explain everything (which theory can?), it correctly drew our attention to the extent of the repressive apparatus and thus made analysts sensitive to the historical possibility – no more – that without such an apparatus operating effectively, the regime would be in deep trouble. For this reason, if no other, the model remained a useful tool for understanding the Soviet Union.[7]

Marxism and the Soviet Union

At the heart of the totalitarian model was a strong emphasis on the role of force in holding together what supporters of the theory ultimately regarded as a most peculiar, almost unnatural system. Ironically, the view that the Soviet system did not correspond to the standard laws of history, and should thus be regarded as transitional in nature, was also implicit in much Marxist writing on the USSR, most of which began (though clearly did not end) with the work of Leon Trotsky. Forced to come to terms with the quite unexpected phenomenon of Stalinism, Trotsky developed a series of theses about the USSR which were to have an enormous impact upon the way later analysts on the left thought about the Soviet Union.

According to Trotsky, the USSR by the 1930s had evolved into what he termed a 'degenerate workers' state'. What he meant by this, basically, was that although the revolution had successfully eliminated capitalism and the old ruling class, it had in turn spawned a new type of regime controlled by a bureaucratic elite determined to defend its own privileged position. The system over which this new group presided had (he agreed) great economic strengths. Indeed, at times, Trotsky talked glowingly about Soviet economic achievements and the need to defend what he termed the social gains of October. However, in the end, the system was not viable. Situated as it was in a sea of world capitalism, the USSR's transition to something else was a foregone conclusion. He obviously hoped that Stalinism would, in time, be replaced by true Soviet democracy, though this would depend as much, if not more, upon developments in the West as it did upon events in the USSR. On the other hand, Trotsky did not rule out a return to the market, led, in fact, by the very same bureaucrats who in the 1930s were proclaiming the virtues of Soviet socialism and predicting the collapse of capitalism. The Soviet future thus remained decidedly uncertain.

Trotsky influenced and inspired others, including his biographer, Isaac Deutscher. Building upon Trotsky, Deutscher developed an interesting thesis about the USSR. Though no apologist for the system, he insisted that the economic policies undertaken by Stalin had been both inevitable and necessary: inevitable, given the failure of revolution in the West and necessary because there was no other way to modernize a backward country. In the process, a new ruling group hostile to internationalism and opposed to egalitarianism had been thrown up which Deutscher described as 'a hybrid element'; and though not a ruling class in the proper sense of the word, it nonetheless possessed certain features in common with other exploiting classes. But this was perhaps of less importance than the underlying contradictions of Stalinism itself. Born of backwardness, the repressive Soviet state could not long survive under conditions of economic maturity. Furthermore, according to Deutscher, by creating a new and mature Soviet working class, the system had spawned its own grave-digger that would challenge the political dictatorship and ultimately refashion Russian society in its own image. And having thrown off the chains of Stalinism, it would go on to remake the Soviet Union by taking control of government and transforming the state into an 'instrument of the nation's democratically expressed will'.

The optimistic view that the system could not last for ever was also advanced by a number of other writers on the Marxist left, including the dissident American Trotskyist – Max Shachtman. According to Schactman, a new form had come into being in the Soviet Union (which he termed 'bureaucratic collectivist') whose 'ruling class' was unique in only one sense: its sheer brutality. There was certainly nothing progressive about this group or the system over which it stood guard. Yet there was no need for pessimism. The revolutionary tradition of the Russian people, he concluded, would ensure that the workers would at some point rise up, overthrow the prevailing order, and establish a genuine socialist democracy. This view was also supported by the Italian Marxist Bruno Rizzi in his highly original work of 1939. Rizzi, in fact, generalized the whole Soviet experience on to the world stage, as did the one-time American Trotskyist – James Burnham. However, whereas Burnham drew very bleak political conclusions from what had happened in the Soviet Union (and suggested that socialism was now globally impossible because the working class had demonstrated its inability to rule) Rizzi argued that Stalinism must inevitably give way to communism.

The German writer and author, Rudolf Hilferding, was perhaps less certain about the Soviet Union's political future. Nevertheless, he wrote with great insight about the system's peculiar dynamics and unique features. Hilferding was especially keen, however, to deny what some Marxists seemed to be suggesting by the end of the 1930s: namely that the USSR was a new species of capitalism or state capitalism (a line of analysis later taken up by Milovan Djilas in Yugoslavia, Charles Bettelheim in France and Tony Cliff in Britain). According to Hilferding, such a theory wilted under serious economic examination. A capitalist economy, he argued, was a market economy, governed by the laws of the market whose 'autonomy' formed the basis of the capitalist system of production. In the USSR, the state had exclusive control over the economy and the means of production, so it was impossible for these 'laws' to function. For this reason, the Soviet system could not possibly be described as 'capitalist'. But nor could it be described as 'socialist' for that implied the socialization of the means of production in a society which was 'democratically self-governed'. Russia, he concluded, had a 'totalitarian state economy' in a situation where politics was determining economics, rather than the reverse. And though this situation could continue for a while, it would not persist for ever.

The assumption that the USSR had to be explained in its own terms, and not through the use of categories derived from a study of capitalism, was also held by the South African analyst, Hillel Ticktin. Ticktin who had spent a number of years in the USSR in the early 1960s before taking up a post in the University of Glasgow (where he established the journal *Critique* in 1973) argued that the USSR was a historically unviable formation more contradictory in nature and thus less likely to survive than capitalism. The general tendency in the system, he insisted nearly 20 years before the USSR finally disintegrated, was towards decay and degeneration. In effect, the Soviet economy had no 'central dynamic' or more precisely its central dynamic was 'self-contradictory'. The chief problem, according to Ticktin, was the atomized nature of Soviet society which resulted from a fundamental conflict between a ruling elite that had little real control over the economy (which he denied was properly planned) and an alienated working class determined to do as little work as possible, as badly as possible. The result was vast waste and inefficiency which could not be sustained over time. In the end, the system was bound to decline. As he noted in 1984, 'the system' was 'drawing to a close' and there was little that could be done about it. Indeed, in his view, the Soviet system was completely unreformable and the only result of perestrioka would be to hasten the USSR's final disintegration.

The foregoing contributions using Marx's theory as a referent are relatively useful in that each of the perspectives, however dissimilar, made direct or indirect reference to the transitional character of the Soviet system. Certainly, most of the writers cited here assumed that because of its 'class nature' and betrayal of socialist ideals the prevailing order could not last, and that therefore the Soviet Union would simply have to change into something else. Many, however, tended to base their judgement on a general assumption of crisis, rather than a detailed study of the Soviet economy. Moreover, few could have anticipated that when the USSR finally did implode, the socialist baby would be thrown out with the Soviet bath water. Furthermore, with the one exception of Ticktin, none really made more than the vaguest of vague generalizations about the Soviet Union's social structure. In fact, of all modern Marxists, Ticktin came closest of all in anticipating the demise of the system – and did so, one suspects, not just because he studied the subject more closely than most, but because he tried to do more than just inject a little history into laws already formulated by classical Marxism.[8]

Elite Models

If theorists on the left could be attacked for being politically naïve about the future of the Soviet Union once the old system had been displaced, elite theory (developed as a critique of Marxism by Pareto and Mosca at the turn of the century) might be criticized for the opposite tendency: of pessimistically assuming that under all circumstances and every condition, elites were bound to emerge. For this reason, no doubt, the elite model seemed particularly well suited to the study of the USSR, and works employing the theory began to appear in the late 1950s. These tried to explain the Soviet political process by seeking to describe the composition of the ruling stratum, the sources from which it recruited additions to its ranks, and how it dealt with challenges from subordinate groups. Amongst the most interesting studies in this genre were those by Raymond Aron, C. Wright Mills, Robert Dahl and Alfred Meyer, who together attempted to look at the USSR as a new type of society which nonetheless had failed to escape the iron logic of elite rule.

Different writers tended to emphasize different features of the Soviet elite, though many seemed as keen to use their work to say something positive about the West as to say something useful about the Soviet Union. Thus although Aron concluded that the Soviet Union was a classless society, it was, in his opinion, ruled by an elite which wielded far more power than political leaders did under conditions of democracy. This view, however, was disputed by Mills who argued that the power elite in both the United States and the Soviet Union exhibited similar characteristics: and if there was a difference between the two, it was more formal than real. Not surprisingly, the great American 'pluralist' - Robert Dahl - supported Aron, and like the French philosopher contrasted the situation in the USSR with what pertained in the West in general and the USA in particular. In his view, there was really no comparison at all, for whereas a single elite organized through the Communist Party controlled the USSR, in the USA there were several elites in direct competition with each other. Alfred Meyer took a somewhat different perspective. He agreed that that there was an elite in the Soviet Union. Nonetheless, recruitment into this group was not dependent upon personal wealth or the ownership of property, but talent, conscientiousness and, of course, loyalty to the party line. Thus although the situation was hardly meritocratic, it was at least open and mobile.

Whilst many writers were content just to describe the structure of the Soviet elite (with a definite tendency to focus on the Communist Party), others looked for significant divisions within the elite itself. The hunt, of course, was not an innocent one and was in large part motivated by a desire to detect major conflict at the top. Albert Parry, for one, was in no doubt that such divisions existed - between technocrats and party bureaucrats - and that the former represented a serious challenge to the monopoly power of the Communist Party of the Soviet Union. This line of analysis was also pursued by the British sociologist Frank Parkin, who believed there was a fundamental contradiction between the ruling political elite (the party and state bureaucracy) and the intelligentsia as a whole. Furthermore, in his view, no political equilibrium was achievable until and unless the latter was allowed access to political power. This view did not go unchallenged, however, and in a seminal article, Stephen White pointed out that there was no such cleavage between either the Party elite, the managers or the creative and scientific intelligentsia. All three sectors in his view contained personnel who were well educated, skilled and technologically oriented, some of whom favoured reform and others who did not. Jerry Hough appeared to agree and like fellow American, Raymond Garthoff, even wondered whether or not there was in fact an 'omnipotent' Party elite in the USSR. The reality was more complex in his view, and rather than there being one elite there were, in his opinion, several top groups with competing interests and different points of access into a complex decision-making process.

There is little doubt that elite theory contributed enormously to our general understanding of the former USSR. Unfortunately, its potential was vitiated by profound disagreements and a lack of clarity about who exactly was a member of this group and the extent to which divisions within it were significant or insignificant. Where the theory was suggestive and useful, however, was in pointing to the potential for conflict at the top, and the challenge to the system as a whole represented by those who identified their interests with the cause of economic change. From this perspective, the most useful contribution would appear to have been made by Parkin (significantly, a non-Sovietologist) who focused upon the threat to the ruling elite's monopoly of power posed by an intelligentsia alienated from a system whose reform it increasingly sought from the late 1970s onwards.[9]

Ideological Perspectives

Amongst Sovietologists there was no fixed or clear view about Soviet ideology, what it actually constituted, and how important it was in determining the actions of Soviet leaders. That said, it was virtually impossible for those who studied the Soviet system before its disintegration to ignore the phenomenon. Basically, analysts adopted one of four approaches to the study of official Marxism-Leninism.

First, there were those like Daniel Bell who denied that ideology played very much of a role at all, and that the only thing which motivated the Soviet leadership was (in the words of Mihajlo Mihajlov) a 'thirst for power' – a view also held by the atomic physicist and later dissident Andrei Sakharov. A second position, adopted by another former oppositionist, Alexander Solzhenitsyn, took almost the opposite perspective. According to Solzhenitsyn, one could not underestimate the importance of Marxism. Indeed, in his opinion, it was precisely the Soviet leaders' blind adherence to Marxism which had led to the Soviet disaster in the first place. Thus ideology was no mere veneer or superficial gloss, but was the underlying motor force of Soviet history from the revolution in 1917 to the fall of the Soviet Union over 70 years later.

A third and less essentialist view was taken by the scholar of international relations: Hans J. Morgenthau. For Morgenthau, Marxism-Leninism had to be viewed less as the cause of all Soviet evils and more as the fundamental source of regime legitimacy. From this analysis, of course, flowed the important insight that any erosion in its influence would be profoundly destabilizing for the USSR (a view widely held by a range of other writers too, such as Meyer, Bauman, Bauer, Inkeles, and Kluckholm). Finally, there were a few who instead of analysing Marxism as the source of Soviet behaviour, either contrasted the Soviet Union in its concrete manifestation with the original doctrine, or looked at the ways in which the doctrine itself was adapted to Soviet conditions. The social theorist, Barrington Moore, managed to do both in fact and argued – persuasively – that ideology as such did not lead to Soviet actions but was rather modified and transformed as a result of Soviet behaviour. In this sense, ideology did not determine politics (Solzhenitsyn's position), but was determined by politics. This was not to deny the role of ideas in the development of the Soviet Union, but rather pointed to a more subtle and complex relationship between ideology on the one hand and the real movement of history on the other.

As our brief survey shows, there was no real consensus amongst Sovietologists about the exact role that ideology played in the Soviet system. For this reason some have therefore concluded that ideology ought to be left to 'gnawing criticism of the mice' and discounted altogether. The problem with this, however, is obvious: something called Marxism-Leninism did happen to exist in the old USSR, and this cannot be discounted altogether. Moreover, if we accept that ideology played its part in both justifying the actions of successive political leaders and legitimizing the system in some vague way, we can at least surmise that once Soviet leaders decided to abandon even this residual connection to the official doctrine – as Gorbachev did increasingly after 1985 – there was every chance that the Soviet Union would change irrevocably. Ideology might not have driven the USSR; however, it did help hold the country together and once it began to wither away, the possibility of the system remaining intact was very much diminished.[10]

Social and Political Science

There is no easy way of characterizing (rather than caricaturing) the contribution made by the social sciences in general, and political science in particular, to our knowledge of the former USSR. Yet amongst many analysts there was an underlying inclination, if not to deny the difference between the USSR and the rest of the world, at least to try to understand the Soviet system as if it were less abnormal than was suggested by the totalitarians. Some writers, moreover, really did believe that modern societies and systems confronted similar problems, and that the basic form of decision-making in political systems was not very different. Not surprisingly, those who argued in this way tended to view the former USSR as perhaps having more in common with other systems in other parts of the world than had hitherto been argued.

We can plot this attempt to normalize the study of the former USSR by looking briefly at four theoretical models used by different social scientists: developmental, bureaucratic, industrial society and institutional pluralism. I shall then say something about Soviet stability.

Developmental

This model arose from the application of lessons drawn from the experience of development in the countries of the Third World. The central idea, basically, was that industrialization under all conditions disrupted traditional societal cohesion and so required a centralized and authoritarian political system to manage the process. John Kautsky, the premier defender of this approach, suggested that the dynamics of change in the USSR after

1929 with its strong emphasis on rapid industrialization under the guidance of a dynamic elite had a good deal in common with the experience of the Third World in the post-war period. Communism therefore should not be regarded as something unique and distinctive, but as an alternative means of modernization without the market.

A version of this particular argument was also advanced by American political scientists Almond and Powell. However, they were less interested in comparing the USSR with the Third World than in seeing whether the dynamics of Soviet industrial development contained within it the seeds of future change. Their interesting conclusion was that the USSR was literally 'bound to pluralism' as the limits of socialist planning became increasingly clear. A similar thesis was put forward by David Apter, who like Almond and Powell believed that as the country experienced further modernization, traditional ideology would be replaced with the more universal values of productivity, output and efficiency. As these became the norm the elite would be impelled to introduce Western-style economic reforms and open the country up in order to sustain continued development.

The developmental model was not without its merits. Indeed, as both David Lane and Stephen White suggest elsewhere in this book, at least one way of explaining the crisis of the Soviet system in the late 1980s is in terms of the contradictions thrown up by dynamic change taking place within an increasingly dysfunctional political and economic framework. Yet the model was not without its problems – the most important one being that it actually said little about the specificities of the Soviet system itself. The issue of development in general is obviously important: what this general theory could not explain however is why the USSR in particular faced the problems it did, when it did, and was unable to resolve them.[11]

Bureaucratic

Whereas writers such as Almond and Powell sought to place the Soviet experience in a wider comparative 'developmental' context, the advocates of the bureaucratic model implied that in the USSR the party as an ideological vanguard had effectively been replaced by a vast bureaucratic apparatus. Moreover, this tendency to bureaucracy was one common to both capitalist and socialist societies. Thus according to Meyer, politics in the Soviet Union was no different and possibly no better than elsewhere, insofar as it was dominated by a large complex bureaucracy operating in a similar fashion to big corporations, military establishments and government institutions in the West. Both Rigby and Kassof agreed, though pointed out that the Soviet Union was obviously different, being a 'command society' in which one party decided and delegated tasks whilst others simply carried out their orders.

Whilst not disputing this, John Armstrong believed there were interesting parallels to be drawn between the USSR and the West. In both economic systems there was, he noted, a substantial degree of endorsement for 'hierarchical administrative principles'. One-man management control over industrial enterprises was as much a feature of the Soviet Union as of Western societies. And administrators in both systems were motivated by similar things, including material rewards and high social standing.

Like any ideal type, the bureaucratic model had its strengths and weaknesses. Its most obvious strength was that it drew our attention to a fundamental feature of all complex societies. Its most obvious weakness was that like most general theories, it ignored the simple fact that in the absence of the market and private enterprise, the whole Soviet system was in a very special sense one huge bureaucracy. As Paul Hollander has pointed out, Communist bureaucracies were quite unique and any attempt to equate them with those of, say, an American corporation suggests a high degree of misunderstanding of the way the Soviet Union functioned – and malfunctioned – before 1989. Michael Garder has also observed that next to the average Soviet bureaucrat, 'the most conservative Western bourgeois' acted and thought like 'a revolutionary'. The observation is not only well made, but also points to at least one of the reasons why the Soviet system was unlikely to endure over the long term. In reality, a bureaucratic system which stifled innovation and whose leaders feared change rather than welcomed it, had little chance of surviving in a world where other states were less inhibited and more willing to experiment with the novel and the new.[12]

Industrial Society

According to this thesis – which was widely popular in the 1960s – the nature of all modern societies are shaped by the logic of technology and industry: and all advanced industrial countries, it was argued, required a flexible and open political system to remain viable. Otherwise their economies would decline. To prevent this occurring, Soviet rulers would, it was asserted, be forced to adapt their policies to meet the economic challenge. This process of adaptation would in turn undermine the totalitarian state, and in time make the Soviet state virtually indistinguishable from what existed in the democratic West. As Galbraith put it, 'the empire of industrialism will [one day] embrace the whole world' – including presumably the Soviet world – 'and such similarities as it decrees will penetrate the outermost points of its sphere of influence'.

The notion that industrial technology had an imperative that transcended ideology and would impel all systems to behave in a more or less identical way, was propounded by several writers. Wirth, for example, spoke with great power and conviction of the universal imperative of industrialism and its likely impact on the USSR. Fainsod also predicted that the needs of 'a progressively complex and highly industrialized society' would lead to 'a greater dispersal of authority, a more pluralistic society, and freer expression' in communist Russia. Michael Gehlen made much the same point and talked of the universal logic of industrialism. The American writer, Jeremy Azrael, even predicted that under the pressure of social and economic advance, Soviet rulers would have to forsake their 'monolithism' in favour of greater pluralization. Indeed, according to Azrael (writing in 1968) powerful forces were already at play in Soviet society, and he anticipated these would soon lead to the emergence of 'a truly democratic polity'.

Like its close cousin, the developmental model, the theory of industrial society was not without its strengths. But it suffered the same tendency of attempting to deduce the very specific nature of the Soviet system from its industrial character. This not only smacked of a certain reductionism, but in the end actually failed to explain the odd dynamics of the Soviet Union and its subsequent economic decline. Clearly, not all 'industrial societies' are alike or suffer from the same problems. In the Soviet case, of course, one of the most important features of its industry was its technological back-wardness and inability to compete in the larger global economy – and to be blunt, industrial society theorists simply could not explain this. In effect, what was really required was not some meta-theory purporting to describe the structure of all industrial societies, but a concrete analysis of why the Soviet industrial system in particular functioned so badly, for so long and with such devastating implications for the USSR's survival.[13]

Institutional Pluralism

While the totalitarians tended to stress the monolithic character of the USSR, this particular school of thought argued that there was some degree of institutional pluralism within the system. Supporters of this viewpoint, moreover, insisted that no state – including the Soviet state – could survive for long without a measure of order, rationalization and predictability, and thus required institutions such as the courts, government bodies and universities to manage the country. As time passed, these institutions would, it was felt, acquire greater autonomy and eventually the regime would find itself being constrained by them. When that happened the dictatorship would gradually be weakened until it was finally replaced by something more democratic.

This pluralist perspective was particularly popular with a number of political and social scientists. David Lane, for one, believed there were definite similarities between the ways in which the Soviet political system and those in the West functioned with competing elites and different interest groups vying for influence and power. Skilling also saw essential similarities between the two, as did the influential American writer on Soviet affairs, Jerry Hough. In fact, according to Hough, interest groups abounded in the Soviet Union, and functioned much as they did in the West. Hough even seemed to imply that the Soviet government after Stalin's death operated in much the same way as governments in the West. This was made clear in his rather odd rewrite of what had until then been Merle Fainsod's fairly orthodox text on Soviet politics. In this highly revised work, Hough made it appear as if the political system in the USSR was no more (and no less) 'plural' than those which existed in the United States and Western Europe; moreover, whereas Fainsod had been keen in his original 1953 work to emphasize the brutal and bureaucratic nature of Russian rule after the revolution of 1917, Hough pointed to the open character of Soviet government. In this way, a picture was suggested of Soviet reality which was almost the opposite of that earlier painted by the totalitarians.[14]

Soviet Stability

The inclination by certain theorists to move beyond the totalitarian thesis with its stress on the role of control from above was carried to its logical conclusion by a number of Western writers who focused increasingly from the late 1960s onwards on the stable nature of the Soviet system. Underlying this approach was the belief that the Soviet Union had at last evolved into a modern industrial state led by a relatively mellow political leadership supported by a well-educated, relatively content populace. This line was strongly advanced in the work of Churchward who concluded that the late Soviet regime was regarded by its own citizens as being legitimate. According to Churchward, even the intelligentsia accepted the existing system and were content to abide by its restrictions. Stephen White, too, seemed to be of the opinion that the system was relatively secure and that the majority of the Soviet population supported (because they believed in) the existing political regime. Many other analysts also stressed the extent of Soviet stability, noting that this was not just based on repression (though that remained critical) but on the country's impressive economic achievements and the party leadership's ability to adapt and reconcile itself to the wishes of sundry interest groups. Levi, for example, believed he had found strong evidence to support the argument that the USSR was a good deal more secure than some right-wing critics had earlier assumed.

The view that the USSR had achieved real stability was a very widespread one amongst a later generation of Sovietologists trying to move beyond what they saw as the overly simple Cold War argument that the system was only held together by fear. Even amongst strong critics of the system there was an overwhelming consensus that in spite of its many difficulties, the USSR would endure. Thus Walter Laqueur, writing in 1989, argued that serious change was not on 'the historical agenda' and that a transition to a new political system would take years rather than months. This view was also shared by a number of Soviet dissidents, including the highly critical Alexander Solzhenitsyn. Like many dissidents, he was thoroughly hostile to the existing regime. Nonetheless he still felt the system was likely to endure. His *Letter to the Soviet Leaders* indeed only advocated rather mild reforms, and far from arguing for democracy in fact made a strong case for a new authoritarian system shorn of its Marxist-Leninism.[15]

The Realist Model

As we have seen, amongst many analysts of the former Soviet Union there was a general inclination to assume that the Soviet system would endure in one form or another. Moreover, even those who anticipated some form of change or even accepted that the USSR had some very basic problems, never really grasped the full extent of the Soviet crisis and why this was making the situation increasingly difficult for the leadership by the late 1970s and early 1980s. In fact, it is quite remarkable how most social scientists – misled by their own novel theories of the Soviet Union – seemed to underestimate the seriousness of the situation facing the Soviet Union in the years just before Gorbachev took over.

'Realists', however, did not share this casual attitude, and whilst seeing little prospect for reform, recognized the underlying fragility of the system. The first to do so, perhaps, was George F. Kennan, the famous State Department official. According to Kennan, the Soviet Union was a potentially 'vulnerable' and 'impotent' state. As he made clear in his famous 'X' article of 1947, though the Soviet Union might have appeared threatening to the West, this did not mean the Soviet system was a secure one. In effect, his whole theory of containment was based upon the twin notions that the USSR was not only much weaker than the West, but that if the West could successfully limit its expansive tendencies, in time the Soviet Union would be impelled to adjust to international realities and address some of its major domestic problems. As he warned – rather prophetically as it turned out – if anything were to happen 'to disrupt the unity and efficacy of the Party as a political instrument, Soviet Russia might be changed overnight from one of the strongest to one of the weakest and most pitiable of national societies'.

Richard Lowenthal also detected what he saw as basic flaws in the structure of Soviet power. In large part this was the logical result of a failed economic system and the heavy hand of the party upon the Soviet economy.

But the Soviet crisis in his view was also the product of the very measures taken by the party to insure the survival of the Soviet Union. Thus by cutting the intelligentsia off the from the West and controlling the dissemination of truthful information within the country, the political elite could only weaken the system over time; and the longer it employed such methods, the deeper would be the final crisis. Zbigniew Brzezinski certainly accepted this line of analysis, but added for good measure that two other factors threatened the survival of the Soviet Union: the failure to attract into the ranks of the political elite 'the ablest, most energetic and innovative elements of society' and nationalist demands. Brzezinski more than most, in fact, took seriously the threat posed to the USSR by growing nationalism within Soviet borders. So too did the British academic resident in the United States – Robert Conquest. Conquest could see no way out for the Soviet Union. The political system he argued was 'radically and dangerously inappropriate to its social and economic dynamics' and an 'unforeseen catastrophe' might easily trigger the overthrow of the regime.

The view that the Soviet system was neither reformable nor savable was also held by a number of other writers of a 'realist' persuasion. Hence Linden, writing in 1983, argued that the continuation of the system could not be guaranteed. The critical dilemma for Soviet rulers was that a torpid leadership and a stagnant economy called for urgent, far-reaching reforms which could only be enacted with the participation of the dynamic and creative forces in society. But the inclusion of these was bound to endanger the 'rule of the partystate'. The USSR thus faced a stark choice: of accepting reform from above which might in time lead to the end of the system or doing nothing. The last course might have seemed the safer but ultimately might lead to upheaval or chaos.

The historian Richard Pipes (who for a time acted as adviser on Soviet affairs to the Reagan administration) was equally convinced that the USSR was in the middle of 'a serious systemic crisis which sooner or later [would] require action of a decisive kind'. A number of intersecting problems lay at the heart of the Soviet malaise: a costly empire; a corrupt, self-interested, parasitic Party elite, so estranged from the bulk of the population as to be in 'grave danger of losing control'; and a stagnant and sick economy. Pipes, however, did not consider a revolution likely (or even desirable) but hoped instead for far-reaching changes introduced by the Soviet leadership. However, such change in his view would not come about without a good deal of pressure from the West itself. This is why a robust American strategy was essential. The American writer, Richard Burks, certainly accepted the policy logic of Pipes' argument. However, he went so far as to predict that the Soviet system would disintegrate within the next five to ten years as a result of a gradual loss of political control, growing economic problems and increasing popular disaffection with the regime. Shtromas took more or less the same view, though suggested this would probably come about not as a result of popular disaffection, but because of a deep division within the elite itself; between what he called the 'partocrats' and the 'technocrats'. This in turn would lead to a wider split in the system as a whole, followed by a revolution from above, which would then usher in a form of Bonapartist dictatorship.

Needless to say, the realist case did not find much favour amongst most mainstream Sovietologists who attacked it in turn for being unduly pessimistic, decidedly neo-conservative and cataclysmic and alarmist. George Breslauer was one such critic, and more or less dismissed the views of the realists, arguing that those who held to what he termed the 'instability-as-cumulative crises' image, were self-evidently wrong. Moreover, not only did they overstate the crisis in his view, they also underestimated the ability of the Soviet leadership to respond to new challenges. There were several measures it might take. It could, for example, improve the economy by adjusting budget reallocations and foreign trade and investment policies. It could, in addition, increase economic aid to the republics to soothe nationalist fervour. And it could grant greater economic independence for Eastern Europe to mitigate opposition there. The system obviously faced difficulties, but there was no reason to assume that these could not be successfully addressed.[16]

So Why Did Soviet Studies Fail?

Time and events were to prove Breslauer quite wrong. But it was not just Breslauer but most of the Soviet Studies profession who were unable to anticipate what subsequently happened in the former USSR. The larger issue is why?

Robert Conquest, more than most, has provided a basis for answering this question. In an article written over 20 years before the demise of Soviet power, he pinpointed some of the chief reasons why so many theorists were 'getting it wrong', even then. His analysis still rings true today. According to Conquest, social scientists were simply not focusing on essentials or on what he believed were the 'salient issues' – and one of the main reasons for this was a growing inclination by a number of writers to deny the unique nature of the Soviet Union and its fundamental problems. This in turn was linked to (and was in part the result of) a growing proclivity amongst writers to force comparisons with other systems upon the USSR. Though the reasons behind this were not entirely illegitimate, what it led to in effect was a denial of the Soviet Union's *sui generis* character. As he put it, with the USSR 'we are in the presence of a modern technological economy that is subject to change at a totally different sort of tempo, and with qualitatively different effects, from those which characterized politically comparable societies in the past. Nor are analogies from the present wholly applicable either, since the Soviet political structure is critically different from that of economically comparable societies.'[17]

Conquest's observation also raises a second point about who got it right and why. Here I would argue that the theories which came closest to predicting the collapse of the Soviet system were precisely those which did in fact regard the USSR as being distinct and in some ways 'abnormal' or 'aberrant'. For this reason the approaches which turned out to have been most perceptive were either developed by Marxists critical of the USSR for deviating from socialism, or totalitarians who assumed that the Soviet Union was in the end only held together by force. Though adherents to both schools were unlikely to agree politically (and did not!) both could at least see that the system was fundamentally flawed and almost certainly transitional in nature. In this way the work of, say, a Ticktin on the one hand, and a realist like Brzezinski on the other, probably had more in common than either would have cared to admit at the time – or have since!

Of course, nobody could have predicted to the month, day or hour when the system would implode. Indeed, almost no one expected the USSR to collapse when it did, even those who had been most pessimistic about its longer-term prospects. And needless to say, the man most responsible for that collapse – Mikhail Gorbachev – was probably as surprised as anyone else when it did. However, to stress the decisive role played by Gorbachev and to make great play of his errors, miscalculations and inconsistencies should not obscure the much larger problems facing the USSR long before Gorbachev came on the scene. Gorbachev might have been better advised to act differently or to have done nothing at all. Some have even suggested that he should have taken the 'Chinese path' and opted for perestroika without glasnost; in other words, reform the economy but leave the political system alone. Possibly so, but in all probability this would only have bought him time. It would neither have addressed the Soviet Union's basic weaknesses nor resolved the more basic contradiction between the need for economic reform and the forms of political control which had hitherto kept the USSR stable. Indeed, those who now think that Gorbachev should have gone along the road taken by China seem to forget that contained within the current Chinese model there is still an unresolved tension between dynamic economic change and political centralization. And as China will no doubt discover – one day – an open market economy is basically incompatible with a closed, repressive polity. Thus it is not Gorbachev who should have learned from China, but China that should now be learning from what happened to the former USSR: and the most important lesson to be learned is that communism does not necessarily have to end with an explosion, but can be brought to a conclusion by a confused, but at least peacefully orchestrated process.

For providing me with the research material upon which this chapter is based, I owe a deep debt of gratitude to Dr Sally Harris.

Notes

1   Bertram D. Wolfe, 'The Durability of Soviet Despotism', *Commentary,* Vol. 24, No. 2, August 1957, pp. 93-104.

2   See Robert Jervis, 'The Future of World Politics: Will it Resemble the Past?', *International Security,* Vol. 16, No. 3, Winter 1991/92, pp. 39-73.

3   For an earlier attempt by the author to theorize these issues, see Terry McNeill, 'Images of the Soviet Future: The Western Scholarly Debate', in Alexander Shtromas and Morton A. Kaplan (eds), *The Soviet Union and the Challenge of the Future,* Vol. 1 (Paragon House Publishers, New York, 1988).

4   Hannah Arendt, *The Origins of Totalitarianism,* 5th Edition (New York; Harcourt Brace, 1973); Sigmund Neumann, *Permanent Revolution: Totalitarianism in the Age of Civil War,* 2nd Edition (New York: Frederick A. Praeger, 1965); also, Carl J. Friedrich and Zbigniew K. Brzezinski, *Totalitarian Dictatorship and Autocracy,* 2nd Edition (Cambridge, Mass.: Harvard University Press, 1965).

5   Carl J. Friedrich, 'The Evolving Theory and Practice of Totalitarian Regimes' in Carl J. Friedrich, Michael Curtis and Benjamin R. Barber (eds), *Totalitarianism in Perspective: Three Views* (New York: Praeger Publishers Inc., 1969), p. 126.

6   For the discussion on totalitarianism see, amongst others, Karl Popper, *The Open Society and Its Enemies,* 4th Edition (Princeton, NJ: Princeton University Press, 1963), pp. 1-2; Barrington Moore, Jr, *Political Power and Social Theory* (New York: Harper & Row, 1965), pp. 74-5; Harry Eckstein and David E. Apter, *Comparative Politics: A Reader* (New York: The Free Press, 1963), p. 437; Hugh Seton-Watson, 'Totalitarianism Reconsidered', *Problems of Communism,* Vol. XVI, No. 4 July-August, 1967, p. 56; Karl Wittfogel, *Oriental Despotism* (New Haven, Connecticut: Yale University Press, 1963), p. 440; Herbert J. Spiro, 'Totalitarianism', *International Encyclopaedia of the Social Sciences,* Vol. 16 (London: Macmillan, 1968), p. 112; Herbert Marcuse, *One Dimensional Man, The Ideology of Industrial Society* (London: Routledge & Kegan Paul, 1964), p. 120; Mary McAuley, *Politics and the Soviet Union* (Harmondsworth: Penguin Books, 1977), p. 161; Paul Hollander, 'Observations on Bureaucracy, Totalitarianism, and the Comparative Study of Communism' in Richard Cornell (ed.), *The Soviet Political System: A Book of Readings* (Englewood Cliffs, N.J.: Prentice-Hall Inc., 1970), pp. 59-60; and George W. Breslauer, *Five Images of the Soviet Future: A Critical Review & Synthesis,* Policy Papers in International Affairs (Berkeley: University of California, 1978).

7   For a defence of totalitarianism see Hugh Seton-Watson, Note 6 above; Leonard Schapiro, *Totalitarianism* (London: Macmillan Press, 1972), p. 110; Hans Kelsen, *The Political Theory of Bolshevism: A Critical Analysis* (Berkeley: University of California, 1948), p. 6; Carl J. Friedrich, 'Whither Russia? Totalitarianism: Recent Trends', *Problems of Communism,* Vol. XVII, No. 3, May-June 1968, p. 43;

Bertram D. Wolfe, Note 1 above, pp. 95-7; Boris Meissner, 'Whither Russia? Totalitarian Rule and Social Change', *Problems of Communism*, Vol. XV, No. 6, November-December 1966, p. 57.

8   On critical Marxist perspectives on the USSR, see Leon Trotsky, *The Revolution Betrayed* (London: Plough Press, 1957); Leon Trotsky, *The Class Nature of the Soviet State* (London: New Park Publications, 1968); Isaac Deutscher, *The Unfinished Revolution: Russia 1917-1967* (New York: Oxford University Press, 1967); Isaac Deutscher, *Russia, What Next?* (London: Hamilton, 1953); Max Shachtman, *The Bureaucratic Revolution* (New York: The Donald Press, 1962); Bruno R(izzi), *La Bureaucratization du Monde* (Paris: Edite pour L'auteur en dépôt aux messageries Hachette, 1939); Milovan Djilas, *The New Class* (London: Unwin Books, 1966); Tony Cliff, *State Capitalism in Russia* (London: Pluto Press, 1974); Charles Bettelheim, *The Transition to a Socialist Economy* (Hassocks: Harvester Press, 1975); Ernest Mandel, 'Ten Theses on the Social and Economic Laws Governing the Society Transitional Between Capitalism', *Critique*, No. 3, 1974, pp. 5-21; Rudolf Hilferding, 'A 1940 Social Democratic View of Stalin's Russia', *The Modern Review*, June 1947, pp. 266-71; James Burnham, *The Managerial Revolution* (Harmondsworth: Penguin, 1945); Hillel Ticktin, 'Towards a Political Economy of the USSR', *Critique*, No. 1 (1973), pp. 20-41; Hillel Ticktin, 'The Contradictions of Soviet Society and Professor Bettelheim', *Critique*, No. 6 (1976), p. 40; Hillel Ticktin, 'Is Market-Socialism Possible or Necessary?', *Critique*, No. 14 (1981), p. 15; and Hillel Ticktin, 'Andropov: Disintegration and Discipline', *Critique*, No. 16 (1984), pp. 111-122.

9   On elite theory see Vilfredo Pareto, *Les Systèmes Socialistes*, 2nd Edition (Paris, 1926); Gaetano Mosca, *The Ruling Class*, translated by Hannah D. Kahn (New York: McGraw-Hill, 1939); David Lane, *Politics and Society in the USSR*, 2nd Edition (Oxford: Martin Robertson & Co., 1978), p. 191; Raymond Aron, 'Social Structure and the Ruling Class', in Lewis S. Coser (ed.), *Political Sociology* (New York: Harper & Row, 1966), pp. 81-2; C. Wright Mills, *The Power Elite* (London: Oxford University Press, 1956), pp. 3-4, 292-3; Robert Dahl, 'A Critique of the Ruling Elite Model', *The American Political Science Review*, Vol. L11, No. 2 (June 1958), pp. 463-9; Alfred G. Meyer, 'USSR, Incorporated', in Donald W. Treadgold (ed.), pp. 21-2; Albert Parry, *The New Class Divided. Science and Technology Versus Communism* (London, Macmillan Press, 1966), pp. ix, 5, 300, 301, 302; Timothy McClure, 'The Politics of Soviet Culture 1964-1967', *Problems of Communism*, Vol. XVI, No. 2 (March-April 1967), pp. 26-43; Frank Parkin, 'System Contradiction and Political Transformation', *European Journal of Sociology*, Vol. 13 (1972), p. 50; Stephen White, 'Contradiction and Change in State Socialism', *Soviet Studies*, Vol. XXVI, No. 1 (January 1974), pp. 41-55; Jerry Hough, 'The Soviet System: Petrification or Pluralism?', *Problems of Communism*, Vol. 21, No. 2 (March-April 1972), p. 27; and Raymond Garthoff, *Soviet Military Policy: A Historical Analysis* (London: Faber, 1966), p. 58.

10 For Soviet ideology see Daniel Bell, *The End of Ideology* (New York: Glencoe Free Press, 1960), pp. 369, 370, 373, 374; Robert V. Daniels, 'The "Withering Away of the State" in Theory and Practice' in Alex Inkeles and Kent Geiger (eds), *Soviet Society. A Book of Readings* (London: Constable & Company Ltd., 1961), pp. 113, 126; Mihajio Mihajlov, *Underground Notes* (London: Routledge & Kegan Paul,

1977), pp. 87-8; Andrei Sakharov, 'On Alexander Solzhenitsyn's *A Letter to Soviet Leaders*', in Viadimir Maximov (ed.), *Kontinent 1: The Alternative Voice of Russia and Eastern Europe* (London: André Deutsch, 1976), p. 22; Alexander Solzhenitsyn, *Letter to Soviet Leaders* (London: Index on Censorship, 1974), pp. 42-9; Hans J. Morgenthau, 'Alternatives for Change', *Problems of Communism*, Vol. XV, No. 5 (September-October 1966), pp. 38-40; Alfred G. Meyer, 'The Functions of Ideology in the Soviet Political System', *Soviet Studies*, Vol. XV, No. 3 (January 1966), pp. 273-85; David Lane, Note 9 above, p. 49; Z. Bauman, 'Twenty Years After: the Crises of Soviet-Type Systems', *Problems of Communism*, Vol. 20, No. 6 (November-December 1971), p. 51; Raymond A. Bauer, Alex Inkeles, and Clyde Kluckholm, *How the Soviet System Works: Cultural, Psychological and Social Themes* (Cambridge, Mass: Harvard University Press, 1956), pp. 29-35; Barrington Moore, Jr, 'Marxist Ideology and Soviet Reality', in Alex Inkeles and Kent Geiger (eds), this note, p. 75; Daniel Bell, 'Ideology and Soviet Politics', in Richard Cornell (ed.), Note 6 above, p. 10; John N. Hazard, *The Soviet System of Government* (University of Chicago Press), p. 229; and Karl Mannheim, *Ideology and Utopia* (New York: Harcourt Brace & World, 1965).

11   On the developmental model, see John Kautsky, *Communism and the Politics of Development* (New York: John Wiley & Sons Inc., 1968); Gabriel A. Almond and G. Bingham Powell, Jr, *Comparative Politics: A Developmental Approach* (Boston, Mass: Little, Brown & Co., 1966), pp. 277, 278, 279; and David E. Apter, *The Politics of Modernization* (University of Chicago Press, 1965), pp. vii, x, 305, 427-8, 460.

12   On bureaucracy, see Alfred Meyer, *The Soviet Political System: An Interpretation* (New York: Random House, 1965), pp. 477-8; T.H. Rigby, 'Traditional, Market and Organizational Societies in the USSR', *World Politics*, Vol. 16 (July 1964), pp. 539-57; Alan Kassof, 'The Administered Society: Totalitarianism Without Terror', *World Politics*, Vol. XVI, No. 4 (July 1964), p. 558; John A. Armstrong, 'Sources of Administrative Behavior: Some Soviet and Western European Comparisons', *The American Political Science Review*, Vol. 59 (1965), pp. 643-55; Robert V. Daniels, 'Soviet Politics Since Khruschev', in John W. Armstrong (ed.), *The Soviet Union Under Brezhnev and Kosygin* (New York: Van Nostrand Reinhold Co., 1971), pp. 22-3; David Lane, Note 9 above, p. 172; Paul Hollander, Note 6 above, p. 62; and Robert Strausz-Hupé, 'Some Historical Parallels', *Problems of Communism*, Vol. XV, No. 6 (November-December 1966), p. 3. The Garder quote can be found in Michel Tatu, 'The Beginning of the End?', *Problems of Communism*, Vol. XV, No. 2 (March-April 1966), p. 45.

13   The discussion on 'industrial society' is based on C. Kerr *et al.*, *Industrialism and Industrial Man: the problem of labor and management in economic growth* (London: Heinemann, 1962), p. 46; Professor J.K. Galbraith, BBC Reith Lectures, *The Listener* (15 December 1966); L. Wirth, 'Urbanism as a Way of Life', in A.J. Reiss, Jr (ed.), *On Cities and Social Life* (University of Chicago Press, 1964), p. 75; Arthur Schlesinger, Jr, 'A Muddling Evolution', *Problems of Communism*, Vol. XV, No. 4 (July-August 1966), p. 45; Merle Fainsod, 'Whither Russia? Roads to the Future', *Problems of Communism*, Vol. XVI, No. 4 (July-August 1967), pp. 21-3; Michael P. Gehlen, *The Communist Party of the Soviet Union* (Bloomington: Indiana University Press, 1969), pp. 141-2; Jeremy Azrael, 'Bringing Up the Soviet Man: Dilemmas and Progress', *Problems of Communism*,

Vol. XVII, No. 3 (May-June 1968), p. 31; A. Giddens, *The Class Stucture of the Advanced Societies* (London: Hutchinson University Library, 1973), pp. 22, 228, 268-9; Sidney Hook, 'Whither Russia? Fifty Years After', *Problems of Communism*, Vol. XVI, No. 2 (March-April 1967), pp. 76-9; and Roy Medvedev, 'What Lies Ahead for Us?', *New Left Review*, Nos 87-8, 1974.

14   On institutional pluralism, see David Lane, Note 9 above, p. 233; H. Gordon Skilling, 'Interest Groups and Communist Parties', *World Politics*, Vol. 18 (1966), pp. 441-2, 446; Jerry Hough, 'The Man and the System', *Problems of Communism*, Vol. 25, No. 2 (March-April, 1976), pp. 1-17; Mary McAuley, Note 6 above, p. 162; and Merle Fainsod and Jerry Hough, *How the Soviet Union is Governed* (Harvard University Press, 1979).

15   The analysis here of the USSR as a stable system is based on L.G. Churchward, *The Soviet Intelligentsia: An Essay on the Social Structure and Roles of Soviet Intellectuals During the 1960s* (London: Routledge & Kegan Paul, 1973), p. 128; Stephen White, 'The USSR: Patterns of Autocracy and Industrialism', in A. Brown and J. Gray (eds), *Political Culture and Political Change in Communist States* (London: Macmillan, 1977), p. 44; Merle Fainsod, Note 13 above, p. 23; Arrigo Levi, 'The Evolution of the Soviet System', *Problems of Communism*, Vol. XVI, No. 4 (July-August 1967), pp. 24-9; Walter Laqueur, *The Long Road To Freedom: Russia and Glasnost* (London: Unwin Hyman, 1989), pp. 310, 311; and Alexander Solzhenitsyn, Note 10 above, pp. 20-6.

16   On 'realism' see George F. Kennan, 'The Sources of Soviet Conduct', in Alex Inkeles and Kent Geiger (eds), Note 10 above, pp. 93, 96, 97; Richard Lowenthal, 'The Permanent Revolution is On Again', *Commentary*, Vol. 24, No. 2 (August 1957), pp. 105-12; Zbigniew Brzezinski, 'Reflections on the Soviet System', *Problems of Communism*, Vol. XVII, No. 4 (May-June 1968), pp. 44-5; Robert Conquest, 'Immobilism and Decay', *Problems of Communism*, Vol. XV, No. 5 (September-October 1966), pp. 35-7; George W. Breslauer, Note 6 above, p. 25; Carl A. Linden, *The Soviet Party-State: the Politics of Ideocratic Despotism* (New York: Praeger Publishers, 1983), pp. vii, viii, xii; Richard Pipes, 'Can The Soviet Union Reform?', *Foreign Affairs*, Vol. 63, No. 1 (Fall 1984), pp. 47-61; Richard V. Burks, 'The Coming Crisis in the Soviet Union', in Alexander Shtromas and Morton A. Kaplan (eds), *The Soviet Union and the Challenge of the Future* (New York: Paragon House Publishers, 1984), pp. 115-65; Alexander Shtromas, 'How the End of the Soviet System May Come About', in Alexander Shtromas and Morton A. Kaplan (eds), this note, pp. 201-300; Leopold Labedz, 'False Dilemmas, Real Alternatives', *Encounter*, Vol. LV (December 1980), pp. 33, 34; Jerry F. Hough, Note 9 above, pp. 25-7; George W. Breslauer, Note 6 above, pp. 22-34, 34-41.

17   Robert Conquest, Note 16 above.

4

Soviet Studies and the Collapse of the USSR: in Defence of Marxism

HILLEL H. TICKTIN

Introduction

Sovietology during the post-war period mirrored the course of the Cold War but in varying ways in different countries at different times, and part of the purpose of this chapter is to explore the relationship between the production of knowledge about the USSR and the rhythms of the conflict between the United States on the one hand and the Soviet Union on the other after 1947. This in turn is related to the more central question of why Sovietology failed to predict the end of the Soviet system. There have already been a number of assessments of Sovietology's intellectual record, though few of these thus far have really come to grips with the main problem. Moreover, in the USA at least the debate has tended to oscillate endlessly between those who seem to think that Sovietology is above and beyond criticism and others whose primary purpose has been to advance their own neo-conservative project. Such a discussion between two weak poles is not going to take us very far.[1] In my view the failure of Sovietology can be ultimately attributed to the inability of the different schools of thought to develop a mature political economy of crisis based upon a critical sociology of the different groups and their interests within Soviet society. Later in the chapter I will attempt to develop such an analysis and show why the various schools (with one obvious exception!) failed to explain - let alone predict - the collapse of Stalinism; and why in turn the same Sovietologists (in the main) have got the so-called transition to capitalism wrong as well. First, however, I will outline the viewpoint of the different schools. I will go on to examine the different social groups in Soviet society. I will then take up some methodological issues before explaining the end of the Soviet Union and why the transition to capitalism has not succeeded.

Five Theories in Search of Soviet Reality

The first 'school' worth mentioning here were those whose basic aim was to defend the USSR against its several critics. In Britain this included Communist Party veterans such as Andrew Rothstein who was head of the School of Slavonic and East European Studies in the University of London in the immediate post-war period until his subsequent dismissal,[2] other members of the Communist Party such as Maurice Dobb of Cambridge who wrote an influential economic history of the USSR,[3] and Jack Miller, the founder of the key journal *Soviet Studies* who wrote somewhat more nuanced pro-Soviet articles and books[4] (though he later left the Party and shifted his political stance to a more orthodox Soviet Studies position[5]). The early issues of *Soviet Studies* tended to be readable descriptions of the USSR, whose political orientation was nonetheless clear.[6] Later reincarnations of this same tendency even tried to downplay the role of Stalin and the numbers killed in the purges.[7]

There were secondly those who identified openly with capitalism, and who regarded the USSR as abnormal or an aberration. They considered all non-capitalist systems as being necessarily oppressive and unstable. Taking their cue from neo-classical economics and the work of such writers as von Mises, Barone and Hayek, those who adhered to this viewpoint believed that these regimes (and particularly the USSR) were not viable over the long term. Though this school was highly critical of the Soviet Union and had important things to say about it, none of the scholars associated with it really understood the concrete processes of change taking place within Soviet society itself. It was just taken for granted that a non-market society could not work. In the United States this tendency witnessed a marked renaissance in the Reagan years under the intellectual prompting of Richard Pipes.[8] In Britain, however, few subscribed to this position.

In the third category were those who saw the USSR as oppressive but doomed to last for a very long time indeed. This view was implicit in Orwell and was explicitly enunciated by Solzhenitsyn.[9] It was in all probability the dominant school in Sovietology for many years. It was also the view of a number of dissident writers including Zinoviev, as well as quite a few (but not all) émigrés. Much of the descriptive work on the USSR – from the Harvard Project through to the studies done by Friedrich and Brzezinski in the 1950s and 1960s – also assumed the system would last.[10] In fact, it was only rather late in the day that the much-cited Brzezinski concluded that the Soviet Union was unlikely to survive. Overall, the strength of this position was its ability to list features of the regime and describe a chilling reality which others sometimes hesitated to do. Its enormous weakness was its inability to describe the corrosive forces at work in the society.

The fourth grouping may be called those who wished to be 'fair to both sides' and included a number of liberal and social democratic influentials such as Alec Nove[11] and much later Stephen Cohen.[12] Though derided as a latter-day form of apologetics by the right on both sides of the Atlantic, this approach had a wide appeal in the larger academic community – especially from the 1960s onwards.[13] These authors certainly provided a detailed statistical and economic analysis of what was actually happening in the USSR, and whilst many writers of this genre were critical of the USSR, many of them emphasized the fact that the system had achieved many things and had certain advantages.[14] The work of Bornstein and Fusfeld fell into this category,[15] as did Mary McAuley's widely used text-book on Soviet politics.[16] Some within this group were even more favourable to the USSR, including a number of scholars at Birmingham University in the UK.[17] Others concentrated on looking at the Soviet system in a more or less functionalist way. The latter were not necessarily favourable to the system, but simply wanted to discover how it worked. Indeed, Robert V. Daniels in a robust defence of Sovietology in 1993 even went so far as to suggest that this approach had helped scholars explain the breakdown of the Soviet system.[18]

The fifth and final category consisted of those who held that the USSR was basically unviable as a political economic system. This viewpoint was particularly associated with the journal *Critique*. Bob Arnot, Michael Cox, Don Filtzer, Dave Law, G.A.E. Smith, Suzi Weissman and the present author were amongst those associated with this position.[19] Although *Critique* published on a wide range of issues, within Sovietology it always existed as the outside left pole within the profession (and was often treated accordingly by the Sovietological establishment). Barely tolerated at times by those in the academic mainstream, the basic *Critique* thesis that the Soviet system had a past but no long-term future was more often than not derided by those who thought they knew better. There were, of course, others who were left wing and critical of the Soviet system, but they seldom provided a theoretical or empirical basis for their position. Antonio Carlo, for example, discussed the crisis in Eastern Europe and evolved a law of increasing waste but did not come to any clear conclusions about the system's ultimate destination.[20]

From the CIA to Leon Trotsky

Unlike other more 'normal' academic disciplines, Sovietology was from the very beginning a highly politicized subject. Nor could it have been otherwise given that on the one hand the USSR was regarded as a monstrous threat by the ruling class in the West, and on the other was the subject of constant dispute by those on the Marxist left. For these reasons, the study of the

Soviet Union was inevitably influenced by organizations and groups standing outside the academic mainstream.

One obvious source of outside influence was the bourgeois state itself. Indeed, one does not have to adhere to the conspiracy theory of history to realize that there always remained a close relationship between the Western contestants in the Cold War and many of those who wrote about the Soviet Union. This is not to suggest that all Sovietologists worked for the intelligence services, or even that the work they produced was any the weaker as a result – only to point to a connection. This connection worked through key individuals. It also shaped and in some cases even generated and defined certain types of research. For instance, in both the United States and the United Kingdom, the military and secret services obviously played a key role in the wider academic discussion about Soviet foreign and defence policies. In the same way, quite legitimate academic interest in oppositional groups and currents in the Soviet bloc was encouraged (and sometimes financed) not just because it was interesting but also because it could be used in the wider Cold War struggle. The Soviet Union too had its relations with important figures, including, amongst others, Maurice Dobb and Andrew Rothstein. Nor does one have to assume that these were the only cases. Indeed, just by being friendly to certain individuals (and providing them with access), the Soviet state helped shape the intellectual agenda in Sovietology. Equally, the CIA and the US military openly and covertly financed scholars to conduct research. When the Harvard Project could openly pay tribute to the US Air Force, one must conclude that it got what it paid for.[21] This is not to denigrate the study itself, or the work carried out by or at the behest of the American government. Indeed, some of the best work done on the USSR was sponsored by the American state, one very good set of examples being the regular reports released by the US Congress Joint Economic Committee.

Other governmental institutions, such as the Foreign Office in the UK and the State Department in the United States, also conducted research on the Soviet Union and regularly called upon academics for advice. In the United States, Brzezinski and Pipes even practised what they preached in the Carter and Reagan administrations respectively. Private think tanks like RAND, and others such as the Brookings Institute, did serious research on the USSR too. Though both represented different wings in the American debate, neither organization questioned the need for the market in the former Soviet Union. In this context it is no surprise to discover that Ed Hewett who was at one time at Brookings acted as an adviser to Yeltsin on privatization.

At the other end of the spectrum were the many varieties of socialism – from the Mensheviks whose writings on history exerted a real influence, right across to the anarchists (whose diatribes against the Bolsheviks went down particularly well with both liberals and the conservatives). But without doubt the single most influential figure on the left was Trotsky. His detailed reflections on the Soviet Union from 1923 onward until his death in 1940 constitute a major source, and not surprisingly had a big impact on the way people thought about the origins of Stalinism and the nature of the USSR. In fact, many who wrote on the Soviet Union in other disciplines developed their original interest in large part because of an earlier commitment to Trotskyist organizations. Alvin Gouldner and Seymour Martin Lipset, for example, had at one time belonged to – or had been close to – US Trotskyist groups. James Burnham, whose book *The Managerial Revolution* played a big role in post-war discussions about the nature of the modern capitalism, also grew up in Trotskyism – and indeed his study was the by-product of an intellectual faction fight within the American Trotskyist movement. Burnham, of course, shifted to the right. However, drawing upon his previous work, he made a major intervention into the foreign policy debates on the republican right in the 1950s. He also helped shape Reagan's thinking about the Soviet Union.[22] George Orwell was another thinker who was unmistakably influenced by Trotsky, even though he was never a Trotskyist himself.[23] Even the much-disputed term 'totalitarian' was widely used by members of the Left Opposition (and Trotsky in particular) in their discussions about the USSR in the 1930s. The German Marxist Rudolph Hilferding also deployed the concept to make sense of the Stalinist economic system.[24]

The only way that pro-Soviet writers could deal with the intellectual influence of Trotsky was either to denigrate all criticism of the USSR or to argue that attacks on the Soviet Union 'aided' the United States. This tactic was largely successful – at least until the late 1960s. Another method was to scoff at terms like totalitarian and atomization. Apologists also talked incessantly about the various achievements of the Soviet Union, from its growth rates to Sputnik, to the number of doctors and engineers, to the health service, and, of course, about the degree to which the USSR had liberated women. The Communist Parties and those influenced by them were also relatively successful in placing their people within academia. Meanwhile independent leftists were frozen out unless they moved into esoteric fields or ones which no longer had any social scientific relevance. Trotsky's secretary, Jean van Heijenoort, for instance, became a mathematical logician and so found a way of existing through the worst years of the Cold War.

If many originally became interested in the USSR because they had once been or were on the left, the pressures upon them to conform once they entered the academic profession were immense – and few were able to resist the temptation to join the mainstream. Those who did not do so, moreover, found themselves being impelled by the insidious logic of the Cold War to defend the USSR, warts and all, against its right-wing critics. Even those who were more openly Marxist – and there were very few in Sovietology itself – still retained a residual sympathy for the Soviet Union. This was more or less the position of the important American writers Paul Baran and Paul Sweezy. Both through their own writings and the journal *Monthly Review* the two authors (together with Leo Huberman and Harry Magdoff) exerted an enormous influence on both the US and British left over the years. Baran, of course, theorized the Soviet economic experience and advocated it for other underdeveloped countries. Sweezy meanwhile shifted towards Maoism and during the 1960s became increasingly critical of the USSR, to the point where he finally declared that a new class had come to power.[25] Nonetheless, those and others like him who found their hopes fulfilled in this or that country – whether it was China, Cuba, Nicaragua or Albania – always seemed to regard the USSR as a mother socialist country which had unfortunately deviated from the true course. Even the Soviet Union's critics on the Trotskyist left and around the journal *New Left Review* still continued to defend the USSR against the United States, almost until the bitter end. As the *Monthly Review* once put it, 'on every major' international 'issue between the United States and the USSR, the Soviet Union has been right' and deserved the support of the left.[26]

Totalitarianism

As Bob Arnot shows elsewhere in this volume, the underlying assumption of much Western writing on the former USSR was that the market was the only viable basis upon which to construct a 'normal' economy.[27] In the same way, a number of writers on the USSR took it as given that the abolition of private property was bound to lead to the creation of a totalitarian system; on the again 'natural' assumption that freedom presupposed capitalism and that by tampering with the eternal laws of the market this would only propel countries to go down what Hayek termed in 1944 'the road to serfdom'.

The genesis and meaning of the term totalitarian has been discussed at length. According to standard accounts it emerged as a Cold War concept in the 1950s, then came under attack by a new cohort of liberal Sovietologists in the 1960s and 1970s, only to get a new lease of life after the fall of the USSR itself in 1991. It has certainly become the standard way of referring to the former USSR in Russia today, and those in the West who once challenged the totalitarian perspective are seen by most members of the Russian intelligentsia as being naïve at best and apologists at worst who simply did not understand the appalling and unique character of the Soviet system.

Though the term is more often than not associated with the conservative right, in fact it was (as we have earlier suggested) part of the political vocabulary used by Marxists critical of the USSR in the 1930s. Victor Serge indeed used it frequently in his writings. But for people like Serge and Trotsky the notion of totalitarianism was not synonymous with communism (which it was in the writings of the right). Nor did they make facile comparisons between Nazi Germany and Soviet Russia. Rather it was deployed to describe the power of a peculiar type of non-capitalist regime which had emerged on the broken back of a defeated workers' revolution. Trotsky also drew political inspiration from the term, arguing that the only solution to the problem posed by Stalinism was a political revolution made by the Soviet masses in the name of Soviet democracy.[28]

In the hands of the more orthodox totalitarians all of this was forgotten, including, by the way, the fact that it had been Marxists like Trotsky and Serge (and not just Benito Mussolini and Hannah Arendt) who had originally used the term. Moreover, in their rush to claim the notion as theirs and theirs alone, the right managed to transform the whole meaning of the concept – in at least two critical ways. First, it was divested of all economic content and turned into a narrowly defined political term. Secondly, whereas Marxists critical of the USSR had explained the rise of Stalinist totalitarianism in terms of the political expropriation of the masses, writers of a conservative persuasion saw the masses as the problem. Drawing intellectual inspiration from nineteenth-century critiques of democracy developed by philosophers such as Nietzsche and Heidegger, the totalitarians quite explicitly linked the rise of the totalitarian phenomenon in the twentieth century with the growth of popular politics. There was no doubt in Arendt's mind, for example, that totalitarianism represented the 'madness of the mob' that had fallen under the 'leadership of *déclassé* intellectuals'. This line was also pursued by the influential historian and political scientist Leonard Schapiro. What distinguished totalitarianism for him was its 'mass democratic character'. Virtually paraphrasing Nietzsche's animated attacks against *vox populi*, Schapiro in a flight of elitist fantasy could even write that 'the mass appeal of Bolshevism delves much deeper into the dark recesses of the mob mind. It draws response from the fear of freedom, the envy, the anti-intellectualism, the chauvinism – in short all the characteristic ambience of the mass man ... with his own mass morality, his crude egalitarian and levelling aspirations and his herd paranoia.'[29] The contrast with Trotsky and the earlier left could hardly have been greater.

If nothing else, the elitist 'spin' given by the conservative right to an important concept did at least show how profoundly anti-democratic many of the totalitarians were in outlook. It is for this reason no doubt that the notion now seems to appeal to the Russian intelligentsia. With their almost Victorian hatred of the working-class (or what Andrei Sinyavsky prefers to term their fear of the 'people') it is quite natural the totalitarians should take refuge in a model built upon a profound antipathy to the Russian *narod*. There is, however, something ironic in all this, for it could be argued that this almost morbid, pathological fear has been used by dictators throughout Russian history to justify authoritarian – or in Stalin's case, totalitarian – rule. Indeed, a strong case could be made that their anti-democratic outlook helped prolong the system to which they were so opposed by lending support to the argument that the USSR required a strong state to contain the dark instincts of the Soviet masses. Significantly, Yeltsin used very much the same rationalization to justify his abuse of power in Russia.

Its elitism aside, the basic problem with the post-war totalitarian school was not so much its fierce denunciations of the Soviet system – in this it certainly came closer to the truth than many Western liberals – but in its failure to understand how the system functioned and why in the end it went into terminal decline. In effect, totalitarianism was a static superstructural description of Soviet political life which entirely failed to grasp the fact that there were social groups in the USSR with very clear interests.

The Missing Social Groups

The Elite

It is somewhat ironic that Western scholars who declined to notice the fact that there was a ruling group in their own societies had no problem in talking about the existence of such an entity in the Soviet Union.[30] That said, most Sovietologists had enormous problems dealing with this layer, identifying who exactly was in it, and what its relationship was to the wider economic system.[31] Most writers, for example, were inclined to limit the concept of an 'elite' to the tiny number of people in the Communist Party hierarchy. Moreover, most assumed that this group was fixed in time and place and would thus never contemplate transforming itself from individuals ultimately dependent on their position within a bureaucratic division of labour to an ownership class in its own right.

Part of the problem, of course, had to do with the lack of any real discussion in the Soviet Union itself about this group. Being a 'socialist' society, it always denied an elite existed; and it certainly made it very difficult for researchers to do serious work on the subject. Thus all that one could turn to by way of evidence were one's own observations on the ground, oral discussion, passages in Soviet poems and novels, extracts from the émigré literature, and various snippets from Soviet articles, statistics and books. This was not ideal, but a picture could at least be put together which suggested that there was a system of real privilege in the USSR.

But this was only part of the problem. The more important obstacle had less to do with the dearth of information and more with a refusal by most Western analysts to look beyond the Communist Party. This in turn was connected to a rather naïve and simple-minded belief that the Soviet elite was ideologically legitimized by something termed Marxism, or to use the correct phraseology 'Marxism-Leninism', which made it impossible for them to think beyond the Soviet economic system. The result of all this was to inhibit discussion of this critical social group in at least three ways.

First, by narrowing down the notion of an 'elite' and identifying it with the Communist Party of the Soviet Union hierarchy, Sovietology gave the impression that this layer was extraordinarily small. But common sense alone might have suggested that if the Soviet system had been ruled for the best part of half a century by a few 'evil ideologically blinkered men', then it would not have endured as long as it did. Equally, by focusing almost entirely on top-level functionaries, Western writers ignored the true extent of the elite – which did not just consist of high-level ruling officials (though they were important in the system), but of heads of enterprises, economic planners, a large part of the KGB, university directors, heads of institutes, academicians and many, many more: a group of at least 5 million people. Soviet statistics even talked of 9 million 'leaders', representing between 3 to 7 per cent of the population.[32] Finally, and perhaps most importantly, because the elite was conceived of in mainly ideological terms – as the guardians of a political doctrine opposed by definition to the market – their material interests were ignored. Admittedly, writers on the different interest groups like Skilling painted a fairly useful picture of the different subgroups within the elite.[33] What they failed to ask, however, was whether or not the elite as a whole had an interest in changing the nature of property relations, to its own (obvious) advantage. As history was to show – and as Trotsky had virtually predicted on the basis of very imperfect knowledge in the 1930s – it was self-evident that members of what he then termed the 'bureaucracy' would in the end prefer to own property rather than be dependent on their position. If nothing else, it would make them richer. It would certainly make them less insecure. And it would be possible for them to transmit their legally owned assets (rather than just plain advantage) to their children. But to have arrived at that conclusion would have involved a leap of political and theoretical imagination which Sovietologists were not prepared to make, until it was too late. By then, of course, the old elite had abandoned the Soviet system in favour of something more to their own socioeconomic taste.

The Intelligentsia

If Sovietology found it difficult to theorize the nature of the Soviet elite and its long-term trajectory, it had an equally difficult time explaining the attitudes and interests of the intelligentsia. In the Soviet Union the term was deployed quite simply to designate those with higher education. This in itself created a problem for Western writers, who generally liked to think of the intelligentsia in the classically nineteenth-century Russian sense of the word; that is, a fairly small group of individuals who were intellectuals in the genuine sense of the word, and broadly speaking progressive in outlook. The notion of an intelligentsia defined merely in terms of its position in the social division of labour (and who incidentally had few critical or progressive ideas) did not seem to fit. Middle class might have been the usual term for the social group to which they belonged, but it made little sense in the former Soviet Union, where the categories used were functional occupational groups, as opposed to nebulous social groups divided according to income and power.

But this was not the only problem. Precisely because university professionals in the West saw themselves mirrored in their Soviet counterparts, they felt a degree of solidarity with this group – especially those opposed to the regime. Though this was laudable at one level, at another it led to a romantic and uncritical attitude towards the intelligentsia as a whole. As a result, some of the more base attitudes exhibited by the intelligentsia – such as its appalling views on the 'lower' orders and Soviet Jews – tended to be ignored.[34] Moreover, those who dared suggest that the intelligentsia were not idealists at all, but rather a very narrowly focused group more concerned with improving their own position, were attacked for undermining the struggle for democracy. Even when Solzhenitsyn berated these 'smatterers' for their conformism and crude materialism, few in the West wanted to listen.[35] Nor was there any recognition, finally, that this layer – like the elite – had a very real interest in moving towards the market. In the Western literature there was, of course, an extended discussion on Soviet intellectual dissent, but very little on the political economy of this group and why they favoured a new set of economic arrangements which they hoped (incorrectly) would work to their advantage.

Herein lies their tragedy. Far from getting what they wanted as a result of Soviet collapse, the intelligentsia have suffered grievously in the so-called transition period. Their former aspirations to enter the elite have come to nothing. Their dreams of economic independence have been shattered. Indeed, the overwhelming majority of them have seen their living standards plummet since 1991 – to the extent that most can only survive now by doing two and sometimes three or four jobs. Under such conditions, it is hardly surprising to discover that their views have changed and that they are no longer the great defenders of capitalism. Most, however, remain confused and demoralized, though a few have begun to move (at last) to the left.

The Working Class

The working class also posed an intellectual problem for Sovietologists. Students of the Soviet economy analysed the functioning of the system as if they did not exist, whilst political scientists seemed to ignore them altogether – and only began to take much notice once workers became more active in the Soviet bloc as a whole in the late 1970s. Indeed, having been ignored by Sovietology for so long, after the events in Poland, academics (even the well-known supporter of trade union power, Leonard Schapiro!) started to take the workers far more seriously. This led to a burgeoning literature, much of it very useful at a descriptive level, but nearly all of it taking it as read that because the workers had an unwritten 'contract' with the regime – 'we'll accept the rules of the game if you provide us with job security' – the regime was likely to continue. One might even go as far as to suggest that it was the belated discovery of the workers, and their apparent integration into the Soviet system, which was a key factor in preventing many Sovietologists from predicting the demise of the USSR.

Since the demise of the former Soviet Union, the discussion about the workers has intensified; largely because they have now become more organized and active as a group. But the real question remains why, in spite of the apparent pain imposed by economic change, have workers not taken more militant action?[36] The answer is not difficult to discover. It is not because they are passive *per se*, or ideologically confused, but rather because there has been no serious transition to the market. The reason for this is also obvious: because the regime now (as in the past) fears what would happen if it went for full-scale reforms involving mass bankruptcies and layoffs. The living standards of workers might have dropped very considerably, but the situation is just about bearable for them (though not for the pensioners, the intelligentsia, or many women, who have been hit harder than men since 1991). For this reason they remain, as one analyst has put it, the 'quiet class'.

The Poverty of Theory and the Role of Prediction

Before moving on to examine the question of Soviet collapse and the nature of the transition, it might be useful to raise a few methodological questions first.

Nobody would dispute the fact that the USSR had certain rules and functioned in a particular way: and the task which Sovietologists set themselves was to explain these rules and understand how the Soviet system operated. But to accept that the Soviet Union 'functioned' does not help us explain whether or not the population was contented and, more generally, whether or not the system was operating at a higher or lower level of contradiction than capitalism. In fact these type of questions were effectively ignored by mainstream academics who regarded such problems as being either too abstract or too big. Moreover, because they were not susceptible to the standard methods employed by the orthodox social sciences, there was not much point in asking them. Hence, they were not asked – and the sort of questions that were asked tended to be trivial or irrelevant.

The consequence of all this was to produce a mass of facts and perhaps a little bit of 'middle-range' analysis based upon Soviet data but not much in the way of theory. Some, of course, would argue (and have) that theory as such can only be as good as the amount of information available; and that because information was limited it was impossible to develop a proper theory of the former USSR. But this is facile. After all, we now have more information about Russia today than we ever had about the Soviet Union, but that does not mean we therefore understand what is happening in Russia. There are enough opinion polls in Moscow to run through a supercomputer to gain a coherent overview, but in essence they often tell us little that we did not know already. They also do not explain the forces at work in the wider society.

The empiricist character of Sovietology meant, in effect, that the subject was in intellectual terms at least something of a backwater in which there seemed to be little or no room for either serious theory or indeed theoreticians. Any cursory examination of the various journals only shows how impoverished the discipline was. Indeed, one of the very few efforts to engage with the problem was made by Nove, who no doubt had many fine qualities but one of them was not theory.[37] But at least he tried. Others did not even bother and simply provided descriptions of Soviet reality rather than any explanation of why the system performed in the very odd way that it did. This was especially true of economists, even the more competent ones like Abram Bergson.[38] The tools of orthodox economics were in fact quite useless when it came to the USSR, and the best and the most we got was better or worse descriptions of how the Soviet economy functioned or malfunctioned (and why a market was necessary) rather than a developed explanation as to why labour productivity was so low, why it was difficult to introduce new techniques, and why the plans were never fulfilled.

This absence of real theory might also help us explain why Sovietology appeared to end up in the hands of people who were sometimes little better than translators. Translation is an honourable profession – made more honourable by those who went further and put the parts of the jigsaw together to produce an interesting picture of Soviet society. But in Soviet Studies it seemed to be especially easy to make a career out of one's linguistic skills and having a few conversations with a number of well-placed Soviet officials. In fact, what passed for serious analysis was often little more than a coherent refashioning of the original Soviet material. Given that this sort of work could not be done in the USSR itself, it did serve a purpose. But whilst such work was useful enough, it was hardly earth-shattering theoretically. Nor was it even particularly scholarly. However, it was safe, and because it asked no difficult questions and came to no dangerous conclusions, it did at least ensure a sound, successful and rewarding professional career for a number of academics.

This brings us finally to the issue of prediction – a problem confronted by Michael Cox in his introduction to this volume although avoided since 1991 by the American Sovietological hierarchy. The issue thus far has been brushed aside as it was, for instance, at the 1993 conference of the American Association for the Advancement of Slavic Studies by Gail Warshovsky Lapidus. Sovietologists, she felt, should simply ignore the charge that they had somehow 'got it wrong'. It was not their job to predict the future; they were social scientists not soothsayers and thus could not have been expected to anticipate the fall of the USSR. Much the same point has been made by others in the profession – on both sides of the Atlantic.

This refusal by the gatekeepers of knowledge to engage with Sovietologys's failed past was perhaps to be expected. However, the bland and blunt assertion that prediction itself is either impossible or unnecessary simply beggars belief. For one thing, Sovietologists did engage in prediction. The only problem was that their particular 'prediction' – that the USSR would continue in being – turned out to be wrong! The idea, moreover, that social scientists should not engage in such activities (even though they do) is methodologically naïve. Of course, nobody can ever be expected to predict the exact moment when a particular event will take place. But that does not mean we should not try to plot the general direction in which history is moving. A social science after all has to explain events, and any explanation worth its salt should contain within it in embryonic form an indication about the shape of things to come. If it does not do so, then it is not science but mere narrative.

The issue about prediction, however, raises an even bigger problem which the defenders of Sovietology appear not to understand. If it can be shown that academics working in the field got the collapse of the Soviet Union wrong – which indeed most of them accept – would this not suggest that their understanding of the Soviet system was also profoundly flawed? Put another way, if the overwhelming majority of experts could not even begin to anticipate where the Soviet Union might be going to, was this not because they had little understanding of where it was coming from? We cannot separate out the two questions as if they were totally unconnected. Past, present and future are not after all distinct entities but part of a continuum. And if Sovietologists had little idea about the Soviet Union's future, it would imply that they had little idea either about how the system operated in the first place.

The Failure of the Traditional Left

If more traditional Sovietologists turned out to be rather poor academics, those on the left proved to be even worse Marxists; and instead of trying to discover the Soviet Union's basic laws of motion, they did little more than just repeat slogans whose purpose (it seems) was less to understand the society than to define the politics of this or that particular group. Furthermore, instead of taking the Soviet Union as it was, the left in the main tended to superimpose categories on Soviet society which made little or no sense. For this reason, amongst others, Marxists could easily be dismissed as cranks – or worse – who knew nothing about the USSR and whose statements about it could be brushed aside as being intellectually worthless.

Even those who perhaps should have known better did little more than just describe the outward appearances of the Soviet system. For example, in the early work of Max Shachtman we find a lucid discussion about the origins of Stalinism (based largely on Trotsky),[39] but beyond that, all we are then provided with is a statement about the USSR being 'bureaucratic collectivist', an assertion that the ruling group in the USSR was a class, and a truism that workers and peasants within the USSR were together being exploited by a particularly unpleasant bunch of gangsters.[40] The theory of state capitalism suffers from a rather different affliction: of attempting to take the laws of motion of capitalism and trying to fit them to the USSR, but with little recognition of the fact that the Soviet Union was in no way capitalist. Indeed, one of the more obvious problems with this particular theory was that it could not in the end explain why Soviet-style 'capitalism' disintegrated between 1989 and 1991 but capitalism elsewhere in the world continued to function.[41] The workers' state theory was equally incapable of explaining what happened to the former USSR. In fact, precisely because the advocates of this semi-apologetic notion like Mandel assumed that 'planning' was by definition on a higher economic plain than capitalism, they were utterly stunned when the theoretically superior form disintegrated leaving the self-evidently inferior form intact.[42]

One could go on. The issue here though is not whether these 'theories' were wrong (history has settled that question) but why they were wrong. Once again we return to the main point: that these theories were not in fact theories at all, but either static characterizations at best, or at worst political statements whose ultimate function was not to explain the dynamics of the Soviet system but to hold this or that group together – normally around a particular guru figure whose wisdom could never be challenged. It was perhaps because these constraints did not exist in Eastern Europe that some of the more interesting work was done there rather than in the West. Indeed, some of the best left-wing studies were not done by Marxists active in the West, but by rather inactive Marxists in the East who at least knew these societies from the inside, who could read the material in the original language, and who could draw upon their own experience to explain what was actually going on. Whether in the end they were any more successful in anticipating the demise of these systems than Marxists in the West is doubtful. However, they did manage to paint a more realistic picture of these countries which others were then able to draw upon. Moreover, writers like Campeneau in particular did show that the systems in the East as a whole had no real dynamic – and that if they persisted at all it was only because of fear and repression.[43]

Rethinking Soviet Collapse

As many readers will no doubt recall, the present author had for many years argued that because the USSR had no underlying economic dynamic (being neither capitalist nor democratically planned) it was doomed to stagnate and die. This thesis, however, commanded almost no support whatsoever within the larger Sovietological profession, many of whom were quite exasperated by my suggestion that what some of them saw as a threat – and others a stable formation – was in fact likely to pass from the stage of history some time in the near future. Whether it was my Marxism or my prognosis, or even a combination of the two, which bothered other academics was difficult to tell. The fact remains that my analysis had little impact on the way mainstream Sovietologists viewed the former USSR. In their collective view – though not mine – the Soviet system would last.[44]

Now, of course, that the Soviet Union has disappeared from the international stage, the same wise men and women have discovered all sorts of reasons to explain that which they once thought inconceivable. The American writer, Alexander Dallin, has summarized these arguments in a useful analytical article surveying the different explanations as to why the Soviet Union collapsed.[45] Dallin makes a number of good points including the one made by Stephen White and Robert Daniels in this book: that many academics did in fact spot the Soviet crisis coming – Marshall Goldman, amongst others, being one.[46] This is true, but the question remains: was this crisis seen as being terminal or one which could in the end be negotiated by the Soviet elite?

There are two levels of analysis which need to be distinguished here: the immediate and the essential. The two often get confused as is shown in the work of, say, Michael Ellman. Ellman sees the immediate cause of Soviet collapse as being Gorbachev and his various policies. He thus implies (though is not consistent on this point) that the disintegration of the USSR was largely accidental, or more precisely owed as much to the withdrawal of the Communist Party from the economy as it did to any necessary tendential law to decline. It also follows from his analysis that there was no essential reason why the former USSR had to implode. It could have continued in being – though for how long is never exactly made clear by Ellman, who in his work seems to oscillate between the argument that the system was probably not viable over the long run and that its collapse should not be seen as inevitable.[47]

The problem with those like Ellman who argue that it was, in the end, an accident of history which led to the dissolution of the Soviet Union, is that their analysis begs a number of important questions. The most obvious is why did Gorbachev feel impelled to experiment with reform in the first place probably knowing full well that it involved huge risks? Would this not suggest that the USSR was already in crisis, or as I would prefer to put it, in an advanced state of decline? The second question is why, in fact, did the USSR fall apart so quickly and so easily because of something as contingent as a flawed policy? Again, does this not tell us something about the fragile nature of the Soviet system? And if it does, then isn't the real task not to 'blame' Gorbachev or overstate his role in history but to work out exactly why the former USSR was so vulnerable; and why in the end a confused strategy designed to arrest its decline only accelerated its more rapid dissolution?

This leads me to make what I think is an important theoretical distinction which is often not made: between breakdown and disintegration. From one point of view, the Soviet Union dissolved into its constituent national parts by the end of 1991 when it fell apart politically. It did not break down as in Yugoslavia, where the constituent parts went to war. Yet the Soviet Union as such ceased to exist and so reached a natural terminus. This breakdown, however, did not come out of the blue but was the end-result of a longer period of political-economic disintegration lasting over a ten- to 20-year period. During this time, industrial rates of growth fell to zero (and worse), agriculture effectively stagnated, and material prospects declined considerably. This of itself did not necessarily have to lead to major change. However, precisely because the regime relied to an extraordinary degree for its stability upon its ability to maintain industrial expansion and (after Stalin) to improve living standards, there was every chance that it would change if growth and living standards fell.

This in turn raises another issue about the nature of the regime itself and why it was so unstable in the first place. The answer to this problem would require a book in itself. Suffice to say here that once it was formed by the mid-1930s, the Stalinist system was always in crisis and the only means by which it could survive was by the most thoroughgoing repression – to an extent even underestimated by the totalitarians. This, however, carried a very high economic price, for without democracy it became impossible to plan or raise the productivity of an alienated workforce. There was, it is true, a degree of political relaxation after 1953. Living standards were also raised. However, this did not make the regime more popular, though it did buy it a breathing space by making life less intolerable for the major social groups in Soviet society – including for the elite itself who now at least could enjoy their privileges in peace. Nor did these reforms make the system any more viable. If anything it made it less so as the regime was forced to make more and more concessions to an increasingly powerful working class. The elite was thus trapped. It could not reimpose terror. On the other hand, the more concessions it made in order to buy social peace at home, the less able it was to sustain economic growth. The only way it could keep the show on the road was simply by adding more and more factors of production to the economy. But this became increasingly costly. Moreover, the whole thing could only be sustained so long as there was a steady supply of labour. When this dried up – as it did in the 1970s – the regime began to run out of options and started to manifest all the symptoms of a system in the early stages of terminal decline: ideological fatigue so-called, declining life expectancy, increasing corruption at the top, and, of course, deep divisions within the ruling elite itself between those who now saw there was no option but serious reform and those who feared (correctly) that reform could easily undermine the system.

This is where Gorbachev (via his mentor Andropov) enters the scene. It is certainly true, as Ellman has argued, that Gorbachev accelerated rather than reversed the process of decline; and, moreover, unleashed forces he neither understood nor could control. This is self-evident. He was no genius after all and almost certainly understood little about the impact his reforms would (and did) have upon Soviet society. That said, his apparent empiricism should not hide the fact that he did have an agenda when he arrived on the historical stage (backed by the KGB and shortly thereafter by Thatcher and Reagan). And at the heart of this agenda was an underlying determination to change the system and to protect the position of the elite by moving towards the market with Western support. Neither he nor his advisers knew exactly how to do this. Hence the confusion. Nor was it at all certain whether the West was prepared to back him with offers of massive aid. Thus the delay. But there is little doubt where his policies were bound to lead to in the end. Whether it was done slowly (as he preferred) or more rapidly was basically a tactical question. In the last analysis, all roads led to the same market destination. Admittedly, Gorbachev could not deliver the goods; however, he did pave the way for what later happened under Yeltsin. In the process, of course, the old economic rules were torn up, and as a result the system went into economic free-fall. But whilst all this was happening the elite at least got what it wanted: a title to property and the right for the first time to be defined as a 'class' in its own right.

Conclusion: a Transition to Capitalism?

Different Western writers have apologized in different ways for their respectful heroes, Gorbachev and Yeltsin. Gorbachev, it is argued, stamped his permanent mark on history by ending the Cold War. Yeltsin, we are informed, has done the same by destroying communism and laying the foundation for market democracy in Russia. The now irrelevant Gorbachev is probably best left to his Western admirers – he has few in Russia. Yeltsin meanwhile is struggling with Russia's appalling problems which are leading anywhere but towards that 'state of nature' which economists refer to as capitalism. Indeed, as has been pointed out by Stephen Cohen in this book, the transition has turned into a tragedy of epoch proportions. However, there is little point just blaming Yeltsin or his increasingly rich cronies. A large part of the responsibility for what has happened also has to be laid at the door of those Western experts so-called (and their Sovietological allies) who urged Russia along the path of economic reform. One might respect them more, of course, if they had got it right. But they have not. Thus instead of the transition taking a 'few' years, Western commentators are now saying it will take several; and having promised that a strong dose of reform would help clean the Augean political stables, we find that those running Russia today are the same old crooks (quite literally) who ran it before – except now they have more money to spend and invest – usually abroad.

When the old order collapsed in 1991, Sovietology not only disappeared as a subject, but at the same time came of age insofar as many of its practitioners now became directly involved in the management of Russia. And it says a great deal about their lack of understanding that they really did believe that a viable capitalism could be constructed on the debris left behind by the Soviet Union. What is truly appalling, however, is that so many of them were prepared to go along with, indeed advocate, policies knowing that if they were successfully implemented, they would lead to large-scale unemployment and the closure of masses of industrial enterprises. The fact that the strategy could never work – and has already failed – does not absolve them from responsibility. Moreover, the idea that ordinary Russians should be asked to tighten their belts on the promise that things were likely to get better in the future would be laughable if it was not so terrible. What our experts seem to forget (probably because they do not know) is that it was Stalin no less who called on people to make sacrifices for the sake of future generations in the 1930s. Why the people should do so again, 50 years later, defies logic.

Stephen Cohen has correctly observed that history will judge those who have advised Russia since 1991 most harshly – perhaps even more harshly than I have judged Sovietology here in this chapter. The twin failures are not unrelated, however. After all, many of the same people who were unable or unwilling to anticipate the demise of the Soviet Union are more or less the same individuals who failed to predict what would happen in Russia after 1991 if the country went for the market. Moreover, they got things wrong twice for basically the same reason: they never really understood the nature of the USSR. But even if mainstream Sovietology isn't prepared to admit that it made mistakes, one gets the distinct feeling that many who originally accepted that there was no alternative to capitalism for Russia have now come to realize the error of their ways. One certainly hopes so. However, they have to do more than just accept that they have made a mistake or two. Their other task now is to suggest an alternative for Russia that will advance the interests of all of its citizens and not just a few. To do this though will require them to be as critical of a capitalist world which suggested that Russia go down the path of reform, as they have belatedly become of the new order in the former USSR. Only then will they begin to develop a proper understanding of Russia's tragic present and its uncertain future.

Notes

1   See for example P. Manson, 'The Owl of Minerva and the Fall of the USSR', *Sociologisk Forskning*, 1994, Vol. 31, No. 4, pp. 3-32, and *The National Interest*, No. 31, Spring 1993.

2   Andrew Rothstein: *Wreckers on Trial: A Record of the Industrial Party Trial Held in Moscow Nov-Dec 1930* (Modern Books, London, 1931) and his *Soviet Foreign Policy during the Patriotic War, documents and materials* (2 vols), (Hutchinson, London, 1946).

3   See Maurice Dobb, *Soviet Economic Development since 1917*, (Routledge & Kegan Paul, London, 1948; revised 1966).

4   See Jack Miller's untitled essay in *Soviet Studies*, Vol. 1, No. 1, June 1949.

5   See Jack Miller, *Life in Russia Today* (Batsford/Putnam, London/New York, 1969).

6   The first issue of *Soviet Studies* (Vol. 1, No. 1, June 1949) declared that it would neither attack nor defend the USSR (p. 2). The contributors were all known for their past or present association with the Communist movement and included Rudolf Schlesinger, Jack and Molly Miller, and Maurice Dobb. Four years later, E.H. Carr (who, of course, was not a communist!) wrote on the death of Stalin that 'it is perhaps in the role of Peter that history will best remember him.

Paradoxically, posterity may yet learn to speak of Stalin as the great westernizer'. *Soviet Studies,* July 1993, p. 7.

7   See for instance: J. Arch Getty, *Origins of the Great Purges: The Soviet Communist Party Reconsidered, 1933-1938* (Cambridge University Press, New York, 1985).

8   See the essays by Richard Pipes and Martin Malia in *The National Interest,* note 1 above.

9   See Solzhenitsyn's letter of 27 May 1974 to *Aftenposten,* in *Mir i Nasilie* (Possev, Frankfurt, 1974, p. 48).

10 Carl Friedrich and Zbigniew Brzezinski, *Totalitarian Dictatorship and Autocracy* (Praeger, London, New York, 1969).

11 See Alec Nove, *The Soviet Economy: An Introduction* (Allen & Unwin, 1962), and revised a number of times since. See also Alec Nove: *Was Stalin really necessary? Some problems of Political Economy* (Allen & Unwin, 1964).

12 Stephen F. Cohen, *Rethinking the Soviet Experience, Politics and History since 1917* (New York, OUP, 1984). Cohen, of course, made his reputation with his sympathetic and influential biography of Bukharin.

13 This attitude also corresponded to a lull in the Cold War during the 1960s and 1970s.

14 See Alec Nove, *The Economics of Feasible Socialism* (Unwin Hyman, London, 1983).

15 See Morris Bornstein and Daniel R. Fusfeld, *The Soviet Economy: A Book of Readings* (R.D. Irwin, Homewood, Illinois, 1962).

16 See Mary McAuley, *Politics and the Soviet Union* (Penguin, London, 1977).

17 The key figure at Centre of the Russian and East European Studies was, of course, Bob Davies, co-author with E.H. Carr and author of several books on the Soviet Union. Others in the Birmingham 'school' at one time or another would be Julian Cooper, Ron Amman, John Barber, David Lane and Jonathan Haslam.

18 Robert V. Daniels wrote that 'Soviet and East European studies went as far as any scholarship could in anticipating the crisis of the system'. See his 'The State of the Field and its Future', *AAASS Newsletter,* January 1995, p. 11.

19 Hillel Ticktin, *The Origins of the Crisis in the USSR: Essays on the Political Economy of a Disintegrating System* (Myron E. Sharpe, New York, 1992); Bob Arnot, *Controlling Soviet Labour* (Macmillan Press, London, 1988), and Michael Cox, 'The Cold War and Stalinism in the Age of Capitalist Decline', *Critique,* No. 17, 1986, pp. 17-82.

20 Antonio Carlo, 'The Crisis of Bureaucratic Collectivism', *Telos,* No. 43, Spring 1980.

21 See the acknowledgements in Raymond A. Bauer, Alex Inkeles and Clyde Kluckholm: *How the Soviet System Works* (New York, Vintage, 1961).

22 James Burnham, *The Managerial Revolution,* (Penguin, London, 1962).

23 Orwell was most obviously influenced by Trotsky in three of his books: *Animal Farm, Homage to Catalonia,* and *1984.* Whether he ever understood Trotsky is not clear, but that he saw him as the authentic hero of the revolution is beyond doubt. Victor Serge, who was a left oppositionist until the end of his life, established a friendship with Orwell.

24 See Rudolf Hilferding's 1940 essay on the totalitarian nature of the Soviet economy reprinted under the title 'A 1940 Social Democratic View of Stalin's Russia', *The Modern Review,* June 1947, pp. 266-71.

25 See the Review of the Month (written by the editors Paul Sweezy and Leo Huberman): 'The Split in the Socialist World', *Monthly Review*, Vol. 15, No. 1, May 1963, where the editors declare that 'the Chinese as its [Marxism-Leninism's] most faithful and powerful champions seem certain to become the spiritual leaders of all genuine revolutionary movements in the world'.

26 See *Monthly Review*, Vol. 13, No. 6, p. 242.

27 See Chapter 12, in this volume.

28 'Through the medium of the totalitarian state, the Soviet worker is sometimes exploited by foreign capitalism.' Victor Serge, *Destiny of a Revolution* (Jarrolds, London, 1937), p. 262. 'L'Etat est moi' [I am the state] is almost a liberal formula by comparison with the actualities of Stalin's totalitarian regime.... The totalitarian state goes far beyond Caesaro-Papism, for it has encompassed the entire economy of the country as well.' L.D. Trotsky: *Stalin* (Hollis & Carter, London, 1947), p. 421.

29 Quoted in Leonard Schapiro, 'Totalitarianism in the Doghouse', in Leonard Schapiro (ed.), *Political Opposition in One Party States* (Macmillan, London, 1972), p. 262.

30 For a useful survey of the sociological literature on the USSR see S.M. Lipset and Richard B. Dobson: 'Social Stratification and Sociology in the Soviet Union', *Survey*, Vol. 19, No. 3, Summer 1973.

31 See Mervyn Matthews, 'Top Incomes in the USSR, towards a definition of the Soviet elite', *Survey*, Vol. 21, No. 3, Summer 1975, p. 13.

32 *Narodnoe Khoziaistvo za 70 Let* (Moscow, 1987), p. 421.

33 See H. Gordon Skilling, 'Interest Groups and Communist Politics', *World Politics*, Vol. 18, No. 3, April 1966, pp. 435-51.

34 See Michael Cox, 'The Politics of the Dissenting Intellectual', *Critique*, No. 5, 1975, pp. 5-35.

35 See Alexander Solzhenitsyn, 'The Smatterers', in his *Under the Rubble* (Fontana, London, 1975), pp. 229ff.

36 For a romantic account of workers see David Mandel, *Perestroika and the Soviet People* (Black Rose Books, Montreal, 1991).

37 Alec Nove, 'Is there a ruling class in the USSR?', *Soviet Studies*, Vol. 27, October 1975, pp. 615-38.

38 Abram Bergson, *The Economics of Soviet Planning* (Columbia University Press, New York, 1964).

39 Max Shachtman, *The Bureaucratic Revolution, the Rise of the Stalinist State* (The Donald Press, New York, 1962).

40 See, however, Antonio Carlo, 'The Socio-Economic Nature of the USSR', *Telos*, No. 21, Fall 1974, and his 'The Crisis of Bureaucratic Collectivism', *Telos*, No. 43, Spring 1980.

41 Tony Cliff, *Russia: A Marxist Analysis* (London, Pluto Press, 1974).

42 See Ernest Mandel in 'Ten Theses on the social and economic laws governing the society transitional between Capitalism and Socialism', *Critique*, No. 3, 'Once again on the Trotskyist definition of the social nature of the Soviet Union', *Critique*, No. 12 and *Beyond Perestroika* (New Left Books, London, 1988).

43 See Pavel Campenau, *The Syncretic Society* (Myron E. Sharpe, New York, 1980).

44 See for example my 'The USSR: the beginning of the End', *Critique*, No. 7, 1976.

45 Alexander Dallin, 'Causes of Collapse of the USSR', *Post Soviet Affairs*, Vol. 8,

October/December 1992.

46   See for instance: Marshall Goldmann: *USSR in Crisis, the Failure of an Economic System* (Norton, New York, 1983).

47   Michael Ellman and Vladimir Kontorovich (eds), *The Disintegration of the Soviet Economic System* (London, New York Routledge, 1992) and Michael Ellman, 'The Many Causes of Collapse', *RFE/RL Research Report*, Vol. 2, No. 23, 4 June 1993, pp. 55-8.

5

Soviet Society and American Sovietologists: a Study in Failure?

VLADIMIR SHLAPENTOKH

The goal of this chapter is to discuss the evolution of American attitudes towards the Soviet Union – from the origins of the Soviet system in 1917 to its demise in 1989. As we shall see, over this 70-odd year period, American intellectuals, including most Sovietologists, tended to oscillate between effusive praise of the Soviet system as a model society and total rejection of the Soviet Union as being abnormal and pathological. Now, when the USSR belongs to history, and when most of the facts about it are known, it is perhaps time to evaluate how well American Soviet Studies did in understanding the nature of this system and in predicting its demise. Of course, the verdict will never be final. Writers are to this day still divided over the reasons for the decline and fall of the Roman empire or the origins of the English civil war. However, unlike historians of the ancient world or the war between 'roundheads' and 'royalists', we do at least have the advantage of having 'known' or even directly experienced the Soviet Union. Moreover, our views are still relatively fresh. Such resources will most likely not be available to future researchers.

Any assessment of American Soviet Studies must perforce be more than just a discussion of a particular academic discipline. In the process of evaluating Sovietology we are at the same time also passing judgement on the nature of American social science in general, considered after the Second World War to be on the cutting edge of research worldwide. Moreover, any discussion of Soviet Studies raises critically important questions too about the relationship between the academic community and the American state which poured vast sums into Sovietology during the years of the Cold War. Finally, an examination of American Sovietology is also likely to tell us a great deal about the United States itself and its ability to understand foreign societies. As I shall try to show, the failure of American Soviet Studies was not just a failure of intellect but a statement about the character of a society which attempted – with only limited success – to comprehend the most important human experiment of the twentieth century.

The Initial Impact of the USSR upon the United States

American attitudes towards the USSR before the onset of the Cold War were shaped as much, if not more, by events in the wider world as they were by developments within the Soviet Union itself. The Soviet Union, moreover, was no ordinary country but the representation of something else: a dream to many, to others an abnormal system which simply could not work, and to some – like the small but influential groups of American Trotskyists – a great cause which had subsequently been betrayed by Stalin and Stalinism.

Certainly there was no lack of sympathy for the USSR in the United States, especially amongst left-wing intellectuals who saw it as offering a real solution to mankind's problems after the First World War. Amongst the long list of influential American admirers one should not only include here the popular chronicler of the Russian Revolution – John Read – but a number of other writers as well, Upton Sinclair, Theodore Dreiser, Lincoln Steffens and Lilian Hellman, to name but a few. The new socialist state was for them above criticism, and those who engaged in such attacks according to Sinclair were simply peddling Wall Street 'propaganda' (Lash, 1962, p.124). After having visited the USSR briefly in 1923, Steffens was equally strong in its defence, declaring that 'Russia' had 'proved that you can change human nature sufficiently in one generation' (Steffens, 1936). Edward Ross, a leading American sociologist and critic of what he termed 'outworn individualism' was also an enthusiast and concluded on the basis of his travels during the first year of the revolution that the USSR was destined to become a true socialist society (Ross, 1918, pp. 330–49).

Sympathy for the Soviet Union necessarily increased during the 1930s. Indeed, under the impact of the Great Depression, the New Deal and above all the Second World War, many Americans now found even more to admire in the Soviet Union – this beacon of hope in a world turned upside down by mass employment and the threat of fascism (Harper, 1931). One such admirer, Walter Duranty, *The New York Times* correspondent in Moscow, was perhaps the most outstanding of US 'fellow travellers' and writing in 1935 argued that 'real' socialism had finally been achieved in Russia where all 'the dynamic forces of the country' were being 'applied for and by the community instead of for and by individuals'. Duranty's apologetics were in part conditioned by the collapse of intellectual confidence in Western capitalism. But clearly what made many Americans especially enthusiastic about the USSR was the rising spectre of Nazism and the belief that the Soviet Union was the main bulwark against further right-wing expansion. It was this in particular that led the famous American journalist Louis Fischer (who was a correspondent in Russia for over 14 years) to pull his punches. As he confessed later, though he well understood the repressive character of the Soviet system, and fully understood the nature of the Moscow show trials, he 'hesitated to throw stones in public' because the Soviet Union seemed to be only country determined to stand up to fascism around the world (Fischer, 1941). This same inclination was particularly marked amongst the so-called New York intellectuals, mostly of Jewish origin, who were perhaps the staunchest defenders of the first socialist country – a bulwark in their view against Nazism in particular and anti-semitism in general (Howe, 1982; Podhoretz, 1979; Glazer, 1984; Abel, 1984).

The tendency to turn a blind eye to the USSR's less acceptable features became even more pronounced following the formation of the wartime alliance between the United States and Russia in 1941. Indeed, during the war, public criticism of the USSR became almost impossible. Even the prominent republican Wendell Willkie was moved to defend the Soviet Union against its critics and celebrate Soviet communism as a living example of a 'vibrant, fearless democracy' (Willkie, 1943). Alexander Werth, whose writings were very popular in the United States at the time, was equally lavish in his praise – as was America's second ambassador to the USSR, Joseph Davies. Davies like Werth painted a particularly bright and positive picture of a country in the throes of building a new society (Werth, 1942; Davies, 1942). Davies even seemed to accept the official version of the Moscow show trials as a legitimate response by a besieged state defending itself against its enemies at home and abroad. To make his message acceptable to an American audience he also implied that the Soviet Union was not really communist at all, but a 'normal' developing society employing 'the methods of capitalism and industrialism' to achieve its long-term goals (Davies, 1942; see also Duranty, 1944).

As the case of Davies illustrates only too clearly, many Americans who commended the Soviet Union often did so not because of its (or their) devotion to Marxism, but because they thought they could detect certain trends in the system that were making it ideologically less dangerous and politically less unique. Quite a few authors in fact began to view the USSR more positively, not because it was Communist, but because it had returned to normal after a period of utopian experimentation. Hence, the important historian of the Russian Civil War – William Chamberlin – praised Russia not because of its commitment to revolution but because of Stalin's liquidation of 'crude' Bolshevism and his efforts to build a more 'settled order' (Chamberlin, 1930, pp. 334–8). Eugene Lyons, a future critic of Communist Russia, found during his visit to Moscow many signs of 'normalization' and what he and others characterized at the time as the new Soviet conservatism. Indeed, it seemed to him that by the mid-1930s the regime had at last begun to 'settle down': significantly, only two years before the purges destroyed the old Bolshevik party, he predicted 'the dissolution of the entire party' (Lyons, 1935, pp. 235-7). Some Americans, like Samuel Harper of the University of Chicago, even looked upon the Soviet Union as a 'pluralistic society' and denied its 'totalitarian' character (Harper, 1929; 1938) - as did several other admirers of the Soviet Union, including the US commentator, Freund, and the intellectual leaders of Fabianism in Great Britain, Sidney and Beatrice Webb (see Freund, 1945, p. 627; Webb and Webb, 1937).

The Soviet Union, however, did have its critics, both on the left (notably the American Trostkyists) and on the right. American foreign policy officials also remained deeply wary of the USSR. In fact, the USA only got round to recognizing the country 17 years after the revolution itself - the last major capitalist country to do so. Some prominent intellectuals like William Walling and Charles Crane were equally hostile to the new revolutionary regime, though they (and others like them) took comfort in the fact that Soviet Russia simply could not last for very long. This view was indeed very widespread before 1921. *The New York Times*, for example, regularly predicted the impending fall of the Soviet regime (Carrol, 1965, pp. 7-8; Lash, 1962, p. 121; Graham, 1925, p. 296; Strakhovsky, 1961). When, of course, the USSR did not collapse, the next line of consolation was to argue that socialism was a utopian pipe-dream; and it was left to writers like Ludwig von Mises and Friedrich Hayek to explain why a planned economy without prices could not work (von Mises, 1951). The argument was as basic as it was logical. According to von Mises, it was in fact impossible under socialism to make meaningful economic calculations. Consequently, there was no way (short of physical compulsion) of making people work - primarily because there was no correlation between 'the magnitude of the share which is assigned for the use of each citizen' and 'the value of the service he renders' (von Mises, 1951, p. 154; Hubbard, 1938; Shlapentokh, 1988). Hayek was also confident that a socialist economy could not function, again (mainly) because there could be no rational form of economic calculation without a market. And where there was no system of monetary rewards, the only way of motivating people was by force. This is why, in his view, central planning was incompatible with freedom (Hayek, 1944, pp. 56-91; see also Shlapentokh, 1988).

The USSR as an Abnormal System: Totalitarianism

The end of the Second World War followed in quick succession by the onset of a Cold War in Europe and a shooting war between communism and the United States in Asia, transformed America's position in the world and destroyed any residual sympathy which Americans might have had for the USSR. US policy-makers and intellectuals now groped for a theory to explain what they saw as the pathological nature of the Soviet system and why a determined US effort was now required to contain it. The theory, of course, came to be known as 'totalitarianism', developed mainly, but not only, by the political theorist Hannah Arendt (Arendt, 1966). Not all totalitarians sang from the same hymn sheet. However they did agree about certain basics: first, that October 1917 was a historical aberration that had prevented Russia from evolving into a normal constitutional democracy; that the revolution itself was a *coup d'état* or what Martin Malia later called an 'illegitimate seizure of power'; that the survival of this highly abnormal regime was little short of miraculous; and finally, that the Soviet Union was an ideological power driven to expand outwards (Daniels, 1967; Malia, 1993; Pipes, 1994, pp. 331, 340). Based upon the not unreasonable observation that the twentieth century had witnessed the emergence of an entirely new form of political organization, the concept was adopted almost uncritically during the early years of the Cold War only to be jettisoned in the 1960s and 1970s by a new generation of Sovietologists who not only detected what they saw as important changes in the Soviet system, but opposed the idea of equating Hitler with Stalin and fascist Germany with communist Russia (Friedrich and Brzezinski, 1965; Wolfe, 1956; Armstrong, 1961; Ulam, 1963).

Yet the totalitarians were by no means the united, monolithic group portrayed by their later critics in the United States. There were subtle variations on the same underlying theme. There was, for example, a clear difference of opinion between writers like Rostow and Pipes who saw Marxism as simply providing a rationalization for Soviet actions, and others like Malia, Conquest and Kolakowski who regarded ideology as being the central motor of Soviet behaviour. Indeed, according to Malia, the USSR was perhaps the 'greatest triumph of ideology over real life', while for Kolakowski, Marxism was nothing less than 'the greatest fantasy of our century' (Rostow, 1953, pp. 7–8; Malia, 1990, p. 302; 1994, p. 126; Kolakowski, 1978, p. 523; Conquest, 1967, p. 19). There was an equally clear division between those who saw the USSR as representing a major break in Russian history – the dominant view amongst totalitarians – and others who observed important forms of continuity between tsarist Russia and the Soviet Union. Many historians, in fact, Kennan being one, viewed the USSR as being firmly within the larger Russian tradition with its centralism, lack of individual rights, fear of chaos and dissent, and xenophobia (Kennan, 1961). Tucker too saw a similar line of continuity and following Berdiaev suggested that Lenin and Stalin together had created a 'kind of neo-Czarist order' (Tucker, 1961, 1980, 1991, see also Daniels, 1987a, 1987b; Fainsod, 1963). A number of other writers also saw certain similarities, if not between tsarism and communism, then at least between Russian and Soviet political culture (Inkeles, 1968; Brzezinski, 1960).

There were thus subtle differences of historical interpretation within the ranks of the totalitarians. They were, however, united in at least one respect: in their hostility to the whole Soviet experience. This, of course, would explain why they were constitutionally unable and intellectually unwilling to see anything worthwhile coming out of the revolution. In this they were clearly misguided; the fact remains that the Bolsheviks did bring order to Russia after the October revolution, and out of the chaos did manage to establish some degree of stability. This was no mean feat (Hubbard, 1938, p. 313). In the process they also managed to re-create an empire not so different to that which had exited under tsarism. Indeed, so successful were the Bolsheviks in defending the integrity of the old 'prison house of nations' that a number of nationalist enemies of the October revolution became the regime's most ardent defenders (Shulgin, 1990; Nesterov, 1984; Agurski, 1980; Yanov, 1978).

This, however, was not the only weakness in the totalitarian's intellectual armoury. A second flaw in their analysis was a basic underestimation of the radical shift that took place in the structure of the official ideology after the 1920s and the extent to which Great Russian chauvinism (rather than Marxism) came to shape the outlook of the Soviet leadership. The process by which this occurred was of necessity a complex one, but certainly by the time of the Second World War – when Stalin completely eliminated all references to socialism from Soviet war propaganda and instead deployed a blend of crude nationalism and messianism to hold the nation together – there was very little left of the original revolutionary vision. Yet in spite of this, serious scholars could still write after the war that the regime 'was driven by the logic of Communism' and that it was quite legitimate to measure the record of the post-Stalin leadership against some fixed notion of Marxist ideology. Even Conquest seemed to get it wrong and later wrote (two years after the fall of the USSR) that until Shevarnadze took over as Foreign Minister in the late 1980s, Moscow remained as committed as ever to the view that that the world was an arena where the central line of contestation was between socialism and capitalism, the proletariat and the bourgeoisie (Ulam, 1963; Shlapentokh, 1986; Katsenelinboigen, 1990; and Dallin, 1992, pp. 286–7).

Finally, if the totalitarians generally underestimated the ideological distance travelled by the Soviet regime, they tended to overestimate the Soviet Union's known capabilities. This did not mean they ignored Soviet problems (Pipes, 1984; Brzezinski, 1969); indeed many implied in their writings that the economic system was so flawed that it was bound to fail. But in spite of this, they seemed to be most impressed by the Soviet record, and until the 1970s at least saw the Soviet economy as having genuine potential. Thus in the early 1960s Huntington and Brzezinski could write that both 'the Soviet and American systems' were 'effective, authoritative and stable' though in their own different ways (Huntington and Brzezinski, 1964). Brzezinski in fact continued to believe in the potential of the Soviet system and noted in 1970 that there could be 'no doubt that in the years to come the Soviet Union will accomplish many remarkable scientific feats, especially in the internationally prestigious realm of space investigations and in scientific areas related to defense' (Brzezinski, 1970, p. 8). The American Sovietologist Frederick Baarghorn was equally impressed and observed in 1966 that gradual, though erratic progress was being made in the USSR towards what he called 'empirical rationality' (1966, p. 384).

It is true, of course, that after 1980 a number of Western scholars began to detect the early signs of an economic crisis in the Soviet Union. Nonetheless, they still insisted that with such a high proportion of GNP being spent on the military, the USSR still represented a major threat to the free world. Therefore, the West under American leadership had to mobilize all its resources to withstand Soviet expansionism. Furthermore, although the Soviet Union might have been in crisis, this did not mean it was on the verge of collapse. Indeed, it was really only after 1989 (and not before) that conservative writers began to assert that Soviet industrial power had been one of 'the great illusions of the century' and that if 'Soviet Communism collapsed like a house of cards, it was because it had been always a house of cards', or as one observer put it, a 'jerry-built structure' that 'ultimately did not work'. This may have seemed obvious after the event. Before the fall took place, however, most totalitarians appeared to have been more impressed by Soviet power than by Soviet weakness (Malia, 1993, pp. 80-1, 88; Conquest, 1993).

The USSR as a 'Normal' Country

With the death of Stalin and the elimination of some of the worst features of Stalinism, the totalitarian model came under intense scrutiny by a new generation of more liberal and left-wing scholars who had matured intellectually in the 1960s. Rejecting the notion that the USSR was a *sui generis* system standing outside history, the new cohort, as they were sometimes called, started to look for points of comparison between the USSR and other countries in the West - accusing the right amongst other things of being unwilling to conduct such research (Dallin, 1973, p. 574). Their attack upon the old totalitarian syndrome proved to be most successful (especially in the United States), and by the late 1970s the 'pathological' approach to the study of the former Soviet Union had been successfully challenged by those in the profession who viewed the USSR as being a more or less 'normal' country.

The 'normalizers' drew inspiration from different theoretical sources including the then fashionable theories of 'modernization' and 'industrial society' (see Rostow, 1967; Aron, 1962; and Bell, 1973). Though these two theories said rather different things, both assumed there were universal social and economic laws which shaped the way societies evolved over time. This idea, of course, could be deployed (and was) to attack the totalitarians who took it as read that the USSR was a unique social and economic formation. Using the ideology of modernization, 'normalizers' could also point to important social changes taking place in the Soviet Union and argue that it was these developments from below – urbanization, improved education and rises in living standards – rather than the way power was exercised from above, that were of increasing importance in determining the shape of Soviet politics (Tucker, 1977).

The new school of Sovietological research was equally keen to rethink Soviet history. More sympathetic to the ideals of socialism than their conservative opponents, a majority of the new scholars viewed the revolution in October rather positively; and though not uncritical of Lenin, many saw a major difference between his policies (and those developed by Bukharin in the 1920s) and those later pursued by Stalin (Cohen, 1973; Lewin, 1975). In this way they challenged the standard totalitarian line which saw a simple and direct connection between the politics of Bolshevism and the practice of Stalinism. Furthermore, though not uncritical of Soviet policies in the 1930s, some of the more radical critics (the so-called 'revisionists') denied these made the USSR totalitarian. Some authors indeed went so far as to suggest that even Stalin had far less power and control over events than had been portrayed in more traditional accounts (Getty, 1985). Moreover, there was (they suggested) more popular support for his policies than had hitherto been assumed and fewer deaths arising from collectivization and the purges than had once been calculated by 'cold warrior' scholars like Conquest. Finally, though they agreed there had been clear 'losers' under Stalin, large numbers had also benefited from his policies – including the majority of workers, millions of peasants, masses of women and, of course, the new intelligentsia (Lewin, 1975). Basically, as long as one conformed, one could look forward to a better life under Soviet rule.

But it was not just the Soviet past which the new cohort sought to rethink but the Soviet present too; and if there were some amongst their number who accepted that perhaps totalitarianism was a useful way of describing Soviet life under Stalin, there were none who thought it made much sense to apply it to the post-Stalin era. Indeed, they accused those 'traditionalists' who persisted in employing the term of having failed to come to terms with the changes that had taken place in the USSR since 1953 (Fainsod, 1963; Conquest, 1965; Hollander, 1981). In fact, the Soviet Union had changed so much according to Stephen Cohen – one of the new generation of writers – that old terms had to be jettisoned and new ones found to describe the Soviet political system. 'Stalinism no longer defines Soviet reality', he asserted (Cohen, 1980). Other influential American Sovietologists seemed to agree, noting, amongst other things, that the Soviet system no longer used 'massive coercion' (Dallin, 1973, p. 563), that Soviet foreign policy was probably more defensive than aggressive (Dallin, 1973, p. 564), and that the party was a far more complex and plural political organization than represented in the classic totalitarian accounts (Fainsod and Hough, 1979; Tucker, 1980, p. 1193). Hence what was the point persisting with a model that no longer accurately portrayed political life in the new Soviet Union?

The New Soviet Studies

The attempt to rethink the Soviet system and move our understanding of the USSR beyond what many saw as the pernicious influence of totalitarianism was facilitated in part by the growing influence of positivist methodology in the United States. With its emphasis on quantitative analysis and simple empirical techniques, this encouraged scholars not to search for the deeper essence of the system but rather to focus on that which was immediate and observable (Breslauer, 1992, p. 230). Positivism also legitimized attacks upon the concept of totalitarianism, which was now regularly assailed in the new literature for not being rigorously academic and properly scientific (Skilling and Griffiths, 1970; Breslauer, 1992). The new methodology in turn justified the more widespread use of hard (official) data – with the inevitable result that Western scholars tended to come up with a more positive picture of Soviet society (at least they did until glasnost revealed more of the truth). Finally, in the new non-dogmatic era, Soviet Studies in the United States became increasingly inclined towards studying the small and the measurable rather than the large and the theoretical; and it is no coincidence that as American scholars became more involved in detailed empirical research of this or that election to this or that local government, the less interesting their findings tended to be. It is quite remarkable in fact how little genuine theory was actually produced by the new scholarship. Theory and theorizing about the Soviet system was left (or so it seemed) to more marginal figures in the profession or to the much-derided émigré community.

Whilst positivism eroded both the critical and theoretical faculties of most Sovietolgists, two other innovations also had an impact upon the way in the which the USSR was assessed in the post-Stalin era: one claiming that capitalism and socialism were drawing together, and the other suggesting that there was not much difference between the ways in which the Soviet and Western political systems functioned. The first theory (known as 'convergence') enjoyed momentary popularity in the 1960s when it was fashionable to argue that all systems were governed by the same socioeconomic laws and would in time become more alike (see Schuman, 1957; Mills, 1958; Sorokin, 1964; Meyer, 1965; 1970, pp. 325–6; and Bell, 1973). Fortunately, the theory soon came under sustained attack and did not survive into the 1970s. What emerged in its wake instead was a perhaps more widespread viewpoint. This accepted that while there were important political and economic differences between state socialism and Western capitalism, there was much they had in common: first in terms of the problems they confronted, second in terms of the overall level of social provision, and finally and most importantly, in terms of the ways in which the two political systems operated at the highest level. In this way the black and white difference between the USSR and the West, which had been central to the totalitarian school of thought, now gave way to a more 'subtle' and 'balanced' analysis which led those who adhered to the new methodology to the inevitable conclusion that even if the Soviet Union was not exactly the same as the United States, it was at least less abnormal than had been suggested by the totalitarians (Lubrano and Solomon, 1980; Solomon, 1983).

The attempt to shed new light on the nature of the Soviet Union of course meant ignoring the repressive features of the system and the extensive forms of surveillance (these again could be left to the émigrés and the academic dissidents). It also involved an intellectual sleight of hand whereby one multiplied the number of genuine political and economic actors involved in the political process. But for all its obvious weaknesses the approach did exert an influence on the ways in which American political scientists understood how politics operated in the USSR.

Basically, there were at least four ways in which the 'normalizers' attempted to rethink the operation of the Soviet political system.

Group Conflict and Institutional Pluralism

The first was to argue that ordinary interest groups, very much like those which functioned in the West, comprised the core of the Soviet politics. Several Sovietologists saw this 'conflict model of society' with its focus on plural actors and complex institutions as perhaps the most powerful challenge to the concept of totalitarianism with its stress on the dominant role of the single ruling party. The seminal book in this genre was the 1970 volume edited by Skilling and Griffiths (1970). This was followed by several other studies of different groups, each, it was argued, playing a crucial role in the decision-making process. Jerry Hough went even further and not only discovered several interest groups but argued that since Stalin's death there had been a 'devolution of power to the major institutional centers' – quite a different picture to that painted by the totalitarians who saw all strategic decisions emanating from the Kremlin (Hough, 1971, 1972, 1977; Dallin, 1973, p. 573; 1992, p. 283).

Participatory Bureaucratism

An equally important intellectual step taken by the 'normalizers' was to introduce the concept of 'bureaucratic participation'. This rejected the idea that the Soviet Union was run by a supreme leader, and instead suggested the system was open at many points to the influence of several different bureaucratic players, not all of whom agreed about 'who should get what, when and how'. There were, naturally enough, reformers and conservatives within the bureaucracy, as there were different generations with different perspectives (Bialer, 1980, 1982, 1983; Hough, 1980). Some Sovietologists even projected the notion back in time and concluded that Stalin too had to take account of other viewpoints and voices (see McCagg, 1978; Getty, 1985).

The Role of Experts

Like any normal functioning system, the Soviet Union depended upon its experts and it was they, it was now argued, rather than the politicians alone who played a decisive role in the important decisions. The concept of 'professionalization of Russian politicians' in fact became very popular among Sovietologists in the 1970s (Bialer, 1980, pp. 167–73), and several scholars started a search for Soviet experts who quietly shaped the policy of the Kremlin. As Dallin noted, 'the men in the Kremlin ... are increasingly dependent on the advice of specialists whose competence in science and technology or in world affairs, appears to be on the increase' (see Dallin, 1992; also Griffiths, 1972; Hough, 1977; Solomon, 1978; Gustafson, 1981; Lapidus, 1978).

Participatory Democracy

Finally, some 'normalizers' suggested that although the USSR was hardly a Western-style democracy, the Soviet citizen could still play a role in the post-Stalin political system, either by writing letters to the press, attending meetings, joining the Communist Party or even lobbying local elites. Nor was this view held by figures marginal to the discipline. Gail Lapidus, for example, argued in 1975 that 'the level of mass political participation' in the USSR had 'increased dramatically'. Two years later Hough thought he could detect an 'increased vitality of public policy debates'. The same scholars, not surprisingly, took more than a passing interest in the levels of active (and apparently significant levels of) participation by the Soviet people in elections and in such institutions as trade unions and Communist youth leagues (Lapidus, 1975a, pp. 115, 118; Hough, 1977, p. 37).

The Soviet Union Abroad

The new cohort also displayed a marked determination to reassess the nature of Soviet foreign policy. This was critical insofar as the totalitarians in their view had presented a particularly menacing image of the USSR which could only lead to Cold War attitudes and policies. It was thus vital to search for signs of a less belligerent Soviet foreign policy which would challenge the bleak conservative view that the USSR was hell-bent on world domination and that the only thing standing between the Soviet Union and its goal was high military spending.

Sovietologists set about their task by focusing on at least three key questions.

The first concerned the Cold War and revolved around the large issue of which of the two main powers was the more responsible for either having started or having prolonged the conflict. The normalizers were not simple apologists. However, they advanced a number of empirical propositions which all led to the same basic conclusion: that it was not the USSR but the United States as the more powerful of the two superpowers which shared the greatest responsibility for the breakdown of relations after World War II and for keeping the Cold War going thereafter. True, some writers did not blame the USA alone; a few indeed saw the Soviet Union as being equally responsible for creating international tension. But for most, it was the USA – either because of its deep-seated anti-communism or because of the strength of the military-industrial complex – which had set the pace after 1947.

There was also a feeling amongst most liberal Sovietologists that even if the USSR did occasionally assert itself in the world arena (as it did after 1945 and again after 1975) it did so basically for defensive rather than aggressive reasons and was as much motivated – if not more – by insecurity rather than any great ideological ambition to convert the world to communism. Moreover, if it had ambitions, this should hardly have come as a surprise or have caused great concern in the West. After all, great powers in the past had attempted to increase their weight in the international order; and all the USSR was trying to do after the war, and once more in the late 1970s and early 1980s, was (to use Bialer's phrase) find a place for itself 'under the sun'. To attack them for acting in this way was, in his view, a case of double standards (Bialer, 1980, p. 229; 1987, p. 261).

The third and final issue on which the new Sovietologists took a clear stand was superpower détente in the 1970s – a policy to which conservatives like Pipes and Conquest were strongly opposed. This alone would have legitimized the policy in the eyes of many in the Soviet Studies profession who viewed the 1972 breakthrough most positively, and who after the signing of SALT I found as many arguments as possible to support the cause of arms control and the improved East–West dialogue. No doubt for the same set of reasons they were fundamentally opposed to Ronald Reagan and his policies. Indeed, according to most Sovietologists, Reagan's tough stance against what he termed the 'evil empire' was based upon two false assumptions: a much exaggerated view of the Soviet threat and the equally incorrect notion that the USSR was in terminal decline. Both assumptions were wrong, in their view, and both were bound to lead to an unnecessarily aggressive American stance.

The Soviet Economy

Perhaps the most difficult problem facing Sovietologists was the issue of the Soviet economy. Though by no means opposed to the market, most students of Soviet planning in the post-war period disagreed with the classical right-wing argument that a functioning socialist economy was a contradiction in terms. By the early 1960s a few even wondered whether the USSR might not even be winning the economic race (Granick, 1960, pp. 287–95). Certainly most economists were very impressed by the speed of recovery after the war and looked in awe at Soviet growth rates throughout the 1950s and the 1960s. Several liberals believed that planning had significant advantages over the market (Galbraith, 1967; Vasilli Leontiev, 1960). Furthermore, in spite of its known weaknesses and problems, few doubted the system would endure. As Paul Gregory and Robert Stuart noted in 1974, the 'long-run ability of the Soviet system to function. without private ownership of the factors of production and without profit motivation is no longer seriously questioned ... and it would be foolish to question its economic viability'. This, moreover, was the common view amongst most economists. As Levine observed, even those sensitive to Soviet technological retardation did not doubt its ability to sustain the basic needs of society and satisfy the needs for Soviet defence (Levine, 1974, pp. 1–17).

Such optimism began to fade rapidly from the late 1970s onwards. Yet this did not change the basic outlook of most economists, the majority of whom assumed that with a combination of reforms here and readjustments there, the USSR would be able to go on. Once again it was left to the highly influential Bialer to sum up the position of his colleagues in the Sovietological profession. In 1980 the economy was, he agreed, in trouble.

However, this did not mean that 'time' was 'running out' for 'the Soviet system'. This was the stuff of fantasies entertained by the neo-conservatives in the Reagan administration. The Soviet Union, he concluded, possessed 'enormous reserves of stability'; and all the leadership had to do was make the necessary economic 'adjustments' to ensure that the system remained 'effective' (Bialer, 1980, p. 305; Campbell, 1983, p. 120).

Conclusion

As we have seen from our broad survey, the most important factor determining the nature of the American debate about the USSR after 1917 was not so much the quality of information available to scholars and analysts but the views and beliefs of Americans themselves. These in turn were profoundly influenced by events in the wider world and not just by developments in the Soviet Union. In this respect the depression, the coming of war, then the Cold War had as much impact upon the way Americans looked at the USSR as did the Russian revolution, collectivization and Stalin's death. The USSR was also fiercely contested terrain dividing socialist from communist, communist from Trotskyist, liberal from traditional conservative, and traditional conservative from neo-conservative. Whether this high level of politicization worked to the advantage of serious scholarship must be open to question. What is not in doubt is the extent to which politics shaped the course of Sovietology in the United States – particularly in the post-war period when first conservatives with their enemy images and later liberals with their easy going attitudes towards the USSR dominated the debate (see Shlapentokh, 1990).

But if the study of American Soviet Studies tells us as much about American politics as it does about the nature of the Soviet Union, it also casts doubt on the claims made by American social science to be truly scientific. Much was made of the great methodological revolution in the 1960s and it was assumed, all too easily, that if only Soviet Studies could be integrated into the intellectual mainstream then all would be well. This turned out to be quite wrong. No doubt some good work was done. But as we have noted the net effect of Sovietology's attempts to borrow from the hard positivist social sciences was to retard understanding of the USSR, not advance it. The hopes of such scholars as Frederic Fleron and Roger Kanet that the application of the most refined social science methods would revolutionize Soviet Studies were not realized (Kanet, 1971; Fleron, 1968).

One might have hoped that the inability of Soviet Studies to interpret the collapse of the USSR would have provoked a major debate within the profession. But this has not been the case at all. Indeed, I know of no prominent Sovietologists of the stature of a Hough, Dallin or a Moshe Lewin who has recanted their mistakes or even thought seriously about what went wrong. Just the opposite seems to have occurred. In fact, in their 'after the fall' survey articles, both Breslauer and Dallin almost completely avoided any self-criticism, as well as any critique of their colleagues (Breslauer, 1992; Dallin, 1992). Getty, moreover, was so bold as to announce that the new information coming out of the archives about the 1930s did not shed any new light on the politics of the period! (Getty, 1993, pp. 41-2). However, conservatives have been equally defensive, and instead of using the disintegration of the USSR as a way of critically evaluating their past, they have used it to assert their impeccable historical record (Malia, 1993; Conquest, 1993; Pipes, 1993). The fact remains that both major schools in American Sovietology, 'totalitarians' and 'normalizers', committed numerous blunders in their analysis of Soviet society. Yet in none of the post-mortems thus far has this been recognized or accepted by those actually engaged in the study of the former Soviet Union.

That said, it is perfectly obvious that the totalitarians almost certainly came closer to understanding the peculiar and pathological nature of Soviet society than did their academic rivals. Furthermore, unlike their liberal and left-wing opponents, they had good reason to celebrate the passing of a system to which they had been so opposed for so long. No doubt they will have drawn much comfort too from the fact that Russian intellectuals - once they acquired some degree of freedom - immediately joined the totalitarian camp, in the process turning Western conservatives like Pipes and Conquest into their new-found heroes whilst branding their Western adversaries as apologists for the Soviet system. They acquired this status, however, not because they were intellectually superior, but rather because they were highly critical of the old status quo. Herein lies their problem. Now that they have turned into Yeltsin's new defenders there is every chance they will lose the influence they once had (Malia, 1995). It will certainly not be the first time in history that yesterday's critic turned out to be today's apologist. Nor one suspects will it be the last. In the meantime, we can but hope that other more detached voices will emerge and make a better job of analysing the dynamics of post-communist Russia than did those who studied and failed to predict the demise of the Soviet system.

References

Abel, L. 1984. *The Intellectual Follies.* New York: Norton.

Adams, A. and J. Adams. 1971. *Men versus Systems: Agriculture in the USSR, Poland and Czechoslovakia.* New York: Free Press.

Agurski, M. 1980. *Ideologia Natsional-Bolshevisma.* Paris: YMCA Press.

Arendt, H. 1966. *The Origins of Totalitarianism.* New York: Harcourt.

Armstrong, J. 1961. *The Politics of Totalitarianism*. New York: Basic Books.

Anonymous. 1983. *American Writers on the Soviet Country*. Leningrad.

Aron, R. 1962. *Dix-huit leçons sur la société industrielle*. Paris: Gallimard.

Baarghorn, F. 1966. 'Changes in Russia: The Need for Perspective'. *Problems of Communism*, XV, 3 (May-June), pp. 39-42.

Batsel, W. 1929. *Soviet Rule in Russia*. New York: Harvard University Press.

Bauer, R.A., A. Inkeles, and C. Kluckholm. 1956. *How the Soviet System Works*. New York: Vintage Books.

Bell, D. 1973. *The Coming of Post-industrial Society*. New York. Basic Books.

Berdiaev, N. 1937. *The Origin of Russian Communism*. London: Saunders.

—1947. *The Russian Idea*. London: Macmillan.

Bialer, S. 1980. *Stalin's Successors*. London: Cambridge University Press.

—1983. 'The Political System', in R. Byrnes ed., *After Brezhnev*. Bloomington: Indiana University Press.

—1986. *The Soviet Paradox*. New York: Knopf.

—1987. *Soviet Union in Transition*. Boulder: Westview Press.

Birman, I. 1981. *Secret Incomes of the Soviet State Budget*. Boston: Kluwer.

Breslauer, G. 1992. 'In Defense of Sovietology', *Post-Soviet Affairs*, 8, 3, pp. 197-238.

Brzezinski, Z. 1956. *The Permanent Purge*. Cambridge: Harvard University Press.

—1960. 'The transformation of Russian Society', in Cyril Black, ed., *Aspects of Social Changes since 1861*. Cambridge: Harvard University Press.

—1962. *Ideology and Power in Soviet Politics*. New York: Columbia University Press.

—1966. 'The Soviet Political System: Transformation or Degradation', *Problems of Communism*, XV, 1 (January-February), pp. 1-16.

—1969. *Dilemmas of Change in Soviet Politics*. New York: Columbia University Press.

—1970. *Between Two Ages*. New York: Viking.

Burnham, J. 1941. *The Managerial Revolution*. New York: John Day.

Campbell, R. 1983, 'The Economy', in *After Brezhnev*, ed. by R. Byrnes. Bloomington: Indiana University Press.

Carrol, M. 1965. *Soviet Communism and Western Opinion 1919-1921*. Chapel Hill: University of North Carolina Press.

Chamberlin, W. 1930. *Soviet Russia: A Living Record and a History*. Boston: Little, Brown.

—1943. *The Russian Enigma*. New York: Scribner's.

Cohen, S. 1973. *Bukharin and the Bolshevik Revolution: A Political Biography*. New York: Knopf.

—1980. 'Friends and Foes of Change: Reformism and Conservatism in the Soviet Union', in S. Cohen, ed., *The Soviet Union since Stalin*. Bloomington: Indiana University Press.

Conquest, R. 1963. 'After Khrushchev: a Conservative Restoration?', *Problems of Communism*, 41-6.

—1965. *Russia after Khrushchev*. New York: Praeger.

—1967. *Power and Policy in the USSR. The Struggle for Stalin's Succession, 1945-1960*. New York: Harper & Row.

—1993. 'Red to Go', *Times Literary Supplement*, July 9.

Dallin, A. 1973. 'Biases and Blunders in American Studies on the USSR', *Slavic Review*, vol. 32, No. 3. pp. 560-76.

—1982. 'Osteuropaforschung in den Vereinigten Staaten', *Osteuropa*, vol. 32, no. 8, pp. 625-44.

—1992. 'Causes of the Collapse of the USSR', *Post-Soviet Affairs*, 8, 4, pp. 279-302.

Daniels, R. 1967. 'The Bolshevik Gamble', *Russian Review*, No. 26, October 1967, pp. 331-40.

—1987a. 'Moscow's Rubber Marx', *The New Leader*, December 28.

—1987b. 'Russian Political Culture and the Post-Revolutionary Impasse', *The Russian Review*, vol. 46, pp. 165-76.

Davies, J. 1942. *Mission to Moscow.* Sydney and London: Angus & Robertson.

Di Palma, G. 1991. 'Legitimation from the Top to Civil-society: Politico-Cultural Change in Eastern Europe', *World Politics*, 44, 1, pp. 49-80.

Duranty, W. 1935. *I Write As I Please.* New York: Simon & Schuster.

—1944. *USSR. The Story of Soviet Russia.* Philadelphia-New York: J.B. Lippincott.

Fainsod, M. 1953. *How Russia Is Ruled.* Cambridge: Harvard University Press.

—1963. *How Russia Is Ruled*, 2nd ed., Cambridge: Harvard University Press.

—1967. 'Roads to the Future', *Problems of Communism*, XVI (July-August), pp. 7-13.

Fainsod, M. and J. Hough. 1979. *How the Soviet Union is Governed.* Cambridge: Harvard University Press.

Fischer, L. 1941. *Men and Politics.* New York: Duell, Sloan & Pearce.

Fleron, F. 1968. 'Soviet Area Studies and the Social Sciences: some Methodological Problems in Communist Studies, *Soviet Studies*, No. 3, 313-39.

Freund, H.A. 1945. *Russia from A to Z.* Sydney: Angus & Robertson.

Friedrich, C.J. and Z. Brzezinski. 1956. *Totalitarian Dictatorship and Autocracy.* Cambridge: Harvard University Press.

Fukuyama, F. 1992. *The End of History and the Last Man.* New York: Free Press.

Galbraith, J. 1967. *The New Industrial State.* Boston: Houghton Mifflin.

Getty, J.A. 1985. *Origins of the Great Purges: The Soviet Communist Party Reconsidered, 1933-1938.* Cambridge: Cambridge University Press.

—1993. 'The Politics of Repression Revisited', in J.A. Getty and R.T. Manning, (eds), *Stalinist Terror: New Perspectives.* Cambridge: Cambridge University Press, pp. 40-64.

Glazer, N. 1984. 'New York Intellectuals: Up from Revolution', *New York Times Review of Books*, February 26.

Graham, S. 1925. *The Dividing Line of Europe.* New York: Appleton.

Granick, D. 1960. *The Red Executive.* London: Macmillan.

Gregory, P. and R. Stuart. 1974. *Soviet Economic Structure and Performance.* New York: Harper.

Griffiths, F. 1972. 'Images, Politics and Learning in Soviet Behavior Toward the United States', PhD dissertation, Columbia University.

Gustafson, T. 1981. *Reform in Soviet Politics.* Cambridge: Cambridge University Press.

Harper, S. 1929. *Civic Training in Soviet Russia.* Chicago: The University of Chicago Press.

—1931. *Making Bolsheviks.* Chicago: The University of Chicago Press.

—1938. *The Government of the Soviet Union.* New York: Nostrand.

Hayek, F.A. 1944. *The Road to Serfdom.* Chicago: University of Chicago Press.

Hindus, M. 1929. *Humanity Uprooted.* New York: J. Cape & H. Smith.

—1931. *Red Bread.* New York: J. Cape & H. Smith.

—1933. *The Great Offensive.* London: H. Smith & R. Haas.

Hollander, P. 1981. *Political Pilgrimage: Travels of Western Intellectuals to the Soviet Union, China, and Cuba*. New York: Oxford University Press.

Hough, J. 1971. 'The Party Apparatchiki', in H.G. Skilling and F. Griffith, eds, *Interest Groups in Soviet Politics*. Princeton: Princeton University Press.

——1972. 'The Soviet System: Petrification or Pluralism?' Problems of Communism. XXI, (March-April). pp. 25-45.

——1977. *The Soviet Union and Social Science Theory*. Cambridge: Harvard University Press.

——1980. *Soviet Leadership in Transition*. Washington, DC: Brookings.

Howe, I. 1982. *A Margin of Hope: An Intellectual Biography*. San Diego: Harcourt.

Hubbard, L. 1938. *Soviet Trade and Distribution*. London: Macmillan.

Huntington, S.P. and Z. Brzezinski. 1964. *Political Power: USA/USSR*. New York: Viking Press.

Inkeles, A. 1968. *Social Change in Soviet Russia*. Cambridge: Harvard University Press.

Jowitt, K. 1992. *New World Disorder: The Leninist Extinction*. Berkeley: University of California Press.

Kanet, R. 1971. *The Behavioral Revolution and Communist Studies*. New York: Free Press.

Katsenelinboigen, A. 1990. *The Soviet Union: Empire, Nation and System*. New Brunswick: Transaction.

Kennan, G. 1961. *Russia and the West under Lenin and Stalin*. Boston: Little, Brown.

Kohler, P., ed., 1951. *Journey for our Time: The Journals of Marquis de Custine*. New York: Pellegrini and Cudahy.

Kolakowski, L. 1978. *Main Currents of Marxism: its Rise, Growth and Dissolution*. Oxford: Clarendon Press.

Lange, O. 1938. *On the Economic Theory of Socialism*. Minneapolis: University of Minnesota Press.

Lapidus, G. 1975a. 'Political mobilization, participation, and Leadership', *Comparative Politics*, October, pp. 91-118.

——1975b. 'USSR Women at Work: Changing Patterns', *Industrial Relations*, vol. 14, No. 2, pp. 178-95.

——1978. *Women in Soviet Society*. Berkeley: University of California Press.

——1984. 'Ethnonationalism and Political Stability: the Soviet Case', *World Politics*, 36, 4, 555-80.

Lash, C. 1962. *American Liberals and the Russian Revolution*. New York: Columbia University Press.

Lewin, M. 1975. *Russian Peasants and Soviet Power: a Study of Collectivization*. New York: Norton.

——1995. *The Drive and Drift of a Superstate: Russia, USSR, Russia*. New York: The Free Press.

Levine, H. 1974. 'An American View of Economic relations with the USSR', *The Annals of the American Academy*, July, pp. 1-17.

Lipset, S.M. 1972. 'Academia and Politics in America', in T. Nossiter, ed., *Imagination and Precision in the Social Sciences*. London: Faber.

——and E. Ladd. 1972. 'The Politics of American Sociologists', *American Review of Sociology*, pp. 67-104.

——and R. Dobson. 1973. 'The intellectuals as critics and rebels: with the special reference to the United States and the Soviet Union', *Daedalus*, 101, pp. 137-98.

Lubrano L. and S. Solomon, eds, 1980. *The Social Context of Soviet Science.* Boulder: Westview Press.

Lyons, E. 1935. 'Russia postpones Utopia', *Scribner's Magazine.* 98 (October), pp. 235–7.

—1940. *Stalin: Czar of all the Russias.* New York: J.B. Lippincott.

—1966. 'The Realities of a Vision', *Problems of Communism,* XV (July–August), pp. 42–4.

McCagg, W. 1978. *Stalin Embattled.* Detroit: Wayne State University Press.

McCormick, A. O'Hare. 1929. *The Hammer and The Scythe: Russia Enters the Second Decade.* New York: Knopf.

Malia, M. (Z). 1990. 'To the Stalin Mausoleum', *Daedalus,* 119, 2, pp. 295–344.

—1991. 'The Hunt for the True October', *Commentary,* 92, 4, pp. 21–8.

—1993. 'A Fatal Logic', *The National Interest,* No. 31 (Spring), pp. 80–90.

—1994. *The Soviet Tragedy.* New York: Free Press.

—1995. 'The Nomenclature Capitalists', *The New Republic,* May 22.

Meyer, A. 1965. *The Soviet Political System: an Interpretation.* New York: Random House.

—1970. 'Theories of Convergence', in C.A. Johnson, ed., *Change in Communist Systems.* Stanford: Stanford University Press.

Mills, C. Wright. 1958. *The Causes of World War Three.* New York.

Moore, B. 1954. *Terror and Progress – USSR.* Cambridge: Harvard University Press.

Nesterov, F. 1984. *Sviaz' Vremen.* 2nd ed. Moscow: Molodaia Gvardia.

Orwell, G. 1961. *1984.* New York: New American Library.

Pipes, R. 1957. 'The Soviet Impact on Central Asia', *Problems of Communism,* 6, (March-April), pp. 27–32.

—1984. *Survival is Not Enough.* New York: Simon & Schuster.

—1990. *The Russian Revolution.* New York: Knopf.

—1994. *Russia Under the Bolshevik Regime.* New York: Knopf.

Podhoretz, N. 1979. *Breaking Ranks: A Political Memoir.* New York: Harper & Row.

Rabinowitch, A. 1976. *The Bolsheviks come to power: the revolution of 1917 in Petrograd.* New York: W.W. Norton.

Ross, E. 1918. *Russia in Upheaval.* New York: The Century Co.

Rostow, W.W. 1967. *The Dynamics of Soviet Society.* Cambridge: MIT Press.

Sarnoff, D. 1968. *Looking Ahead: the Papers of David Sarnoff.* New York: McGraw-Hill.

Schumann, F. 1957. *Russia since 1917: Four Decades of Soviet Politics.* NY: Knopf.

Seton-Watson, H. 1956. 'The Soviet Ruling-Class'. *Problems of Communism,* V (May-June), pp. 310–23.

Shlapentokh, V. 1986. *Soviet Public Opinion and Ideology: Pragmatism in Interaction.* New York: Praeger.

—1988. *Soviet Ideologies in the Period of Glasnost.* New York: Praeger.

—1990. *Soviet Intellectuals and Political Power.* Princeton: Princeton University Press.

Shtromas, A. and M. Kaplan, eds, 1987. *The Soviet Union and the Challenge of the Future.* New York: Paragon House.

Shulgin, V. 1990. *Gody: Dni. 1920.* Moscow: Novosti.

—1991. *Tri stolitsy.* Moscow: Sovremennik.

Skilling, H. G. and F. Griffiths, eds, 1970. *Interest Groups in Soviet Politics.* Princeton: Princeton University Press.

Skocpol, T. 1979. *States and Social Revolutions: A Comparative Study of France, Russia, and China.* Cambridge: Cambridge University Press.

Solomon, S., ed., 1983. *Pluralism in the Soviet Union*. London: Macmillan Press.

Solzhenitsyn, A. 1974. *The Gulag Archipelago*. London: Collins & Harvill.

—1976. *Lenin in Zurich*. New York: Farrar, Strauss & Giroux.

Sorokin, P. 1964. *The Basic Trends of our Times*. New Haven: Yale University Press.

Stalin, J. 1952. *Voprosy Leninisma*. Moscow: Politizdat.

Strakhovsky, L. 1961. *American opinion about Russia: 1917–1920*. Toronto: University of Toronto Press.

Steffens, L. 1936. *The Letters of Lincoln Steffens*. New York: Harcourt, Brace.

Taracouzio, T. 1940. *War and peace in Soviet diplomacy*. New York: Macmillan.

Trotsky, L. 1937. *The Revolution Betrayed*. Garden City: Doubleday.

Tucker, R. 1961. 'The question of totalitarianism', *Slavic Review*, No. 20 (October), pp. 377–81.

—1974. 'Communist revolutions, national cultures, and divided nations', *Studies in Comparative Communism*, No. 3, 235–245.

—1977. *Stalinism: Essays in Historical Interpretation*. New York: Norton.

—1980. 'Communism and Russia', *Foreign Affairs*, pp. 1178–83.

—1982. 'Swollen State, Spent Society: Stalin's Legacy to Brezhnev's Russia'. *Foreign Affairs*, 60, 2, pp. 414–35.

—1987. 'The Stalin Period as an Historical Problem', *The Russian Review*, vol. 46, pp. 424–7.

—1988. 'Giving up the Ghost', *New Republic*. October 17, pp. 20–3.

—1991. 'Czars and Commiczars', *The New Republic*, January 21, pp. 29–34.

Ulam, A. 1963. *The New Face of Soviet Totalitarianism*. Cambridge: MIT Press.

von Mises, L. 1951. *Socialism: an Economic and Sociological Analysis*. New Haven: Yale University Press.

Webb, S. and B. Webb. 1937. *Soviet Communism. A New Civilization*. London: Longmans, Green.

Werth, A. 1942. *Moscow 1941*. London: Hamish Hamilton.

Willkie, W. 1943. *One World*. New York: Simon & Schuster.

Wolfe, B. 1956. *Communist Totalitarianism*. Boston: Beacon Press.

Yanov, A. 1978. *The Russian new right: Right wing ideologies in the contemporary USSR*. Berkeley: Institute of International Studies.

Zinoviev, A. 1976. *Ziauschie Vysoty*. Lausanne: L'Age d'Homme.

—1978. *Svetloie Buduscheie*. Lausanne: L'Age d'Homme.

—1982. *Homo Soviecticus*. Paris: L'Age d'Homme.

—1985. 'Ne vse my dissidenty. O sotsial'noi oppositssii v Sovetskom obshschestve', *Kontinent*, 44, 175–90.

6

Soviet Society and American Soviet Studies: a Study in Success?

ROBERT V. DANIELS

The argument has been advanced in this book and elsewhere that 'Sovietology' – and in particular the form of it practised in the United States – failed to predict the collapse of Communism. This proposition has come to be accepted even amongst people who used to engage in that occult art themselves, but since 1991 have been at pains to disown it. However, as I hope to show in my contribution to this volume, the question assumes too much. We have to pick it apart and put to ourselves a series of more specific queries in order to grasp the impact of 1991 on the study of Russian/Soviet affairs. First, what exactly was 'Sovietology'? Moreover, what in actuality, was 'Communism' – and what do we mean by its 'collapse'? Finally, was there a failure of prediction, or did in fact 'we' the academic experts do a good deal better at anticipating the fall in 1991 than many of our detractors have since suggested?

Let us begin, then, with a brief discussion of Sovietology itself. We shall then go on to examine its rise in the United States in the post-war period, the events of 1991, and whether or not 'we' got it wrong. I shall conclude this chapter by asking the question which others in this study have also tried to answer: namely, what is the nature of the post-Soviet 'transition' and does post-Soviet Studies have a future?

Sovietology

Sovietolgy, of course, was never a discipline unto itself, let alone a monolithic academic cult, as some of its detractors seem to suggest. It was merely the specialized study of the Soviet Union from the standpoint of the familiar academic disciplines: history, economics, geography, occasionally sociology and anthropology, and above all political science. Political science, economics, and sociology, with their orientation towards the present, moved along with events up to 1991 and naturally enough took the existing Soviet Union as their frame of reference. Soviet specialists in all these fields might have been less methodologically sophisticated than the more theoretical 'mainstreams' of their respective disciplines, and they often drew more insight from each other than from their non-area colleagues. Tension between the area focus and the disciplinary focus still marks Russian studies in the USA, as well as American aid-and-advice programmes directed toward the former Soviet bloc. If anything, this strain threatens to be more disruptive to the continued pursuit of Sovietological 'successor studies' than the collapse or transformation of the object of study itself.

In common usage, the term Sovietology has come to imply a much narrower approach in Russian/Soviet studies, primarily in political science, as a line of inquiry focused above all on leadership politics and behaviour. Herein lies the much-derided practice of 'Kremlinology', an art of interpolation developed by necessity out of the paucity of objective evidence (not unlike medieval history). At the same time, other modes of study carried on by Slavists have been overlooked or underappreciated by the public. Obviously, if Sovietology is defined as the study of contemporary Soviet leadership, the demise of the Communist regime leaves Sovietologists stranded, with 'nothing left to do' (Cox, 1994, p. 1). But political scientists are certainly capable of leaving the old era to the historians and moving into the new one. Now they are taking up the subject of 'transitology' to describe, compare, and analyse regimes undergoing 'transitions to democracy' (Schmitter, with Karl, 1994, p. 173). Furthermore, as time marches on, the subject matter of political science inexorably passes into history, and the historians (including the many members of political science faculties who have done some of the best work in Soviet history) should be able to keep the old body of Sovietology very much alive.

An objection has arisen in the minds of some commentators, who feel that encompassing Soviet material within the purview of the familiar disciplines implies a presumption that the Soviet Union as such was a 'normal' subject of study, and hence not so different from the West (Malia, 1994). This suggests to the critics a certain moral denseness amongst Soviet specialists, if not actual softness on totalitarianism. Perhaps such criticism is a legacy of the Cold War and a parting shot at value-neutral social science. But now value-neutral analysis of the successor regime in Russia may be suspect on different grounds, for insufficient appreciation of the leaderships' protestations of democratic and free-market values.

Soviet Studies in the United States

Sovietology in the USA has an intense, if brief, history. Russian studies in American universities actually goes back to the turn of the century, before the Soviet Union was ever heard of, initiated by such luminaries as Samuel

Harper at Chicago, Archibald Cary Coolidge and Leo Wiener at Harvard, and George Noyes at Berkeley (Byrnes, 1978a, 1978b). Between the wars the field benefited from an infusion of émigrés, but in disciplinary terms it remained largely confined to language, literature, and a history that was mostly pre-revolutionary. In America, as in Europe, the revolutionary Communist challenge to bourgeois society was primarily addressed not by scholars but by activists, as diverse left-wing parties and groups disputed the merits and demerits of the Soviet experiment. Only with World War II came the burgeoning of serious American social science work on foreign areas, with the infusion of government and foundation money into the major university centres. These operations were all informed by the new concept of 'area studies' that had taken shape during the war, in training personnel for military and intelligence purposes in any, and nearly every, exotic part of the world, and in researching the strengths and weaknesses of the enemy. The most famous product of this work was the study of Japanese national character led by the anthropologist Ruth Benedict at the behest of the American government (Benedict, 1946).

The Cold War simply shifted the focus of this pragmatic effort, along with the funding for it, to the study of the Soviet Union. The new research institutes, notably the Russian Research Centre at Harvard and the Russian Institute at Columbia, were set up in the late 1940s with the policy-oriented, interdisciplinary approach in the forefront. Training and research in this vein across the country enjoyed a major new stimulus when the National Defense Education Act went into effect in 1958 (unfortunately the new programmes were usually misnamed 'Russian', to the neglect of the Soviet minorities). In the context of subsequent controversy about government-funded research, it is important to underscore the academic integrity and scholarly benefit achievable even with military sponsorship, for example the Harvard Refugee Interview Project of 1950–51 funded by the Air War College and summarized in book form by its directors (Bauer, Inkeles, and Kluckholm, 1956). Latter-day allegations of governmental manipulation of such research do not ring true for people who actually participated in those endeavours (O'Connell, 1990). The scandalous presidential address to the American Historical Association in 1949 calling for the subordination of scholarship to patriotism was the opinion of a Tudor historian, not of a Sovietologist (Read, 1950).

Considering the political climate of hysterical anti-Communism in the 1950s, the growing field of Soviet Studies remained on the whole remarkably objective in its approaches. This assertion may seem far-fetched to younger practitioners in the field, raised on debates over Cold Warriors and the theory of totalitarianism. But as Robert F. Byrnes noted some years ago, 'specialists in the Russian and East European fields were never subject to the pressures which afflicted those who studied the Far East, especially

China, during the 1940s and 1950s' (Byrnes, 1964, p. 62). Indeed, even the much-criticized 'totalitarian' model was not merely an artefact of Cold War propaganda. First coined by Benito Mussolini in a positive sense, the term was familiar before World War II and was used to bracket the Nazi and Communist dictatorships together. Moreover, anti-Stalin Marxists – including Leon Trotsky and Rudolf Hilferding – also deployed the term to distinguish Stalinism from socialism (Trotsky, 1937; Hilferding, 1940). Hannah Arendt's well-known treatise popularized the concept in the early Cold War years and became the basis for much non-specialist polemical comment (Arendt, 1951). However, as developed by Carl Friedrich and Zbigniew Brzezinski, the concept did convey a reasonable working image of the Stalinist regime, even if it was weak on the origins and potential and national peculiarities of the Communist system (Friedrich and Brzezinski, 1956; Odom, 1992; Gleason, 1995). Other treatments, notably that of Merle Fainsod, took a more historical and developmental view of the singularities of Stalinist totalitarianism (Fainsod, 1953). Daniel Bell published an early summation of the various approaches to Stalinism and their predictive value (Bell, 1958).

Soviet Studies therefore did not feed the politicians' hysteria about Communist expansion, but rather operated to defuse it with empirical knowledge of the system's past and current problems. Works in the vein of the Communist master plan for world domination were largely the product of non-specialists and often of non-academics (Leites, 1951; Possony, 1953; Hoover, 1958). Indeed, most broad historical and political descriptions of the Soviet Union in the 1940s and 1950s were undertaken by either British scholars and émigrés, who thereby provided the framework for subsequent American work (Dallin, 1944; Timashev, 1946; Maynard, 1948; Crankshaw, 1948; Deutscher, 1949; Hunt, 1951; Carr, 1951-64; Schapiro, 1960; Lichtheim, 1961). A series of more specific studies, mainly from Harvard, explored the divergence of theory and practice in the Soviet system (Moore, 1950; Berman, 1950; Bauer, 1952; Meyer, 1953, 1957). Other works detailed the operation of particular aspects of the system (Inkeles, 1950; Brown, 1953; Curtiss, 1953; Field, 1957; Counts, 1957; Fainsod, 1958; Fisher, 1959). European scholars who shifted their base to the USA in more recent decades may be counted as an additional plus for American Soviet studies (Conquest, (ed.), 1986; Lewin, 1988).

Meanwhile, the empirical side of Soviet studies received an important boost in 1956 when Nikita Khrushchev opened the USSR to tourism – and incidentally to American academics travelling under the aegis of the federally funded Inter-University Committee on Travel Grants, the predecessor of the broad exchange programme of IREX, the International Research and Exchanges Board (Byrnes, 1964, pp. 63-4).

If there was any major intellectual split within Sovietology, it centred on interpretation of the role of Marxist-Leninist ideology, whether it still operated as a guide to action (Leites, 1951; Linden, 1966), or only as a rationalization of power interests after the fact (Enteen, Siegelbaum, and Daniels, 1995). But on the whole, to the later disgust of critics both on the right and on the left, Soviet Studies tried to remain value-free.

Soviet Studies in the USA were strengthened by the area studies approach, wherein students, curricula as well as research institutes focused on the area with its language or languages (and in the Russian and East European case, the common fact of Communist rule), and brought the various academic disciplines into collaboration to these ends (Lambert *et al.*, 1984). Instruction based on the area studies concept was initiated in 1946–7 by the Harvard Regional Studies programme and by the Columbia Russian Institute certificate programme. Subsequently, in 1960, the area movement gained professional form with the reorganization of the American Association for the Advancement of Slavic Studies from a publishing entity into a membership organization, meeting at first quadrennially and after 1968, annually (Atkinson, 1991). The area studies context not only gave specialists in particular disciplines an awareness of area specifics, but made them more sensitive to the background and insights that other disciplines offered for their own work (Keenan, 1994).

The roles of the various disciplines in Soviet studies have changed considerably over time. In the initial Harvard effort, the more 'social' of the social sciences – sociology, anthropology, and psychology – had pride of place, with emphasis on Parsonian structural-functional analysis and the exploration of national character. (Bauer, Inkeles, and Kluckholm, 1956.) Columbia's approach, under the leadership of Geroid T. Robinson, was both more historical and more ideological. Subsequently, the social science contribution to Soviet Studies lapsed in the face of minimal fieldwork opportunities. Ultimately special funding was undertaken through the Social Science Research Council, by means of graduate student fellowships and subsidies for a new faculty, but the results were meagre until the collapse of the Communist bloc opened the opportunity for fieldwork.

Economic analysis of the Soviet system flourished for years, but then began to be recaptured by the mainstream, even before the successor regimes undertook to abandon the planned economy (Gerschenkron, 1964; Millar, 1992). History as a discipline was not prominent in post-war Soviet Studies for a generation, most of the good historical work being done by political scientists or journalists (Fainsod, 1958; Schapiro, 1960; Ulam, 1968; Tucker, 1973). Then, in the later 1960s and 1970s, history took off, but primarily in the direction of social history (e.g., Fitzpatrick, 1979; Koenker, 1981). Political science remained from beginning to end the key discipline in Soviet Studies, though it tended to be historically and institutionally oriented, with a focus on top leaders and decisions and an acknowledged reliance on guesswork, in contrast to the behaviourist and quantitative mainstream of the discipline (Adams, 1964; Rush, 1965; Linden, 1966). It is understandable that this branch of Soviet Studies came to be equated with 'Sovietology' and 'Kremlinology'.

A new intellectual stage in Soviet studies was reached in the 1960s and 1970s, as the totalitarian model was called into question and the focus of scholarly interest shifted toward conditions and movements among the mass of the Soviet (usually Russian) people. This shift has sometimes been attributed to the political influence of the New Left (*The National Interest,* Spring 1993), or to the thawing of the Cold War in the era of détente. Actually the alleged influence of the Cold War on scholarly opinion was exaggerated by the new cohort. Probably more relevant were changes of fashion in the mainstream disciplines, notably social history, combined with the new access to those Soviet archives of low political sensitivity.

In sum, Sovietology did not constitute a peculiar discipline, a unique method, or a single set of conclusions. Its critics notwithstanding, Sovietology was no different in principle from the mobilization of scholarly expertise for the study of any other 'exotic' area of the globe. What threatens it now is not so much changes in the region it studies as the shallow sense that its area of the globe is no longer so different as to warrant any continued concentration of specialized scholarly effort (Hegenbotham, 1994; Huber *et al.*, 1995). This facile assumption, fed by the professed democratic ideology of the post-Communist regimes, may prove to be badly misleading both for theoretical understanding and for practical policy bearing on a group of countries that will long remain *sui generis*.

Communist Collapse?

To evaluate the merits or demerits of Soviet Studies as highlighted by the collapse of Communism, we have to reconsider some questions that may seem too obvious even to think about. What really was this entity called 'Communism'? What exactly happened that is termed a 'collapse'?

The conventional wisdom, expressed by most observers in Western governments and media as well as a few senior Sovietologists themselves, is that Communism was a 'utopian experiment', based on the insidious theory of Marxism-Leninism, defying human nature, but cruelly foisted upon hapless populations until at length the Soviet empire proved incapable of keeping up in the global competition for power. (Laqueur, 1995.) Ideological commitment to their elusive goal, it is said, drove the Communist leaders to erect the system of totalitarianism with all its horrors and similar in character to the regime found in Nazi Germany before World War II. This is the thesis of what I would call the 'doctrinal generation of totalitarianism', which engages in a sort of ideological determinism according to which evil results are due simply to evil ideas, independent of historical circumstances. The resulting system, therefore, could not be altered in its 'essence': it could only be overthrown from without, or (a possibility that no one expected) it could break down internally and be replaced by something altogether different. Gorbachev's perestroika, in this reasoning, was a futile attempt to salvage the Communist system without giving up its putative essence, whereas the Yeltsin regime, heir to the collapse, is presumed to have represented a wholly new departure.

This picture, for all its prevalence, does not withstand close scrutiny. The Soviet record since the revolution manifests a profound transformation, proceeding through a series of markedly different stages and reflecting the traditions and conditions of the Russian scene as well as the ambitions, obsessions, and usually misbegotten choices by successive political leaders. Generally speaking, the more closely one looks into the details of any social system and its development, the less accurately do 'models' such as totalitarianism fit the facts or tell us something we could not observe directly. This is not to say that Soviet reality did not approach the totalitarian model, but as Moshe Lewin has pointed out, the theory did not allow for either the complex development or the dissolution of the Soviet state itself (Lewin, 1988, p. 3). Instead, as some of its critics have contended, the totalitarian model became an emotional rallying point for moralistic anti-Sovietism in the later Cold War era. Westerners who questioned it on scholarly grounds ran the risk of political denunciation – and still – do (Joravsky, 1994, pp. 847–51).

The so-called collapse of Communism is another formula that needs to be re-examined. 'Collapse' is a facile popular image of what was actually a complex, step-by-step, and still incomplete process of change in the society or societies of the Soviet Union. Moreover, it obscures the elements of continuity in the successor regimes and their problems (Jowitt, 1991).

The key to this experience of transition was a sequence of events at the political centre, inherently unpredictable, that eviscerated the authority and legitimacy of the Communist Party dictatorship. Democratization and decentralization, set in motion by Mikhail Gorbachev in 1988–9, quickly became irreversible. By the time of its 28th Congress in 1990, more than a year before its débâcle in the August Putsch, the party had become a hollow shell (Gill, 1994). By the last months of the Soviet Union, governance was arguably less personalistic than it was to become later on in the majority of the successor states, including Russia. What came nearest to an abrupt collapse was the ideological rationale of official Marxism-Leninism, but this had long since become a mere liturgical façade, believed in by none but the few who now make up the unregenerate Communist splinter parties. (Leonid Brezhnev is reported to have told his brother that faith in the doctrine was only for the gullible masses: See Brezhneva, 1995.) Russian nationalism and great-power pride was the real ideology of the Communists, and this mentality persists virtually unabated along much of the political spectrum in Russia today.

The command economy and the principles of state socialism held on a little longer, whilst Gorbachev's attempts at reform and reinvigoration undermined the actual performance of the system. Boris Yeltsin, as President of the Russian Republic in opposition to Gorbachev from mid-1990 on, espoused a more drastic break with the economic past, and put it into effect following the dissolution of the Soviet Union. However, this economic change was not so much a collapse as it was the introduction of new principles from above by political command – an old story in Russia. Serious economic breakdown was a characteristic not of Communism but of the system that replaced it, though the troubles were blamed on the Old Regime – just like the Communists' years of harping on about the survival of capitalism.

Combining both the spontaneity of the political changeover, and the directed character of the economic transition, was the crisis of the Soviet nationalities and the liquidation of the Union. The latter event has been represented by the Yeltsin government as Russia's assertion of independence, along with the other republics, against an anti-national Soviet dictatorship. But this is absurd. The Soviet Union always was a revived version of the Russian Empire, and Russia was its core. It is more accurate to think of the break-up of the Union as a process of decolonization, driven by the minorities' assertion of autonomy as soon as Moscow began to democratize. Yeltin's alternative Russian government in Moscow simply endorsed and accelerated this movement in order to strike against Gorbachev's more slowly reforming regime. *De facto* independence of the colonies and formal dissolution of the Russian Empire came easily once the August coup had crippled the Union government. But within his Russian jurisdiction Yeltsin revealed no sympathy toward the separatist aspirations of lesser national minorities.

It is a metaphorical excess to term the events of 1991 a 'revolution', even if this notion seems to preserve the purity of the totalitarian model, that is, a system that remained solid until abruptly overthrown. There was no sudden, violent breakdown in the nation-wide structure of power comparable to 1917. All of the elements of the so-called collapse of Communism started gradually, defying the totalitarian model, and none has yet been completed, which defies the simplistic image of a transition to market democracy.

Certainly, democratic politics have not scored any net progress in the former Soviet Union since the Communist Party surrendered its monopoly in 1990. Under Yeltsin, Russia moved step by step back to personalistic authoritarianism, particularly after the coup from above of September-October 1993 gave the President the power to ignore the legislative branch at his pleasure (Daniels, 1995c). At the same time, prodded by Russian nationalists, Yeltsin's government took steps to restore its hegemony over the former imperial space, in a horizontal mode of bilateral ties outside the Russian Federation and in a mode of vertical subordination within it. This is a process that economic, cultural, ethnic, and strategic realities make very logical, if not inevitable. Finally, the economy, if it could be brought out of its state of chaos and criminality, might remain more durably reformed than other aspects of Russian life, but this is not a facet of the Communist collapse so much as a product of governmental initiatives taken before as well as after the political overturn. Overall, Russia is still Russia, with its problems and obsessions rooted partly in the Communist past, partly in a political culture that is much older, and partly in the unique series of events that undid the old system of government.

Getting It Right? Sovietology and the Soviet Crisis

Analysed into its elements, the so-called collapse of Communism becomes a large order to expect of any sort of prior prediction. Exact forecasting of political events in an inherently uncertain world is beyond the claims of any social science, excepting only quasi-religious doctrines such as Marxism (which despite its pretensions could not even predict the Russian Revolution). Nevertheless, when we consider the specific elements that went into the transformation of the Soviet/Russian realm between 1985 and 1991, it is worth noting not how intellectually complacent 'we' had all become, but how much broad awareness there was in Sovietological research regarding the changes, stresses, and weaknesses that already marked the Soviet Union. (See Breslauer, 1992.)

Signs of an impending crisis were perhaps clearest to Western economists (U.S. Congress, 1973, 1976, 1979, 1982; Millar, 1982; di Leo, 1983; Goldman, 1983). It was obvious to them that the methods of the command economy, no doubt effective as one alternative approach to extensive development, had become counterproductive when resource limits and foreign technological advantages imposed on the Soviets the need to shift to intensive development. A steady decline in the rate of economic growth between the 1960s and the 1980s made it impossible to reconcile the demands of consumers, investment, and the military competition with the West, whilst the requirements of the information society collided with

Russian habits of official secrecy, and the grey economy corrupted the whole society. These problems, of course, were equally obvious to Soviet reformers, the people who, under Gorbachev, initiated the disruptive efforts to decentralize and marketize the economy that in turn set the stage for real economic crisis under Yeltsin (Aganbegyan, 1987).

Sovietologists and social historians were long aware of the truly dialectical contradiction between the social modernization promoted by the Soviet regime, and the rigid and dysfunctional behaviour of the regime itself (Ryavec (ed.), 1978; Connor, 1979; Lewin, 1988). This is the typical recipe for revolution. An urbanized and educated populace with rising expectations pressed for material improvements and personal freedom, whilst the frustrations imposed by party controls undermined national morale. Soviet critics, up to the very top, themselves highlighted weaknesses in incentives and income fairness (Andropov, 1983; Zaslavskaya, 1983).

Soviet Studies has frequently been faulted for neglecting the non-Russian minorities, yet in this area too an impending crisis had long been evident to specialists (Armstrong, 1955, 1990; Simmonds (ed.), 1977; Misiunas and Taagepera, 1983; Suny (ed.), 1983; Conquest (ed.), 1986; Olcott, 1987; Hajda and Beissinger (eds), 1990; Nahaylo and Swoboda, 1990). Soviet propaganda about the 'rapprochement' if not 'merger' of nationalities was singularly unconvincing. Despite a considerable degree of ethnic mixing through internal migration and intermarriage, it was clear that the façade of unity was maintained only by the secret police, and that any degree of democratization at the centre would be a signal to the forces of national autonomy on the periphery (Motyl, 1987). As it appeared on the eve of Gorbachev's accession to power, 'in the minority regions particularly, there is reason for [the rulers'] anxiety if political liberalization should signal the opportunity to resist control from Moscow' (Daniels, 1985, p. 365).

Historians and political scientists also saw signs of inevitable change, even if its eventual depth took them by surprise. For one thing, analyses of generational differences in the Soviet leadership pointed to a major break when the cadre of Stalinist conservatives, growing old in office from the time of the purges of the 1930s, finally fell by the wayside (Bialer, 1980; Hough, 1980). Political scientists noted the erosion of totalitarian discipline and ideological authority, and the formation of interest group politics and enclaves of professional autonomy beneath the skin of party conformity (Skilling and Griffiths (eds), 1970; Hough and Fainsod, 1979, pp. 547-8, 571-2). For this insight, incidentally, Sovietology was roundly denounced by some of the same defenders of the totalitarian model who subsequently faulted the alleged failures of Sovietological prediction.

Taken as a whole, the work of Western Slavists and Sovietologists in their various disciplines was remarkably accurate and insightful in defining the elements of the crisis that overtook the Soviet Union. Their judgements went as far as any social science scholarship could responsibly go, without resorting to wild guesswork. What could not be accurately foreseen, in the nature of the matter, was how these elements of crisis would play out at the political level where the decisions of leading personalities and the effects of chance events could be decisive. On this plane, contingencies and indeterminacies amongst alternative lines of development can never be ruled out. Above all, the August Putsch of 1991, widely anticipated and hardly surprising in its conservative intent, had totally unpredictable consequences, first in its ignominious failure, and second in the ultimately fatal destabilization of the government that it had unsuccessfully tried to overthrow.

As reforms unfolded and crises sharpened in the USSR between 1985 and 1991, Western scholarship was in most respects closely attuned to the new developments (Walker, 1993). Again, economics – the most concrete of the social sciences – was the most accurate and perspicacious about Soviet needs and shortcomings, more so than the Soviet leadership itself (Goldman, 1983; Hewett, 1988; Aslund, 1989, 1991; Campbell, 1991). Studies of culture and the media tracked Gorbachev's introduction of glasnost, and had little difficulty anticipating its impact (Burbank and Rosenberg, 1989; Laqueur, 1989; Nove, 1989). In politics and particularly in foreign policy matters, Sovietology fell behind events, reluctant as it was to take Gorbachev's 'New Thinking' seriously enough, soon enough. If the profession had a general fault, it was not lack of insight but excessive caution, perhaps reflecting the continuing influence of prominent exponents of the totalitarian model who insisted that the Communist system could never seriously change from within. Notions that democratization and accommodation with the West could really be under way under perestroika were widely dismissed by some as 'Gorbymania.' In nationality matters, the Achilles' heel of democratization, events bore out the reality of change under perestroika, as local nationalists seized the opportunities offered by loosening at the centre, and Russian conservatives reacted against threats to the integrity of the empire (Motyl, 1990; Goble, 1991). Beissinger and Hajda are amongst those who have faulted Soviet studies for neglecting the nationalities. But their own work refutes the charge: 'There is a nationalities component to every facet of Soviet politics .... The most likely outcome, short of a revision of *glasnost*, is sustained crisis .... In an era of reform, the nationalities problem presents Soviet leaders with their most serious challenge, one that virtually guarantees that Soviet political evolution will be neither smooth nor simple' (Beissinger and Hajda, 1990, pp. 305, 320). Gorbachev was caught in the middle, and responded erratically, whilst Yeltsin's decision to play the nationality card against Gorbachev was highly predictable if one considered the personal animosity between the two. Truly surprising, on the other hand, was Soviet tolerance of the Communist débâcle in Eastern Europe. Here we have a series of events that in some cases, above all in East Germany and Czechoslovakia, really did amount to a 'collapse'. Undoubtedly it was impressions of 1989 in the former Soviet bloc that lent a sense of collapse to events in the Soviet Union itself in 1991.

In my own conceptualization of developments since 1985 I have used the perspective of revolution as a long-term process. Applied to Russia, this notion embraces the moderate phase of 1917, the extremist phase of 1917–1921, the Thermidorean reaction of 1921–1928, and the prolonged post-revolutionary dictatorship of 1928–1985 (sliding into the functional equivalent of a monarchical restoration by the late 1930s, followed by abortive cycles of reform after 1953). The entire process finally came to a close in what I term the moderate revolutionary revival (Daniels, 1985, 1987, 1995b). This formula designates the effort to return to some point of departure between early revolutionary radicalism and the Old Regime, though the range of choices is wide. (One might conceive of Gorbachev as representing a leftist alternative, and Yeltsin a rightist one.) The period of this revolutionary endgame is accordingly unstable and unpredictable, until a functioning constitutional government is finally arrived at. I have found the moderate revolutionary revival a useful construct for relating both the Gorbachev and Yeltsin periods to what went before, and for anticipating some of the changes and struggles that the most recent years have witnessed.

Transition? What Transition?

Notwithstanding its impressive record of achievement, American Sovietology went into a state of shock after the political earthquakes of 1989 and 1991. Numerous high-profile commentators – some within the profession, more outside it – seized on these events to denounce the entire practice of Sovietology as worthless because it had 'failed to predict' the unpredictable demise of Communist rule (Malia, 1990, 1994; *The National Interest*, 1993). Many practitioners in the field, swamped by media amplification of the anti-Sovietological view, succumbed to the mood of professional breast-beating.

As I have noted, the actual crises of 1989 and 1991, governed as they were by personalities and contingencies, could not have been closely predicted from any model or precedent. (See Daniels, 1995c.) Historians should be able to understand this truth better than those social scientists who try too hard to make events appear to be law-governed. What happened was just as surprising to all the political actors in the Soviet Union and Eastern Europe as it was to observers in the outside world. But this does not rule out the role of expertise in attempting to comprehend the background and consequences of the upheaval.

Intellectually in retreat since 1991, Sovietology has been guilty of much more serious errors both of commission and of omission in addressing events since that turning point, when the new orthodoxy of 'transitional studies' took hold in Western work on the former Soviet bloc. In this framework it was assumed beyond rational demonstration that democratic government and market economics would be the uniform outcome, subject only to debate about the best path and pace to this end. The process was not thought essentially different from comparable experiences in southern Europe, Latin America, and elsewhere in the Third World. Russian and Central European policy-makers who were most closely attuned to Western theory acted according to the premises of this school, and often appeared to validate the theory. Yet in detail the policies prescribed by transitology, intentionally undertaken to realize a predicted outcome, have been quite confounded by events.

In economics, the Russian disciples of the transitology school attempted to apply simultaneously the 'shock therapy' of monetary austerity and the institutional reorganization of state socialism into private capitalism, presumably following the experience of Latin America and Central Europe. The financial outcome was the opposite of intention and prediction: runaway inflation, extinction of investment, plummeting of production, and mass impoverishment – in short, true collapse! Haste in trying to change the economic power structure, without first providing the necessary legal and financial framework, reminded one of the impetuosity of the Bolsheviks in the original extremist phase of the revolution. In behavioural terms, the outcome was predatory speculation and the metastasis of criminality, whilst the old 'New Class' of the Communist nomenklatura turned itself into a phalanx of self-aggrandizing entrepreneurs. None of this was foreseen, obviously, or Western advice would no doubt have steered the reforms quite differently.

Transitology was equally defied by political developments. Taking account neither of the personal factor nor of Russian political culture, it failed to foresee the subversion of fragile new democratic institutions by supposedly democratic leaders in the successor republics. It pinned its democratic hopes and expectations on the personality and pronouncements of Boris Yeltsin so uncritically that the unfolding of his authoritarian instincts and his break with the legislative branch of government in 1993 prompted some of his Western apologists to the patent falsification of the history of these events (Daniels, 1993). No one seems to have expected the survival of the nomenklatura as a social force in enterprise administration and local government. The Yeltsin regime evoked illusions of democratic and capitalistic wish-fulfilment mirroring the self-deception of fellow-travellers on the opposite end of the political spectrum in the 1930s.

Nationality studies, entranced by the seeming victories of self-determination in 1989 and 1991, failed to anticipate the ongoing curse of inter-ethnic conflict as well as the economic and security pressures for reintegration in the Commonwealth of Independent States. (An exception is Slider, 1994.) Missed almost completely, until it became obvious, was the consolidation of political power in most of the former Soviet republics and many Russian regions by former Communist officials, now turned nationalist but still operating in the old authoritarian manner. The revival of reform Communists in Eastern Europe was equally unanticipated and underappreciated. The force of Russian nationalism and chagrin over the dissolution of the empire were particularly underestimated until the startling showing of Vladimir Zhironovsky and his 'Liberal Democratic' party in the elections of December 1993. In sum, Western Sovietology, by now post-Sovietology, shamed by its alleged failure to predict the Communist collapse, has in the main allowed itself to be mesmerized by the democratic and nationalist claims of the successor regimes, whilst putting its critical predictive powers on ice.

Towards a Post-Soviet Studies

Since 1992 American Sovietology, or rather the hastily renamed field of 'Russian, East European, and Eurasian Studies', has been caught in a mood of pessimistic soul-searching. It has lost confidence in the merit of its analyses. It has lost the sense of a unifying context that had been provided by the geographic compass of Communist regimes. It has seen financial support for training, research, and publications begin to dry up; presumably we no longer need to 'know our enemy'. Practitioners of Soviet Studies, losing their sense of relevance, have begun to rejoin the mainstreams of their respective disciplines (usually theoretical, statistical, and parochially American), and they may fail to replicate their expertise on the area. All this at a time when the actual needs, opportunities, and talent for study of the former Communist realm were never more compelling. The Slavist profession in the USA is running on the oil left in the pipeline.

Confronted by such professionally disconcerting conditions and events, American post-Sovietology is in danger of embracing new simplicities that may render its analytical and predictive powers less effective than they actually were before perestroika. Some of the deceptively universalistic tendencies in political science have already been noted. History of the area is being carried away by the mainstream fashions of social history and gender studies at the expense of the political history of the Communist regimes now documented by newly accessible archives. Economics, once the star discipline in Sovietology, has dismissed the planned economy as a synonym for Stalinism, and has lapsed into simplistic mainstream assumptions that the post-Communist economies are almost 'normal', or if not, should be made so by shock therapy (Millar, 1992).

Under the circumstances, within the American scholarly community as well as in the target region, do post-Soviet studies have any future? If they do, the outcome depends on intellectual effort and serious self-criticism, though not the kind of breast-beating that has been so fashionable since the end of the Communist regimes in Europe.

First, post-Sovietology needs to recognize the path it took to post-Soviet error. It was too sceptical of Gorbachev and too trusting of Yeltsin; too reserved about the possibility and progress of reform under Communist aegis; too uncritical of reform in its radical, post-Communist version. Like much of Sovietology in the old days, it read the successive regimes too literally: Gorbachev was still a Communist and therefore he could not really change; Yeltsin was an anti-Communist (notwithstanding his identical background) and therefore his every action had to be legitimate.

Secondly, post-Sovietology must emphasize that the Communist background is still relevant. To be sure, Communism has passed from the purview of the present-minded disciplines to the historical. Nevertheless, it still gives a unity of experience and circumstance to all the countries of the former Soviet bloc, however diverse their post-Communist lines of development may be.

Thirdly, post-Sovietolgy should be chary of simplistic or rigid paradigms. This was the most obvious drawback with Sovietology in the Soviet period, with its partiality to glib formulas such as totalitarianism or pat explanations such as Marxist ideology. Now new catch-phrases have taken over – transitions to democracy, market economy, national self-determination – without enough critical reflection about their meaning and their relationship to actual events. Though Sovietology's effort to be value-neutral in the spirit of modern social science has been denigrated by ex-Cold warriors, post-Sovietology needs to hew again to this standard, at least to the extent that it distinguishes between wish and reality.

Finally, area specialists in their respective disciplines must keep their common area studies identity intact so that they can continue to learn from each other as they have in the past. Someone needs to understand the singularities of the region as a whole, not to mention individual countries, as against the global generalities propounded by the traditional academic fields. Otherwise, expertise on the region will sink out of sight into the respective disciplinary mainstreams, leaving afloat only the earliest pieces of Russian and East European studies, namely a little language work and antiquarian history. This would be a sad conclusion to one of the most exciting facets of American scholarly accomplishment in this century.

References

Adams, A.E., 1964. 'The Hybrid Art of Sovietology', *Survey*, no. 50 (January 1964).

Aganbegyan, A., 1987. *The Economic Challenge of Perestroika*, edited by M.B. Brown, Indiana University Press, Bloomington.

Andropov, Y.V., 1983. 'Uchenie Karla Marksa i nekotorye voprosy sotsialisti cheskogo stroitellstva v SSSR',1 *Kommunist*, no. 3.

Arendt, H., 1951. *The Origins of Totalitarianism*, Harcourt, Brace, New York.

Armstrong, J., 1955, 1990. *Ukrainian Nationalism*, Columbia University Press, New York.

Aslund, A., 1989. *Gorbachev's Struggle for Economic Reform*, Cornell University Press, Ithaca.

Atkinson, D., 1991. 'Soviet and East European Studies', in National Council of Area Studies Associations, *Prospects for Faculty in Area Studies*, AAASS, Stanford, Cal.

Balzer, H.D., ed., 1991. *Five Years That Shook the World: Gorbachev's Unfinished Revolution*, Westview Press, Boulder, Col.

Bauer, R.A., 1952. *The New Man in Soviet Psychology*, Harvard University Press, Cambridge, Mass.

Bauer, R.A., A. Inkeles, and C. Kluckholm, 1956. *How the Soviet System Works*, Harvard University Press.

Beissinger, M., and L. Hajda, 1990. 'Nationalism and Reform in Soviet Politics', in Hajda and Beissinger, 1990, pp. 305–20.

Benedict, R., 1946. *The Chrysanthemum and the Sword*, Houghton Mifflin, Boston.

Berman, H., 1950. *Justice in Russia*, Harvard University Press, Cambridge, Mass.

Bialer, S., 1980. *Stalin's Successors: Leadership, Stability, and Change in the Soviet Union*, Cambridge University Press, New York.

Brezhneva, L., 1995. *The World I Left Behind: Pieces of a Past*, Random House, New York.

Brown, E.J., 1953. *The Proletarian Episode in Russian Literature, 1928–1932*, Columbia University Press, New York.

Burbank, J., and W.G. Rosenberg, 1989. 'Perestroika and Soviet Culture', Special Issue, *Michigan Quarterly Review*, vol. 28, no. 4 (Fall 1989).

Byrnes, R.F., 1964. 'USA: Work at the Universities', in *Survey*, no. 50 (January 1964), pp. 62–8.

——1978a. 'Russian Studies in the United States. Before the First World War', in H.-J. Torke, ed., *Forschungen zur osteuropaischen Geschichte. Werner Philipp zur 70. Geburtstag*, Harassowitz, Berlin. Reprinted in Byrnes, 1994.

——1978b. 'Archibald Cary Coolidge: A Founder of Russian Studies in the United States', *Slavic Review*, 38:4. Reprinted in Byrnes, 1994.

——1994. *A History of Russian and East European Studies in the United States: Selected Essays*, University Press of America, Lanham, Md.

Campbell, R.W., 1991. *The Socialist Economies in Transition: A Primer on Semi-Reformed Systems*, Indiana University Press, Bloomington.

Carr, E.H., 1951–64. *A History of Soviet Russia*, Macmillan, New York.

Connor, W.D., 1979. *Socialism, Politics and Equality: Hierarchy and Chance in Eastern Europe and the USSR*, Columbia University Press, New York.

Conquest, R., ed., 1986. *The Last Empire: Nationality and the Soviet Future*, Hoover Institution Press, Stanford, Cal.

Counts, G.S., 1957. *The Challenge of Soviet Education*, McGraw-Hill, New York.

Cox, M., 1994. 'The End of the USSR and the Collapse of Soviet Studies', *Coexistence*, 31:1.

Crankshaw, E., 1948. *Russia and the Russians*, Viking, New York.

Curtis, J.S., 1953. *The Russian Church and the Soviet State*, Little, Brown, Boston.

Dallin, D., 1944. *The Real Soviet Russia*, New Haven, Yale.

Daniels, R.V., 1985. *Russia: The Roots of Confrontation*, Harvard University Press, Cambridge, Mass.

—1987. 'Il risveglio del rivoluzionario russo', in *Il procietto Gorbaciov*, Rinascita, Rome. English version in Daniels, 1988, reprinted in Daniels, 1995a.

—1988. *Is Russia Reformable? Change and Resistance from Stalin to Gorbachev*, Westview Press, Boulder, Col.

—1993. 'The Riddle of Russian Reform', *Dissent*, Autumn 1993.

—ed., 1995a. *Soviet Communism: From Reform to Collapse*, D.C. Heath, Lexington, Mass.

—1995b. 'The Revolutionary Process, the Moderate Revolutionary Revival, and Post-Communist Russia', in Martine Godet, ed., *De Russie et d'ailleurs: feux croises sur l'histoire, pour Marc Ferro*, Institut d'Etudes Slaves, Paris.

—1995c. 'Prospects for Democracy in Russia', in M. Kraus and R. Liebowitz, eds, *Russia and East Europe after Communism*, Westview Press, Boulder, Col.

Deutscher, I., 1949. *Stalin: A Political Biography*, Oxford University Press, New York.

di Leo, R., 1983. *L'Economia sovietica tra crisi e riforme (1965-1982)*, Liguori, Naples.

Enteen, G., L.H. Siegelbaum, and R.V. Daniels, 1995. 'The Dynamics of Revolution in Soviet History: A Discussion', *Russian Review*, vol. 54, no. 3 (July 1995).

Fainsod, M., 1953. *How Russia Is Ruled*, Harvard University Press, Cambridge, Mass.

—1958. *Smolensk under Soviet Rule*, Harvard University Press, Cambridge, Mass.

Field, M.G., 1957. *Doctor and Patient in Soviet Russia*, Harvard University Press, Cambridge, Mass.

Fisher, R.T., 1959. *Pattern for Soviet Youth*, Columbia University Press, New York.

Fitzpatrick, S., 1979. *Education and Social Mobility in the Soviet Union, 1921-1934*, Cambridge University Press, Cambridge.

Friedrich, C., and Z. Brzezinski, 1956. *Totalitarian Dictatorship and Autocracy*, Harvard University Press, Cambridge, Mass.

Gerschenkron, A.P., 1964. 'The Study of the Soviet Economy in the USA', *Survey*, no. 50, January 1964.

Gill, G., 1994. *The Collapse of a Single Party System: The Disintegration of the Communist Party of the Soviet Union*, Cambridge University Press, Cambridge.

Gleason, A., 1995. *Totalitarianism: The Inner History of the Cold War*, Oxford University Press, New York.

Goble, P., 1991. 'Imperial Endgame: Nationality Problems and the Soviet Future', in Balzer, 1991.

Goldman, M.I., 1983. *USSR in Crisis: The Failure of an Economic System*, Norton, New York.

Hajda, L., and M. Beissinger, eds, 1990. *The Nationalities Factor in Soviet Politics and Society*, Westview Press, Boulder, Col.

Hegenbotham, S.J., 1994. 'Rethinking International Scholarship: The Challenge of Transition from the Cold War Era', *Items* (Social Science Research Council, New York), June-September 1994.

Hewett, E.A., 1988. *Reforming the Soviet Economy: Equality vs Efficiency*, Brookings Institution, Washington.

Hilferding, R., 1940. 'State Capitalism or Totalitarian State Economy?', *Sotsialisticheskii Vestnik*, New York, 1940; English translation, *Modern Review*, June 1947.

Hoover, J.E., 1958. *Masters of Deceit*, Holt, New York.

Hough, J.F., and M. Fainsod, 1979. *How the Soviet Union Is Governed*, Harvard University Press, Cambridge, Mass.

Hough, J.F., 1980. *Soviet Leadership in Transition*, Brookings Institution., Washington.

Huber, R.T., B.A. Ruble, and P.J. Stavrakis, 1995. 'Post-Cold War "International" Scholarship: A Brave New World or the Triumph of Form over Substance?', *Items* (Social Science Research Council, New York), March 1995.

Hunt, R.N. Carew, 1951. *The Theory and Practice of Communism*, Macmillan, New York.

Inkeles, A., 1950. *Public Opinion in Soviet Russia: A Study in Mass Persuasion*, Harvard University Press, Cambridge, Mass.

Joravsky, D., 1994. 'Communism in Historical Perspective', *American Historical Review*, vol. 99, no. 3.

Jowitt, K., 1991. 'Weber, Trotsky, and Holmes on the Study of Leninist Regimes', *Journal of International Affairs*, vol. 45 (Summer 1991).

Keenan, E., 1994. 'What Have We Learned?' (Presidential address to the AAASS, November 1994), in *Newsnet*, January 1995.

Koenker, D., 1981. *Moscow Workers and the 1917 Revolution*, Princeton University Press, Princeton.

Lambert, R.D., et al., 1984. *Beyond Growth: The Next Stage in Language and Area Studies*, Association of American Universities, Washington.

Laqueur, W., 1989. *The Long Road to Freedom: Russia and Glasnost*, Scribner's, New York.

—1995. *The Dream That Failed: Reflections on the Soviet Union*, Oxford University Press, New York and Oxford.

Leites, N., 1951. *The Operational Code of the Politburo*, McGraw-Hill, New York.

Lewin, M., 1988. *The Gorbachev Phenomenon: A Historical Interpretation*, University of California Press, Berkeley.

Lichtheim, G., 1961. *Marxism: An Historical and Critical Study*, Praeger, New York.

Linden, C.A., 1966. *Khrushchev and the Soviet Leadership, 1957-1964*, Johns Hopkins University Press, Baltimore.

Malia, M., 1990. 'To the Stalin Mausoleum', (by 'Z') *Daedalus*, Winter 1990.

—1994. *The Soviet Tragedy: A History of Socialism in Russia, 1917-1991*, The Free Press, New York.

Maynard, J., 1948. *Russia in Flux*, Macmillan, New York.

Meyer, A.G., 1953. *Marxism: The Unity of Theory and Practice*, Harvard University Press, Cambridge, Mass.

—1957. *Leninism*, Harvard University Press, Cambridge, Mass.

Millar, J.R., 1982. *The ABC's of Soviet Socialism*, Cambridge University Press, New York.

—1992. 'Rethinking Soviet Economic Studies', Ford Foundation Workshop Series, 'Rethinking Soviet Studies', Kennan Institute, Washington, DC., 23 October 1992.

Misiunas, R.J., and R. Taagepera, 1983. *The Baltic States: Years of Dependence, 1940– 1980*, University of California Press, Berkeley and Los Angeles.

Moore, B., 1950. *Soviet Politics: The Dilemma of Power*, Harvard University Press, Cambridge, Mass.

Motyl, A.J., 1987. *Will the Non-Russians Rebel? State, Ethnicity, and Stability in the USSR*, Cornell University Press, Ithaca.

—1990. *Sovietology, Rationality, Nationality: Coming to Grips with Nationalism in the USSR*, Columbia University Press, New York.

Nahaylo, B., and Victor S., 1990. *Soviet Disunion: A History of the Nationalities Problem in the USSR*, The Free Press, New York.

The National Interest, Spring 1993.

Nove, A., 1989. *Glasnost in Action*, Unwin-Hyman, London and Boston.

O'Connell, C., 1990. 'Social Structure and Science: Soviet Studies at Harvard', Ph.D. dissertation, UCLA, Los Angeles.

Odom, W.E., 1992. 'Soviet Politics and After', *World Politics*, vol. 45 (October 1992).

Olcott, M.B., 1987. *The Kazakhs*, Hoover Institution Press, Stanford, CA.

Possony, S., 1953. *A Century of Conflict: Communist Techniques of World Revolution*, Regnery, Chicago.

Read, C., 1950. 'The Social Responsibilities of the Historian', *American Historical Review*, January 1950.

Rush, M., 1965. *Political Succession in the USSR*, Columbia University Press, New York.

Ryavec, K.W., ed., 1978. *Soviet Society and the Communist Party*, University of Massachusetts Press, Amherst.

Schmitter, P.C., with T.L. Karl, 1994. 'The Conceptual Travels of Transitologists and Consolidologists: How Far to the East Should They Attempt to Go?', *Slavic Review*, 53:1.

Schapiro, L., 1960. *The Communist Party of the Soviet Union*, Random House, New York.

Simmonds, G.W., ed., 1977. *Nationalism in the USSR and Eastern Europe in the Era of Brezhnev and Kosygin*, University of Detroit Press, Detroit.

Skilling, H.G., and F. Griffiths, eds, 1970. *Interest Groups in Soviet Politics*, Princeton University Press, Princeton.

Slider, D., 1994. 'Federalism, Discord, and Accommodation: Intergovernmental Relations in Post-Soviet Russia', in T.H. Friedgut and J.W. Hahn, eds, *Local Power and Post-Soviet Politics*, Myron E. Sharpe, Armonk, NY.

Solomon, S.G., 1993. *Beyond Sovietology: Essays in Politics and History*, Myron E. Sharpe, Armonk, NY.

Suny, R.G., ed., 1983. *Transcaucasia: Nationalism and Social Change. Essays in the History of Armenia, Azerbaidzhan, and Georgia*, Michigan Slavic Publications, Ann Arbor.

Survey: A Journal of Soviet and East European Studies, no. 50, January 1964.

Timasheff, N., 1946. *The Great Retreat*, Dutton, New York.

Trotsky, L., 1937. *The Revolution Betrayed: What Is the Soviet Union and Where Is It Going?*, Doubleday, Doran & Co., Garden City, NY.

Tucker, R.C., 1973. *Stalin as a Revolutionary*, Norton, New York.

Ulam, A., 1968. *The Bolsheviks*, Macmillan, New York.

U.S. Congress, Joint Economic Committee, Government Printing Office, Washington 1973, *Soviet Economic Prospects for the Seventies.*

—1976, *The Soviet Economy in a New Perspective.*

—1979, *The Soviet Economy in a Time of Change.*

—1982, *The Soviet Economy in the 1980s Problems and Prospects.*

Walker, E.W., 1993. 'Sovietology and Perestroika: A PostMortem', in Solomon, 1993.

Zaslavskaya, T., 1983. 'Doklad o neobkhodimosti bolee ugublennogo izucheniya v SSSR sotsiall' nogo mekhanizma razvitiya ekonomiki', *Arkhiv Samizdata*, AS 5043. Translated as 'The Novosibirsk Report', *Survey*, vol. 28, no. 1 (Spring 1994).

7

Rethinking the Transition: 1991 and Beyond

STEPHEN WHITE

Introduction

Just as 1917 was a turning point in world affairs, so too was 1989. Or perhaps 1991, if the formal dissolution of the USSR is the crucial event. The decision to dissolve the world's first socialist state was taken in something of a scramble: the Supreme Soviet that took the decision was inquorate; the decision should in any case have been put to the full Congress of People's Deputies, or (almost certainly) to the people in a referendum; and the Treaty of Union of 1922 had not, in fact, provided for the withdrawal of any of its parties or for the abrogation of the treaty as a whole. For most of Gorbachev's opponents, in any event, it was not the end of the USSR that was crucial but the defeat of the attempted coup in August 1991 and the suspension of Communist Party authority. For Boris Yeltsin, speaking just after the coup had collapsed, the Soviet people had 'thrown off the fetters of seventy years of slavery' (*Izvestiya*, 23 August 1991, p. 1). For the critic Alla Latynina, a 'Russian liberal democratic state' had been born (*Literaturnaya gazeta,* 28 August 1991, p. 7). For *Izvestiya*, speaking editorially on 22 August, democracy had 'taught the people not to be silent': a reference to Pushkin's Boris Godunov, in which the population of the time, invited to welcome the False Dmitrii, had (in a celebrated phrase) 'said nothing'.

A few years later, it was less clear that there had been such fundamental changes. Just as 1917 failed to usher in a European and then global transition to Soviet and communist rule, so too 1989/91 led to a contradictory process of change in which many ruling elites remained in place and former communist parties in power, and ordinary citizens had no greater influence upon the shaping of public policy than they had enjoyed beforehand - in some respects, they thought themselves, even less. Certainly, a communist monopoly of power had ended. But it had ended, at least in the USSR, in the later stages of communist rule, not after the failure of the coup. There had been improvements in human liberties, in religious freedoms, in the independence of the media and the courts; but again most of these changes had their origins in legislation of the late Soviet period. There had clearly been a change of regime, in that government was, for the most part, in the hands of different people espousing a different set of policies. But it was less clear that there had been a change of system, or a more fundamental departure from long-standing patterns of centralized and authoritarian rule.

It might well be the case - as Michael Cox has noted - that social scientists failed to 'predict' the end of Soviet power (1994). But there had always been a wide diversity of views, the consensus within which was that the Soviet system had begun to encounter deeply rooted obstacles from at least the late 1960s. For many, this had led to a form of rule that (by the late 1980s) was fragile and unreformable; for some, there had been a patrimonial system since much earlier times and the problems that the Soviet authorities confronted by the 1980s were not very different from those of late tsardom: integrating an ethnically diverse state in which Russians were (at that time) less than a majority, devising a form of rule that would combine effective executive action and popular accountability, and generating a standard of living that would satisfy a sufficient proportion of the population to ensure the survival of the regime itself. As we know, both the tsarist and the Soviet leaderships failed to resolve these tasks; and there was little indication by the late 1990s that the post-communist presidency of Boris Yeltsin would be more successful in doing so, or in shifting the locus of political authority from an all-powerful state to an active and informed citizenry within a secure framework of rights.

Sovietology and the Soviet Crisis

Did Sovietologists - as others in this volume have suggested - fail to predict the transition from communist rule? There is no simple answer to this.

There were many, certainly, for whom there were few prospects of a change in communist rule during the 1980s, not only in the USSR but throughout Eastern Europe. For Samuel Huntington, writing in 1984, the likelihood of democratic development in Eastern Europe was 'virtually nil' (p. 217). For Andrzej Korbonski, writing towards the end of the decade, there was 'little difference between the situation in 1988 and that twenty years ago', and there was no reason to expect 'radical changes in Soviet relations with Eastern Europe, at least in the forseeable future' (in Carnovale and Potter (eds), 1989, p. 22). For Jerry Hough, as late as 1990, Soviet difficulties had been 'grossly exaggerated'; the real story of that year had been the 'further consolidation of Gorbachev's political position', and he was 'almost certain to remain in power at least until the 1995 presidential election' (in Dallin and Lapidus (eds), 1991, pp. 226, 247). There were few who argued that governments of the Soviet type had secured the consent of those who nominally elected them. But there was, it appeared, a basis for stability in the implicit 'social contract' that appeared to have been concluded between the authorities and the society over which they ruled, based upon an exchange of political rights for a stable and assured standard of living (Cook, 1993).

There was some support for these views, moreover, within the broader social science literature. For at least one influential body of theory, the legitimacy of a regime was a function, at least in part, of the length of time it had been in continuous existence. No regime, it was hypothesized, could be said to be moving away from repudiation unless it had survived long enough to have been the predominant influence upon the political memories of more than half of its adult population. Regimes that had been in existence for two or three generations, conversely, could gradually acquire legitimacy as an increasing proportion of their populations grew up knowing no other kind of system than the one in which they had themselves been raised (Rose, 1971, p. 35). The Soviet system, by the late 1980s, abundantly satisfied these criteria. It had been in existence for more than 70 years and more than 90 per cent of the population had been born since its establishment, nearly 70 per cent of them since the Second World War (*Itogi*, 1992); it should gradually have gained legitimacy, on this interpretation, as those with a conscious recollection of the pre-revolutionary order became a small and steadily diminishing proportion of the population as a whole. The Soviet view was not entirely different: a popular commitment, it was thought, would gradually develop as 'survivals' of the old order faded steadily into the past and new, socialist forms of thinking took their place (Syzrantsev, 1977, p. 225).

Views of this kind, however, were only a part of the spectrum and probably a minority within Western Sovietology. From at least the 1960s there were very different suggestions, for instance that the 'new class was divided' between communists and technocrats (Parry, 1966). Another influential interpretation was that there would be 'convergence' between the Soviet system and its Western counterparts (Johnson (ed.), 1970); a Trotskyist variation on this theme was that the bureaucracy was 'breeding its own gravediggers', as education and social change overwhelmed the centralized structures that had been inherited from late Stalinism (Deutscher, 1967, pp. 59-60). By the late 1970s, as economic growth slowed down, the emphasis shifted away from benign processes of social change to a deepening tension between the ruling group and the society, and within the ruling group itself. By the early 1980s there was a widespread agreement the USSR was 'in crisis' (Goldman, 1983), that its agriculture was 'in crisis' (Hedlund, 1984), and that the East European economies were also 'in crisis' (Drewnowski (ed.), 1982). For Pipes, the Soviet Union already fitted Lenin's description of a 'revolutionary situation' (1984, p. 50); for Burks, 'the ingredients for some kind of explosion [were] increasingly in place' (1984, p. 71).

For most of these writers, and for many others, the weakness of Soviet rule was more than a matter of short-term harvest failures or other difficulties: it was the product of a more fundamental contradiction between communist authoritarianism and the open and bargaining culture that corresponded to its economic maturity. Perhaps the most influential exponent of this view was Talcott Parsons (as David Lane notes in more detail in the next chapter) a sociologist – and member of the Russian Research Center at Harvard – who drew his inspiration from Darwin and much older theories of social change. All states, for Parsons, had to develop a range of capacities or 'evolutionary universals' that would allow them to adapt to the requirements of modern society, amongst them a 'democratic association with elective leadership and fully enfranchised membership' (1964a, pp. 340-1). The communist states, in Parsons's view, would prove incapable of competing with liberal-democratic systems in the long run, and would be compelled to make adjustments in the direction of electoral democracy and a plural party system if they were to survive. This meant that the party would have to share political responsibilities with the wider citizenry: or that it would have to 'relinquish its monopoly of such responsibility' (ibid., p. 356). As a result of their own internal dynamics, Parsons wrote, the communist states would therefore be bound to develop towards the 'restoration – or where it has not yet existed, the institution – of political democracy'; this was the 'only possible outcome – except for general destruction or breakdown' (1964b, pp. 396-8).

A more developed version of this theory took the form of political modernization: the view, as Robert Dahl put it, that 'because of its inherent requirements, an advanced economy and its supporting social structures automatically distributes political resources and political skills to a vast variety of individuals, groups and organizations'. The monopoly of political power enjoyed by communist leaders, according to Dahl, was therefore being undermined by the programmes of social and economic development that they themselves had sponsored. The more communist leaders succeeded in transforming the social and economic structures of the countries over which they ruled, the more their political skills were threatened by obsolescence; but if they sought to retain their dominance by force alone they would be confronted by the enormous costs of managing a modern society in this anachronistic way. The change from Stalinism to post-Stalinism, Dahl suggested, was already a 'profound step towards liberalization'; further steps were inescapable as a centrally dominated political system became increasingly difficult to reconcile with the pluralistic pressures of a modern economy and society (1971, pp. 64-5, 76-9, 218).

Dahl was not the only scholar in the 1970s and 1980s to point to an 'iron law of pluralism'. The Soviet historian and commentator Roy Medvedev spoke of democratization as an 'inevitable tendency'; Ghita Ionescu suggested that 'pluralization and institutionalization' were an 'inevitable trend' which accompanied the 'process of economic, social and political development'; Karl Deutsch identified an 'automatic trend towards pluralization and disintegration'; Merle Fainsod expected the 'emergence over time of a looser, more pragmatic, and pluralistically based party in which the differentiated interests of an industrial society find freer expression (cited in White, 1978, pp. 105-6). Gabriel Almond, in perhaps the most far-reaching of such analyses, spoke of the 'pluralistic pressures of a modern economy and society' and of a 'secular trend in the direction of decentralization and pluralism'. As their societies and economies developed, Almond suggested, communist systems would face the 'inevitable demands of a healthy, educated, affluent society' for both more material and what Almond called 'spiritual consumer goods' (such as opportunities for participation and a share in the decision-making process). Already, Almond wrote, 'Russian success in science, education, technology, economic productivity and national security have produced some decentralization of the political process. I fail to see how these decentralizing, pluralistic tendencies can be reversed, or how their spread can be prevented' (Almond, 1970, pp. 27 and 318-9).

There was little evidence, as the Prague Spring was crushed and dissidents were incarcerated, that these pluralistic pressures were exerting the positive influence that had been so widely expected. But as economic growth slowed down in the late 1970s and early 1980s, the prevailing Western interpretation became an increasingly bleak and uncompromising one. For Tucker (1981-2), Brezhnev's Russia was a 'spent state and a swollen society'. For Bialer (1986), it was 'external expansion, internal decline'. There was an environmental crisis (Komarov, 1980), and a widening gap between rich and poor (Matthews, 1986); there was also a widening network of privilege and corruption (Matthews, 1978; Simis, 1982; Clarke (ed.), 1983). And despite the reforms of the perestroika years, it was clear that deeper, more systemic choices could not be avoided (see for instance White, 1990, p. 219). Indeed for some the changes that took place in the late 1980s were evidence that that modernization theory had been right all along, as the East European systems found themselves unable to resist the imperatives of economic maturity and social complexity as well as the spread of international and electronic communications. For Pye, these were nothing less than 'inevitable forces of history' (1990, p. 6); for Lewin, similarly, the changes of the 1980s were evidence that Soviet society needed a state that could 'match its complexity', although there was still the possibility of a 'democratized one-party system' (1988, pp. 146, 151).

There was clearly no uniformity of view among Western students of Soviet affairs, and relatively few who argued that communist rule would collapse in – specifically – the late 1980s. But the view that Soviet socialism was in a deep and systemic crisis was very widely shared, and almost certainly the consensus. Joseph Berliner, in a study of the recent writings of presidents of the American Association for the Advancement of Slavic Studies, found that they had argued with some consistency that the post-Brezhnev USSR was a 'spent society'; that there were 'severe problems of corruption, ethnic tensions and social strain'; that productivity was likely to decline; and that the central problem was the 'dictatorship' of a party bureaucracy that contained the 'seeds of its own destruction' (1994, p. 11). And some were prepared to go even further. Zbigniew Brzezinski, in particular, was arguing in early 1988 that it was 'no exaggeration to affirm that there are five countries now in Eastern Europe all of which are ripe for revolutionary explosion. Nor is it an exaggeration to say that this could happen in more than one simultaneously' (cited in Hankiss, 1990, p. 142). Brzezinski's book *The Grand Failure*, completed in late 1988, dealt with the 'birth and death of communism in the twentieth century'; the cover of the paperback edition (Brzezinski, 1990) could claim that it had been the 'Book That Foretold the Collapse of Communism in Eastern Europe and in Russia'.

Change of Regime? Change of System?

The transition, when it came, was certainly a curious one. Unlike most of Eastern Europe, where a mass politics had ousted communist administrations and placed very different governments in power, the Soviet transition centred around the defence of a predominantly communist parliament led by a former member of the Politburo. Yeltsin was President at this time of the Russian Soviet Federal Socialist Republic; his running-mate, who stood beside him outside the White House, was still a party member; so too were more than 80 per cent of the deputies. There was relatively little popular involvement in the transition: there was no national and indefinite strike in response to Yeltsin's appeal, and the crowd that defied the curfew outside the White House was about 15,000 (a year later many more Muscovites 'remembered' they had been there: *Izvestiya*, 17 August 1992, p. 3). Yeltsin's appeal, in any case, was for the Soviet constitution to be respected and for the Soviet President and General Secretary to be released from his detention in the Crimea (Dobrokhotov *et al.*, 1992, pp. 71–2). The Communist Party was suspended, and then banned; but it revived again in early 1993 and soon became the largest and best supported, not just at the elections to the State Duma but still more so at local elections throughout the country. Not surprisingly, perhaps, most Russians in the summer of 1994 thought that the Communists were 'still in power' (*Argumenty i fakty*, 1994, no. 23, p. 2).

It was certainly the case that former Communists were still in most of the positions of authority. Yeltsin himself had been a loyal party member for more than 30 years, and a member of the Politburo. His prime minister, Viktor Chernomyrdin, had been a member of the Central Committee. More broadly, there was substantial evidence that the old communist nomenklatura had lost little of its former influence. Within the early post-communist government all but one of the ministers was a former party member. Within the Yeltsin leadership as a whole, 75 per cent were former nomenklaturists; within the Russian government, 74.3 per cent; amongst Russian parliamentarians 60.2 per cent had a background in the nomenklatura; and at the regional level a massive 82.3 per cent were former nomenklaturists. Even the business elite were often (41 per cent) from the former nomenklatura. And their experience was, on average, a reasonably extended one: for the Yeltsin elite as a whole the average period in the nomenklatura had been 11.5 years, ranging from 10 years amongst the members of the President's own administration to 14.5 years among the regional elite (Kryshtanovskaya, 1995, pp. 64-5). As Gorbachev's press secretary Andrei Grachev put it, it was a sort of 'revolution of the "second secretaries", even less competent than their predecessors', they had always wanted to take power from the upper levels of the bureaucracy, and having done so went on in Orwellian fashion to call it an exercise in popular democracy (1994, p. 9).

Were democrats, more generally, in command of the political system by this time? Only 19 per cent thought so, in the summer of 1994; more than half took a different view (*Argumenty i fakty*, 1994, no. 29, p. 2). And had the defeat of the attempted coup in August 1991 seen the 'end of the communist regime'? A year later, 41 per cent agreed but 41 per cent disagreed; two years later the jury was still out, with 43 per cent in agreement that the collapse of the coup had brought about the end of communist rule but 45 per cent taking the opposite view (*Izvestiya*, 20 August 1993, p. 4). Asked to evaluate the political system in the summer of 1994, more than half rated the former communist regime positively; 13 per cent were unsure, and 36 per cent were hostile. When asked about the 'current system, with free elections·and a multiparty system', opinions were more or less reversed: 48 per cent were hostile, 35 per cent positive, and 16 per cent unsure (Rose and Haerpfer, 1994, pp. 24-7). A greater degree of freedom of speech was still widely valued, as was the closer relationship that had developed with the West; but there were more, in November 1994, who thought multiparty elections had harmed Russia than who thought they had been beneficial (33 per cent as against 29 per cent); the same was true of the right to strike (Levada, 1995, p. 10).

What about human rights more specifically? Just 22 per cent, in a Eurobarometer survey that appeared in 1994, thought they were broadly respected; more than three times as many (75 per cent) thought they were not. Former Soviet republics were consistently the most likely to believe that there had been no fundamental improvement in their human rights, with Armenians and Ukrainians being even more pessimistic than Russians (*Central and Eastern Eurobarometer*, no. 4, March 1994, Annex figure 8). All the former Soviet republics, again, were most likely to express dissatisfaction with the development of democracy in their country (15 per cent of Russians were satisfied, but 71 per cent took the opposite view). In both respects there was a sharp contrast with Central Europe, and with the Baltic states (ibid., figure 7). What about more particular freedoms, such as freedom of conscience and freedom of the press? The picture that emerged from the views of ordinary citizens was a very mixed one (see Table 7.1).

Of a list of eight freedoms, five or six were seen as greater in the summer of 1994 than they had been under communist rule, with relatively little differentiation across the generations; but there was a wide range of variation, with a much clearer belief that basic civil rights had been secured (such as the freedom to worship), than that a more effective mechanism had been developed by which citizens could control the government that spoke in their name. Indeed there was less belief that government could be influenced, and less that it treated citizens fairly, than had been the case in the years before perestroika – let alone the liberalized USSR of the last years of communist rule.

There had, in fact, been substantial support for the attempted coup in 1991. According to Gorbachev himself, speaking afterwards to

Table 7.1: Political freedoms before and after communist rule

Political freedoms	Better	Worse	Same/ Don't know
Everyone has a right to say what he thinks	67	7	15
One can join any organization one likes	67	4	29
One can travel or live anywhere one wants	41	28	31
People like me can have an influence on government	6	20	74
One need not be afraid of illegal arrest	23	15	63
Everyone can decide individually whether or not to take an interest in politics	53	4	43
Government treats everyone equally and fairly	7	32	61
Everyone has freedom of choice in religious matters	77	2	21

Source: Adapted from Rose and Haerpfer, 1994, pp. 27–9.

journalists, support ran as high as 40 per cent (*Izvestiya*, 20 September 1991, p. 3); for *Pravda* editor Afanas'ev it was as high as 70 per cent (1994, p. 99). Representative or otherwise, up to 70 per cent of the letters that were sent to the Russian Prosecutor about the arrested conspirators were in their support (*Pravda*, 26 October 1991, p. 3); and sentiments of this kind were certainly apparent in some of the letters that were sent to the Soviet press after the coup had been launched but before it had been defeated. 'May your hands be firm and your hearts pure,' wrote a Moscow pensioner. 'Force everyone to obey the Constitution, and introduce some public order.' Or as a group of automobile workers wrote to *Izvestiya*, 'We welcome order and discipline, we welcome the new leadership' (31 August 1991, p. 3).

And what kind of a victory had there been for democracy after the coup had collapsed? Perhaps there had been some sort of victory in Moscow and St Petersburg, but in Bashkiria, wrote V. Beloboky, the only difference was that prices were rising even faster; as another writer put it, the local 'totalitarian regime' had remained and even 'strengthened itself' (ibid., 21 October 1991, p. 3).

What about the ending of the USSR, and of Soviet citizenship? An overwhelming majority, in March 1991, had expressed their support for the retention of the USSR as a 'renewed federation': there was a turnout of 80 per cent, of whom 76.4 per cent voted in favour (*Izvestiya*, 28 March 1991, pp. 1, 3). An equally substantial majority, three years later, regretted the eventual dissolution of the USSR: 68 per cent thought the decision had been ill-advised (just 12 per cent approved), and for a still more substantial 76 per cent it had depressed living standards (Rose and Haerpfer, 1994, p. 41). Substantial numbers, in fact, still regarded themselves as Soviet citizens: 61 per cent did so in the summer of 1994, with varying degrees of certainty (*Moskovskaya pravda*, 20 July 1994, p. 3). Indeed, a form of federal union might have continued, even after the end of communist rule, if circumstances had been otherwise: most of the former Soviet republics had agreed, in November 1991, to establish a new Union of Sovereign States, with a single parliament and presidency, and it failed to materialize because of the Ukrainian referendum on 1 December which delivered a large majority in favour of full independence. A reformed USSR would have made little sense without its second most important member; the result was a rather looser Commonwealth of Independent States, although one that has nonetheless gradually restored some of the forms of association, particularly at the economic and military levels, that were a feature of the USSR it had replaced.

What about much broader and deeper values? There was certainly little support for a return to communist rule (23 per cent agreed largely or entirely with a reversion to the previous system, but 62 per cent were

Table 7.2: Russian value systems (1994)

Western values	Soviet values	Personal values
1. Entrepreneurship	1. Atheism	1. Fairness
2. Wealth	2. Enthusiasm	2. Personal integrity
3. Efficiency	3. Guaranteed social rights	3. Love of labour
4. Inviolability of private property	4. State rights over individual rights	4. Feeling of obligation
5. Profitabilty of labour	5. Struggle	5. Education
6. Free choice of opinions and behaviour	6. Feeling of obligation	6. Hospitality
7. Professionalism	7. Patience	7. Professionalism
8. Non-interference	8. Labour discipline	8. Equality before the law
9. Labour discipline	9. Education	9. Guaranteed social rights
10. Guarantees of political right	10. Hospitality	10. Unselfishness

Source: Argumenty I fakty, 1994, no. 24. p. 2 (March 1994 poll, n = 2468; characteristics selected from a list of 37).

opposed: Rose and Haerpfer, 1994, p. 29). But in terms of the basic orientations that underpinned such choices, there was a much greater degree of convergence between 'communist' values and those with which ordinary Russians were willing to identify themselves than with what were seen as 'Western' values. (See Table 7.2.) More generally, there was strong support for freedom, a 'unitary and invisible Russia', Christianity and glasnost; Marxism-Leninism was generally unpopular (15 per cent in favour, 37 per cent against), and so too was socialism (24 per cent in favour, 33 per cent against), but capitalism was hardly a more general preference (25 per cent were positive, 28 per cent against) (Boeva and Shironin, 1992, pp. 30-1).

Most popular of all, in nearly all surveys, was the view that Russia should develop 'according to our own traditions': a decisive majority (78 per cent) took this view in the summer of 1994, with just a small minority that thought Russia should develop along the lines of its European neighbours (Rose and Haerpfer, 1994, p. 23).

And what about the society in which they lived, about public ownership and the market? Some form of market principles had been popular in 1990 and 1991 (more than half of those who were asked favoured a rapid or more gradual transition in that direction). As the reality of a market became apparent, however, there was a steady withdrawal of support and a corresponding rise in the proportion that favoured planning (see Table 7.3).

The same impression emerges from Eurobarometer's annual studies of Russian and East European opinion. For Russians, in 1991, a market

Table 7.3: Attitudes to the market and planning, 1992–94

	1992			1993			1994
	Feb.	Mar.	Dec.	Mar.	Jun.	Oct.	Dec.
Favour the market	52	42	42	33	39	33	26
Favour planning	27	32	30	35	34	33	41
Hard to say	21	25	28	32	26	34	26

Source: Ekonomicheskie i sotsial'nye peremeny: monitoring obshchestvennogo mneniya,
1995, no. 1, p. 25.

economy was the preferred option (42 per cent as compared with 34 per cent), but by 1994 opinion had moved decisively in the other direction, with 58 per cent believing that a market economy was 'wrong for Russia' and only 29 per cent believing it was 'right' *(Central and Eastern Eurobarometer,* no. 4, March 1994, p. 32). And there was throughout a much higher level of support for a modest but assured income than for a higher but more speculative one; in line with the principles of market entrepreneurialism. In 1994, more than half those who were asked by the All-Russian Centre for the Study of Public Opinion favoured a 'modest but reliable income and certainty in the future' (54 per cent); they were more than twice as numerous as those who preferred to 'work hard and earn well but without any guarantees for the future' (23 per cent, which was down on the 27 per cent that had taken this view in 1989) (Levada, 1995, p. 9).

There had certainly been important changes in the relationship between regime and society over the late communist and post-communist period. But arguably, the crucial changes had taken place in the late communist period, including the consolidation of fundamental freedoms in all-union legislation. There had, for instance, been a scheme for the privatization of industry, approved by the Soviet parliament in July 1991 on the basis of a law on property that had been approved the previous year *(Vedomosti S'ezda narodnykh deputatov-SSSR i Verkhovnogo Soveta SSSR,* 1991, no. 32, art. 904, and ibid., 1990, no. 11, art. 164). The Soviet parliament, in its final session, agreed a 'Declaration of the rights and freedoms of the individual' that guaranteed equality before the law, freedom of speech and assembly and the right to own property and to engage in business (ibid., 1991, no. 37, art. 1083). A law on the press of June 1990 abolished censorship and established the right of individuals as well as private and state bodies to publish their views in any form (ibid., 1990, no. 26, art. 492). And there were fundamental changes in freedom of conscience, with a law of October 1990 that affirmed the right of parents to give their children a religious upbringing and of the churches themselves to take a part in public life, to found schools and universities and to issue their own publications (ibid., no. 41, art. 813). Most fundamental of all was the formal end of the Communist Party's political monopoly in March 1990 and the enactment of legislation later in the year that allowed the formation of other parties and movements (ibid., no. 42, art. 840). Russians, at this time, thought they were as 'free' as Americans (and 'freer' than American blacks) (Gibson, 1993); and more thought they were 'free' than were inclined to do so in post-communist Russia three years later (Sedov, 1994, p. 15).

A 'Transitional' Conclusion

It will be some time before we can begin to draw even preliminary conclusions about the processes of change that swept across communist Europe in the late 1980s. For some it was the end of a dream, even the end of history: 'Communism: World Tour, 1917–1989', as an inventive T-shirt described it. For others it was too soon to draw any conclusion of this kind. Were these, for a start, regimes that had anything to do with a doctrine that had conceived of a more equal society based on the self-emancipation of the working class, or with a movement that had campaigned for the vote for women, for the right to strike, for the defence of elected governments against Francoists in Spain, and for the abolition of apartheid in South Africa? Were the communist regimes of Eastern Europe not more adequately described as 'bastard socialism', by analogy with the 'bastard feudalism' of late medieval Europe: regimes that used the vocabulary of classical Marxism but were more decisively influenced by Stalin and an authoritarian, 'Asian' political tradition? And as post-communist parties sought to join the Socialist International they had once despised, was this not, more than anything, a judgement on the attempt to impose centralized forms of organization upon the workers' movement in other countries, from the '21 conditions' for affiliation to the Communist International in 1920 to the financial subventions that had sustained a small but loyal pro-Moscow following up to the 1980s?

There are certainly several lessons from the transition for a scholarly community that began life as Sovietologists and now find themselves students of comparative politics in the post-communist 1990s. The first is to acknowledge, along with Robert Daniels in the previous chapter, that there has not been a single 'transition' but a complex series of changes or indeed non-changes. Some of the communist governments of the late 1980s were overthrown by force (as in Romania); in others the regime itself initiated the process of change, and it took place through consultation (as in Hungary and Poland). In some an economically 'liberal' government took power and retained it (the Czech republic); in others the former communists largely survived (in Romania, Serbia and Slovakia); in others still the former communists were re-elected (as in Hungary, Poland, Lithuania and Bulgaria). Three states collapsed (the former USSR, the former Yugoslavia and what was formerly Czechoslovakia); one disappeared altogether (the former GDR); but the others survived. And there was little sign, at least not in 1998, that the remaining communist governments were about to fall: in Cuba, in China, in Vietnam and in Laos. Even North Korea seemed to have enough repressive resources left to withstand a famine. This was far from the universal adoption of liberal capitalism that had at first been proclaimed as the 'end of history' – a notion which was in its own way a Western version of the discredited Soviet orthodoxy that had societies moving inevitably from feudalism to capitalism and then on to socialism, but never backwards or laterally.

The process of change had in any case to be located in a longer time perspective and with a greater willingness to disaggregate the processes that were involved. In virtually all the communist-ruled nations the 'transition' took place over a lengthy period: there were contested elections from the late 1950s (in Poland), parliaments themselves became more assertive, and courts became more independent. Within the ruling parties a pattern of personalist leadership was gradually replaced by the rule of a group of oligarchs; the single ruling party lost its unity and, by the late 1980s, had become a framework for the expression and (sometimes) resolution of divergent interests, and itself one amongst a number of legal parties and movements. All of these regimes were 'communist' up to the end of the 1980s; but it was a label that had lost most of its explanatory value as it extended across a variety of regimes from the Ceausescu dictatorship in Romania, 'market Stalinism' in China, to the flourishing alternative societies of Hungary and Poland. In just the same way the 'transition' has been a varied one – not only across countries, but also across the political and social system, as programmes of privatization were launched and then suspended, as former communists returned to power, and as regional groupings like Visegrad emerged in place of the uniformity of the Warsaw Pact.

What remained as both Urban and Fish and Ron Hill point out in later chapters was what some have called 'transitology', based on an acknowledgement that the end of communist rule not only represented something less than a wholesale change of system, but that the new systems in formation had their own very special characteristics (they were not, as some have suggested, a mere recapitulation of the Latin American experience). Nor was it even clear that it could be called a 'transition', in the sense of a rapid change of state. Rather, just as Soviet systems had their own peculiar features, the post-communist ones had theirs which included weak parties, strong executives, powerful (often criminal) business elites, mass publics with very limited rights, a low sense of efficacy, a preference for economic rather than procedural forms of democracy, and a general lack of the civil society of public self-regulation that sustained liberal democracy in the capitalist West. This was the end, at least in Europe, of the monopolistic rule of Marxist-Leninist parties; but for the societies concerned it was the beginning and not the end of a new form of history, the history of post-communism. There was every sign, by the late 1990s, that it would be nasty, brutish, and rather extended.

References

Almond, G. (1970) *Political Development*. Boston: Little, Brown.

Afanas'ev, V.G. (1994) *4-ya vlast' i 4 Genseka*. Moscow: Kedr.

Berliner, J. (1994) 'The voice of American Sovietology', *NewsNet: The Newsletter of the AAASS*, vol. 34, no. 1 (January), p. 11.

Bialer, S. (1986) *The Soviet Paradox*. London: Tauris.

Boeva, I. and V. Shironin (1992) *Russians between State and Market: the generations compared*. Glasgow: Centre for the Study of Public Policy, University of Strathclyde, SPP 205.

Brzezinski, Z. (1990; first published 1989) *The Grand Failure: The birth and death of communism in the twentieth century*. New York: Collier.

Burks, R.V. (1984) 'The coming crisis in Eastern Europe', *East European Quarterly*, vol. 18, no. 1 (March), pp. 61-71.

Carnovale, M. and W.C. Potter, eds (1989) *Continuity and Change in Soviet-East European Relations*. Boulder CO: Westview.

Clarke, M., ed. (1983) *Corruption*. London: Pinter.

Cook, L.J. (1993) *The Soviet Social Contract and Why it Failed*. Cambridge MA: Harvard University Press.

Cox, M. (1994) 'The end of the USSR and the collapse of Soviet Studies', *Coexistence*, vol. 31, pp. 1-16.

Dahl, R. (1971) *Polyarchy: Participation and Opposition*. New Haven: Yale University Press.

Dallin, A. and G.W. Lapidus, eds (1991) *The Soviet System in Crisis*. Boulder CO: Westview.

Deutscher, I. (1967) The *Unfinished Revolution: Russia 1917-1967*. Oxford: Oxford University Press.

Dobrokhotov, L.N. *et al.* (1992) *Krasnoe ili beloe? Drama avgusta-91*. Moscow: Terra.

Drewnowski, J., ed. (1982) *Crisis in the East European Economies*. London: Croom Helm.

Gibson, J.L. (1993) 'Perceived political freedom in the Soviet Union', *Journal of Politics*, vol. 55, no. 4 (November), pp. 936-74.

Goldman, M. (1983) *The USSR in Crisis*. New York: Norton.

Grachev, A. (1994) *Dallshe bez menya: Ukhod Prezidenta*. Moscow: Progress-Kulltura.

Hankiss, E. (1990) *East European Alternatives*. Oxford: Clarendon Press.

Hedlund, S. (1984) *Crisis in Soviet Agriculture*. New York: St Martin's.

Huntington, S. (1984) 'Will more countries become democratic?', *Political Science Quarterly*, vol. 99, no. 2 (Summer), pp. 193-218.

Itogi (1992) *Itogi Vsesoyuznoi perepisi naseleniya 1989 goda*. Tom II, chast' 1. Minneapolis: EastView.

Johnson, C., ed. (1970) *Change in Communist Systems*. Stanford CA: Stanford University Press.

Komarov, B. (1980) *The Destruction of Nature in the Soviet Union*. London: Pluto.

Kryshtanovskaya, O. (1995) 'Transformatsiya staroi nomenklatury v novuyu rossiiskuyu elitu, *Obshchestvennye nauki i sovremennost'*, no. 1, pp. 51–65.

Levada, Y. (1995) ' "Chelo'vek sovetskii" pyat' let spustya', *Ekonomicheskie i sotsial'nye peremeny: monitoring obshchestvennogo mneniya*, no. 1, pp. 9–14.

Lewin, M. (1988) *The Gorbachev Phenomenon*. London: Radius.

Matthews, M. (1978) *Privilege in the Soviet Union*. London: Allen & Unwin.

—(1986) *Poverty in the Soviet Union*. Cambridge: Cambridge University Press.

Parry, A. (1966) *The New Class Divided: Science and Technology versus Communism*. New York: Macmillan.

Parsons, T. (1964a) 'Evolutionary Universals', *American Sociological Review*, vol. 39, no. 3.

—(1964b) 'Communism and the West: The Sociology of the Conflict', in A. and E. Etzioni, *Social Change: Sources, Patterns and Consequences*. New York: Basic Books.

Pipes, R. (1984) 'Can the Soviet Union reform?', *Foreign Affairs*, vol. 63 (Fall), pp. 47–61.

Pye, L. (1990) 'Political science and the crisis of authoritarianism', *American Political Science Review*, vol. 84, no. 1 (March), pp. 3–19.

Rose, R. and C. Haerpfer (1994) *New Russia Barometer III: The Results*. Glasgow: Centre for the Study of Public Policy, University of Strathclyde, SPP 228.

Sedov, L.A. (1994) 'Mezhdu putchem i vyborami', *Ekonomicheskie i sotsial'nye peremeny: monitoring obshchestvennogo mneniya*, no. 1, pp. 14–15.

Simis, K. (1982) *Secrets of a Corrupt Society*. London: Dent.

Tucker, R.C. (1981–2) 'Swollen state, spent society: Stalin's legacy to Brezhnev's Russia', *Foreign Affairs*, vol. 60, no. 2 (Winter), pp. 414–35.

White, S. (1978) 'Communist systems and the "iron law of pluralism" ', *British Journal of Political Science*, vol. 8, no. 1 (January), pp. 101–17.

—(1990) *Gorbachev in Power*. Cambridge: Cambridge University Press.

8

Social Theory, the Collapse of State Socialism and After: Convergence or Divergence?

DAVID LANE

Introduction

Compared to the advanced capitalist countries of the West, the ideological, historical and structural features of the state socialist systems led all serious students to classify them as a different type of modern society. The major organizing principles on which these differences hinged may be summarized in terms of eight dimensions: property ownership, goals, efficiency, effectiveness, solidarity, rule application, integration and gratification. (See Table 8.1.)

Capitalism, as an ideal type, was (and still is) based on private ownership, commodity exchange and the hegemony of a ruling class. Communism, as a social system, as defined by Soviet Marxists, was determinant on changes in the relations and means of production conjoined with the political hegemony of the Communist Party. These alternative organizing principles (value systems, forms of organization and ways of doing things) were not disputed as defining characteristics of capitalism and state socialism respectively. Political debate ranged over their efficacy, moral justification and their trajectory of change.

Table 8.1: Organizing principles of capitalism and state socialism

Resource	Capitalism	Socialism
Property	Private	Public/state
Goals	Freedom	Equality
Efficiency	Market	Planning
Effectiveness	Democratic	Central control
Solidarity	Pluralist	Collectivist
Rule application	Law	Politics
Integration	Private	Public
Gratification	Leisure	Labour

On the basis of these characteristic features, advocates of the distinctiveness of capitalism and socialism constructed their morally superior positions. 'Totalitarianism', in emphasizing the monistic 'command' political system, condemned the subjugation of mankind to the modern state. Soviet Marxism on the other hand emphasized its superiority as a social model of development under the class leadership of the Communist Party. For quite different reasons both these approaches denied that systemic changes could be internally generated. Under totalitarianism the powers of the ruling elites were so great and the people so massified that movements for reform or revolution could not develop (see Bauman 1991). Likewise, for the supporters of Soviet Marxism, the class structure of socialism was such that internal contradictions were precluded because of the absence of an ascendant class with its own distinctive roots in the ownership of the means of production. Reproduction took place with little systemic changes. The relationship between state and society was one of cohesion, durability and stability.

Whatever their theoretical merit, the notion of totalitarianism and its mirror image, Soviet Marxism, at least had the virtues for the dominant classes in both systems of legitimating their own rule. They were also useful political devices and could be used (and were) to portray the enemy in a particular way during the Cold War. Yet neither are of much use in helping us explain the upheavals which convulsed the Soviet Union in the late 1980s and early 1990s. Indeed, in his chapter to this book and elsewhere (1994) Michael Cox argues that the way knowledge was structured in the West almost made it impossible for scholars in general to understand the underlying flaws of state socialist systems. As a result, those organized in the particular discipline of Soviet Studies were unable to anticipate the fall of the Soviet Union. This chapter looks at the problem from a different perspective and concludes that an important school of sociologists did in fact analyse the systemic imbalances under state socialism: they claimed that to function efficiently and effectively all modern societies had to adopt similar essential processes. This view was by no means accepted by mainstream sociology, and in Soviet Studies itself had few followers. Indeed, the idea was openly rejected by those who held to the view that the USSR was a *sui generis*, totalitarian system. The collapse of state socialism clearly calls for a re-examination of both standpoints. In other chapters the totalitarian model is discussed at some length, so here I will concentrate primarily on what I see as the value of a Parsonsian approach to the study of the Soviet system and its contradictions. I will also examine the post-communist system in Russia within the same framework and suggest that a neo-liberal developmental strategy might not be the only, let alone the best, form of the 'transition'. The components of an alternative strategy are then briefly discussed.

Industrial Society

It is pertinent to recall that following the Second World War some of the most influential sociologists believed that what I have called the 'organizing principles' of state socialism could not be sustained. It was denied that public property, collective welfare and equality, a dominant public sphere, planning and comprehensive collective control could sustain the development of the productive forces. It was held further that the socialist 'alternative' would most likely lead to the collapse of the system and its subsequent transition to the superior economic form to be found in the Western capitalist countries. Rather more charitably, many writers wrote in ideologically neutral terms referring to 'advanced industrial society' and the notion of 'convergence', though in practice the theories entailed a one-way convergence to capitalism, or 'democratic pluralism'.

Pitrim Sorokin in 1944 stressed the similarity of psychological, cultural and social values between the USA and the USSR (Sorokin 1944: 6) and, in 1949, Talcott Parsons described 'capitalist and socialist industrialisms … as variants of a single fundamental type' (Parsons 1964a: 333). He described the Soviet Union as a 'counterpoint' of the capitalist West, as a 'specification' of the more general pattern of 'instrumental activism' (Parsons 1971, Chapter 7). Parsons was joined by Clark Kerr (Kerr 1962) who postulated the theory of an 'industrial society', the common features of which were later discussed by Parsons in his 'Characteristics of Industrial Societies' (Parsons 1960). The conclusions of both writers were of course grounded – albeit implicitly – in the Durkheimian theory of structural differentiation. This argued that 'evolving adaptive capacity' led to the formation of complex forms of organization requiring market exchange and the division of labour. Structural differentiation also involved the development of organic solidarity, stratification and social pluralism. Over time, the 'inclusion' of units would have to give rise to democratic forms of government which ensured solidarity. The development of the productive forces (the process of 'adaptation') was dependent on adjustments in the value (belief), political and social systems. A consequence of the increasing division of labour was the necessary development of pluralism. Economic inequality was a necessary incentive to promote growth and economic efficiency, and without it, societies would stagnate.

Such writers, who were largely but not exclusively American, believed that the evolution of world history led to societies of an 'industrial type'. Whilst Parsons' theory is widely dismissed as a paradigm of 'stasis', this view is incorrect as it ignores the evolutionary perspective in his writing. (See Parsons 1966c: 4, where he points out that if certain structural conditions are not met, then 'regression' occurs, one example being the fall of the

Roman Empire.) Evolution would lead to developing countries copying the structural and functional features of American society. As Parsons put it: 'The United States' new type of societal community, more than any other single factor, justifies our assigning it the lead in the latest phase of modernization ... American society has gone farther than any comparable large-scale society in its dissociation from the older ascriptive inequalities and the institution-alization of a basically egalitarian pattern.' (Parsons 1971: 114)

Moreover, the United States as the most advanced society would become a model for the rest of the world. Parsons's theory clearly implied that the possibilities for the creation of an essentially different kind of advanced society - such as communism or totalitarianism - was limited. The 'totalitarian' character of the USSR was not, he claimed, compatible with an effective industrial type system. One of the most important consequences of advanced social and political differentiation, he believed, derived from the advanced division of labour which over time would lead to the destruction of totalitarianism. 'It can ... be definitely said that the further this differentiation of the social structure proceeds, the more difficult it becomes to press it into the mould of a rigid line of authority from the top down' (Parsons 1964b: 397-8). The political hegemony of the state was essentially a systemic variable of the communist societies which would have to be modified for a modern society to work efficiently and effectively.

Taking Parsons as the point of theoretical departure, the present author pointed out some time ago that the development of state socialist societies would lead to increases in levels of structural differentiation and to 'exchange between the various subsystems [becoming] more reciprocated' (Lane 1976: 70). Without such changes, evolution would not occur and society would not develop: it would stagnate or decline. Parsons in a prescient passage anticipated that the communist societies would 'either make adjustments in the direction of electoral democracy and a plural party system or "regress" into generally less advanced and politically less effective forms of organization' (Parsons 1964c: 356). Such views were echoed by many other writers, particularly Daniel Bell and John Kenneth Galbraith. Bell (1961) in an influential work, cogently argued that the Marxist conception of a new classless order would, inevitably, be replaced by the striving for individual advancement and status differentiation. Politics would become a matter of administering industrial society, reconciling group interests and managing tensions, rather than the expression of class struggle or ideological preferences. Bell was unique in applying this concept to state socialism (Bell 1966). Galbraith took a dual convergence approach, anticipating the growth of enterprise autonomy under both capitalism and socialism. The independence of business undertakings from the bureaucracy he saw as being analogous to the 'exclusion of the capitalist from effective power' in

Western firms (Galbraith 1967: 390). Ownership of the means of production vested in the state had to be split from control of the means of production. Galbraith doubted whether the market exchange characteristic of capitalism could continue to be effective and he believed that the state as a co-ordinator would become a more important characteristic of capitalism and socialism. Galbraith correctly foresaw that under state socialism the party activist would follow the shareholder in relinquishing direct control of the industrial enterprise.

The conclusion to be drawn here is that a sophisticated theory of state socialism existed in the sociological literature, moreover this pointed to the systemic incompatibilities of centralized control and structural inadequacies under state socialism. Writers such as Jerry Hough (see particularly Hough 1977) and myself argued that inside state socialism was a pluralistic social system trying to get out. We never asserted that these societies were 'pluralistic' in a Western liberal-democratic sense, as some critics have wrongly asserted. Rather, it was suggested that Soviet political institutions would in time be forced to react and respond to societal forces. My own view was to analyse state socialism in terms of Parsons's four-functional paradigm, suitably adapted to include classes and property relationships (Lane 1981). These views, however, remained a minority position amongst specialists on communist states where state socialism was regarded as a distinct 'totalitarian' type of modern society.

British Sociology

Unlike American writing of the 1960s – which had been deeply influenced by the writing of Talcott Parsons – the dominant trend in British sociological thought was to insist on the diversity of types of industrial societies. The nomothetic explanation of Parsons was to some extent replaced in Britain by emphasis on the idiographic features of modern societies.

It was Alex Inkeles more than Parsons who inspired the dominant school of British sociology. While he analysed Soviet society in terms of 'industrial society', he concluded that the industrial order was compatible either with 'democratic or totalitarian political forms' (see Inkeles and Bauer 1959: 390; Inkeles 1969: 431). John Goldthorpe (1966) in an influential article 'Social Stratification in Industrial Society', originally delivered at the 1964 Annual Conference of the British Sociological Association, insisted that social stratification and economic order may be subject to 'political regulation'. Thus industrialism could assume a totalitarian form. As he noted:

> The experience of Soviet society can be taken as indicating that the structural and functional imperatives of an industrial order are not so stringent as to prevent quite wide variations in patterns of social stratification, nor to prohibit

the systematic manipulation of social inequalities by a regime commanding modern administrative resources and under no constraints from an organized opposition or rule of law (Goldthorpe 1966: 657–8).

Goldthorpe, basing his views on empirical data derived from specialists working in the field of Soviet Studies, generalized his position by arguing against common features of differentiation, consistency and mobility in industrial societies. He also argued against the Parsons/Kerr idea that Soviet-type societies should be placed on a 'lower' level than the United States.

Another influential 'British' voice at the time was that of Anthony Giddens. Like Goldthorpe, Giddens also recognized that capitalism and state socialism could be interpreted as encapsulating 'alternative frameworks' for the development of the 'industrializing process'. His words are indicative of the political outlook in Britain of the 1970s. He wrote then that, 'state socialist societies ... have genuinely succeeded in moving towards a classless order, but only at the cost of creating a system of political domination rather than in any sense diminishing it' (Giddens 1973: 294). In Giddens's view, divergence lay in the institutional structure. Capitalism ensured division between the economy and the polity. This separated out conflicts between labour and capital which were restricted to struggles of an economistic type. Under state socialism, however, the fusion of economy and polity made the system more unstable. Economistic demands had no boundaries and labour, in seeking economic improvements, challenged the whole system. Rather than stability, as in the totalitarian paradigm, Giddens detected an institutional precariousness (Giddens 1973). Another sociologist working in Britain, Frank Parkin also detected the existence of contradiction under socialism. However, for Parkin the main area of conflict was between knowledge and power. Parkin focused in particular on the emerging role of an 'ascendant class' and concluded that the central fault line in the USSR and Eastern Europe was between the intelligentsia and the ruling bureaucratic class (Parkin 1972).

The Parsonsian Framework

These debates all contributed to our understanding of the tensions and incompatibilities within the state socialist societies which culminated in the policies of reform in the 1980s and the final collapse of the system in 1991. If nothing else, the Parsonsian paradigm did at least point to some of the necessary conditions for a modern society to operate effectively and efficiently. However, as the Parsonsian system is not common currency amongst sociologists and political scientists today, a more detailed explanation of his analysis of society might be useful at this point.

According to Parsons, any advanced society can be broken down into four subsystems: the maintenance of institutionalized cultural patterns (socialization); the societal community (the integrative aspects), the polity, and the economy. These are indicated in Figure 8.2 as L - The pattern-maintenance subsystem; I - the integrative subsystem; G - Goal attainment subsystem (the polity); and A - the adaptive subsystem (the economy). Any society to survive and reproduce itself must thus address all four issues:

1. Pattern maintenance and tension management: the process by which the culture of a society is internalized by individuals through their socialization.
2. Integration: the maintenance of the wholeness of the system, social control is the major mechanism here.
3. Goal attainment: the co-operative effort required to fulfil certain general objectives for the society; the polity is the primary focus with responsibility for this function.
4. Adaptation to the external environment, with role differentiation and the division of labour.

These structures and functions do not occur in isolation, but in terms of complex interchanges. The process of the polity, for example, has to be congruent with those of the economy whilst the value system must be compatible with both. The exchanges between these subsystems give rise to six different subsystems: the loyalty solidarity commitment system (the L-I exchange); the legitimation system (L-G exchange); the labour consumption market system (the L-A exchange); the allocative standard system (I-A); the political support system (G-I); and the resource mobilization system (A-G) (see Figure 8.2).

It is not appropriate here to detail the way in which transactions occur in these interchanges (see Rocher 1974: 63-7). However, to illustrate the point. The exchange between economy and polity is the resource mobilization system: the economy is concerned with the control of productive resources, the polity performs the important role of creating the conditions of the opportunity for effectiveness. The economy in turn provides services (such as employment) in exchange for effort. Money (not shown in Figure 8.2) is a particularly important medium of exchange in the control of productivity, in the allocation of resources, in the determination of wage income, in the assertion of personal claims over resources, and in the ranking of claims over resources.

No single unit monopolizes the exchange transactions constituting the functional subsystems and in practice no society works perfectly to enable the reciprocal exchanges to take place. Inflation and deflation may occur in the economic system of exchange, for example (Parsons 1951: 19). In an evolutionary sense, however, if certain conditions are not met then

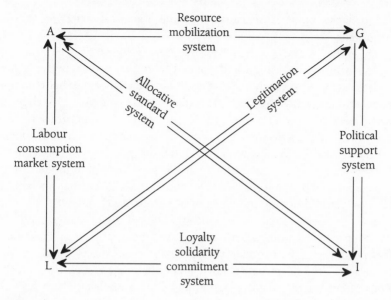

Figure 8.2
A Adaptive subsystem (the economy)
G Goal-attainment subsystem (the polity)
I Integrative subsystem (law [as norms] and social controls)
L Pattern-maintenance subsystem (locus of cultural and motivational commitments)
(Based on: Talcott Parsons, 'On the concept of political power', reprinted in R. Bendix and S.M. Lipset, *Class, Status and Power*, London: Routledge, 1968: 262)

'regression' occurs (Parsons 1959: 19). This is the critical point. Thus there will be dislocation if ideology does not provide a legitimating cement – or if the economy is unable to provide the requisite goods and services in return for labour input. A collapse of a mode of production is most likely to occur when there are multiple exchange problems. Parsons in fact made it clear that social change results 'from the operation of plural factors, all of which are mutually independent ... *no* claim that social change is 'determined' by economic interests, ideas, personalities of particular individuals, geographical conditions and so on, is acceptable. ... Any factor is always interdependent with several others' (Parsons, 1966: 113). For a society to reproduce itself there must be reciprocity of exchange between all four societal subsystems.

Gorbachev and State Socialism

If we accept that Parsonsian sociology is a paradigm of change and not stasis, what then are the implications of this approach for our understanding both of the collapse of state socialism and the transition since the USSR disintegrated?

In an earlier book, I mentioned the imperfections of the forms of exchange in the Soviet Union and pointed to several problems facing the Soviet leadership. These included: the undeveloped relationship between the economy and the polity; the inadequacy of money as a medium of exchange; the deficiency of ideology; the lack of commitment to production; the problem of ranking claims by reference to ideology; administrative definition of priorities; and finally and more generally, the problem of legitimation. Whilst the 'energy' of the political system was predominant in modernizing society under Stalin, the 're-equilibration of society' (in Parsonsian terms) which took place under his successors was only partial (Lane 1981: 127). It was for Gorbachev to spell out the incongruities of the exchanges and try and develop a new synthesis. This at heart was the meaning of perestroika.

The meaning of perestroika was perhaps most clearly outlined by Gorbachev in 1986. Here he provided a critique of state socialism and its methods of bureaucratic control, and outlined inadequacies in the nature of the economic and political systems.

Gorbachev pointed to four major contradictions which might have been taken from Parsons himself: first between the way work was organized and carried out and what was needed to operate a modern economy; second between the form of ownership under socialism and the ways that management and control were performed; third between the goods that were produced and the money that was available to distribute them to consumers; and finally between the centralization of the economy and the need to give economic units independence to organize things efficiently. As Gorbachev pointed out at the time, there was a basic 'lack of correspondence between the productive forces and productive relations, between socialist property and the economic forces of its implementation, in the relations between goods and money and in the combination of centralization and independence of economic organizations' (speech to Party Congress, February 1986. See further discussion, Lane 1992). In essence, his analysis hinged around what Parsons would have termed the adaptive subsystem.

The doubts about the viability of the Soviet system raised by both different social theorists and Parsonsian system analysts were thus echoed by the leader of the world's leading communist state. For instance, Gorbachev seemed to accept a systemic explanation of stagnation similar in character to that earlier advanced by Parsons. He also adopted implicitly the stance of the industrial society theorists with their emphasis on the market, competition, and pluralism in political exchange. However, he still conceived of economic reforms occurring within a reformed structure of state socialism and under the hegemonic leadership of the Communist Party.

In this he was not only politically naïve, but actually managed to ignore the logic of his position which should have led him to adopt a more radical perspective; one which accepted that markets have their own inimitable logic and of necessity have to operate relatively autonomously. In the last analysis, there was a contradiction between the operation of a central plan (as under state socialism) and the market – one which Gorbachev either could not or would not recognize.

But Gorbachev was a critical figure in the move from one order to the next. After all, prior to 1985, reformers so-called had tried to reform the economy without contemplating any significant political and ideological change. But as history showed, it proved impossible to reform the economy without also implementing major changes in the political system as well. However, by changing the political system – as Gorbachev and others started to – one was bound to weaken the structure as a whole by encouraging the growth of markets and weakening the system of command planning. In turn, changes in the economy had ramifications for the value and belief system, in the mechanisms for integration (law) and motivational commitments, and the ways in which the polity was organized and processed inputs. In this way, the Soviet Union and the other Eastern European countries gradually and then more rapidly moved from the fusion of politics and economics to a more pluralistic structure. This involved (in terms of our original Figure 8.2) the collapse of the dominant ideology (Marxism-Leninism) (L) leading to a crisis of legitimation (the G–L exchange); a destruction in the confidence of the leadership and an undermining of the norms of state socialism (I–L exchange); and a collapse in the political support system (G–I).

Whither the Transition to Capitalism?

The implosion of Soviet socialism is clearly important for sociologists, if for no other reason than that it may indicate the limitations inherent in any attempt to restructure 'industrial society'. One school discussed at the beginning of this chapter had indeed long argued that communist systems, by definition, could not be efficient and democratic. According to Brzezinski, economic efficiency needs competition, competition requires markets, and this requires private ownership (1989). From this standpoint, perestroika defeated communism (see Z (1990: 195-344) and Schopflin (1990: 3-16)). Put another way: to modernize the economy, a market was required; the market calls for political pluralism. This in turn entails democracy because real pluralism means the autonomy of political organization in general and competition between political parties in particular. Thus the market leads to a representative-type democracy with interest groups and competing parties.

But is there any alternative to the ways of organizing society other than through capitalism?

The neo-liberal leadership, which has come to power in a number of the former communist states (including the Russian state), appear to have found the appeal of the liberal-democratic model, as advocated, for example, by Brzezinski, overwhelming. But in copying the neo-liberal processes of Western advanced capitalist countries, the leadership of the successor states has also exacerbated internal conflicts and tensions. Problems of exchange – between values, social integration, the role of the polity, the nature of motivational commitments – have once again come to the fore. It is not enough to destroy state socialism. An effective replacement has to be created. The question is, then, has the post-Gorbachev leadership managed to create such a replacement? There are some real doubts about this in Russia.

To all intents and purposes, the shifts which have taken place in policy under the new leadership have redistributed resources in such a way that many find they can no longer afford essentials. The working class in particular has been affected adversely by the greater role being played by private traders, price rises and an increase in (and the threat of) unemployment. The elderly, the poorly educated, the low-wage earners, women and the pensioners have perhaps been hit even harder by the changes brought about in the 1990s. In effect, the social costs of the 'transition' have been borne by those groups least able to defend themselves. Moreover, whilst poverty has risen and inequality increased, over the past few years a new class of 'new Russians' has been formed which in no way appears to be justified or legitimated by the requirements of the economy. Inevitably, these developments have created new forms of tension which have helped undermine loyalty, solidarity and commitment (see McAuley and Manning, in Lane (ed.): 1995). What the radical reformers seem to forget is although individualistic possessive individualism is a motivational commitment socialized in the USA, it is not a widespread part of the cultural commitments of the peoples socialized in Russia – either before or after 1917.

Conclusion – Towards a New Socialism?

The model of state socialism inherited from Stalin has to be viewed in the context of the history and culture of Russia and the USSR. This contained ingredients which were imported from the socialist ideologies then current – in particular a marked attachment to the central role of the state. This statist vision was in turn wedded to a specific view of the party as a political instrument to grasp and maintain power in one of the most backward countries in Europe. It is not surprising that in this context a centralized form of revolutionary power arose. After the Revolution, as a mobilizing strategy of development, state socialism was rather effective. This, of course, explains its past appeal to many countries in the Third World. The ideology of Marxism-Leninism was also a useful ideological tool in countries wishing to overcome backwardness and inertia conditioned by underdevelopment. The Party effectively promoted economic growth and social solidarity secured through mass literacy, full employment and rudimentary but comprehensive forms of education and social welfare.

This not unsuccessful model has now collapsed to be replaced by something very different. As we have argued, this has hardly worked to the socioeconomic advantage of the peoples of Russia. However, the fall of state socialism has also created difficulties for socialists – and if socialism is to be a movement and not just a counterculture, it must have an effective political praxis to guide political action. Socialism as a type of society must not only ensure rapid economic development through a state-led political system, it also has to secure equality and an absence of exploitation concurrent with economic efficiency. A socialist policy, moreover, not only has to be concerned with group rights (the rights of classes) but also with individual ones. Socialist theory also has to consider bureaucratic and professional power as well as class power. It has, in addition, to take account of different forms of identity: national, ethnic, generational and gender. A sociology of socialism also has to create a new synthesis between solidarity, power and efficiency. In the last analysis, the challenge of socialism, not only in the post-state socialist societies but also in the West, is a sociological challenge: of how to combine socialist ideals – collective, egalitarian, reciprocated relationships – with economic efficiency and effective management and political action. This is an agenda requiring what C. Wright Mills would have termed a 'sociological imagination'.

The Parsonsian model, as I have outlined it here, allows one to make some policy recommendations about the future course of development. It can also be used creatively as the basis for a critique of neo-liberalism. The model after all stresses the interdependence and the necessity of reciprocated exchange between subsystems of society. The driving force of Western advisers in the post-communist societies, however, has been to adopt a market-led strategy based upon the privatization of collective state assets. But even if one could overcome the practical problems of privatizing state industry, there seems to be no particular reason why we need a specific class of private owners. It is doubtful whether the distribution of shares in former state industries in the post-communist societies would create a class in support of the new political order (see Nelson and Kuzes and Clarke and Kabalina in Lane 1985). It would be preferable, surely, to 'privatize' the management of state enterprises, rather than the property assets themselves.

It has been argued here that Gorbachev's reform strategy did not think through the implications of changes in the economy to other societal complexes. A similar charge could be levelled against the current neo-liberal reformers who have neglected the cultural system with its historically determined locus of motivational commitments. The loyalty-solidarity-commitment system could readily be enhanced in the future through support for collective norms inherited from the previous system. The current system of legitimation is almost exclusively regarded in the West as being dependent on the political 'market' of voting and electoral choice. However, other features are also necessary in a society which has been a major world power. The inclusion into the world economy of post-communist societies since 1989 has been one of 'dependent modernization': dependent culturally on the mass values of the West, politically dependent on the powers of the major world states, and economically dependent on the economic strength of the USA and Germany. Whilst the neo-liberal leaders in these states initially approved of this strategy, it has not met with universal approval from the ordinary Russian people – many of whom have turned in frustration to indigenous oppositional movements. An alternative policy is thus required which would involve a greater welfare state role, a slower move to the market, the development of socialist entrepreneurs using leased property under state ownership and a political and cultural policy closely linked to established motivational commitments – such as universal welfare, comprehensive education and full employment. To answer the question asked at the beginning of this chapter: divergence or convergence? The question is wrongly put: there is both convergence and divergence. The crucial feature for the development of modern societies is reciprocated exchange which may take very many forms.

References

Bauman, Z. 'Social Dissent in East European Politics'. *European Journal of Sociology*. Vol. 12. 1971: 25–51.

Bell, D. *The End of Ideology: On the Exhaustion of Political Ideas in the 1950s*. New York: Collier Books, 1961.

——'The End of Ideology in the Soviet Union', in M. Drachkovich (ed.), *The Appeals and Paradoxes of Contemporary Communism*. New York: Praeger, 1966.

Brzezinski, Z. *The Grand Failure: The Birth and Death of Communism in the Twentieth Century*. London: Macdonald, 1989.

Cox, M. 'The End of the USSR and the Collapse of Soviet Studies'. *Coexistence*, Vol. 31, (1994) 1–16.

Galbraith, J.K. *The New-Industrial State*. London: Hamish Hamilton, 1967.

Giddens, A. *The Class Structure of the Advanced Societies*. London: Hutchinson, 1973.

Goldthorpe, J. 'Social Stratification in Industrial Society', in R. Bendix and S.M. Lipset, *Class, Status and Power*. London: Routledge, 1966.

Hough, J.F. *The Soviet Union and Social Science Theory.* Cambridge, Mass., Harvard University Press, 1977.

Kerr, C. *Industrialism and Industrial Man.* London, Heinemann, 1962.

Inkeles, A. 'Models and Issues in the Analysis of Soviet Society', in A. Inkeles (ed.), *Social Change in Soviet Russia.* New York: Simon & Schuster, 1969.

—and R.A. Bauer, *The Soviet Citizen.* Cambridge, Mass.: Harvard University Press, 1959.

Lane, D. *The Socialist Industrial State.* London: Allen & Unwin, 1976.

—*Leninism: A Sociological Interpretation.* Cambridge: Cambridge University Press, 1981.

—*Soviet Society under Perestroika.* London: Routledge, 1992.

—(ed.). *Russia in Transition.* London: Longman, 1995.

Parkin, F. 'System Contradiction and Political Transformation', *European Journal of Sociology,* Vol. 13. 1972.

Parsons, T. *The Social System,* Glencoe, Ill.: The Free Press, 1951.

—'General Theory in Sociology', in R.K. Merton *et al., Sociology Today,* Vol. 1, New York: Free Press, 1959.

—'Characteristics of Industrial Societies', in *Structure and Process in Modern Societies,* Glencoe, Ill: The Free Press, 1960.

—'Social Classes and Class Conflict in the Light of Recent Sociological Theory', in *Essays in Sociological Theory.* New York: Collier Macmillan, 1964a.

—'Communism and the West: The Sociology of the Conflict', in A. and E. Etzioni, *Social Change: Sources, Patterns and Consequences.* New York: Basic Books, 1964b.

—'Evolutionary Universals', *American Sociological Review,* Vol. 39, no. 3, June, 1964c.

—*Societies: Evolutionary and Comparative Perspectives.* Englewood Cliffs, NJ: Prentice Hall, 1966.

—*The System of Modern Societies.* Englewood Cliffs, NJ: Prentice-Hall, 1971.

Rocher, G. *Talcott Parsons and American Sociology.* London: Nelson, 1974.

Schopflin, G. 'The End of Communism in Eastern Europe', *International Affairs,* Vol. 66, no. 1, 1990: 3–16.

Sorokin, P.A. *Russia and the West.* New York: Dutton, 1944.

Z, 'To the Stalin Mausoleum', *Daedalus,* Vol. 119, no. 1, 1990.

9

Does Post-Sovietology have a Future?

MICHAEL URBAN AND M. STEVEN FISH

The 'Autumn of the People' of 1989 was a dismal failure of the predictive power of political science.

Adam Przeworski (1991)

Introduction

Political science is all about prediction. Whilst most studies may not attempt to forecast events, the canon of social science inserts prediction into the very structure of our methods and the knowledge that they yield. This much is evident in the conventions of hypothesis testing or of determining the values assumed by 'dependent variables' on the basis of 'independent' ones. In either instance, information from the past is placed in a frame wherein it is assigned the task of confirming/disconfirming statements (hypotheses) that are constructed so as to predict the results of a test based on some collection of facts. The method, then, implies that we are 'predicting' on the basis of theories, models, hypotheses, and data – that which (usually) has already occurred.

Of course, much work in political science does not explicitly conform to the scheme of hypothesis testing. It nonetheless remains within the field because the knowledge that it produces becomes the common property of the field itself, educating political scientists about politics, suggesting ways of thinking about their domain, contributing theoretical concepts, posing problems to be analysed, and often supplying propositions that can be treated as hypotheses and submitted to empirical tests. As a collective endeavour, political science thus draws both its versions of poetry (theory) and prose (narration-description) into the scope of its predictive logic. Finally, since political science is a social enterprise, forecasting events in the world is also part of it. People expect political scientists to know something about politics that will help them answer perennial questions: What next? Where is this leading? What should we be concerned about in the future? Political scientists, being ordinary people, often have the same questions in mind. In any event, political scientists rarely dismiss invitations to discuss the future as being irrelevant to their professional self-concept.

For political scientists working in Sovietology, the collapse of the USSR represented a colossal failure. Even following the East European revolutions, Sovietologists continued to imagine the Soviet system as a permanent, or at least a long-term, prospect. Indeed, by autumn 1989, many had just come around to the notion that some important changes were under way in the USSR. The point here is neither to accuse, nor to excuse Sovietologists for failing to foresee the collapse of the Soviet Union. Rather, it is to call attention to Sovietology's preoccupation with that which at the time was already the remnants of the Soviet regime, to the neglect of those political forces that had recently sprung to life and that would shortly bring down that regime. As the Russian 'revolution' was gathering speed in 1990, Sovietologists fretted about Mikhail Gorbachev's ability to defend his reforms from conservative forces in the Communist Party. When Russia, under the leadership of the nation's most popular politician, was turning itself into a sovereign state, the attention of Sovietologists remained fixed on the latest Communist Party of the Soviet Union (CPSU) Congress, which was deemed important simply because it was a CPSU Congress. This preoccupation with the leadership - itself a hallmark of Sovietology - ultimately debilitated political analysis. In some respects it trained us to ignore real politics altogether.

If there is a future for post-Sovietology, it would appear to require taking stock of our past. Where and why did we fail?

Retrospect and Prospect

For the past century, Russia has served as one of the great proving grounds for the central conflicting ideas and ideologies of our age. This historical circumstance, so much more than the allure of Russian culture or the threat posed by Russia's possession of weapons of mass destruction, explains why the country has occupied a larger place in Western imaginations than have other major countries such as India, Brazil, Japan, or Indonesia. Russia was, after all, the motherland of Leninism, the most compelling, coherent, and (despite its brutality and spectacular demise) successful challenge witnessed in our century to the ideological hegemony of liberalism and the geopolitical predominance of the United States and Western Europe.

Because Leninism's global claims involved us, we were involved. Scholarly detachment was thus the first casualty of the Cold War. As Mary McAuley once noted with respect to the first generation of students of Soviet Russia, no one could remain neutral when writing about Soviet politics. This has remained true ever since (McAuley, 1977, p. 15). But our loss of detachment was due not only to the external challenge presented by Leninism. It was also tied to conditions in our own societies. It is important to remember that Sovietology was born at a time when the difference between dissent and disloyalty was erased from American public discourse, a time when people suspected of communist associations or communist sympathies were purged from government, cultural institutions, trade unions and universities in the United States. But Sovietology was not merely coextensive in origin and thus subject to the domestic chill of the Cold War. The actual process of waging the Cold War constructed it (White, 1975; Cox, 1986).

One may begin by considering the role played by Sovietology's first reigning paradigm, the totalitarian model (Friedrich and Brzezinski, 1965). To be sure, this model was not the only version of 'totalitarian' theory available at the time, but its particular construction made it especially serviceable to Cold War Sovietology. Although cast as a contribution to comparative political science, the model was highly limited in range and intellectual depth, consisting merely of a checklist of the system's constituent features (terror, personality cult, and so on). The illocutionary interests embedded in the model become clear when we consider that a parallel conception – one more rigorously formulated and intellectually challenging – had been worked out by members of the Frankfurt school (Horkheimer, 1947; Marcuse, 1964). This, however, was ignored by most Sovietologists of the time, just as the sophisticated totalitarian theory of the Budapest school (Feher, Heller, and Markus, 1983) would be overlooked a generation later. The point of Sovietology's attachment to a particular concept of totalitarianism was less to compare different sociopolitical systems than to *distinguish* the Soviet system from Western democracies. Its black-and-white categories implied that the forms of domination evident in 'their' system counted as domination, whilst the absence of those same forms indicated the existence of a free society in 'ours' (Brzezinski and Huntington, 1964). The only real comparison of interest to this school of thought was the parallel drawn between Stalin's (and, later, Khrushchev's) Russia and Hitler's Germany. This was a comparison effective in marshalling a Cold War consensus against a little known and poorly understood system by associating it with a very different one whose infamy was incontestable.

With Sovietology thus isolated from the field of comparative politics by the hermetic category of totalitarianism, it fell to the 'revisionists' or 'pluralists' in the 1960s to attempt a reintegration of Sovietology into political science. This reintegration was facilitated by appropriating certain concepts and methods (interest groups and statistical analysis) then current in the study of American politics and applying them to the Soviet Union. The symmetry between totalitarians and pluralists was striking. The subtext of the former read: 'Theirs is the opposite of our [Western democratic] politics.' In reply, the latter maintained: 'We both share (essentially) the same institutions and processes.' One view invited us to think of the USSR as if it were Nazi Germany – the other, as if it were the United States! Neither though directed attention to the Soviet Union itself as a social formation *sui generis* that required theorizing.

In practical terms, both major approaches found in Sovietology served the ends of public policy, especially in the United States. The totalitarian model furnished an enemy image that helped justify enormous defence expenditures and American intervention in a host of Third World conflicts on the grounds that carbon copies of Soviet totalitarianism must not be permitted to take root. The pluralist image, which achieved prominence in Sovietology during the period of détente, helped to destigmatize the Soviet Union, thus facilitating public and elite acceptance of arms control agreements that both institutionalized strategic parity and reduced the growth of defence expenditures at home. The extent to which the concerns of public policy affected scholarship cannot be ascertained precisely. But the fact remains that the outlines of Sovietology's research agenda were barely distinguishable from the topics of interest to governmental agencies. Indeed, government funding of policy research was generally regarded as an unmixed blessing for the academic community. Policy studies commissioned by the government already had been identified by many Sovietologists as 'basic research'. Distinguishing Sovietologists as a scholarly community from their counterparts in related government agencies was rendered problematic by the fact that the U.S. State Department's *Problems of Communism* functioned as that community's principal journal, just as government officials regularly participated in scholarly conferences. Did they share 'our' language or we 'theirs'? Or was there in fact any difference?

In the professional circles of political science, the appropriation of concepts and methods familiar to those outside Sovietology brought payoffs of another kind. If one used the standard language of political science and employed statistical techniques, one stood some chance of publishing in the discipline's most prestigious journals. Never mind that this work often involved analysis of voting, accounts of political participation, and discussion of public opinion in a land in which no real elections ever occurred, no meaningful political participation was possible, and public opinion could scarcely be known. The use of concepts with cross-national credentials, accompanied ideally by correlation coefficients and tests of statistical significance, was sometimes sufficient to admit this brand of analysis to the mainstream of political science.

The end of the Cold War has robbed the field of the template that shaped its debates and informed its methods and conclusions for so long. But the end of the Cold War does not necessarily mean that we Western scholars will cease defining Russia through the prism of our own experience, or that Russian intellectuals will stop conceiving of the essence of their own society in opposition to that which they – often mistakenly – believe exists in the West. In the wake of the demise of actually existing socialism, the oppositional schemes of communism/socialism/planned (or command) economy versus democracy/liberalism/capitalism/market economy no longer engage the imagination. But the 'Russian idea' versus the 'American way', or the 'Russian collective spirit' versus 'Western individualism', wait in the wings as candidates ready to replace the old mutually defining pairs of opposites. Without a conscious effort to depart from such habits of thinking and concept formation, post-Sovietology may prove to be no less successful than was Sovietology.

Now that official communism is extinct, the lands of the former Soviet Union and East Europe are not merely the graveyards for an old order: they are also the new battlegrounds of contending great ideologies and models of social organization claiming universal significance. The centrality of the Russian experience in grand struggles helps explain how a notion as parochial, apparently banal, and (in contrast with Leninism) non-exportable as the 'Russian idea' could be accorded the status of a messianic world-historical force and remain – or again become – the source of so much attention and debate in both Russia and the West. To be sure, no one – least of all in Russia itself – is sure of what the 'Russian idea' is. But all are aware that it defines itself at least in part in opposition to materialism, rationalism, individualism, and liberalism.

What does the Russian experience tell us about history and about the future? One view holds that the death of the Soviet experiment – the century's greatest challenge to the West – represents the global triumph of liberalism, in theory even if not yet in practice (Fukuyama, 1992). Some who are less confident about the universality of liberalism's appeal assert that the demise of Sovietism actually shifts the criteria for evaluation of liberalism, thereby setting the stage for new and unforeseeable challenges to its fundamental tenets and solutions, especially in those countries in which it has long been hegemonic (Schmitter and Offe, 1994). Many observers hesitate to proclaim the triumph or crisis of liberalism as a result of Sovietism's demise, insisting on waiting to see what will happen in the lands of post-socialism, and especially in Russia. If liberal democracy fails there, those who have expressed the view that democracy's future is very likely geographically circumscribed and that liberalism and democracy are somehow profoundly Western things will be at least partially vindicated. Liberal-democratic universalists will be sorely disappointed and will have to lower the high expectations that they have brought to their assessments of what has appeared to be a global march of democracy.

Another, perhaps even more disconcerting possibility is that the death of Soviet-style socialism has already begun to reveal the inadequacies of the liberalism/socialism, capitalism/socialism, and authoritarianism/democracy dichotomies that have guided our thinking about politics and societies for many decades, thus leaving us – be we liberals, conservatives, socialists, or something else – nearly as adrift as are the subjects of our study, whose current crisis of ideology, principles, and faith has recently become the object of so much of our concern and even pity.

Imposition and Immanence

Post-Sovietology is no less a foreign enterprise than Sovietology was. Since we Western Sovietologists are overwhelmingly not members of the particular societies that we study, we are 'foreigners' there, just as 'there' is a foreign place for us. Inevitably we bring to our subject our own cultural and professional baggage: concepts, habits of mind, ways of looking and, probably, some measure of hope and fear for the fate of the society in question. Our analyses of the post-Soviet world therefore involve the *imposition* of foreign elements on to the object of analysis itself. This imposition is not in itself a liability. Indeed, in our view, it has tremendous potential to enlighten not only post-Sovietologists, but also emerging social scientists in the former Soviet Union itself. In order to realize that potential, however, post-Sovietologists would have to pay greater heed than did our forebears to that which is *immanent* in the domain we study. We would be well served by taking seriously the concepts, theories, analyses, characteriza-tions, and reflections produced by subjects within the societies that are the focus of our research. We have not yet acquired this habit, despite – or rather because of – our long history of relying upon misleading official Soviet press sources and personal contacts with select groups of Soviet officials and academics who were charged by their government with creating a façade of open debate, pluralism, and free thinking.

The problem of imposition is especially acute for those identifying with mainstream political science, which often neglects the possibility that concepts about the social world are themselves socially constructed. Much of mainstream political science is grounded in a positivist epistemology that casts the political scientist as a pure observer, recorder and analyst of data. This wilful innocence means that the political scientist supposedly has no motivation other than an interest in knowledge *per se*. He or she only assembles and analyses the data, which is 'out there' waiting to be discovered. This approach is rife with possibilities for runaway imposition and for neglect of that which is immanent in the social system under consideration.

In order to maintain a creative balance between imposition and respect for immanence, we need to pay particularly close attention to our sources. In our opinion, the best sources of information and understanding available to us are real human subjects. Above all we have in mind the practitioners of the activities we study – the labour organizers, the activists from the nascent political parties, the new demagogues, the new entrepreneurs and the old 'red directors'. It is remarkable that many of we students of Russia still regard an article in *Pravda or Izvestiya* as a more reliable source than an extensive personal interview or kitchen-table conversation with a real actor.

Our second indispensable source of information and understanding will be scholars who reside in or who have emigrated from the countries we study. During the first several years of the post-Soviet period, much has been made in the West of the urgent imperative of transferring Western social science concepts, techniques, and pedagogical methods to our counterparts in the former Soviet Union and East Europe. With much the same gusto that American business schools, governmental organizations, non-governmental organizations and corporations have assumed the burden of transmitting a work ethic, entrepreneurial skills and culture, and advanced accounting techniques to embryonic private businesses in post-socialist countries, many American scholars have now embarked upon the task of training social scientists in all manner of Western theory and research methods. Joint projects that involve transferring Western expertise to Russian, Ukrainian, Latvian, or Polish hands enjoy priority among American funding agencies, and there is no shortage of scholars ready to take up the anglophone's burden in virgin lands. Analysts in the post-socialist world will no doubt benefit from the expertise that their Western counterparts have to proffer. But Western scholars would now do well to acknowledge the possibility that the direction of intellectual diffusion will run more strongly the other way.

Indeed, the record of the Soviet period shows plainly that most of those scholars who produced genuinely sophisticated and penetrating work on communist systems were residents of, or émigrés from East Europe or the Soviet Union. Unfortunately, the objectivity of such scholars was often held in question in the West, and much of their work was neglected or marginalized in Anglo-American Sovietology. These scholars were a diverse lot. They included conservatives such as Leszek Kolakowski and Marxists such as Ferenc Fehér, Agnes Heller, and Maria and Gyorgy Markus. Many of them, such as Andrew Arato and Andrew Janos, were thoroughly 'Western', making all or most of their professional careers in the West. Others (amongst them Zygmunt Bauman, Janos Kis, Victor Zaslavsky, Vladimir Shlapentokh, Aleksandr Yanov, Ivan Szelenyi, György Konrad, Elemer

Hankiss and Jadwiga Staniszkis) emigrated later in their careers or never permanently left their homelands. All, however, enjoyed intimate familiarity with the realities of real existing socialism. That was critical.

Generalizing about such a varied array of scholars is difficult. But several traits and orientations may be regarded as common to most of them, most of the time. First, the theories they created were usually more abstract than those developed in Anglo-American Sovietology. They admirably straddled political philosophy and social science inquiry and generated genuine abstractions that fruitfully linked concepts to one another. These writers often eschewed the middle-range theorizing prominent in Anglo-American Sovietology, wherein concepts unfortunately sometimes came to function less as meaningful abstractions than as categories for sorting data. For the most part, these writers anchored their theories firmly in either Marxist, Durkheimian, Weberian, or other European intellectual traditions. In addition to drawing more explicitly on certain grand philosophical traditions (and less on contemporary social scientific models), the scholars under discussion were often less hesitant to reveal their own political-philosophical orientations and less concerned with maintaining liberal 'objectivity' than were their Anglo-American counterparts. In the final analysis, they were usually concerned with the 'essence' and the 'nature', rather than the mechanics and operation, of the societies, states, and regimes under their scrutiny. Since they were perhaps less concerned than their Anglo-American counterparts with finding niches in established academies, the threat of being proven wrong, or with a desire to be policy relevant, such scholars often embraced opportunities to engage in both polemics and prediction, but usually eschewed punditry. Finally, such scholars' work often manifested a large measure of anti-empiricism. Not only was their theory often quite abstract (even at the expense of sometimes being opaque), but the evidence adduced to support the theory was often thin and the techniques used to acquire data and insights exceedingly low-tech. Most of the scholars under discussion relied far more on their intimate familiarity with life in the societies from which they came than on opinion surveys, content analysis of the press, or other empirical techniques.

Review of the orientations and methods found in the work of those who made the most perceptive contributions to the study of Soviet-type systems is instructive for the practice of post-Sovietology. Above all, it highlights three points: (1) some methods of inquiry might be better than others, and some of those that recently have become fashionable in post-Sovietology may not be expected to yield the most illuminating findings; (2) no theoretical or philosophical orientation or tradition may be regarded as inherently superior, because what matters is how a theory is developed and deployed to illuminate and explain the experience of the subjects of study; and (3) high-quality theory, within whatever tradition or orientation, normally involves a *systemic* approach and aims for a reasonably high degree of abstraction. Attention to theory will be indispensable to a successful post-Sovietology, providing us with both rudder and compass for the strange seas we seek to chart.

Understanding and Explaining Post-Soviet 'Reality'

As Western analysts conducting fieldwork on post-Soviet terrain, we confront conditions chaotic enough to dislodge our respective centres of intellectual gravity. The phenomena and people we study sometimes cannot help but perplex us. A scam artist who has embezzled the public out of trillions of roubles in a pyramid investment scheme runs for a seat in the Russian parliament with the express wish of using the immunity from prosecution afforded by deputyship to avoid prison – and wins (Yasmann, 1994b). A group of self-proclaimed irreconcilable oppositionists in Russia, composed of communists, nationalists, and disgruntled democrats, forms a bloc which declares as its goal 'to unite all *left and right non-systemic opposition forces* on a *centrist* position in the interest of the Russian people' (emphasis added) (Yasmann, 1994a).

Understandably, one response to the confusion that we encounter (and experience) is to impose some order on it by focusing on what seem to be manageable research topics and employing conventional comparative politics concepts and methods in so doing. This tendency to retreat into the intellectual security of the familiar would seem to be particularly strong amongst those of us who have held the view that the primary research obstacle that we faced as Sovietologists was access to the data. With barriers to access now down, it would appear that at last the time has arrived when genuine empirical social science is possible in Russia. Accordingly, a tendency arises to single out particular sectors of the political world – say, voting results in legislatures or public opinion – and to frame them as discrete areas of investigation and to analyse data on them with the help of empirical-statistical methods. *Mensurabitur, ergo est.*

Whilst this approach has much to recommend it from the standpoint of initiating some conceptual clarity, it must be tempered by other ways of looking if it is to achieve significant results. In this respect, we might profit from bearing in mind that social science – contrary to the ideology of scientism and positivist epistemology – is neither innocent nor neutral. The applicability of its methods under the circumstances prevailing in Western societies has derived directly from the fact that social science has been *applied* to these societies for generations. Social scientists working in educational, penal, occupational and medical institutions have not simply been studying some reality detached from their investigations; they have figured directly into the process by which these and other institutions have 'normalized' social life (Foucault, 1977, 1980). It is therefore difficult to imagine that such methods of investigation can be readily transferred to the former republics of the Soviet Union, where social science has barely existed and where social life has not been normalized in a manner recognizable for Western specialists. By slicing up the social world in terms of the categories common to Western social science, then, post-Sovietologists are necessarily assuming the existence of a normal social-institutional infrastructure on which these methods are predicated. In the absence of such an infrastructure, and minus the rudder and compass of a theoretical orientation, we are likely to be sailing in circles and drawing some very bogus charts.

Already disturbing in this respect are some of the first impulses evinced by post-Sovietology, now that the data seems to be there. Perusal of leading journals reveals that the method that has quickly established hegemony in efforts to understand post-socialist societies is the public opinion survey. Specialists on the former Soviet Union and East Europe who have had no experience in survey research, as well as specialists in survey research who have had little or no knowledge of the former Soviet Union and East Europe, have thrown themselves with great enthusiasm into measuring populations' attitudes toward every possible object, including the market, democracy, liberal values, other ethnic groups, the constitution, the legislature, and the president. Indeed, in much of the new literature, most major changes and events, including elections, political party development, the adoption of a new constitution, strikes, and demonstrations are regarded as less significant in and of themselves than as indicators of public attitudes, which in turn are treated, explicitly or implicitly, as the components of political culture.

The rush to survey public opinion is undoubtedly motivated by a commendable desire to advance knowledge about societies that have been only dimly understood in the West. Survey research, moreover, does serve certain ends quite well, such as dissecting election results. But does the measurement of attitudes by means of surveys necessarily provide the most fruitful way to study Russia and other post-socialist societies? Several considerations counsel scepticism.

The first would be the extreme difficulty - perhaps even impossibility - of meaningfully measuring public opinion during a revolution, which is, after all, what began in East Europe and the former Soviet Union in the late 1980s and what has continued to go on there. The events of the late Soviet and early post-Soviet periods should have served as warnings concerning the evanescence of preferences in countries devoid of stable political identities and seized by the continuous occurrence of momentous events. One poignant example is found in the differences in outcome of the referenda in Ukraine in 1991. In March, nearly three-quarters of Ukrainians supported in a referendum Gorbachev's call for a 'renewed Union' (and thereby registered opposition to separation from the USSR); in December, in the post-putsch referendum on Ukrainian statehood, nine-tenths voted for independence.

The second problem with reliance upon opinion surveys concerns how they are done. Do the questions researchers ask yield answers that lend insight into what it is that they intend to understand and explain? Do we understand what our respondents mean? For that matter, do they understand us? May negative responses to the question of whether one would like to see an expansion of the gypsy population in one's city, under conditions in which members of the group in question (gypsies) have been experienced by respondents (say, Muscovites) exclusively in the role of thieves and assailants, be regarded as demonstration of a portentous, resurgent popular xenophobia? Similarly, can we always count as strong evidence of tolerance replies to questions whose validity and reliability as measures of tolerance have supposedly been established by cross-national studies? In contrast with the first problem, this second difficulty seems at least potentially soluble. Hypothetically, it could be surmounted by asking the right questions and by interpreting answers correctly. But the ability to do so would then depend on intimate familiarity with the context in which the survey was carried out and extensive knowledge of the country gained from long-term firsthand exposure. In this respect, an orientation toward understanding may be regarded as an important requisite of effective explanation (Schutz, 1945).

The third cause for scepticism regarding the utility of opinion surveys concerns the tenuousness of the connection between public opinion and political life. Even in the very unlikely event that one can meaningfully measure public opinion during a revolution and devise questions that elicit answers that lend real insight into popular beliefs, what do attitudes, however measured, really tell us about politics? As scholars such as Dankwart Rustow and Sidney Tarrow have shown, what matters in politics, especially during times of deep and rapid change, is not what values people hold in the abstract, but rather what concrete actions they are actually willing and able to take (Rustow, 1970; Tarrow, 1992).

Given its drawbacks, how can one explain the vogue for surveying opinion? Several possibilities stand out. First, the countries in question were closed to the outside world for such a long time that researchers, now given the chance, are naturally eager to use every method available to crack the enigma. Opinions could not be expressed freely – through responses to surveys, autonomous political participation, or any other means – for several generations. Given the resultant information vacuum, it is little wonder that researchers are now eager for the numbers on every aspect of political and social life. Second, survey research yields findings and results relatively easily. Polling requires no specialized knowledge of the society under survey. At any rate, one can always hire one of the numerous public opinion research agencies or sociological research institutes that have recently sprung up in Moscow and elsewhere to do the work. Some such agencies, if kindly informed in advance, are glad to furnish evidence for whatever conclusions the customer purchasing the data seeks support. Surveying also enjoys the lustre – to funding agencies as well as to parts of the academy – of science. Currently, nothing attracts large research grants like elaborate public opinion survey projects. Particularly competitive applications involve large teams of specialists and include collaboration with native scholars and the promise of transferring to the latter training in methods commonly used in Western social science.

If we are now to avoid repeating old mistakes under new circumstances, we are obliged to raise what might be considered indelicate questions. If we can recognize the imprint of governmental influence on Sovietology, perhaps we should now be mindful of the ways in which influences emanating from governmental, commercial, and financial institutions may shape our post-Sovietological research agendas. In the parlance of rational choice theory, what is the structure of incentives that we are facing here? If the questions we find ourselves asking (How receptive are Ukrainians to the market? What do Russians think of foreigners?) are identical to those questions to which answers are eagerly sought by private business and government agencies, and if the methods we employ are precisely those demanded of us by funding agencies, might we not benefit from pausing occasionally to check that our scholarly autonomy is in good repair? For whom are we producing knowledge and what kind of knowledge are we producing? The present authors do not pretend to have answers to these questions, but we are convinced that they must be raised and debated if post-Sovietology is to elevate its intellectual contribution to comparative politics.

The main methodological alternative to opinion surveying is ethnographic research that aims to establish intimate familiarity with the subjects of study. Such an approach normally involves fieldwork, by means of which the researcher attempts to enter the world of his or her subjects with a readiness to be instructed by it. Thus, in sharp contrast to the conventions governing the opinion survey, this orientation proceeds from the understanding that the more clearly the field-worker has in mind what he or she is after, the less likely it is that he/she will discover what the natives' cultural practices and representations are about and how they define them, construct them and manipulate them (Schneider, 1968, p. 10). Research tools may include extensive interviewing as well as attending meetings, conferences, and all manner of seemingly mundane private and public gatherings. Interviews based on pre-set and uniform questions put to all respondents may not serve as well as in-depth, open-ended conversations with actors or analysts that allow them to recount and explain their experiences as they understand them. Effective ethnographic research is not necessarily limited to field research. It may also entail intensive study of written sources; particularly those that reflect or express currents of thought that are not necessarily captured in the regular mass media. For analysts of social movements and social mobilization, manifestos, handbills, placards, and programmes serve as such sources; for observers of political parties, internal party documents might prove particularly useful; students of political culture might find literary sources of great benefit.

Use of ethnographic methods cannot always impart knowledge and understanding as deep and intuitive as that possessed by native scholars or émigrés. But it can, if pursued tenaciously, provide a good substitute for native understanding. Indeed, the experience of long-term firsthand exposure coupled with the 'outsider's' perspective may constitute a felicitous combination, as is abundantly evident from the work of Alfred Stepan on Latin America, Sidney Tarrow on Western Europe, Benedict Anderson on Southeast Asia, and Robert Bates on Africa. Ethnographic approaches to research do not, of course, guarantee high-quality scholarship. But they do enable the researcher to learn from his or her subjects – a crucial aspect of learning about one's subjects that is lost in survey research. In our own research, we both have been struck by the frequency with which actors themselves, in the course of interviews, informal personal conversations, speeches, or discussions, offer insights into – or even tentative answers to – the truly big questions that inform the scholarly enterprise. Of course, actors' perspectives and answers can never be regarded as definitive, and the observer must always take pains to avoid a loss of distance and scepticism. Still, it is remarkable how often subjects can, and do, provide not only information but also insights into broader theoretical questions.

Patrimonies and Paradigms

Theory building is, of course, primarily the responsibility of the researcher, and one of the main tasks that students of the former Soviet Union and East Europe now face is developing theory that transcends the limitations of Soviet-era scholarship. As in the area of methods, in the realm of theory the experience of Sovietology provides important insights for post-Sovietologists. First, it suggests the virtue of engaging in genuinely abstract theorizing about the nature and essence of post-Soviet regimes, states, and societies, as well as the importance of informing empirically oriented work with a theoretical component. The widespread discrediting of the totalitarian model in Anglo-American Sovietology in the 1970s was unfortunately accompanied by a clear departure from high-range theorizing and grand model building. Whatever one might think of the validity of the totalitarian model, in the hands of certain East European scholars it did encourage truly systemic thinking. Although the totalitarian system has disappeared from the post-Soviet space, these same countries are to one degree or another littered with its debris. The need for theory in post-Sovietology remains as acute as ever.

A second consideration engendered by the experience of Sovietology is that effective theorizing and penetrating analysis are not the monopoly of any particular paradigm or philosophical tradition. Experience counsels against prescribing or proscribing particular theoretical approaches. The important things are boldness, clarity, and originality, not working within the right paradigm or avoiding getting it wrong in one's analysis and predictions. Some theoretical approaches may be better suited than others to the study of post-Soviet politics, but substantial contributions are possible within any of the major paradigms now current in the social sciences.

Rational choice theory may be the most problematic choice under present-day conditions. As one of the approach's leading exponents acknowledges, the theory's appropriateness and utility decline as actors' goals become more fuzzy, as the rules of interaction become more fluid and less precise, and as institutions in general become weaker or break down entirely (Tsebelis, 1990, pp. 32-3). Under conditions in which preferences and identities are poorly defined and in deep flux, such as they are in many post-socialist countries, an unvarnished rational choice framework of whatever variety may not always yield the most illuminating analyses. Still, many of the assumptions that inform rational choice approaches may be of considerable utility, as is evident from the fine work that has been produced within the tradition even on societies in transition (Przeworski, 1992).

Socioeconomic modernization theory may provide an even richer framework for analysing post-socialist politics. The way in which modernization theory has often been used in recent Sovietology has earned justifiable opprobrium. Many scholars, in an effort to explain the rise of Gorbachev and his associates to power, located a plethora of apparitions in the Soviet Union, including a new middle class and a civil society, and attributed these phenomena to rising educational attainment, urbanization, and other aspects of modernization. Some such writings minimized the enormous differences between Western and Leninist types of modernization. Still, there is no logical reason why socioeconomic modernization approaches cannot form the basis of an important school of thought in post-Sovietology. Indeed, the field would doubtless benefit from a neo-modernization approach that focused on the nature and legacy of the peculiar form of modernization that the Leninist regime carried out. The effects of Soviet-type modernization on present-day social structure and social relations – and consequently on popular mobilization (and demobilization), party formation, progress toward (or regress from) democracy, class formation and conflict, and the criminalization of the economy – are enormous. And within paradigms that emphasize the importance of socioeconomic determinants, Durkheimian theories by no means exhaust the possibilities. Marxist approaches may serve as equally fruitful frameworks. Much of the finest conceptual and theoretical work found in studies on the Soviet Union and East Europe – including some of the most perceptive and searing critiques of the Soviet-type regime – were produced by Marxists such as the scholars of the Budapest school. Indeed, shunning Marxist analyses altogether in the post-Soviet world (and thus in post-Sovietology) would constitute no less of an error than it was during the Soviet era. Not only the record of Sovietology, but also that of studies on bureaucratic authoritarianism and regime change in Latin America, demonstrates the potential richness of Marxist theory for studying problems of state–society relations and regime transformation. Whilst it is doubtful that versions of Marxism that focus exclusively on structural factors and ignore human agency can contribute more than background information to the study of post-Soviet politics, approaches that are mindful of the issue of consciousness would appear especially promising. Indeed, the transformations under way in the post-Soviet world provide an array of challenging targets for those interested in how certain forms of transparent domination have been historically superseded by more opaque, subtle and, therefore, perhaps even more effective ones.

Certain political culture approaches are no less promising. Some of the early post-Sovietology carried out within a Weberian framework has already helped to sharpen and focus debates over the effects of the legacies of Russian, Slavic, and Soviet political culture on post-Soviet politics. What is more, several theorists employing Weberian political culture approaches have built theories sufficiently coherent and encompassing as to make possible bold and provocative predictions about the course and direction of post-Soviet political development (Tucker, 1992; Jowitt, 1992). Working within a very different tradition but nevertheless also within a cultural framework, some adherents of post-modern approaches have begun grappling with problems of post-Soviet transition. Research strategies that include a linguistic dimension may offer a particularly valuable vantage on the social world. A focus on the production of meaning in speech acts not only transcends positivism's dissection of the world into such categories as fact/value or behaviour/meaning but helps to join the enterprises of understanding and explanation. Unravelling the meanings manifest and suppressed in political language represents an exercise in understanding, just as the use of research methods associated with discourse analysis yields forms of explanation already grounded in understanding itself. Far from merely recapitulating what subjects have said, or going through the motions of analysis by quantifying the frequency at which certain words have appeared in their utterances, discourse analysis represents a promising tool for discovering, investigating and explaining political life. It is encouraging to note the contributions made recently in our field by such established journals as *Slavic Review* which has featured studies devoted to the analysis of discourse, culture and identity.

As well as any of the approaches that we have mentioned, linguistically based strategies highlight the creative interplay between theory and data that is the hallmark of sound methods. When the concepts that we deploy are in fact theoretical abstractions, they directly construct their referents and order relations amongst them. Contrary to positivist provisos, theory and data are interdependent. And it is precisely this interdependence that joins the seemingly disparate research orientations – abstract theorizing on the one hand, fieldwork on the other – advocated in this chapter. The degree to which we are prepared to be instructed by our subjects will represent the measure of our capability to theorize about them.

References

Arendt, H. *The Origins of Totalitarianism* (2nd ed.). New York: Meridian, 1958.

Brady, H.E., S. Verba, and K.L. Schlozman. 'Beyond SES: A Resource Model of Political Participation'. *American Political Science Review,* Vol. 89, No. 2 (June 1995).

Brym, R. 'Anti-Semitism in Moscow: A Re-examination'. *Slavic Review,* Vol. 53 (Fall 1994).

Brzezinski, Z., and S. Huntington. *Political Power: USA/USSR.* New York: Viking, 1964.

Cox, M. 'The Cold War and Stalinism in the Age of Capitalist Decline', *Critique,* No. 17 (1986).

Feher, F., A. Heller, and G. Markus. *Dictatorship over Needs.* London: Basil Blackwell, 1983.

Foucault, M. *Discipline and Punish.* New York: Pantheon, 1977.

— in *Power, Knowledge,* C. Gardner (ed.). New York: Pantheon, 1980.

Friedrich, C., and Z. Brzezinski. *Totalitarian Dictatorship and Autocracy* (2nd ed.). New York: Praeger, 1965.

Fukuyama, F. *The End of History and the Last Man.* New York: Free Press, 1992.

Gilison, J. 'Understanding Anti-Semitism in Russia: An Analysis of the Politics of Anti-Jewish Attitudes' and 'Misunderstandings of Anti-Semitism in Russia: An Analysis of the Politics of Anti-Jewish Attitudes', *Slavic Review,* Vol. 53 (Fall 1994).

Hesli, V., A. Miller, and W. Reisinger. 'Comment on Brym and Degtyarev's Discussion of Anti-Semitism in Moscow'. *Slavic Review,* Vol. 53 (Fall 1994).

——and K. Morgan. 'Social Distance from Jews in Russia and Ukraine'. *Slavic Review,* Vol. 53 (Fall 1994).

Horkheimer, M. *Eclipse of Reason.* New York: Oxford University Press, 1947.

Jowitt, K. 'The Leninist Legacy', In Ivo Banac (ed.), *Eastern Europe in Revolution.* Ithaca, NY: Cornell University Press, 1992.

Kolomeits, V. Personal communication to Michael Urban, 28 September 1994.

Marcuse, H. *One-Dimensional Man.* Boston: Beacon, 1964.

McAuley, M. *Politics and the Soviet Union.* Harmondsworth: Penguin, 1977.

Przeworski, A. 'The "East" Becomes the "South"? The "Autumn of the People" and the Future of Eastern Europe'. *PS: Political Science and Politics,* Vol. 24. March 1991.

——'The Games of Transition.' In S. Mainwaring, G. O'Donnell, and J.S. Valenzuela (eds), *Issues in Democratic Consolidation: The New South American Democracies in Comparative Perspective.* Notre Dame, IN: University of Notre Dame Press, 1992.

Rustow, D.A. 'Transitions to Democracy: Toward a Dynamic Model'. *Comparative Politics,* Vol. 2, No. 3. April 1970.

Schmitter, P.C., and C. Offe. 'The Paradoxes and Dilemmas of Liberal Democracy'. unpub. MS, March 1994.

Schneider, D. *American Kinship: A Cultural Account.* Chicago: University of Chicago Press, 1968.

Schutz, A. 'Some Leading Concepts in Phenomenology', *Social Research,* Vol. 12. February 1945.

——'Concepts and Theory Formation in the Social Sciences.' *Journal of Philosophy,* Vol. 51 (1954).

Tarrow, S. 'Mentalities, Political Cultures, and Collective Action Frames: Constructing Meanings Through Action'. In A.D. Morris and C. McClurg Mueller (eds), *Frontiers in Social Movement Theory.* New Haven, CT: Yale University Press, 1992.

——*Power in Movement: Social Movements, Collective Action and Politics.* Cambridge: Cambridge University Press, 1994.

Tsebelis, G. *Nested Games: Rational Choice in Comparative Politics.* Berkeley: University of California Press, 1990.

Tucker, R.C. 'Sovietology and Russian History'. *Post-Soviet Affairs,* Vol. 8, No. 3 (1992).

White, S. 'Political Science as Ideology: The Study of Soviet Politics.' In B. Chapman and A.M. Potter (eds), *W. J. M. M. Political Questions: Essays in Honour of W. J. M. Mackenzie.* Manchester: Manchester University Press, 1975.

Yasmann, V. 'Petr Romanov Named Leader of Irreconcilable Opposition.' *RFE/RL Daily Report,* 26 October 1994a.

——'Sergei Mavrodi Is Elected to the Duma.' *RFE/RL Daily Report,* 2 November 1994b.

10

Russian Political Evolution: a Structural Approach

RICHARD SAKWA

Introduction

The academic discipline of Sovietology was no more than a small, and by no means the most significant, part of the attempt by writers, émigrés, intellectuals and others to understand the origins not just of communism (in its various guises) but of Russia's ambiguous relationship with modernity and the West. Ideological commitments, reasons of state, academic partisanship and personal prejudices accompanied the rise and fall of the Soviet system, factors which in no small way still influence our understanding of post-communist developments. This chapter does not pretend to escape the traditional constraints of the discipline, but tentatively suggests an approach encompassing both the dynamics of revolutionary socialism and the elusive search for a political order embracing Russia's distinctive developmental path and civilizational identity. Only by placing the fall of the Soviet Union in a longer historical and a larger theoretical perspective can we begin to understand the dimensions of the Russian problem, a question that is by no means resolved.

Stability and Order

Tocqueville noted that 'A democratic republic exists in the United States'; and the principal object of his book on America was to explain the causes of its existence (Tocqueville, 1981, p. 170). The study of communism and post-communism is faced by a very different problem; we are forced not only to examine what happened but to look at the potential and the beliefs of the key actors for the emergence of something different. Russia in the modern era appears torn by the belief that it should be something other than it is. In the twentieth century this sense of displacement took the form of the grand recivilizing projects of communism and post-communism, both with common origins in Enlightenment universalism and a belief in progress.

Twice in the twentieth century orders have dissolved, in 1917 and 1991, giving rise in both cases to periods of disorder before, in one form or another, new orders have been reconstituted. In both cases Russia became the site for changes imposed upon politics rather than emerging through politics (Barnard, 1991, p. 138). The impositions became doubly burdensome because both transformatory projects were derived from values generated abroad, and in particular Western Europe. The Soviet regime declared itself to be transitional, preparing the way for the onset of full communism, whilst post-communism, too, has taken on the mantle of provisionality whilst preparing for full capitalism. The familiar dialectic between ends and means has once again reasserted itself: politics was subordinated to an apparently choiceless and alternativeless world.

Whilst the tension between democracy and order has accompanied debates on the fall of both old regimes, there is perhaps a more profound tension, namely between stability and order. Whilst the English, American and French revolutions had each in turn given rise to a new political order – *Ordnungspolitik* (despite equivocations, restorations and the like) – the Bolshevik revolution reflected not the maturation of social processes but their interruption. In the interview between Joseph Stalin and H.G. Wells of 23 July 1934, Stalin noted that 'even if the Americans you mention [in the New Deal] partly achieve their aim ... they will not destroy the roots of the anarchy which is inherent in the existing capitalist system' (Wells, 1950, p. 4). As far as Stalin was concerned, political power was required as a lever for change. 'The new political power creates the new laws, the new order, which is revolutionary order ... for order that corresponds to the interests of the working class' (Wells, 1950, p. 18). Revolutionary socialism was to give rise to a new order that assumed inherent systemic stability qualities in a society based on the hegemony of the working class in a world where capitalist exploitation had been abolished.

However, it could be argued that the ultimate reason for the dissolution of the communist regime was that it was unable to generate a new political order. The Bolshevik regime explicitly rejected the notion of a political order in the expectation that the abolition of exploitative classes would allow the emergence of an immanent self-managing order. The abolition of politics (understood in the conventional sense), the suppression of civil society, and the espousal of the formula of one class, one party, one truth, foreclosed the option of establishing a new political order, hence the Bolsheviks were forced to maintain their rule by stability politics involving greater or lesser degrees of coercion (Hoffman, 1984, pp. 129–49).

The Soviet system can thus be understood within the framework of the tension between stability and political order. A *political order* is based on hegemony and systemic forms of governance, whereas a *stability regime* veers between mobilization and stagnation and is based on expanded adminis-tration. We can no more than allude to the pre-1917 system to suggest that late tsarism had also increasingly become a system based on stability-management as the legitimacy derived from popular belief that it was grounded in natural order was eroded. Tsarist Russia, like its Bolshevik successor, had failed to establish itself as an *Ordnungspolitik*, and hence became prey to modernizing impulses appealing to universal norms of political adaptation.

The revolutionary socialist project sought to transcend the instability at the heart of capitalist democracy by establishing a fundamentally new social formation marked by the abolition of politics and the allegedly rational administration of the public good. The Soviet system can thus be characterized as a stability regime in three senses: it had (or sought to) overcome (according to its self-definition) capitalist crisis tendencies and operated according to 'steady state' rules of a post-political economy world; its 'order' in the profound sense was not political but based on the management of a pre-ordained and pre-political stability in which traditional 'bourgeois' law and all of its accoutrements could be transcended; and it gave birth to rule of a *regime* rather than a *system*.

The distinction between *regime* and *system* is central to comparative politics, with the latter suggesting a rule-bound legal-rational form of state management involving usually the ordered circulation of elites and a degree of public accountability, whilst regime rule denotes usually arbitrary and to a degree authoritarian government above politics with weak popular reciprocity. The combination of the terms stability and regime is thus a way of stressing the link between ideology and organization, between the intellectual project and its political consequences.

At the heart of the stability regime was the belief in an immanent order in a world where the laws of political economy no longer operated and where politics had been transcended (Polan, 1984). The emancipatory potential associated with the stability regime of revolutionary socialism sought to extend human potential by overcoming alienation and fulfilling what Marx called 'species being', the full range of capacities inherent in the human person, above all by abolishing the separation between the political and the social (Kolakowski, 1991). The viability of such hopes need not detain us here, but Soviet communism swiftly became a 'dictatorship over needs' for the reason, amongst others, that communism became the alternative to capitalism rather than its successor (Feher *et al.*, 1983). It inherited a society of scarcity rather than abundance, but even in the best of circumstances it is not clear how 'stability' could have been managed without politics. Nove has pointed out just how unfeasible traditional revolutionary socialist aspirations were (Nove, 1983).

Circumstances in revolutionary Russia were far from propitious for the implementation of a revolutionary socialist programme, and thus the management of stability took on emergency forms for both theoretical and practical reasons and gave rise to what has been called a 'syncretic society' (Hudelson, 1993, p. 26). Indeed, the instability at the heart of the social order was its defining feature, veering from extremes of violence to periods of stability corroded by inherent stagnatory tendencies. Whilst the eight-month-long Provisional Government in 1917 was explicitly provisional, the system born in October was in certain respects, too, no more than a 74-year-long regime of crisis management. Whilst there may well be forms of modernity differing from that prevalent in the West, revolutionary socialism was unable to provide a viable form of post-capitalist development. Thus Bolshevik rule, like the Provisional Government before it (and late tsarism), became yet another example of a failed 'transition'.

Transformation and Adaptation

At this point we can introduce another pair of related concepts, *transformation* and *adaptation*. At the heart of the revolutionary socialist project was the attempt to transform all existing social relations according to a set of predetermined goals, albeit a project allowing flexibility over meaning and time. The abolition of the market is clearly a central goal of revolutionary socialism, but the means of achieving this is open to interpretation. The Soviet regime was sustained by belief in a revolutionary transformatory project in economic and social relations, and was predicated on the assumption that a 'new Soviet person' would emerge. The utopian aspirations of the transformatory process, however, came into conflict with the developmental tasks generated by the transformatory project itself (see Lowenthal, 1970). The ultimate structural cause of the high level of coercion was the dissonance between patterns of subjectivity and the transformative aims of the Bolshevik regime, conventionally described as a gulf between regime and society. The regime's transformatory mission rendered the 'stability regime' far from stable; but without its transformatory purpose and the striving for the imputed stability inherent in a proletarian polity, the system would no longer have been a 'stability regime'. In other words, stripped off its revolutionary purpose, the 'stability regime' would have become just another dictatorship.

The transformatory project can be contrasted with processes of adaptation. By adaptation we mean something more than 'inclusion', defined by Jowitt as 'attempts by the Party elite to expand the internal boundaries of the regime's political, productive, and decision-making systems, to integrate itself with the unofficial (i.e., non-apparatchik) sectors of society rather than insulate itself from them' (Jowitt, 1992, p. 88). As far as the Bolsheviks were concerned, their world transformatory project was threatened by the traditions and social patterns of the society in which they found themselves and with which they could make peace only on pain of losing their identity. Adaptation means the establishment of a reciprocal relationship between state and society, although it does not necessarily mean that regime forms of rule give way to systemic, let alone democratic, forms of governance.

Adaptative regimes do not necessarily adapt themselves to everything in society, but their overall tendency is to make peace with underlying social realities. Broadly speaking, whilst the transformatory project is ideologized, processes of adaptation are deideologized. Adaptation suggests that the regime–society division gives way to some form of congruence between system (polity) and society. This is no longer based on instrumental policies of inclusion but suggests a broader form of consensus, the creation of a new political community, the reconstitution of order based on politics. Dissonance (of which dissent was only one symptom) gives way to congruence. This should not be taken as implying that a society can have only one form of political system, but that there is a dynamic interaction between the system and society mediated by a reconstituted political sphere.

Gellner notes that the Bolsheviks, having won the Civil War, 'could not be seduced into compromise and routinization because they were politically too successful' (Gellner, 1994, p. 49). Adaptation in the USSR did, of course, take place in a variety of formal and informal ways, ranging from Stalin's 'big deal' concession to middle-class values (Dunham, 1976, pp. 3–23) to Brezhnev's 'little deal' – based on a rudimentary form of 'social contract' in which rising standards of living were promised in exchange for political passivity (see Millar, 1985). The post-Stalin years saw the rise of what Breslauer dubbed 'welfare-state authoritarianism' (Breslauer, 1978/1984) against the background of the 'neo-Stalinist compromise' in which the regime reduced the level of coercion at the price of popular political exclusion (Zaslavsky, 1982). However, once the purging stopped and the Party began to adapt socially (usually in corrupt forms), if not politically, to the society, then its days as a vanguard organization were clearly numbered (Brzezinski, 1966).

Beyond the Stability Regime: Gorbachev

The exit from the stability regime formally began under Gorbachev. The tendency of his reforms in their last phase was to move beyond instrumental policies of 'inclusion' towards adaptation. Thus a classic example of inclusion would be 'glasnost', which by the end of Gorbachev's rule had largely given way to an open-ended adaptive freedom of speech (Murray, 1994). Thus transformation gave way to incipient adaptation. The final shreds of commitment to the stability regime were eroded, symbolized by the acceptance of the market (albeit at first the 'socialist' market), and attempts were made to institutionalize systemic forms of rule through elections, a revamped legislature, and so on, all accompanied by the decline of the Party's leading role as the manager of stability.

In foreign affairs perestroika saw the evolution of competitive coexistence (the form of coexistence predominant between 1945 and 1985) into cooperative coexistence, with Gorbachev believing that Soviet-type systems, based on what he called 'the socialist choice', would be able to continue indefinitely in a parallel but non-competitive relationship with the capitalist democracies. In the event, the increasingly apparent lack of viability of Gorbachev's hopes for a parallel modernity led to a series of Soviet capitulations to a Western-dominated international system. Gorbachev's hopes that 'new political thinking' would be able to modify the international system, with an enhanced role for the United Nations and the like, gave way to the USSR's largely unnegotiated adaptation to the existing world order.

The continuation of gradualistic adaptive policies of the Gorbachev type might have allowed the country to avoid another revolutionary transformatory storm through a process of what might be called transformation through adaptation. The late stages of perestroika in effect constituted a radical repudiation of the core principles of the Soviet regime, but did so through a peaceful process of adaptation to domestic society and the international system. It might be noted that Asian countries have proved themselves particularly adept at strategies of transformation through adaptation, with Japan in the Meiji restoration period leading the way in transforming itself into a modern industrial power and adapting (to a degree) to the international economic system whilst at the same time maintaining traditional patterns of social organization and belief systems, albeit now harnessed to the development of a modern industrial economy. This appears to be the dynamic of contemporary East Asian societies in which the logic of modernization and the compulsion to Westernize diverge (Gray, 1994), signalling a growing gulf between international adaptation and domestic cultural and civilizational diversity. Mechanisms of transformation through adaptation appear to be strongest in what Samuel Huntington (1993) has called 'Confucian civilizations', above all Japan, and weakest in Russia.

Transformation and Adaption: Yeltsin

In contrast with the Bolshevik regime, Yeltsin's rule was initially marked by a distinctive twofold project: transformative and adaptive. The transformative element was intended to overcome the Bolshevik legacy and to introduce the elements of market rationality – ideologically generated goals that were in certain respects reminiscent of earlier attempts at grandiose social engineering. The transformatory task perpetuated some of the behavioural codes of the old regime, giving rise to the condemnation of the Yeltsin regime as no more than inverted Bolshevism stamped by a new form of authoritarianism turned now from destroying the market to its establishment 'by Bolshevik methods' in a process dubbed 'market Stalinism' by Boris Kagarlitsky.

The adaptive element, however, mitigated the Bolshevistic features of the new system. Rather than the regime setting its face against traditional notions of political and national community, the regime began to adapt to them. Although both gave rise to regime forms of rule, there are fundamental differences between the two great transformations to build new social orders in Russia in the twentieth century. Whilst both the Soviet and Yeltsin regimes shared directive transformative features, the direction and purpose of the historical change was crucial. The utopian project of the Bolshevik sort was unable to adapt to the society and national traditions because in doing so it would have lost its identity, meaning and *raison d'être*. Once the notion of politics was rehabilitated (as it began to be during perestroika), then the assumptions underlying the belief in post-bourgeois stability were threatened, and in turn the whole purpose of the Soviet regime evaporated. It was a real 'nowhere land': a sort of 'sixteenth republic', hovering above the existing fifteen; in the political sense claiming the inheritance of a post-political community based on substantive knowledge of the 'general will'; and in the economic sense based on notions of post-market stability. The counter-utopian programme of post-communist Russia, on the other hand, was precisely prone to adaptation as it moved from nowhere to somewhere, and in adapting made possible the shift from regime to system forms of rule.

Yeltsin came to power committed to a new transformatory project which at first suggested the wholesale transformation of the past and a commitment to adaptation to Russia's historical traditions, the national community and the international system. These processes soon came into contradiction with each other. The programme unleashed an enormously destructive transformative storm on the country but appeared able neither to adapt nor to transform. Thus whilst transformation through adaptation of the Japanese type can be enormously successful, and indeed appears to be effective in China today, the attempt to achieve adaptation through transformation of the Yeltsin type was profoundly contradictory and destabilizing. The post-1991 order was based on the attempt to incorporate 'the people' into a reciprocal relationship with the political order, but the understanding of popular sovereignty was mediated by transformatory goals and fears of premature adaptation. The agenda of the liberal transformation (property and individual rights) took priority over constitutionalizing political order and democracy, giving rise to new forms of regime rule.

Problems of Adaptation

References to adaptation are found throughout the literature, yet the concept is rarely analysed. Von Laue, for example, stressed the problem faced by Russia, at the margins of the European state system and confronted by the 'unconscious aggressiveness of a universal model' which resulted in 'the inescapable adaptation to Western achievements' (Von Laue, pp. 4, 150). In this section a preliminary attempt will be made to examine the notion and its implications. Claus Offe noted 'a Pandora's box full of paradoxes' in the post-Cold War epoch (Offe, 1991), and indeed the problem of adaptation is particularly prone to paradoxes. Some of the central problems can be traced back in Russian history and some are of more recent provenance. They can briefly be outlined as follows.

Domestic versus International Adaptation

Whereas adaptation in Central European countries proceeded relatively smoothly after 1989, and the 'return to Europe' appeared natural and desirable, in the former USSR adaptation has proved far more problematical. The very notion of adaptation to a Western-centred world system has always been contested in Russia, and there was no reason to think that after 1991 this would be any different. Whilst Poland, for example, considered itself a Western country that by an accident of geography found itself in the East, Russia thought of itself as the bearer of a unique civilization in its own right (Pozdnyakov, 1991). Thus adaptative processes were divided between a Western-oriented approach which prioritized international adaptation and a nativist tradition reasserting Russia's civilizational autonomy.

The international system in which Russia has sought to survive has traditionally been hostile, and the politics of order at the interstate level (which in an anarchic international system can only tenuously take the form of a political order) has usually been accompanied by regimes in domestic affairs committed to the preservation of the state itself, at whatever social and political cost. The establishment of new political orders in post-war Germany, Italy and Japan took place in the context of America acting as the new *Ordnungsmacht*, and indeed the rest of Europe was stabilized by the overlay produced by the bipolar Cold War global system. Russia today is not a defeated power (however much subjectively this might appear to be the case), and the bipolar superpower world is dead.

After 1991, the Western-dominated international system itself, particularly in the form of international financial organizations, took on the role of the Comintern of old, exhorting a weak indigenous government to evermore radical acts of liberal domestic economic transformation. As Strange has noted, the structural transformation of the global economy has resulted in the diminution of state power and forced governments to appear to be acting 'reasonably' by the international community. Otherwise, they would be unable to attract investment, credits and other facilities (Strange, 1994). The contradiction between the nostrums coming from abroad, on the one hand calling for adaptation to international democratic norms whilst on the other hand sponsoring disruptive economic policies (however necessary in a strictly economic sense), has impeded responsiveness to domestic demands, thus intensifying regime forms of rule. The relatively benign international climate in the early post-communist years provided a unique opportunity for the weak post-communist states to consolidate themselves without fear of external aggression, but in Russia the perceived imperative of adaptation to the international system has deprived the new government of some of its legitimacy and thus inhibited the shift from regime to systemic (democratic) forms of rule.

The argument, however, could be tempered by suggesting that by around 1993 a consensus had emerged in Russia over the fundamentals of Russia's national interest. The concept itself was rehabilitated and foreign policy was stripped of its Marxist verbiage. Russia's foreign diplomacy was now designed to serve the national interest and in its turn contributed to the definition of a post-communist national identity. Philip Cerny has stressed the way that foreign policy is 'the specific instrument par excellence at the disposal of elites hoping to mobilize the population of a legally-recognised nation-state towards authority legitimation and political integration' (Cerny, 1979, p. 71). Whilst Kozyrev's foreign policy did not attract universal praise, the gap between his views and that of nationalists and patriots narrowed dramatically as Russia took a more assertive line in the 'near abroad' and in its dealings with the West.

Adaptation can thus take the form of an appeal to the national community that comes into contradiction with international adaptation. The appeal to nationalism is the great alternative in the twentieth century to class-based approaches to political mobilization and is a stability-enhancing stratagem shared by democratic and authoritarian polities alike. A fully fledged nationalist regime, however, would signal the emergence of a new form of stability regime based on an appeal to pre-political forms of substantive community. A stability regime inspired by nationalism would, in all probability, be accompanied by a new type of transformatory project, this time directed towards the mobilization of the ethnic basis of citizenship and ethnic reordering abroad. It is unlikely that a nationalist-stability regime would be able to establish a sustainable political order and would, unless accompanied by exceptional political skills and instruments, in all likelihood prove unviable in the long run.

The tension between transformation and adaptation can be seen as part of the uneasy relationship, characteristic of modernization, between universal and particular (national) factors in the choice of developmental strategies. Marxism is well known as one of the great universalizing ideologies, with the more advanced societies, in Marx's words, only showing the less developed their own future. Kagarlitsky remains an exponent of this view, insisting that 'Marxism is the path to European civilization ... we must accomplish the historical and, for Russian culture, very difficult transition from "European-ism" and "Westernism" to universalism' (Kagarlitsky, 1989, p. 35). This universalizing tendency is at the centre of the Enlightenment tradition, and now, with the decline of revolutionary socialism and other sustained universal alternatives, is borne by liberalism alone. In the contemporary world, however, this liberalism comes as a package with capitalist democracy and is associated with a 'Westernizing' impulse that appears to threaten precisely all that is unique in Russian culture. Proletarian internationalism has given way to liberal universalism (Fukuyama, 1989; 1992).

Transformation as an Obstacle to Adaptation

Since at least the time of Peter the Great, when an accelerated process of Westernization was launched that arguably resulted in the postponement of genuine Westernization (Szamuely, 1974), transformative goals have acted as an impediment to organic development and adaptation. As Von Laue notes, 'copying alien models, a practice unknown in West European countries, set up major barriers between rulers and the ruled' (Von Laue, 1993, p. 4). Each transformatory storm left its mark on society, and later periods of adaptation have to reckon with them. Peter the Great's transformatory endeavour, for example, gave rise to the city of St Petersburg, which became an outpost of Westernism without the West, a bureaucratic city isolated from the rest of Russia and whose artificial development stymied the evolution of consensual norms. By contrast, in Moscow, a city deeply rooted in society and sensitive to popular demands, under late tsarism strategies of class hegemony were tried (for example, by providing cheap tram transport and water to working-class districts) that sought to incorporate the emerging proletariat into an expanding national community based on modern forms of legitimation (Thurston, 1987). The Bolshevik seizure of power was resisted fiercely in the city and was only achieved by bringing in outside forces.

The Petrine and Bolshevik revolutions disrupted the organic pattern of Russian political evolution, and ever since the option of adaptation has been drastically narrowed if not foreclosed, leading to a permanent crisis in regime–society relations. At times when regimes decline and state power weakens, anarchy rather than new orders result. The accustomed division of Russian history into periods of reform and periods of reaction (Crummey (ed.), 1989) can be seen as a symptom of a deeper malaise, the structural impediments to the emergence of political order. The imperial state can be seen as a distinctive form of stability regime, and Russian history as polarized between periods of stability and periods of anarchy, with the problem of political order unresolved.

Adaptation as an Obstacle to Transformation

The enhancement of regime autonomy under Yeltsin was justified on the grounds that Russia faced the danger of premature adaptation, a capitulation to existing social interests (e.g. the so-called military industrial complex and the shards of the old elite system). Under Gorbachev premature adaptation might have condemned the USSR to continued stagnation in that the interests of the old ruling group would have gone unchallenged. The fear of premature adaptation lies at the heart of 'shock therapy', the argument that the exit from the stagnatory effects of the stability regime requires a sharp break, supplied above all by price liberalization, to allow the marketization of the economy and, indeed, of people's minds (Sachs, 1994).

However, the critics of shock therapy contend that in any political process there must be a balance between adaptation to existing realities and rejection of them, and that the radical economic reformers had lost touch with this basic political fact. Whilst the pretensions to pre-political stability of revolutionary socialism might have been rejected, it is not so clear that the welfare gains associated with the social democratic programme of evolutionary socialism should have been jettisoned as well. In other words, those who argue that an evolutionary exit from the stability regime was possible point to the high degree of adaptation that had already taken place within the framework of the old regime, whereas those who favoured a more revolutionary approach insisted that little could be salvaged of the old system and that concessions would give rise to premature adaptation and the end of transformation. Thus, once again, post-communist transformative goals inhibited the development of hegemonic strategies, undermined democratic consensus building and stimulated the development of new forms of regime rule.

Weakness of the Social Subject of Adaptation

Many of the morbid social ills attending the fall of communism are common to most modern societies, but there are some that are system specific and can be explained by what Berliner has dubbed the 'societal-void theory' (Berliner, 1994). The Soviet system destroyed or gutted traditional institutions of authority and control like the church and family, and even those social institutions that survived, like trade unions, were thoroughly subverted from within. The fall of communism resulted therefore in the retraditionalization of society against the background of the struggle for the re-creation of the social forms of modernity.

The very fluidity of the subject of adaptation exacerbated the authoritarianism of the post-communist polity. The transformatory programme impeded the transition from regime to systemic forms of rule and a gulf opened up between civil society and the political system. There were few effective political or social institutions to mediate adaptive processes, and the transformative programme distrusted the emergence of genuine social organizations that it feared might restrict the scope of the changes. Political parties began to fulfil their mediating functions, but overall a regime system of rule predominated even after the transformatory drive was blunted. Both transformation and adaptation appeared still-born.

State Weakness: Territorial Aspects

Adaptation was inhibited by the amorphous nature of the state, shelled out of a USSR with which for many it had always been coterminous. The borders were fragile and the consolidation of popular sovereignty was undermined by the lack of agreement on who constituted 'the people': did it include the 25 million Russian speakers who now found themselves abroad; and what about the 19 per cent of the population in the Russian Federation who were not ethnically Russian? Traditionally the basis for order in Russia had come from the imposition of compulsory unity when faced by external threats and the imperatives of keeping a huge ramshackle geopolitical unit together. Whilst the external threats might now have given way to a relatively benign international climate, domestic geopolitical imperatives have by no means been transcended.

The 'new medievalism' (to use Berdyaev's term) was particularly apparent in the emergence of semi-autonomous regions and republics. Adaptation to the international economy was a highly differentiated process, with local accommodation at the regional level and with peripheral areas (e.g. the Russian Far East) being particularly susceptible to the influence of neighbouring systems. In these circumstances adaptation can give rise to absorption (something that the Bolsheviks had always feared), which might in turn provoke yet a new round of authoritarian state building of the traditional sort.

State Weakness: Institutional Aspects

The legacy of the Bolshevik transformation can above all be seen in the weakness of social structures and institutions. Adaptation implies an existing form of society and polity to which adaptation is sought, but in Russia the hybrid nature of political institutions acted as one of the main blockages to adaptation. The legislature inherited from the old regime, for example, had only a very low capacity to evolve into a genuine parliament. The nascent party system was stamped by its struggle with the one-party state.

Adaptation in the late communist and early post-communist years was mediated by numerous domestic pressures, above all by the general feudalization of politics as competing baronies were carved out of the state administration. The defining feature of post-communism is the retreat from governmentality, which in the context of the stability regime meant the aspiration of the party-state to control all aspects of political and social life, but this has been accompanied everywhere by a decline in governance in its entirety. Whilst Russian history is stamped by the titanic struggle for the survival of the state itself, the post-Soviet state was rudimentary and with a low capacity to enforce the usual attributes of statehood, including tax-collecting, maintaining order, implementing decisions and retaining the monopoly over the legitimate use of force. The ideology of neo-liberalism, highly influential at the fall of the communist regimes, further delegitimized extended state action in the social and economic spheres.

Transformation as a Cultural rather than a Political Project

Whereas Marx had considered the dictatorship of the proletariat a social category, Lenin gave the idea a severely political form, meaning the literal dictatorship of one group over another. Analogously, it might be argued that transformation is a long-term process of growing into modernity. Polanyi used the term to describe the cultural revolution attending the birth of modern capitalist democracy, using the term 'great transformation' to describe the process whereby pre-modern patterns of subjectivity were transformed according to the logic of modernity (Polanyi, 1945). Today in Russia an accelerated 'great transformation' is being imposed on the country in a storm similar in certain respects to the transformatory impulse at the heart of revolutionary socialism. The problem, however, is that revolutionary transformation tends to undermine the social and cultural bases on which a genuine Polanyi-type transformation can take root: in other words, accelerated transformation may well be no transformation at all, as the Bolsheviks had earlier found to their cost.

The notion of a premature adaptation suggests not only concessions to an unreformed society but also limited progress towards the profound transformation of the type described by Polanyi. Yeltsin's regime in practice achieved only modest successes before domestic pressure for adaptation without transformation blunted the campaign. Only limited decommunization took place, and the hopes of the more radical democrats, for lustration laws and the like, went unheeded. Enormous continuities remained, not only in elite structures but also in patterns of elite interaction. More importantly, only limited progress was made towards the transformation of societal orientation towards the subjectivity that could sustain a market democracy and the rule of law.

The Destruction of Normalcy

Let us suppose that Alexander Solzhenitsyn was right and that the Soviet experiment represented no more than a mad dash down a blind alley: what are the consequences of this? Alain Besancon argued that 'if the absence of socialism is caused not by technical but by ontological reasons, if it does not exist because it simply cannot exist, then its introduction will lead only to the destruction of what already does exist' (*Glasnost*, No. 13, 1988, p. 19). Earlier Gyorgy Bence and Janos Kis (writing under the pseudonym of Marc Rakovski) noted Soviet-type systems were *sui generis* new social formations travelling up a historical dead end with limited potential for internal development (Rakovski, 1978). In other words, the search for a stability that not only did not exist but could not exist rendered the Bolshevik project not transformatory but destructive. The destruction of conventional patterns of daily life, the 'normalcy' associated with the last two and a half thousand years of Graeco-Roman Judaic civilization, meant that the destruction of the old regime could not be followed by a 'return to normalcy' because there was no longer anything normal to return to. 'Compared to this', Arpad Szakolczai noted, all talk about 'property', 'markets', or social policy', is 'peanuts' (Szakolczai, 1993, n. 16).

The absence of a generally recognized 'normalcy' to which the country could return following the long Bolshevik 'emergency' has given a disturbing edge to debates in Russia today. It is not clear what can be rejected and what can be adapted from the past or abroad. The past in Russia is itself a deeply unsettling category, not as wholly antithetical to democracy as some have suggested yet harrowed by failed transformations, whilst the 'abroad' for many takes the form of a civilizational threat. The appeal to Russian traditions in a society where the social bases of tradition have largely been destroyed and where political space lacked social and institutional form could not but appear artificial. Their very social artificiality allowed the symbols of Russian statehood, and indeed the tokens of democracy like 'the constitution' to become no more than symbols in political conflict rather than elements of a substantive social process.

Adaptation itself, therefore, is a paradoxical process. The problem of adaptation is one that operates both over time (the past) and space (the form of modernity prevalent in the West today). The spatial form of adaptation suggests that Russia can draw on the experience of the West, whilst the temporal form seeks elements of a 'usable past'. The historical and culturological elements are closely connected, but the question of 'fit' (congruence) between the attitudes and expectations of citizens and the political system is fraught with methodological difficulties, as the long-running debate over the value of the concept of political culture indicates (Welch, 1993). The pitfall of circularity in the argument marginalizes the factors that contribute to change. It is precisely because in Russia core elements of national identity, and even basic notions of the individual's relations with society, remain contested, that post-communist adaptation becomes an exercise fraught with ambiguity. Adaptation even more than usual became a process of open-ended evolution rather than a predefined end state.

Democracy and the Struggle for Order

Two world-historical orders have dissolved in Russia in the twentieth century: it remains to be seen whether a third will arise on their ruins. The dissolution of the tsarist order was followed by a period of disorder that was only partially reversed by the Bolsheviks. Their attempts precisely to build a system that repudiated the classical features of a political order, including the renunciation, for example, of explicit appeals to the national interest in foreign policy or to the traditional national community at home, gave rise to what we have called the stability regime. The dissolution in turn of the stability regime gave way to a new period of disorder as it soon became clear that the antithesis of the communist system, in the first instance at least, was not democracy but a distinctive type of anarchy. The post-communist restoration of order is profoundly ambiguous, being no longer based on the aspiration to achieve some sort of post-political stability but being an order that in certain respects is marked by pre-political features, derived from the logic of transformation itself.

The periods of disorder following the fall of the old regimes is largely derived from Russia's weak adaptive potential. The Soviet system underwent a catastrophic collapse rather than a fall, and the reasons for this have to be sought in the peculiarly destructive features of the 'stability regime'. Long colonization by the Party meant that the state functioned as a peculiarly neo-feudal organization, whilst the institutions of the market and law were rudimentary and often corrupt. The stability regime itself had gutted the social and political institutions that might have contributed to the structuring of political and social space in a democratic way. In this context it is not surprising that the antithesis of the communist order is not democracy but disorder.

The regime born of August 1991 can be defined as a *sui generis*-type of 'authoritarian democracy'. The legitimating ideology was a type of universalized democracy, accompanied by the language of 'rejoining world civilization' and the like, but whose democratic features were undermined by regime forms of rule and the transformatory impulse. The depth of the Soviet destruction of Russian traditions and society, and the gulf between Soviet and Western developmental trajectories, has meant that a contradiction has emerged between domestic and international adaptation. We have suggested, moreover, that the option of domestic adaptation itself was foreclosed because of the absence of a structured political society that might have provided the framework for the transition from regime to systemic forms of rule. The relationship between regime and society has remained at best wary and at worst antagonistic. The relationship between regime and state, moreover, has not been a settled one – with a damaging fluidity in state structures that has increased the regime's relative autonomy and freedom from popular or political control.

The founding process of a new order is the defining moment of that order, but the tension between transformatory and adaptive goals has been reflected in contradictory popular perceptions of the post-communist regime in which everything is held to have changed whilst everything has remained the same. Is it democratic or authoritarian, or some in-between type of soft authoritarianism? At the level of high politics a regime system of government has emerged in which one-party rule has given way to non-party government, and at the level of daily life and social relations much of the style of the old regime has been perpetuated. The attempt to avoid a premature adaptation by maintaining the transformatory impulse has perpetuated the regime system.

The revolutions of 1989–91 have been represented as part of the third great democratic wave in history (Huntington, 1991), but this liberal universalism can be seen to be as much of a utopian project as the stability regime it sought to eradicate. Democracy might well be the result, and given the nature of contemporary international society this is the 'norm' to which all societies have to respond, but this is only one outcome amongst many and is mediated, as we have seen, by problems of adaptation. In the modern world, political order tends to be associated with democratic forms of rule, but there might be alternatives. Whilst the failure (or inability) of the Soviet regime to adapt to 'modernity' and its associated patterns of subjectivity might have been the central process in its collapse, the emerging 'new order' may be far from that intended by the ideologists of the neo-liberal transition and the theorists of 'democratization' (Gray, 1993; Gellner, 1994).

Conclusion

The structural approach and its associated vocabulary outlined above give rise to a number of corollaries. First, revolutionary socialism was predicated on the belief that a transformatory process would give rise to some form of steady state stability. Belief in the immanent 'stability' of a post-market and post-political world entailed certain consequences at the level of political practice, especially when the transformation did not concern the conversion of a developed economy and polity to socialism but involved a sustained developmental dynamic. Development in the Soviet context, of course, proved highly ambiguous and gave rise to a distinctive form of modernization without modernity. Stability in the 'stability regime' proved elusive, and on both the economic and political levels required sustained regime activism to imbue the system with any dynamism. In the absence of regime vitality, and with the option of adaptation foreclosed, the system fell prey to stagnation.

Second, the Gorbachev years represented the end of belief in the potential of transformation to give rise to stability. Stability is here used in two senses: as an ideologized notion of stability in a post-political economy world in which economic and social relations have become transparent (and in which, incidentally, the alleged inherent militarism of international capitalism has been laid to rest); and as a contingent practice designed to sustain stability in the management of a political system. Perestroika represented the shift from the first sort of stability politics to the second, accompanied by elements of deideologization and adaptation. Perestroika opened the door to adaptation. Attempts were made to move beyond the regime systems of rule, in which the ruling elite governed with a low and arbitrary level of reciprocity with society, to a more ordered systemic form of governance, bound by law, rules and popular representation – a strategy which in the end failed.

Third, Yeltsin's rule represented a renewal of the transformatory drive, but this time designed to establish the conditions for capitalist democracy. Transformation, however, stimulated the new system once again to adopt regime forms of rule. Regime capacity to achieve its desired changes, moreover, was inhibited by its simultaneous commitment to adaptation, both to its own society and to international norms of economic and political life. The hybrid system, torn between transformation and an elusive adaptation, gave rise to a form of 'authoritarian democracy', where the achievements in democratic development were undoubted but were mitigated by weak institutionalization, legal arbitrariness and declining state capacity. Post-communist Russian political development thus came to share some of the features of Third World countries, and to a degree its political system could be characterized by the term 'low intensity democracy', a veneer of democratic practices astride growing social inequalities, corruption, and relatively closed forms of regime rule (Gills *et al.* (eds), 1993).

Fourth, adaptation itself is a highly ambiguous process, assuming a set of domestic and international civilizational norms which in the event proved elusive and contingent. The measure of adaptation in the early years of the August regime was largely drawn not from the country itself but measured against apparently universal standards of 'Westernization'. The age of paradox is far from over, and as Gray noted in the context of the shift of economic power to the non-occidental cultures of East Asia, 'in this larger historical context, the Soviet collapse will be seen not as another surge in an irresistible movement of Westernisation but as the beginning of the world-historical reversal of that movement' (Gray, 1994, p. 41).

In the context of the structural approach outlined above, the alleged failure of Sovietology to predict the Soviet collapse becomes a largely meaningless question. For analytical purposes we can distinguish between the related concepts of prediction, the statement of some future event at a more or less specified time precluding other potential outcomes, and anticipation, suggesting the possibility of a variety of outcomes with an open-ended time frame.

A vast body of literature and academic writing from the very first days of Bolshevik power indeed anticipated the inherent lack of viability of a post-market stability regime, quite apart from the enormously disruptive political and social consequences of the project. In this connection we need only cite Andrei Platonov's writings of the civil war years (especially *Kotlovan* and *Chevengur*) and Evgenii Zamyatin's dystopian *We*, the precursor of a distinctive twentieth-century genre. Zamyatin's community (called the United States) was based on the proposition that freedom and happiness were incompatible, and already in 1924 he noted that 'elections themselves have rather a symbolic meaning. They remind us that we are a united, powerful organism of millions of cells' in which there was 'no place for contingencies', like not knowing in advance the result of the elections (Zamyatin, 1924, p. 129). On the academic front, Bertrand Russell's *The Practice and Theory of Bolshevism*, a devastating critique of Bolshevik rule, was first published in November 1920. The moral collapse associated with the rise of Bolshevism was explored, amongst others, by Nikolai Berdyaev, whilst G.P. Fedotov fruitfully explored the tension in the relationship between Russia and the West.

In his justly renowned 'Mr X' article of 1947, George Kennan noted that 'Soviet power, like the capitalist world of its conception, bears within it the seeds of its own decay'. With remarkable prescience he warned that if anything were ever to disrupt the unity and the efficacy of the party as a political instrument, Soviet Russia might be changed overnight from one of the strongest to one of the weakest and most pitiable of national societies (Kennan, 1947, p. 580), an insight whose implications Gorbachev might well have considered with profit. In a similar vein, others had noted in connection with Soviet-type systems that 'the whole vast apparatus of domination which seemed omnipotent and omnipresent the day before, disintegrates the next day' (Féher *et al.*, 1983, p. 21). The stability regime itself eroded the bases on which a functioning political order could be built, and the manner of its collapse was immanent in the system itself. In this respect, the fall of the regime in 1991 added little that was not already well known.

Whilst the factors conditioning the fall of the Soviet system had been anticipated by numerous writers, the disintegration of the USSR as a geopolitical entity was determined by a separate set of factors which had a logic of their own. Whilst we can anticipate the reconstitution of an economic and ultimately a political identity for large parts of the former Soviet Union, it is most unlikely that anything like the Soviet-type stability regime will be restored. Similarly, whilst we can anticipate the emergence of a democratic and prosperous Russia, we cannot with any confidence predict this. The development of a regime system of government following August 1991 indicated only a partial reconstitution of politics, and the perpetuation of stability-managing responses reflected the paradoxes of adaptation and indicated just how hard it would be to create a new political order. Rather than suggesting that some form of liberal democracy is inevitable, the dynamics of post-communist transformation and adaptation suggest that a new political order is in the making whose features can only be hazily discerned. This new order will reflect the society and political culture of Russia, whilst at the same time responding to the demands of modernity within the framework of remodernization.

As others in this volume have observed, it is not at all clear what is the most appropriate social science methodology to understand the grandiose changes taking place in the former communist world. The discipline is being 'normalized', and we find that the skills learned in the old days of Soviet studies are now being applied to new fields and new problems whilst incorporating the methodologies developed in the study of comparative politics. The question remains, however, whether the concepts developed to study communist systems or Western societies are appropriate for analysis of the post-communist world. The attempt to apply basic Western concepts to Soviet studies as part of the reaction against the totalitarian model obscured precisely what was unique about the system. The uncritical application today, too, of such notions as 'democratization ' and 'transition' is liable to obscure our understanding of the profound dynamic of societal, national and political reconstitution taking place now in Russia and other former Soviet states. We must accept that the Owl of Minerva flies at dusk for good reason.

References

Barnard, F.M., 1991. *Pluralism, Socialism and Political Legitimacy*, Cambridge University Press, Cambridge.

Berliner, J., 1994. 'Reflections on the Social Legacy', in J.R. Millar and S. Wolchik (eds), *The Social Legacy of Communism*, Cambridge University Press, Cambridge, pp. 379-85.

Breslauer, G., 1978/1984. 'On the Adaptability of Soviet Welfare-State Authoritarianism', in E. Hoffmann and R.F. Laird (eds), *The Soviet Polity in the Modern Era*, Aldine Publishing Company, New York.

Brzezinski, Z., 1966. 'The Soviet Political System: Transformation or Degeneration?', *Problems of Communism*, Vol. 15, No. 1, January-February, pp. 1-15.

Cerny, P.G., 1979. 'Foreign Policy Leadership and National Integration', *British Journal of International Studies*, Vol. 5, pp. 59-85.

Crummey, R. (ed.), 1989. *Reform in Russia and the USSR*, University of Illinois Press, Urbana.

Dunham, V., 1976. *In Stalin's Time: Middle Class Values in Soviet Fiction*, Cambridge University Press, Cambridge.

Féher, F., A. Heller and G. Markus, 1983. *Dictatorship over Needs: An Analysis of Soviet Societies*, Basil Blackwell, London.

Fukuyama, F., 1989. 'The End of History', *The National Interest*, Summer, pp. 3-18.

——1992. *The End of History and the Last Man*, Penguin Books, London.

Gellner, E., 1994. *Conditions of Liberty. Civil Society and Its Rivals*, Hamish Hamilton, London.

Gills, B., J. Rocamora and R. Wilson (eds), 1993. *Low Intensity Democracy: Political Power in the New World Order*, Pluto Press, London.

Gray, J., 1993. *Post-Liberalism: Studies in Political Thought*, Routledge, 1993.

——1994. *Post-Communist Societies in Transition: A Social Market Perspective*, The Social Market Foundation, 1994.

Hoffman, J., 1984. 'The Coercion/Consent Analysis of the State under Socialism', in Neil Harding (ed.), *The State in Socialist Society*, Macmillan, London.

Hudelson, J., 1993. *The Future That Failed: Origins and Destinies of the Soviet Model*, London, Routledge, 1993.

Huntington, S.P., 1991. *The Third Wave: Democratization in the Late Twentieth Century*,

University of Oklahoma Press, Norman, OK.

——1993. 'The Clash of Civilizations?', *Foreign Affairs*, Vol. 72, No. 3 (Summer), pp. 22-49.

Jowitt, K., 1992, 'Inclusion', in K. Jowitt, *New World Disorder: The Leninist Extinction*, University of California Press, Berkeley.

Kagarlitsky, B., 1989. 'The Importance of Being Marxist', *New Left Review*, no. 178 (November-December), pp. 29-36.

Kennan, G., 1947. 'The Sources of Soviet Conduct', *Foreign Affairs*, July, pp. 566-82.

Kolakowski, L., 1991. 'The Myth of Human Self-Identity: Unity of Civil and Political Society in Socialist Thought', in C. Kukathas, D.W. Lovell and W. Malley (eds), *The Transition from Socialism*, Melbourne, Longman Cheshire, pp. 41-58.

Lowenthal, R., 1970. 'Development vs. Utopia in Communist Policy', in C. Johnson (ed.), *Change in Communist Systems*, Stanford University Press, Stanford, pp. 33-116.

Millar, J., 1985. 'The Little Deal: Brezhnev's Contribution to Acquisitive Socialism', *Slavic Review*, Winter, pp. 694-706.

Murray, J., 1994. *The Russian Press from Brezhnev to Yeltsin*, Edward Elgar, Aldershot.

Nove, A., 1983. *The Economics of Feasible Socialism*, Unwin Hyman, London.

Offe, C., 1991. 'Capitalism by Democratic Design? Democratic Theory Facing the Triple Transition in East Central Europe', *Social Research*, Vol. 58, No. 4, Winter, pp. 865-902.

Polan, A.J., 1984. *Lenin and the End of Politics*, Methuen, London.

Polanyi, K., 1945. *The Great Transformation: The Political and Economic Origins of Our Time*, Gollancz, London.

Pozdnyakov, E., 1991. 'The Problem of Returning the Soviet Union to European Civilization', *Paradigms: The Kent Journal of International Relations*, Vol. 5, No. 1/2, pp. 45-57.

Rakovski, M., 1978. *Towards an East European Marxism*, Alison Busby, London.

Sachs, J., 1994. *Understanding 'Shock Therapy'*, The Social Market Foundation, London.

Strange, S., 1994. 'Rethinking Structural Change in the International Political Economy: States, Firms and Diplomacy', in R. Stubbs and G.R.D. Underhill (eds), *Political Economy and the Changing Global Order*, London, Macmillan.

Szakolczai, A., 1993. *Types of Mayors, Types of Subjectivity*, EUI Working Papers SPS No. 93/5, Florence.

Szamuely, T., 1974. *The Russian Tradition*, Fontana, London.

Thurston, R.W., 1987. *Liberal City, Conservative State*, Oxford University Press.

Tocqueville, A. De, 1981. *Democracy in America*, Random House, New York.

Von Laue, T., 1993. 'Gorbachev in Historic Perspective' and 'Gorbachev's Place in History', in J.L. Wieczynski (ed.), *The Gorbachev Reader*, Charles Schlacks Publisher, Salt Lake City.

Welch, S., 1993. *The Concept of Political Culture*, Macmillan, London.

Wells, H.G., 1950. *Interview with J.V. Stalin*, Current Book Distributors, Sydney.

Zamyatin, E., 1924. *We*, Dutton & Co., New York.

Zaslavsky, V., 1982. *The Neo-Stalinist State*, Harvester, Brighton.

11

Social Science, 'Slavistics' and Post-Soviet Studies

RON HILL

As Michael Cox argues in the opening chapter, the rapid decline and collapse of the Bolshevik-inspired communist systems around the world took the profession of 'Sovietologists' by surprise (see also Cox: 1994). Hindsight and glib commentary might suggest that the members of that profession ought to have predicted it: after all, the point of scholarship is understanding, and understanding implies an appreciation of processes as they unfold, which in turn should allow the observer to identify the direction of change. The broad failure – even amongst some who had most passionately hoped for such a turn of events – has had at least two effects. First, the profession has been forced to face up to this apparent failure, and to re-evaluate its own identity, its strengths and weaknesses; and secondly, scholars based on academic disciplines who until the late 1980s had paid scant attention to the communist-ruled world have now entered the fray as researchers, to a considerable extent displacing those who have spent half a lifetime in the study of the region and its systems. The present chapter argues for a rather more complementary approach, suggesting that both sets of scholars possess knowledge and skills that are vital to the other if the study of those societies is to be successfully integrated into scholarship over the next decade or two.

Communist Collapse and the Scholars

The collapse of the Soviet Union in the last quarter of 1991, preceded by the demise of the Soviet-supported regimes in Eastern Europe and followed by the transformation of other regimes modelled on the Soviet example, has presented the professional students of the former communist-ruled countries with a severe crisis of confidence. Whilst no serious scholar can claim the power of exact prediction, the fact remains that virtually none in the profession convincingly argued that the system that had existed for half a century – three-quarters of a century in the Soviet case (and almost as long in Mongolia) – would not survive into the 1990s; and into the next century.

Certainly, it would not remain unchanged: a variety of changes had indeed taken place since the death of Stalin in 1953, and different 'communist' countries had developed recognizably individual patterns of institutions and practices whilst maintaining certain fundamental principles intact. But very few observers predicted the collapse and abandonment of the system, whether they came from the disciplines of social science or from the multidisciplinary field of area studies. These two groups of scholars had applied their different ranges of skills to the common object of study; they argued occasionally over the appropriate methods for studying the system; and they made their various scholarly contributions from a range of ideological perspectives: some admired the attempt to create a new kind of society based on different principles from those of individualism and capitalism, whilst others were openly hostile to everything the communist system stood for. But they were effectively united in their broad assumption that the system was here to stay. The failure to identify the constellation of fundamental weaknesses in the system has raised once again the arguments over methodology, as a set of political systems that were secretive, exotic and challenging have given way to transitional regimes that are, for the time being at any rate, so much open to study that scholars with no previous interest are venturing in, in an attempt to capture the essence of transformation. The arguments over how to study such regimes have now acquired an urgency that renders whole schools of scholars vulnerable to intellectual attack and jealous of their scholarly *amour propre*.

Communism and the Social Sciences

There has been a long-standing debate in Soviet studies, stemming at least from Fleron's challenging collection of 1969 under the title *Communist Studies and the Social Sciences*, about the appropriate methodological and intellectual approaches to understanding and explaining the world of communism, particularly the former Soviet Union. At issue was the significance of the broad linguistic, cultural and historical background for an understanding of the politics of a system that was, by common consent, 'different' from the bourgeois or liberal democracies familiar in the West. So different did it appear to be, indeed, that conventional conceptual frameworks were inappropriate, since in many cases the forms in which they were operationalized could not be applied to a communist-ruled society. Survey research, interviews with politicians and administrators, election studies, analysis of coalition behaviour, studies of stratification, participation or deviance – these and other standard research concepts and techniques in the social sciences simply could not be applied to the closed societies under communist rule; official statistics including census data, although widely used, were suspect and could not be verified. These and a host of other problems demanded the devising of special techniques that often required diligent quarrying of printed materials (also available on restricted terms: local newspapers could not be subscribed to from outside the country concerned, for example), and this in turn placed considerable emphasis on linguistic competence and general understanding of the context in which political, economic and social behaviour took place.

The argument was very well expressed by Fleron himself, in his Preface to the volume mentioned above. In attempting to study the Soviet Union as a graduate student, he found he had to study subjects that appeared very remote from the area of his principal concern. 'Why', he asked himself, 'learn about these unrelated subjects? Why not just immerse oneself in the study of the geographic area?' Later, after training as a political scientist, he asked why he had to learn about Russian history, literature, economics, geography and the like, rather than concentrating on the study of Soviet politics, which was his real interest (Fleron (ed.), 1969, p. vii).

In fact, the question can be posed in a slightly different way: is it necessary to study the history, literature, economics and geography of the former Soviet Union in order to understand its politics? Are essential 'ingredients' in the understanding or explanation absent if it is not informed by such 'background' material? Without it, is there a risk that misinterpretation might result? Or, less definitively, does such a study enrich our understanding of Soviet politics to an extent that makes the additional time and effort worthwhile?

These questions can, of course, be asked of the study of any country or region: colleagues with a particular interest in Asian, African and other area studies have no doubt been perplexed by the same set of questions. It is therefore germane to our approach to the study of post-Soviet Russian (and Ukrainian, and Uzbek, and Slovak, Hungarian, Polish and Bulgarian) studies. To some extent, the debate reflects the tension – perhaps even conflict – between scholarly disciplines and area studies.

Communist Studies: Methods and Needs

In the days of the Soviet Union, with its 'satellite' systems in Eastern Europe and elsewhere around the globe, including Southeast Asia, the Caribbean (Cuba), the Middle East (South Yemen), and self-styled Marxist regimes in Africa, plus the 'alternative' communist regimes in China, Albania and North Vietnam, and the communist-inspired regimes of Yugoslavia and certain states of India, 'communist' politics seemed to be *sui generis*. As a political system it set out to be different from the 'bourgeois' systems it rejected. And, although it adopted some of the terminology of 'conventional state machinery' (Scott, 1969, ch. 3), it was quite inappropriate to attempt to study it by the methods of Western political science. It was clear that the institutions, however similar their appearance, functioned quite differently from their counterparts in liberal democracies: elections, parliaments, councils and parties were quite different in the way they conducted their business, their interrelations and their functioning – not to mention the obvious differences in the extent to which the different systems attempted to regulate and control the lives of citizens.

Moreover, one particular element in that control rendered conventional study impossible: access to the appropriate information was not open to Western scholars or even to scholars in the countries concerned. Meaningful interviews with politicians, survey research, even identifying pertinent issues through perusal of the press – the standard fare of Western political science methodology – was quite impossible. The result was the devising of analytical concepts and techniques peculiar to the study of communist systems. 'Totalitarianism', 'monohierarchical polity', 'the mono-organizational society', 'the communist party state' (sometimes with a hyphen between 'communist' and 'party', sometimes between 'party' and 'state'): these and other terms distinguished communist studies from the study of other types of political system (the terms quoted above are to be found in, *inter alia,* Arendt, 1951; Friedrich and Brzezinski, 1956, 1965; Laird, 1970; Rigby, 1990). As for methodology, most students had relatively few opportunities to visit the target of their intellectual curiosity – they certainly did not enjoy free access – and were forced, at a distance (but in relative comfort), to engage in 'the arcane art of Kremlinology' (Burks, 1983), observing 'who eats before whom' in order to divine 'who is doing-in whom' (Bell, 1962).

To a considerable extent, the scholarly concerns, even with their restricted methodological repertoire, reflected political needs at a time when the world was riven by ideologically based confrontation. A sophisticated model of Soviet politics was not needed by Western policy-makers whose concerns were to deal with whoever might rule the Soviet Union today or tomorrow. The communist-ruled countries were manifestly centralized systems dominated by one political elite based on the Marxist-Leninist party and not obviously responsive to popular demands. In those circumstances the study of politics in the villages or of voters' attitudes, for example, even if it were possible, was scarcely likely to add significantly to our appreciation of the likely defence posture or economic priorities of the next generation of Kremlin leaders, or help us predict the overthrow of a leading politician.

Communist Studies: An Academic Ghetto

For these reasons, at least, the study of Soviet and communist politics - and economics and sociology - was relegated to a kind of academic ghetto. There was little exchange between Soviet studies and political science, or Soviet studies and economics. The methodologies and conceptual frameworks of the mainstream disciplines were inapplicable and therefore inappropriate to the study of communist systems, and the study of these systems was seen as having very little to contribute to the mainstream disciplines, since it could not answer the questions that had come to dominate the agenda: voting behaviour, studies of community power, party organization, how to induce growth without inflation or to maintain full employment in market economies. The study of communist systems simply had nothing to offer. It is, I believe, not wholly accurate to assert that students of the Soviet Union isolated themselves from the mainstream (see Fleron and Hoffmann, 1993, p. 372), although they may have had reasons of professional vanity for doing so: the fact is that the mainstream itself was not particularly interested in what the Soviet and communist experience had to offer; concepts such as 'totalitarianism' and 'authoritarianism' seemed adequate to depict the communist system (see, for example, Finer, 1970; Crick, 1973). Furthermore, it might be observed that much American scholarship betrayed ignorance of the work done by scholars in Europe and elsewhere, even that published in the English language, whereas the reverse was broadly not true: European scholars could not realistically ignore the work of scholars in the United States. Much of the criticism levelled at Sovietology by Fleron and Hoffmann and other transatlantic scholars is less applicable to British scholars, I believe, and this distinction stems in part from different political circumstances (Europe as a whole has been more prepared to give the Soviet Union the benefit of the doubt) and different intellectual traditions (American-style 'political science' did not reach Europe until the 1960s). European scholars were therefore able to make certain statements about the Soviet Union that in the context of the United States would have branded their author as maverick, misguided, naïve or in some other way unacceptable: the mixed reputation of Jerry Hough is a case in point.

Bridging the Gap

From the late 1960s onwards, in part a response to the growing availability of new kinds of information and greater access to the target countries, attempts were made by some scholars to bridge the gap between 'communist area studies' and mainstream disciplines, notably political science. The work of Gordon Skilling (1966; Skilling and Griffiths (eds),

1971) and others in attempting to apply the concept of interest groups to the study of communist politics attracted considerable attention, and the challenging approach of Jerry Hough (1977) in applying quantitative methods and innovative operational techniques to the comparative studies of Soviet and Western systems led to controversy in the profession without really making Soviet politics acceptable material to the discipline of political science. To a considerable extent, the controversy concerned the unwillingness of Hough and others in the 'revisionist' school to make value judgements about the nature of the communist system. The quest for 'value-free' political science clashed with the older tradition – fed in no small measure by the insights and experiences of the émigré community of scholars – of condemnation of the system for its manifest failure to match Western standards in such areas as human and civil rights. Studies of political culture, by adapting a concept developed in political science, also began to bridge the gap between the discipline and the broad study of a civilization (White, 1979; Brown and Gray (eds), 1977, 1979; Brown (ed.), 1984). Studies of local government, also, attempted to provide a picture of a country's political life that was richer and fuller than Kremlinology permitted (Stewart, 1968; Taubman, 1973; Hill, 1977; Friedgut, 1979; Ross, 1987; Bahry, 1987; Hahn, 1988). But their impact on political science was minimal.

Multidisciplinary Area Studies

On the other side of the equation, throughout the 1960s and into the 1990s, stands the multidisciplinary work of a scholar such as the late Alec Nove. Whilst easy to dismiss as 'Alecdotal', since his evidence was drawn from an exceptionally wide reading of Russian and Soviet history, literature and the press, and somewhat scorned by economists driven by adherence to 'models' that are not rooted in observed behaviour, Nove's eclectic approach may have produced more insight and genuine understanding of how the Soviet Union actually functioned than any theory-driven analysis of the economy (Nove, 1961, 3rd edn 1989; 1977, 3rd edn 1986, 1972, 1975, 1979, 1989). And Arthur Koestler's novel *Darkness at Noon* or George Orwell's insights in *Animal Farm* were for generations of students far more revealing of the reality of Stalinism than the complex, involved and at times emotional technical debates about the number of victims, or political theories of modernization and the use of terror.

Learning the Language

In all of this, however, one thing was never in doubt: it was essential for a specialist on whatever part of the communist world to be able to use materials in the language or languages of the area. A scholar whose reading was restricted to translations or who was obliged to make use of an interpreter was not regarded as capable of making a serious contribution, and may have felt inadequate in the company of émigré scholars and the growing band who had graduated from a Russian or Slavonic Studies programme, or who had troubled to learn the language after obtaining a social science degree. As opportunities for study in the communist world grew from the 1960s, with the establishment and growth of inter-governmental cultural exchange agreements, a year in the field became *de rigueur* for graduate students and, increasingly, undergraduates. Even so, the opportunities for access remained limited, and with that so did both the level of linguistic competence and the opportunities to develop the 'anthro-pological' side of Soviet studies: the capacity to gain acquaintance of the society 'from within' and the insights that might be revealed through participating in everyday life in those societies. When linguistic exercise is limited to reading between the lines of politicians' speeches or studying the details of legislation or official statements, or even reading the frequently stilted prose of commentators and scholars, insights are likely to be modest. Fleron and Hoffmann identify 'mediocre linguistic skills' as one of the weaknesses of American Sovietology. One result may have been an unwarranted deference towards those whose linguistic capacities were beyond challenge, namely émigré scholars. A notable exception to the generalization that 'anthropological' studies were virtually impossible to undertake is the work of Caroline Humphrey, whose study of a collective farm in Buryatiya (Humphrey, 1993) was based on extended fieldwork.

The results of all this endeavour were, in the circumstances, quite impressive. The world of scholarship in the West did manage to overcome some of the difficulties, to amass a solid body of research and gain an understanding which, on some levels, far surpassed that of scholars living in those countries. They, after all, had to contend with ideological barriers to scholarship which prevented them from even asking what in the West were seen as pertinent questions. As a result, as a distinguished legal scholar in the Soviet Union noted in the mid-1960s, much 'analysis' of legal and political questions was reduced to commentary on the political leadership's latest utterances (Burlatskii, 1965; see also Lepeshkin, 1965, pp. 6–7). Even the notoriously cautious and conservative leader Leonid Brezhnev (1966, p. 9) suggested at the Twenty-Third Communist Party Congress that 'it is necessary to put an end to the notion, current among part of our cadres, that the social sciences have merely a propagandistic significance, and are called upon to explain and comment upon practice' – a statement that was eloquent testimony to the level to which social science had descended.

Western students of the former Soviet Union and Eastern Europe may be on the defensive after their failure to predict the collapse of the system; their self-confidence may have been further eroded by Western governments' perception (however inaccurate it may prove to be) that the Cold War has been won by the West and that it is therefore no longer urgent to invest in the study of the 'enemy'. It may nevertheless be premature to reject the understanding that was achieved, or even the eclectic methodology that contributed to the establishment of 'area studies'. As Edward L. Keenan observed in his presidential address to the annual convention of the American Association for the Advancement of Slavic Studies in Philadelphia, on 19 November 1994, 'the flowering of area studies generally (and to a significant extent we Slavists wrote the book on area studies) has been a major event in the intellectual and cultural life of [the United States] – and not only of this country. On our way we learned, and invented, an astonishing array of specific skills and facts about the area of our interest' (Keenan, 1995).

The Future: Post-Communist Studies

The question that now arises, however, concerns the future – not only that of the countries studied by Slavists and those interested in the phenomenon of communism and related concepts, but of the scholarly skills and methodological techniques that were used to penetrate what, in the case of Russia, Winston Churchill famously identified as 'a riddle wrapped in a mystery inside an enigma'. And if the battalions of those engaged in Russian area studies, with whatever focus, managed to penetrate some of the enigma, dispel some of the mystery and begin to solve the riddle, they – like Churchill – still could not forecast the demise of the political system that had been sustained for most of the twentieth century and its transformation within a few years into a society and system comparable in key respects with those of the West. The events of the decade from 1985 have changed Russia, and even more so much of former Eastern Europe, unrecognizably. Or, to be perhaps more accurate about it, the old restrictions do not apply; events appear to be following a logic that bears some resemblance to the Western experience.

The collapse of communist rule, preceded by a deliberate policy of glasnost that opened up enormous new areas of information, has rendered at least some countries of the former Soviet Union (and its erstwhile allies in Eastern Europe) far more open to investigation by Western – and indeed local – scholars using concepts and techniques that have been standard in the liberal democratic context for decades. Electoral studies, empirical investigations of political culture, surveys of public opinion and the like have now become standard in the study of the social and political life of the former communist world. Are Russia and its former allies therefore becoming 'normal' in this respect? Can the methodologies of the social sciences now at last be used convincingly to investigate and explain the new reality? Moreover, the circumstances that required area studies to serve as a substitute for the methodologies and techniques of academic disciplines have now changed: does that mean that the dichotomy between an area studies and a discipline-based approach has now become irrelevant? Is the rivalry – for that is how it was perceived – between the two approaches now over?

It is tempting to suggest that it is. Certainly, the old techniques have been made redundant by the change in the dominant ideology. The abandonment of censorship and the establishment of a competitive press in place of the communist regimes' use of virtually all publications as an official gazette, make the Kremlinologists' skills of reading between the lines for nuances that might reveal disagreements in the leadership or subtle changes of policy quite irrelevant. Indeed, not simply irrelevant, but quite impossible to pursue: the press is no longer filled with verbatim records of the speeches of politicians, or the texts of party and government statements and decrees. Political life has become far more diverse than it ever was under the old regime, the public has become more discriminating in its needs, and the press reflects those changes. The press is now extremely diverse, and it is impossible to identify a 'newspaper of record' – even of official record, a role that was formerly performed by the central newspapers *Pravda, Izvestiya, Trybuna Ludu, Rabotnichesko delo, Rude Pravo or Nepszabadsdg.* At the very least, these publications – where they still exist, and where they do not now represent simply one political margin – need to be supplemented by others to complete the range of views and information. This immediately poses dilemmas for individual scholars and librarians in the West. Quite apart from the purely logistical questions associated with the collapse of the established state-run bureaucratic channels for the export of publications, choices need to be made concerning which publications are to be purchased. The days when subscriptions to a couple of central newspapers, two or three journals and one or two émigré or dissident publications could suffice are clearly over, but it is not yet clear what range is needed, or even what publications are useful for the purposes of scholarship. The escalating cost of procuring publications from the former communist countries is a separate concern, which is as real for libraries under financial pressure as it is for the lone scholar. The unreliability of supply, as apparently secure publications suddenly go under, is a further professional hazard.

In any case, perusal of the press is no longer an adequate research method. Perhaps it never was: by definition it created certain biases, and meant that much – some might say most – of the political reality beyond certain circles in the capital city was excluded from our understanding.

Today, new institutions, which operate in ways quite alien to the communist tradition, demand our attention. To the extent that they are modelled on or comparable with Western institutions, they require the deployment of new techniques for their study, and that has been happening. Methods standard in the West for decades have been introduced that allow us to add new dimensions to our understanding of what is going on in the countries concerned: opinion surveys, elections and referendums, parliamentary votes, opportunities to interview politicians, plus the memoirs of politicians of the recent past – all these innovations, and the accompanying acquisition of the skills to examine them on the part of scholars in the countries concerned, have changed the underlying assumptions about what can be done and what questions need to be asked. These new opportunities have revealed the limitations of the traditional area studies specialists, whose finely honed skills should perhaps now be discarded: they need to be replaced by different techniques, with which possibly most area specialists are unfamiliar, or at least in which their expertise is at best limited. Counting votes, assessing public opinion and its impact, or explicating the process of coalition formation – these are activities that were rarely deployed in the study of communist politics (note, however, exceptions such as Gilison, 1969).

Social Science and Post-Communist Studies

On the other side of the scholarly divide, there has been an understandable excitement in the discipline-based branches of the scholarly community, who now have undreamt-of opportunities to apply their skills and techniques to the study of societies that in the past were closed to them. The timely application of new research methods has the potential of advancing our understanding of economic, social and political processes in societies undergoing transition from authoritarian rule. Comparisons with, say, southern Europe, parts of Africa and perhaps Latin America may teach us much about the nature of change in societies in transition. The Russian and East European area specialists do not obviously possess the intellectual apparatus that would permit them to undertake such studies competently and with confidence. In the past half-decade, therefore, students of political culture or public opinion, for example, who have never previously shown any interest in the area, have been entering the field with enthusiasm, armed with a questionnaire and a substantial research grant. The foundations that disburse the funds for research are more impressed, it appears, by the sharp focus of an academic discipline than by the broad eclecticism of area studies. It is difficult not to experience professional envy at this, or to refer to it without conveying a sense of 'sour grapes'.

From the purely scholarly perspective, there is no doubt that some of the studies undertaken by generalists, comparativists or other discipline-based scholars in recent years are extremely impressive in their methodological sophistication and rigour. Some studies display commendable modesty in the claims made by their authors, whilst producing no doubt serious and well-grounded results, whether based on surveys, interviews or newly released archive material. Some such studies reveal great care on the part of their authors to avoid elementary errors (linguistic, for example), by way of extremely careful drafting, translation, testing and reformulation of questionnaires, screening and briefing of interviewers and so forth. The work for example, under the auspices of the UK Economic and Social Research Council's East-West Programme strikes this observer as a model of punctilious survey design.

Even so, such work tends to be characterized by a precise and deliberately narrow focus, based upon paradigms derived from the experience of quite different societies. There is little doubt, therefore, that the picture that it presents is at best a partial one, which probably misses nuances that closer observers with a broader appreciation of the cultural and historical background would identify - and which may even lead to unwarranted interpretations.

Studies of public opinion - essentially snapshots at a particular time and in particular localities - that are seen as indicating an underlying preparedness for 'democracy' are a case in point. Jeffrey Hahn (1991), for example, shows a commendable restraint in not assuming that his data from the city of Yaroslavl are applicable to the whole of Russia, yet he still purports to make firm statements about the post-Soviet political culture. Hahn's work, and such political culture studies in general, is subjected to critical assessment by Stephen Welch (1987) and Matthew Wyman (1994). Western investigators of public opinion may well have little appreciation of the significance of particular types of question - those concerning communist party membership, ethnic identity or religious beliefs, for example. Indeed, the cultural context in which a survey is administered may be so different from that of Western societies as to render the results suspect - even though a whole new polling industry has sprung up in the former Soviet Union itself, and in the countries of Eastern Europe. It may not yet be possible to take for granted the willingness of citizens to give accurate responses to questions, given past experiences of what might happen to information about political opinions. And, in the wake of the collapse of the communist system, a new orthodoxy makes it difficult for individuals to express ideas that run counter to the prevailing official values of 'democracy' and 'the market'. What this certainly demands is exceptional care in the construction of the survey instruments - and also, of course, in the interpretation of results. Even the vocabulary of politics may have different significance in a different context: words such as 'party', 'government' or 'authority' may possess undertones arising out of the context that are absent in established Western societies: indeed, the translation of the terminology may be a far from simple technical problem. The position of a city mayor or the meaning of the term 'planning', to cite two examples from local government, are quite different in the British and Russian contexts. I led a British delegation to meet local government officials in Yaroslavl province in November 1994, and there was considerable misunderstanding on both sides until the different uses of identical terminology were sorted out. Concepts and practices such as 'rate-capping' (limiting the amount that a local authority may raise through local taxation) was quite untranslatable except by lengthy circumlocution. Area specialists, straddling the two cultures, as it were, may at least be sensitive to some of these issues – possibly even more so than scholars in the countries concerned.

Area Studies and Social Science Disciplines

One of the particular difficulties of the discipline-based approach is that it attempts to find 'explanations' within the terms of the discipline concerned, seeking parsimony in the range of explanatory material deployed. The result may be a disregard for context and particularly a tendency to overlook history. It appears to this author that many of the profound concerns of the Russian people in the immediate post-Soviet period – reflected in a renewed confrontation with national identity – can best be understood by reference to similar debates that took place in the early nineteenth century. Faced, in the Russian case, with the loss of empire and the collapse of a dream that had inspired several generations who had devoted their lives to its attainment, there is a renewed need to examine their own and their nation's identity. This questioning is not entirely new, even in the modem context, for it has been evolving in the past two or three decades through such cultural movements as the village writers and the organizations to protect Russia's natural environment and historical monuments. The Russian nation, other nations of the former Soviet Union and also the two nations of former Czechoslovakia – not to mention the nations of former Yugoslavia – are seeking to regain identities that were to some extent submerged and obliterated in the attempt to create a standard international 'socialist' citizen, and this is leading inevitably to a rediscovery, re-evaluation and reassessment of their historical experience. Unless that is appreciated, and informed by a comparable awareness of that past, the observer is unlikely to appreciate the concerns which opinion surveys may not adequately reveal. What this implies is that a rich explanation – rather than a parsimonious one – must take into account far more than can be gleaned in a brief expedition. It is at such levels of theory that the area specialist, therefore, has a good deal of distinctive understanding to offer that the discipline-based social scientist cannot emulate. The area specialist may know why certain questions are particularly worth investigating, or why others may yield poor results.

Nevertheless, there can equally be no doubt that the social scientists have much to teach the area specialist by way of approaches, concepts and rigorous methodology. They can – indeed, they must – wean those steeped in the history and culture away from a tendency to 'look into their own heart' in order to appreciate what is going on in Russia and elsewhere: although few scholars would risk committing such thoughts to print, at conferences in the past decade I have heard 'explanations' of the kind, 'Moscow is, after all, Moscow', or 'the Balkans are simply behaving like the Balkans', or even 'the Mongols just don't think like that'. Such assertions lack conviction, to put it at its mildest, as sophisticated social science explanations of anything, even though natives and scholars familiar with the country concerned immediately understand the import of these statements.

Equally invalid is the claim of émigrés or scholars living in those countries to have a superior insight simply by virtue of having grown up and lived there. Certainly, they do possess insights that outsiders can rarely, if ever, acquire; but by the same token, their experience can serve as a blinker, by preventing an appreciation of what questions are significant for the outside observer. What discipline-based scholars can certainly contribute is a concern for methodology and conceptualization, for the careful use of terminology, for the generalization of conclusions so as to generate comparative insight and understanding. To assert that every system is *sui generis* is philosophically accurate, but it leads to the banal and actually erroneous conclusion that no comparisons are possible.

Collaborative Inquiry

Clearly, the area studies and social science approaches both have contributions to make, and a symbiotic relationship may develop over time. In my view, however, the inputs of the two approaches are likely to vary as post-communist Russia and Eastern Europe reach different stages of their evolution. In examining the relationship between Russia (or any other country) and the social sciences as a vehicle for its study and understanding, two approaches to the relationship can be identified.

One focuses on the country, and makes use of the scholarly discipline to elucidate its nature, by posing appropriate questions. Thus, the interest group approach and the political culture approach took a theoretical framework developed on the basis of Western experience. That framework pointed towards certain questions that were deemed suitable to ask in order to reach an understanding of specific aspects of the system. Clearly, the research strategy had to be tailored to take into account the accessibility of relevant evidence, but in the end valuable insights were obtained into the nature and extent of continuity and change in the system. In that sense, social science theory posed questions that did not necessarily arise naturally from the study of a country, but at the very least it led the researcher to approach his or her subject with fresh eyes, and to assess how far the system had changed.

The second approach focuses on questions of theory generated by the scholarly discipline, and uses case studies of the country to test the theory. It is in this sense that the former communist countries are invaluable as a living laboratory at the present time. Comparisons with democratic development or the establishment of a market economy in other parts of the world will allow the testing of hypothesis and partial theories, whilst further comparisons between former communist countries concerning how they approach various problems of transformation and with what success should likewise contribute to the framing of middle-range theory. That certainly explains the interest of discipline-based scholars in the problems of the area.

It is clear, however, that both approaches can learn from the other: area specialists, anxious to explore the applicability of social science concepts, need the advice of discipline specialists over the content of the conceptual framework and over the methodology whereby aspects of it are best studied. Social scientists need the background information and the linguistic skills of the area specialist if elementary misinterpretation is to be avoided.

At the present time, in the early stages of the transition from communist rule, the greatest need is for factual knowledge and understanding of Russia and her former allies. There is so much that is not known, and there is such a demand in the world at large (including governments, business concerns, and so forth, who might be interested in making use of the results of scholarly research) for knowledge of the countries concerned, that plain, straightforward but reliable information is in the greatest demand. At this stage, therefore, the social science disciplines can assist the area studies specialists by introducing rigour into the investigation, whilst the area studies can greatly assist in the interpretation of the results of research, particularly by setting them in their historical and cultural context. At a later stage, when a broad understanding according to the canons of discipline-based scholarship has been attained, Russia and other countries that have undergone the transformation can be expected to contribute to an understanding of some of the more complex processes for which new explanatory theory is being devised.

For these reasons, therefore, 'Post-Soviet Studies' must not be seen as a struggle for supremacy between area specialists and social scientists: each has much of value to contribute to the common quest for knowledge and understanding. The most urgent need is for both sets of scholars to recognize their own merits and limitations and to collaborate.

A Whimsical Postscript

Apart from the possible lack of rigorous discipline-based training in the methods of investigation, area specialists may even be confronted by yet another obstacle as they attempt to come to grips with the momentous changes that have affected the objects of their study: do they possess the intellectual curiosity to persevere? Whatever their political and emotional orientation towards communist systems of rule may have been, they were in many cases attracted to their study precisely because these systems were *different* - exotic even. They had something of the aura of forbidden fruit. They posed a certain kind of intellectual challenge which many exponents of 'Soviet studies' found intellectually stimulating. Students of such systems were not required to engage in what may appear as a somewhat arid activity of counting votes, adding up figures representing public opinion, observing parliamentary coalitions forming and disintegrating - what for many students of politics is their very bread and butter - and this was for many a blessing rather than a source of disappointment. Now that the former communist countries are apparently in the process of becoming 'normal' the allure may have evaporated. As a political scientist might observe, if he or she had been interested in such issues, he/she might more profitably have chosen to concentrate on, say, Italian politics: votes (in elections and referendums), coalitions and the like have been present in abundance in the modem period, almost to the point of embarrassing instability - and the country can boast a better climate, better food and far greater accessibility than practically anywhere in the former communist world. If area specialists need to retrain, as they probably do, will they also abandon study of an area in which they have acquired a good deal of hard-won expertise?

References

Arendt, H. (1951), *The Origins of Totalitarianism* (Cambridge MA: Harcourt, Brace).

Bahry, D. (1987), *Outside Moscow: Power, Politics, and Budgetary Policy in the Soviet Republics* (New York: Columbia University Press).

Bell, D. (1962), 'Ten Theories in Search of Reality: On the Prediction of Soviet Behavior', in his *The End of Ideology: The Exhaustion of Political Ideas in the Fifties* (New York: The Free Press).

Brezhnev, L. (1966), Speech to the Twenty-Third CPSU Congress, quoted in *Pravda*, 30 March.

Brown, A. (ed.) (1984), *Political Culture and Communist Studies* (Basingstoke: Macmillan).

—and J. Gray (eds) (1977, 1979), *Political Culture and Change in Communist States* (London: Macmillan).

Burks, R.V. (1983), 'The Arcane Art of Kremlinology: Faults in the Stars, Faults in Ourselves', *Encounter,* March, pp. 20-30.

Burlatskii, F. (1965), 'Politika i nauka', *Pravda,* 10 January, p. 1.

Cox, M. (1994), 'The End of the USSR and the Collapse of Soviet Studies', *Coexistence,* Vol. 31, pp. 1-16.

Crick, B. (1973), *Basic Forms of Government. A Sketch and a Model* (London: Macmillan).

Finer, S.E. (1970), *Comparative Government* (London: Allen Lane, 1970).

Fleron, F.J. Jr (ed.) (1969), *Communist Studies and the Social Sciences: Essays on Methodology and Empirical Theory* (Chicago: Rand McNally).

—and E.P. Hoffmann (1993), 'Post-Communist Studies and Political Science: Peaceful Coexistence, Detente, and Entente', in Fleron and Hoffmann (eds), *Post-Communist Studies and Political Science: Methodology and Empirical Theory in Sovietology* (Boulder, CO: Westview), pp. 371-85.

Friedgut, T.H. (1979), *Political Participation in the USSR* (Princeton, NJ: Princeton University Press).

Friedrich, C.J., and Z.K. Brzezinski (1956, 1965), *Totalitarian Dictatorship and Autocracy* (Cambridge, MA: Harvard University Press).

Gilison, J.M. (1968), 'Soviet Elections as a Measure of Dissent: The Missing One Percent', *American Political Science Review,* Vol. LXII, No. 3, pp. 814-26.

Hahn, J.W. (1988), *Soviet Grassroots: Citizen Participation in Local Soviet Government* (Princeton, NJ: Princeton University Press).

—(1991), 'Continuity and Change in Russian Political Culture', *British Journal of Political Science,* Vol. 21, No. 4, pp. 393-421.

Hill, R.J. (1977), *Soviet Political Elites: The Case of Tiraspol* (London: Martin Robertson).

Hough, J.F. (1977), *The Soviet Union and Social Science Theory* (Cambridge, MA: Harvard University Press).

Humphrey, C. (1993), *Karl Marx Collective: Economy, Society and Religion in a Siberian Collective Farm* (Cambridge: Cambridge University Press).

Keenan, E.L. (1995), 'What Have We Learned? (What Have We Taught? What Have We Forgotten? What Must We Not Forget?)', *NewsNet: The Newsletter of the AAASS,* Vol. 35, No. 1 (January), pp. 1-6.

Laird, R.A. (1970), *The Soviet Paradigm: An Experiment in Creating a Monohierarchical Polity* (New York: The Free Press).

Lepeshkin, A.I. (1965), 'Nazrevshie voprosy razvitiya nauki Sovetskogo gosudarstvennogo prava', *Sovetskoe gosudantvo ipravo,* No. 2, pp. 5-15.

Nove, A. (1961, 1989), *The Soviet Economy* (London: George Allen & Unwin).

—(1972), *An Economic History of the USSR* (Harmondsworth: Penguin).

—(1975), *Stalinism and After* (London: George Allen & Unwin).

—(1977, 1986), *The Soviet Economic System* (London: George Allen & Unwin).

—(1979), *Political Economy and Soviet Socialism* (London: George Allen & Unwin).

—(1989), *Glasnost in Action: Cultural Renaissance in Russia* (London: Unwin Hyman).

Rigby, T.H. (1990), *The Changing Soviet System: Mono-organizational Socialism from Its Origins to Gorbachev's Restructuring* (Aldershot: Edward Elgar).

Ross, C. (1987), *Local Government in the Soviet Union: Problems of Implementation and Control* (London: Croom Helm).

Scott, D.J.R. (1969), *Russian Political Institutions,* 4th edn (London: Allen & Unwin).

Skilling, H.G. (1966), 'Interest Groups and Communist Politics', *World Politics,* Vol. XVIII, No. 3, pp. 435–51.

—and F. Griffiths (eds) (1971), *Interest Groups in Soviet Politics* (Princeton, NJ: Princeton University Press).

Stewart, P.D. (1968), *Political Power in the Soviet Union: A Study of Decision-making in Stalingrad* (Indianapolis, IN, and New York: Bobbs-Merrill).

Taubman, W. (1973), *Governing Soviet Cities: Bureaucratic Politics and Urban Development in the USSR* (New York: Praeger).

Welch, S. (1987), 'Issues in the Study of Political Culture: The Example of Communist Party States', *British Journal of Political Science,* Vol. 17, No. 4, pp. 479–500.

White, S. (1979), *Political Culture and Soviet Politics* (London: Macmillan).

Wyman, M. (1994), 'Russian Political Culture: Evidence from Public Opinion Surveys', *Journal of Communist Studies,* Vol. 10, No. 1, pp. 25–54.

12

From Collapse to Disintegration: the Russian Economic Transition

BOB ARNOT

Introduction

The central question that this volume seeks to address is did Western Sovietologists fail to anticipate the collapse of the former Soviet Union and the Eastern bloc - and if so why? The issue of course is a complex one and not surprisingly different analysts in this book have come up with very different answers. This chapter looks at the role played by Western economists and after suggesting some reasons for their difficulties, considers whether they have learned anything from their inability to predict the demise of the former Soviet Union. In particular the chapter considers whether the economic advice proffered to Russia, in the period from the fall of Gorbachev to the present, demonstrates any critical reflection on past analytical failures. As I will show, little if nothing has been learned and for this reason - amongst others - those who first failed to anticipate the decline of the Soviet Union have also failed to predict the appalling consequences of their own intervention in the affairs of post-communist Russia. Stephen Cohen in the next chapter argues that a large part of the blame for the current crisis in Russia should be laid at the door of the United States. However, Washington alone should not bear all the burden of guilt. We also have to look elsewhere, and especially at the type of economic 'advice' that has been thrust upon Russian reformers by the West as a whole. In this sense it is not just the Americans who are to blame for what Cohen correctly identifies as the Russian tragedy, but the economists too. How this has happened and with what results will be outlined in what follows.

Failed Method

The former Soviet Union posed problems of a very particular kind for mainstream economists. However, with regard to the economists active within Sovietology there is a relatively straightforward answer to the question of why they failed to predict the demise of Stalinism: because the static, partial and ahistoric methodology of conventional, neo-classical economics was unable to comprehend at any time, the dynamics of the former Soviet Union.[1] Specifically, this mode of analysis, by removing from consideration precisely those socioeconomic forces that shaped the destiny of the USSR, failed to identify the developmental and degenerative tendencies within the Soviet system. As a result, those who adhered to this method found it virtually impossible to conceive of the Soviet economy decaying from within or those in charge of the system being unable to find a way out of the impasse. Theoretically, such an outcome seemed quite inconceivable.[2]

But this should have come as no great surprise insofar as the methodology utilized was dependent upon the same categories that had proved just as incapable of identifying the laws of motion of capitalism.[3] This approach was underpinned by an implicit view of the 'normal' functioning of all economic systems, and in contemporary economic analysis the dominant view was that the market was both natural (insofar as it corresponded to man's basically selfish and competitive nature) and eternal.[4] There may have been history before the emergence of the market. However, once the market had come into being there was no possibility of moving beyond it. In this very special sense, history had come to an end.

Within this larger framework it was of course impossible for economists to use such categories as decline or decay, transformation or even change. Economic crises were also very difficult to explain. For orthodox economics the predominant concept remained that of equilibrium, and crises – which were fundamental to the operation of the capitalist system – were viewed as exogenous to its essential nature.[5] As a result the location for disturbances was always looked for outside the operation of the system. The consequence of this kind of approach meant that the majority of Western economists writing on the former Soviet Union were well able (as Stephen White points out in an earlier chapter) to identify specific problems in say agriculture,[6] industry,[7] consumption[8] and technology and R&D.[9] However, the very nature of the discipline precluded a systemic view that located these features as part of a fundamental crisis of the system as a whole. In fact those who took such a view – including Hillel Ticktin on the left and certain analysts on the right – were often seen as madmen on the fringes of both the discipline and sanity. Indeed, to suggest that the Soviet system could not survive or would not survive was to attract opprobrium and ridicule.[10]

Impossibilists and Reformists

A failed method thus made serious systemic analysis of the Soviet crisis very difficult indeed. It could be argued, however, that the economic analysis of the former Soviet Union also reflected two general tendencies that were conditioned by the confidence shown by Western economists in the nature of capitalism itself. The two tendencies could be described as 'impossibilism' and 'reformism'. The proponents of both schools of thought ultimately agreed on the benefits of the market, the necessity of hierarchical social relations of production and, in the final analysis, the economic superiority of capitalism.[11] But their analysis of the Soviet Union differed in certain key respects.

The first tendency arose as a consequence of the debates in the early part of the twentieth century. These concluded that any attempt to transcend capitalism and establish a socialist system would end in economic disaster.[12] For von Mises therefore the early period of Soviet rule represented nothing more than 'a picture of the destruction of an existing order of social production ... all branches of production ... are in a state of entire dissolution. What is happening under the rule of Lenin and Trotsky is merely destruction and annihilation.'[13]

The prospects were also bleak because according to writers like von Hayek, no rational economic system could ever emerge in the USSR.[14] When of course the Soviet Union did industrialize in the 1930s, von Hayek pointed out that this was in no way evidence of the superiority or efficacy of the system, as the absence of 'rational economic calculation' made it impossible to assess the worth or economic usefulness of the accumulation of means of production.[15] For von Mises, a 'socialist management of production would simply not know whether or not what it plans and executes is the most appropriate means to attain the ends sought. It will operate in the dark. ... squander the scarce factors of production both material and human. Chaos and poverty for all will unavoidably result.'[16] With regard to the Russian experience, what it showed was 'a very low level of the standard of living of the masses and unlimited dictatorial despotism'.[17]

By the end of the Second World War the analysis of the former Soviet Union advanced by the 'impossibilist' economists had been partially eclipsed as a consequence of two large shocks to the international system. These gave rise to the second tendency in mainstream economic analysis.

First, the confidence of bourgeois economics was clearly shaken by the experience of the inter-war depression and the apparent successes of the former Soviet Union.[18] The ability of Stalinist central 'planning' to industrialize an economically backward country (no matter how brutal its methods) and, after a disastrous start, to contribute to the defeat of fascism in the Second World War, convinced many economic commentators that not only was socialism now possible (and not impossible) but that it even contained elements within it that could be employed to solve the economic problems of capitalism itself (in the same way that the judicious addition of elements of the market mechanism could be used to improve central planning).[19]

The second shock was caused by the onset of the Cold War. As Michael Cox has argued elsewhere in this volume, the Cold War had a marked impact upon Soviet Studies in general and led, amongst other things, to the USSR now being presented as a formidable enemy in all senses of the word. It also led to the Cold War view of equal but opposite superpowers as well as the new discourse of comparative economic systems, through which most students in the West received their first education about the nature of the Soviet economy.[20] From the outset, the initiates into the discipline were reminded that the study of the Soviet economic system was not only a good thing in itself but would help make them appreciate what they already had. Moreover, a careful study of planning in the Soviet Union might suggest new means of making capitalism function even better. As the American economist Bornstein put it, a study of the Soviet economy not only enriched one's understanding of the Western economic system but sharpened one's 'appreciation of its merits and demerits' and suggested 'organizational and operational changes to improve its performance'.[21]

Inevitably, the questions which economists asked about the Soviet system were broadly the same as those which they asked of capitalism – namely what were the rules and orders governing the interaction of participants involved in the production, distribution and use of goods and services under conditions of scarcity?[22] Certainly, there was never any doubt that the methodology of orthodox economics could be utilized to illuminate these problems. However, instead of trying to look at the system as a whole and its underlying contradictions, the vast majority of Western economists focused on the partial, the descriptive and the empirical. Without doubt, many of the studies undertaken provided significant insights into the day-to-day operation of the system.[23] What was absent, though, was an integrative and historical approach that could lay bare its laws of motion.

The apogee of this reformist methodological approach was the vacuous 'theory of convergence'.[24] This took the superficial similarities of the contending systems and argued that there was a process of convergence evident in all industrialized economies that forced similar problems to be met with similar solutions. According to this thesis, economic systems were simply technical mechanisms in which there were neither relations of power or social relations of production. Hence there were no necessary reasons why economic systems could not be constantly reformed. Indeed, according to convergence theory, through a process of learning and 'rational' adjustment, ultimately an 'optimal system' would finally emerge – one which would almost certainly exhibit the best features of both systems.[25]

The theory of convergence was especially popular in the 1960s and

1970s, though it later came under intense attack.[26] Yet, in an attenuated form, many of its underlying assumptions continued to inform and influence economists of a more liberal or social democratic persuasion who constituted the overwhelming bulk of the Sovietological profession. It was perhaps for this reason, amongst others, that they failed to predict the subsequent collapse of the USSR. After all, if, as they argued, economic systems were capable of rational improvement – and that neither capitalism nor Soviet socialism had any essential features – there was no reason to believe the Soviet Union could not endure for ever. It was hardly surprising therefore that when the USSR did begin to manifest all the visible signs of terminal decline, it was extremely difficult for most liberal economists to draw the obvious conclusion. Even the CIA assumed that the system could carry on, not because it was functioning well, or because it did not face critical choices, but rather because there was always room for improvement. Until the very end in fact the consensus was that in spite of its many obvious problems, the USSR would continue to muddle through – no matter what.[27]

The Neo-Liberal Approach to the Transition in Russia

Having failed to anticipate Soviet economic decline, Western economists after 1991 drew what to them at least seemed the obvious lesson: that planning had been a utopian detour and that the market was the only way forward. As one of the new gurus of the transition (who knew neither Russian nor much about the former USSR) argued at the time, because socialism had been unable to deliver the goods, the introduction of full-blown capitalism was inevitable.[28] There were a few dissenting voices but not many – and none that were significant at the policy level. In this way the profession finally shed any pretence of being objective and detached. Having for years explained to their students that economics was a positive, value-free science, most economists now became straightforward apologists for the market, especially those who participated in what became known as the 'Great Trek to the East' as 'teachers of capitalism'.[29] The ideological veneer which had previously shielded Western economists from criticism by 'ideologues' on the left disappeared almost as quickly as the Berlin Wall itself.[30]

One might have thought that given their poor record in anticipating the demise of the previous economic system, Western economists would have been somewhat reluctant to offer their advice to the new Russian elite.[31] Ed Hewett's unintentionally damning comment that 'western economists know a great deal about how to manage a market economy, but very little about how to create one' would also have suggested the need for some intellectual humility.[32] But this proved not to be the case at all, and where angels feared to tread lest they be proved wrong yet again, the economic fools of the West rushed in offering their advice and expertise – at a price. Indeed, the proponents of the neo-liberal Washington consensus were like highly paid missionaries trying to persuade the natives (in this case the reformers in the former communist countries) to hang tough, grit their teeth, and suffer in the short term in the sure knowledge that all would be well in the future. This advice came from many institutional quarters but the main source of the new wisdom were the neo-liberals who dominated the corridors of power in the International Monetary Fund (IMF) and the World Bank. With little consideration for the human needs of the domestic populace, Western experts urged the countries of the old 'Second' World to take the plunge and integrate themselves into the world capitalist system. There would be pain, but the new democracies would emerge at the end of the day sleeker, more competitive and able to stand on their own feet in the international economy.[33]

It was especially unfortunate for the peoples of the former communist countries that the demise of the old order happened to coincide with a period of free market triumphalism in the West. Inspired in part by the liberal economic views of von Mises and von Hayek, the policy 'advice' offered to countries like Russia nonetheless depended for its successful adoption upon a good deal of external coercion. Indeed, it was somewhat ironic that those now preaching the virtues of freedom used enormous economic pressure in the shape of IMF loans and Western economic assistance to get policy-makers in the East to adopt their brand of economics.[34] It was strange (but not surprising) too that the introduction of the market with its attendant demand to remove the shackle of government from the economy presupposed a large role for Western governments. The West would certainly not be sending massive amounts of aid eastwards to facilitate the transition. There would be no second Marshall Plan. However, this did not preclude massive political intervention from the outside to ensure that the new elites of the East adopted the right course of economic action.

But what was the correct course of action? Here again the wise men of the West left their pupils in the East in no doubt. To arrive in the new economic heaven it was essential in their view to go for bust – and to do so quickly. Drawing upon the lessons of what had happened in Latin America in the 1980s, Western experts urged the short, sharp shock approach.[35] Indeed, what became known as 'shock therapy' rested upon the primitive economic view that all that capitalism required to flourish was macro-economic stabilization, liberalization and privatization.[36] It was assumed that the agents necessary to make the transition would spring from the old order, and once the framework was provided would act as the rational economic 'men' of the neo-classical fantasy. Naturally there were disputes between the contending policy advocates over the question of sequencing and the precise nature of the strategy.[37] Moreover, differences emerged regarding the time period over which it would be necessary to maintain financial and budgetary stringency.[38] But these were of secondary importance: all the participants in the end agreed that the market was the only solution. As one economist noted at the time, all the various institutions, and the economics profession too, 'for once seemed to have reached timely agreement on some novel and pretty fundamental issues of import'.[39]

Economic Decline: Economic Inequality

The record of the transition process has, of course, been different country by country.[40] Some of the smaller countries, with a shorter period of Stalinist planning and which already had elements of market institutions in place, have fared less badly than, for example, Russia and the former Soviet Republics. Here the record has been bleak.[41]

In economic terms, the elusive stabilization sought since January 1992 has still not been achieved.[42] Inflation is still far from under control[43] and the budgetary position continues to fluctuate wildly - largely but not only because of demands for increases in the minimum wage and pensions. The decline in industrial production and GDP has been precipitate and shows every sign of continuing.[44] The fundamental problems of the domestic economy are well illustrated by the enormous outflows of funds that are estimated to run to $1.0 to 1.5 billion a month. In 1997 alone about $21 billion was thought to have left the country. Nor has Russia's trading position improved in any way. Indeed, far from getting better, the situation as a result of the reforms has got worse. Exports continue to be dominated by raw materials (90 per cent of Russia' s hard currency revenue coming from this source), with oil still being as critical now as it was before communism collapsed. At the same time, the import of consumer goods and food keeps going up. The net result has been a major increase in Russia's external debt and the country's further subordination to the West.[45]

If the reforms have done little for the Russian economy they have done even less for the majority of ordinary Russians. It may be the case that Moscow stores are full of foreign consumer goods, but Moscow homes - never mind those in the provinces - are not. The overall decline in living standards can most easily be measured perhaps by the fall in domestic production of consumer goods. In the first six months of 1995 light industry output contracted by 38 per cent, a trend that has continued ever since.[46] It is true, as defenders of the new economic order claim, that there are no longer any queues and that there is a larger assortment of goods available in the shops. However, without the money to buy these commodities, the new freedom to 'choose' is entirely theoretical. Certainly the disparity between average wages and prices would suggest that the living standard of the majority of people has continued to decline since 1991.[47] One problem here of course is the non-payment of wages. One estimate has suggested that up to 12 million workers were not receiving wage payments in 1995, and the figures for the following years indicate that the problem was getting worse rather than better.[48]

Another result of the reforms advocated by Western experts has been a rise in poverty and inequality. Comparative figures indicate that in 1993, 30 to 35 million people could be located somewhere on, or below, the Russian poverty line. Two years later the figure had risen to nearly 50 million, with very high levels of deprivation to be found amongst pensioners, students and unskilled workers. Even members of the intelligentsia, and those from the more educated sections of Russian society were finding life increasingly tough, and many only survived by taking on more than one job.[49] Life for a few, however, was very good indeed – especially for those from the old elite who managed to accumulate vast fortunes by simply handing over public assets to themselves. According to one official source, the richest 10 per cent of the Russian population in 1995 earned 15 times the poorest 10 per cent. But this almost certainly hid the extent of inequality, inevitable perhaps in a country where the emergent bourgeoisie had little or no interest in revealing the extent and scale of its wealth to the tax authorities.[50]

Social Crisis

The increase in absolute poverty has also led to a decrease in the level of food consumption. Figures for 1995 show that food industry production of staple goods had fallen by an average of 12 per cent in that year alone.[51] In early 1995 it was also reported that meat and butter consumption had fallen back to 1970 levels, whilst that for milk products was down to that of the 1960s.[52] These falls in turn had a profound impact on a wide range of social problems. Thus in the 1990s (and for the first time in the post-war period) there was an absolute decline in Russia's population, caused by a combination of a sharp drop in the birth-rate and increasing mortality amongst the general population.[53] Disease and infant mortality – particularly in the first year of life – also began to rise to levels that might have been the norm in the more developed of the developing countries, but not in a nation that was defined as being advanced.[54] According to one source, the general mortality-rate in Russia is now about 1.7 times the birth-rate, with two-thirds of all deaths being due to accidents, crime and early death amongst both men and women.[55] The reduction in life expectancy has been quite marked in fact, especially for men, who in 1987 could expect to live on average until 65, but only eight years later were surviving seven years less,[56] the direct result of a collapsing social infrastructure, the social strains of the transition and the reappearance of diseases that were once thought to have been eradicated.[57]

Another consequence of the 'transition' has been a decrease in safety at work and a marked increase in the number of injuries and deaths on the shop floor.[58] In 1993, for example, over 7500 workers were killed at work, an average of 21 per day. By 1994, however, this average had risen to 30 per day, and in the first five months of 1995 alone, 3000 workers died – and this in spite of the fact that employment and economic activity overall had fallen sharply over the period.[59] It has also been estimated that over 14,000 people a year are now disabled as a result of accidents at work.[60] The economic crisis has also exacerbated another old Soviet problem: alcoholism, which according to a British Medical Association study had reached 'pandemic proportions' only six years after the end of the Cold War and four years after the disintegration of the USSR.[61] The authors of the report noted that more than 26,000 people per year were dying from alcohol poisoning in 1995 compared to 12,000 deaths in 1990. One of the reasons for this, it seems, was the increase in pure alcohol consumption from 10.7 litres per capita in 1987 to 14 litres in 1992. This in turn was the direct result of rises in both the price of foodstuffs and ordinary vodka. Hence, whilst a bottle of vodka in 1984 cost the equivalent of 2 kilos of sausage, a decade later it was costing approximately the same as half a kilogram of sausage. And the sausage itself, like nearly all foodstuffs, had risen in price, tempting the ordinary consumer to spend more on alcohol in general and pure spirit in particular.

The rise in alcoholism and alcoholic-related illnesses and deaths has also been paralleled by a notable increase in other social 'diseases'. One family in six is now reliably reported to have a drug problem. Increased drug consumption has in turn led to a marked rise in drug-related crime.[62] The suicide-rate has increased too, and Russia in 1995 had the third highest suicide-rate in the world (having increased from about 39,000 in 1990 to 62,000 in 1994).[63] In addition, juvenile crime has leaped by over 50 per cent in just under five years, adding to Russia's growing reputation as a country of violence and crime. Significantly, teenagers were reported to be responsible for 60 of the murders committed in Moscow in 1994.[64] In the summer of 1995, Moscow police also reported that one murder occurred every five hours in the city, and that every six hours there was one gang attack.[65] In the first half of the same year, a 7 per cent rise in serious crime was reported in Russia's capital city.[66]

Criminality more generally has become almost a way of life in Russia. In fact, one of the most marked changes since the collapse of the old political order has been the extraordinary increase in crime – including economic crime and crime involving the business community.[67] High-profile crime such as drugs, prostitution and the murder of economic targets has been extensively reported in the West.[68] However, every level of economic activity has apparently offered the possibility for criminal activity. The low pay or lack of pay of minor officials has meant that the incentive to abuse bureaucratic power has increased. The privatization process has also offered a wide range of opportunities for criminal activities and official statistics suggest that over 40,000 commercial entities are now directly controlled by criminal groups. At a more mundane level, the combination of inter-enterprise debt and non-payment from government, coupled with the non-payment of wages and the impoverishment of workers, has provided an enormous spur for theft from enterprises.

Disillusion with the Market

As has been argued elsewhere in this volume, the net result of Western economic advice has been to lead to a growing disillusionment with the market[69] and a steady rise in political movements opposed to those Western countries which have imposed such misery on the Russian people.[70] Certainly, if opinion polls are to be believed, the average Russian is not an especially happy Russian.[71] The response by the West, however, has not been to accept this and adjust policy accordingly but rather take a number of evasive strategies. These have taken several forms.

The first approach has either been to emphasize the positive contribution made by the new Russia to the new international order,[72] or to talk up the 'successes' of the transition within Russia itself. Unsurprisingly, those Western economists who have been most closely associated with Yeltsin and his entourage have turned out to be the most enthusiastic devotees of the new line, and have talked glowingly of what has been achieved in Russia – and in such a short space of time.[73] Unfortunately, for them, this strategy has had little success in convincing potential Western investors; nor has it staunched the outflow of Russian funds to the West.[74] Furthermore, it has made very little difference either to the Russian people who year on year continue to think that far from things getting better, they are getting worse. Indeed, in an opinion poll carried out in 1995, about 70 per cent of the respondents thought that things had declined since the reforms had been introduced, whilst 69 per cent thought the situation would be even worse in 1995 itself. Eighty per cent concluded that Yeltsin's economic policy was failing.[75]

A second approach has been to claim that the reason Russia has struggled is because there has been not enough shock and too little therapy! This argument has convinced hardly anybody. Neither Yeltsin nor Gaidar were half-hearted in their approach to the reform process in 1992. Their programme intended the full shock therapy treatment and it was only *realpolitik* that led to a modification of the original policy. As Gaidar argued at the time, we 'looked into the abyss and pulled back'.[76] The threat of a major social explosion[77] and popular opposition to private property and speculative activity caused the leadership to withdraw from the full implications of the programme and opt for a more pragmatic, populist approach.[78]

The third line of intellectual defence has been to suggest that the problems created by the old system were so deeply entrenched that the transition was bound to be more difficult than anticipated. This assertion has some validity in that the economic psychology of the Russian populace is clearly not easily adapted to the requirements of a market economy. But if this is the case why has the strategy advice not reflected these deep structural difficulties? Is it because the advisers had little appreciation of the nature of the problems faced, or that the model they attempted to transplant was not a universally generalizable form of human social organization but one that required particular cultural and historical prerequisites which were absent in Russia? But if this were so, it would then raise a major question about the market – that it was not 'normal', 'natural' or even 'eternal' but a historically contingent system that could only function successfully under very specific circumstances.

Beyond Neo-Liberalism? The Lessons of History

Significantly, the failure of the transition in Russia has coincided with a period of uncertainty and a lack of confidence in capitalism on a global scale.[79] This in turn has led to a rising tide of dissatisfaction with the economics of neo-liberalism and caused a minor resurgence of what might best be described as neo-Keynesianism. Highly critical of free market economics in general, latter-day Keynesians have increasingly turned their attention to Russia and tried to propose what they think is a serious alternative to a policy which they feel has caused damage to the fabric of Russian society, done nothing to restore the competitiveness of Russian industry, and threatens the stability of the country over the longer term. Believing that industrial regeneration rather than fiscal orthodoxy, social partnership rather than social inequality, is in Russia's best interest, the new reformists have inevitably received a wide hearing in both Russia and the West.[80]

The question has to be posed, however – is their policy advice any more appropriate than that offered by the neo-liberals they criticize: and if put into practice, would it be any more successful? To answer these questions, it might be useful to examine one of the several alternative economic plans put forward by one group of Keynesian economists in the 1990s: the 'American Experts Group'.

The report of the American Experts Group was first delivered at a conference at Moscow State University in the summer of 1995.[81] This had been prepared for the conference but was also presented to an economic committee of the Duma with the claim that it offered an alternative to the neo-liberal approach. The authors were very critical of the attempted shock therapy and the economic policies of the Russian government in the period from 1990 to 1995. They therefore sought to provide an innovative economic policy that was both politically and economically viable: and basically what they put forward as an alternative to neo-liberalism was a form of Western-style, democratic, 'corporatist' capitalism.[82] Drawing upon the lessons of the successful reconstruction of both Germany and Japan in the immediate post-war years, their clear objective was to move beyond what they termed the 'folk tales' of the neo-liberals by creating a new framework which would revive Russia's fortunes.

What the American Experts suggested, in effect, was a combination of an aggressive Keynesian macro-economic policy intervention to boost domestic demand, a strong industrial policy geared to support viable enterprises and wide-scale institutional change.[83] On the surface, their alternative looked very persuasive and appealing. Moreover, by turning to history and trying to show that with the right combination of policies, a viable capitalism could be constructed in Russia (in much the same way as it had been built in Germany and Japan after World War II), it looked on the surface at least as if they had a good, almost unanswerable, case. But however attractive their plan was, it nonetheless contained some fairly basic methodological and historical flaws.

Most critically, their proposal tended to mythologize the development of capitalism in general and said virtually nothing about why Germany and Japan in particular were able to recover after 1947. Though there were many pre-conditions which led to renewed capital accumulation in both countries – including the Cold War (which has now ended) and massive US aid (which Russia has not received and will not get) – the process was only made possible in the first instance because of the neutralization of the labour movement. Let us recall what happened.

In Japan in the immediate post-war period, there was a massive growth in the size and in the radicalism of the workers' movement. Trade Union membership grew from practically zero in August 1945 to almost 5 million by the end of 1946.[84] In spite of this, the new radicalism was soon defeated with the assistance of the occupying American forces, who banned a proposed General Strike in early 1947. This was followed in 1949 with a purge of 'leftists' in a wide range of occupations. Left-wing newspapers were also banned, and management was given either tacit or open approval to suppress independent union power.[85] The strike waves of the early 1950s, particularly in the car, coal and steel industries, then saw massive defeats for the Trade Unions after vicious pitched battles where a combination of police and gangsters helped defeat the organized working class. And it was all this – taken together – which laid the foundation for the later economic miracle; one that was inspired not by a general social consensus but by the 'iron triangle' of conservative politicians, career bureaucrats and big business.[86] As a consequence, by the late 1950s a combative, potentially independent labour movement had been broken and replaced by company unions, 'sweetheart deals' and slogans like 'those who truly love their union love their company'.[87]

A similar process took place in Germany. Here, a workers' movement (much weakened by fascist repression) nonetheless emerged after 1945 in a very strong position. The movement was also very militant, and after the war workers' committees and anti-fascist councils took over production and distribution in a number of areas under the leadership of socialist and communist parties.[88] The basic policy of the Americans in particular was to suppress these committees and councils, whilst German trade unions were shackled by the British occupying forces who used right-wing British trade union personnel to restructure the German unions on lines functional for capitalism.[89] However, this alone would not have undermined the militancy of the workers' movement. What really weakened the movement was the intensification of the Cold War. This not only made it possible for the West German ruling class to marginalize the communist left and create the conditions which led to the gradual deradicalization of German social democracy (which just after the war adhered to a Marxist programme), but also led to a mass migration of people from the East to the West – at least it did until the Berlin Wall was built in 1961. The net result of this influx was to dilute the organized power of labour and bring about a marked rightward shift in West German political life.

In both Germany and Japan therefore, workers were unable to act effectively to defend their interests: as a result the value of their labour power was driven downwards. This process, directed and fostered by the state, gave favourable conditions for capital accumulation and provided the impetus for the post-war 'economic miracles' in the two countries. Of course, some layers of the working population were incorporated by means of social expenditures and the guarantee of (more or less) full employment, whilst others no doubt accepted their lot without resistance. But none of this changes the fact that the foundation of Germany and Japan's prosperity was, in the last analysis, built upon the defeat and containment of organized labour as an independent force. And without that, sustained capitalist recovery would not have been possible.

Lessons for Russia?

Our brief examination of what happened in Germany and Japan in the post-war period holds out little hope for capitalism in modern Russia where organized labour is still very strong indeed. It should not be forgotten (though frequently it is) that almost 50 million Russian workers remain in Trade Unions covering 90 per cent of all workers.[90] Moreover, these unions have real power and judging by the level of strike activity in the 1990s, are willing to use it.[91] Workers also continue to exercise an influence on economic policy by merely threatening to take action. The result of such action, normally, is to restrain the government from doing what it might otherwise have done. It has also forced Yeltsin to make a series of concessions to workers in an attempt to buy them off. This of course would explain the continual populist turns in the economic policy of the Russian government, often imposed on reluctant economic ministers by Yeltsin himself. The inability of the Russian government to follow the logic of the neo-liberal programme, with widespread restructuring, closures and mass unemployment, is further evidence of the negative power of labour.

This is not to suggest that either the labour movement generally, or the Trade Unions through its central organization, can forge economic policy unambiguously in their own interests. The leadership at national level, for example, is riven internally by conflicts between unions in different sectors, different regions and with different political allegiances. Furthermore, politically it is unable to deliver a solid Trade Union vote to any particular bloc. The discussions around the electoral alliance 'Trade Unions in the Election' have amply demonstrated this.[92] That said, Russian workers are clearly in no mood to acquiesce to any programme of economic restructuring – whether it takes a neo-liberal or a more corporatist 'Keynesian' form. Indeed, conditions in Russia make any form of dynamic capitalism virtually inconceivable. First, the pre-condition of a demoralized defeated labour movement or no labour movement at all is absent – and any attempt to defeat labour in Russia today would only invite an immediate social explosion. Secondly, economic regeneration based on the market would require a tough incomes policy, but under Russian conditions – where workers are already sensitized to increasing income inequality and quite literally hate the new Russian bourgeoisie – such a policy would be impossible to impose. And thirdly, the central Trade Union leadership has little real control over the different unions and even less over the workers themselves and thus could not be used as a reliable instrument of discipline. Moreover, given the peculiar combination of factors in Russia – rapid and deep economic decline, high levels of overmanning and enterprise obsolescence, traditional worker hostility to inequality – it would take the most draconian measures imaginable to push through the type of economic policies that would facilitate renewed capital accumulation. And no Russian government (not even an authoritarian Russian government) would be able to push through such measures.

But if conditions in Russia make a revival of the economy highly unlikely, the external environment renders the task almost impossible. Let us not forget that the revitalization of both Germany and Japan after the war presupposed not only a certain set of internal conditions but a definite set of international circumstances as well. Basically, when their model of economic development was initiated in mid-century, the capitalist world system looked very different from what it does now. Today, the international economy is more centralized, concentrated and globalized than it was just after the war. The scope therefore for individual 'national' solutions is that much narrower. But more importantly, in the post-World War II period, the USA was willing and able to underwrite capitalism in the world. Furthermore, it not only had an economic reason for doing so, but it was politically compelled to do so because of the existence of the USSR and the fear of the spread of communism. Whether the post-war system required the Cold War to re-establish its equilibrium is a moot question. But, certainly, the reconstruction of market capitalism under America's powerful tutelage would have been a good deal more difficult without it.

Ironically, the passing of the Cold War (caused by the collapse of the Soviet 'threat') means that the USA no longer has a political imperative to do very much – and certainly not to rebuild the Soviet Union. Nor, to be blunt, has it much of an economic reason for doing so. Russia after all is not – and never will be – as central to the international economy as either Japan or Germany. The sheer costs of a new Marshall Plan would also be extraordinarily high and without an external menace to its interests, the USA is highly unlikely to extend much aid to rebuild Russia: nor for that matter are Japan or Germany. Even the European Union (EU), which does have more of a stake in Russia (and has extended most aid since 1991), is under no great compulsion to rebuild Russian industry. Like the USA, the EU has problems of its own to deal with. Moreover, like the Americans, the West Europeans have no great interest in helping revive Russian industry if the result is likely to be the emergence of a very powerful competitor in the world.

Naturally, the West as a whole does not wish to see the former Soviet Union and Russia descend into complete chaos – a chaos that could be extremely difficult to contain. Hence the logic of the current strategy, which is to provide limited and conditional support for market reforms, to allow for the international exploitation of parts of the Russian economy (energy and raw materials) and to permit a very narrow sector of the domestic population to enrich themselves, integrate into the world finance system and enjoy consumption levels similar to their counterparts in the West. This, of course, will not lead to the economic rebirth of Russia. Nor will it improve the lives of the ordinary Russian people. However, it will keep the Russia elite quiet internationally and prevent disturbance in Russia spilling over into the wider world system. And if the West can gain access to cheap Russian oil and gas, then so much the better.

Conclusion

The basic argument of this chapter has been that mainstream economic analysis failed to understand the operation and eventual disintegration of the former Soviet Union because of weaknesses in its fundamental methodology – and that its inability to theorize the old system has continued into the present. This has resulted in a collapse of living standards for the majority of the Russian populace, and the degradation of economic life as criminality and corruption became endemic with little prospect of improvement in the immediate future.

It has also been argued that a neo-Keynesian approach to the transition would be similarly flawed and unsuitable for contemporary Russia. The historical parallels drawn with either Germany or Japan after World War II are quite false and misleading. Neither the internal situation nor the international context will allow the corporatist Keynesian solution to work. It may have been an appropriate strategy for capitalist renewal at a particular point in the past, but it does not seem to offer much hope to Russia in the present.

Whilst the neo-liberals (reflecting their impossibilist precursors) naïvely presume that the market is natural and that institutions and individuals will emerge to fill the vacuum created by the death of Stalinism, the neo-Keynesians (reflecting their reformist predecessors) fail to address the question of the underlying social relations of production. Ultimately both approaches to the transition in Russia present a fetishized view of capitalism and a reluctance to recognize that capitalism is based upon a process of surplus extraction from the direct producers, not social democratic consensus or monetary orthodoxy. Thus although the Russian ruling group and their supporters in the West might have been able to move beyond the command economy, they have been unable to replace it with a system of domestic capital accumulation that is both viable and self-reproducing. The introduction of a quasi-money economy may have been relatively easy to achieve but the logic of that process has never been followed through. The attempts at privatization rather than being an example of the strength of the transition process are in fact the reverse. It is one thing to transfer the formal ownership of the enterprise, but it is quite another to restructure the enterprise, undertake mass redundancies and close perhaps whole sectors of the economy. But the full reintroduction of capitalist social relations of production requires precisely that, so that labour re-emerges as a commodity. Neither the neo-liberal proposals nor the alternative neo-Keynesian view provides a solution to this fundamental problem. For this reason, Russia can do little more than disintegrate whilst Western economists continue to talk without purpose about something called a transition.

Notes

1   There is a wide range of literature that provides a methodological critique of bourgeois economics. See for example, M. Campbell, *Capitalism in the UK* (Croom Helm, London, 1981), pp. 9–30.

2   For an excellent account of the weaknesses of 'economic science' see Homa Katouzian, *Ideology and Method in Economics* (Macmillan, London, 1980).

3   See for example T. Buck, *Comparative Industrial Systems* (Macmillan, London, 1982).

4   See for example Ed Hewett's comments on the inevitability of the market in *From the Command Economy to the Market*, K. Bush (ed.) (Dartmouth, Aldershot, 1991), p. 106.

5   For an excellent brief survey of this question see Anwar Shaikh, *Crisis Theories in Economic Thought*, Thames Papers in Political Economy, Thames Polytechnic, 1977.

6   See for example, S. Hedlund, *Crisis in Soviet Agriculture* (St Martin's Press, New York, 1984); D. Diamond, L. Bettis and R. Ramsson, 'Agricultural Production', in A. Bergson and H. Levine (eds), *The Soviet Economy: Toward the Year 2000* (George Allen & Unwin, London, 1983).

7   See for example, J.S. Berliner, *Factory and Manager in the USSR* (Harvard University Press, Cambridge, 1957) and D. Granick, *Management of the Industrial Firm in the USSR* (Columbia UP, New York, 1954).

8   See P. Hanson, *The Consumer Sector in the Soviet Economy* (Northwestern UP, Evanstown, 1969).

9   See for example, R. Amman and J. Cooper, *Industrial Innovation in the Soviet Union* (Yale UP, New Haven, 1982); R. Amman, J. Cooper and R.W. Davies, *The Technological Level of Soviet Industry* (Yale UP, New Haven, 1977); and J. Berliner, *The Innovation Decision in Soviet Industry* (MIT Press, Cambridge, 1976).

10 See for example the responses to A. Amalrik, *Will the Soviet Union Survive Until 1984?* (Penguin, Harmondsworth, 1980), suggesting that his work was co-written with the KGB!

11 For example, the coupling of Alec Nove and von Hayek as opposite poles in the market debate is somewhat disingenuous. The distance between Nove and von

Hayek is not as great as might at first seem the case. Nove, rather than arguing as his book title suggests for a 'feasible socialism', always argues for a 'feasible' and humane capitalism. See Alec Nove, *The Economics of Feasible Socialism* (Unwin Hyman, London, 1983) and *The Economics of Feasible Socialism Revisited* (Harper-Collins, London, 1991).

12 See *Collectivist Economic Planning*, edited by F.A. von Hayek (Routledge, London, 1935). As well as von Hayek and von Mises, this collection includes E. Barone's article 'The Ministry of Production in the Collectivist State' as an appendix.

13 Ludwig von Mises, 'Economic Calculation in the Socialist Commonwealth', in von Hayek, Note 12 above, p. 125.

14 Ibid., p. 130.

15 F.A. von Hayek, 'The present state of the debate', in von Hayek, Note 12 above, pp. 204–5.

16 Ludwig von Mises, *Socialism: An Economic and Sociological Analysis* (Jonathan Cape, London, 1936), p. 585.

17 Ibid., p. 589.

18 As Maurice Dobb argued, the USSR seemed to be 'a simple country of progress in a crisis-stricken world'. M Dobb, *Soviet Russia and the World* (Sidgwick & Jackson, London, 1932), p. 12.

19 There is an enormous literature on market socialism. See A. Nove and I. Thatcher (eds), *Market Socialism* (Blackwell, London, 1995) for a selection of key readings.

20 See for example P. Gregory and P. Stuart, *Comparative Economic Systems*, 4th ed. (Houghton Mifflin, Boston, 1992).

21 M. Bornstein, 'The Comparison of Economic Systems: An Integration', in M. Bornstein (ed.), *Comparative Economic Systems: Models and Cases* (R.D. Irwin Inc., Illinois, 3rd ed., 1974), p. 18.

22 See J. Elliot, *Comparative Economic Systems* (Wadsworth, Belmont, 1985).

23 See for example the classic USAF-funded output from the Harvard Project, especially R. Bauer, A. Inkeles and C. Kluckholm, *How the Soviet System Works* (Vintage Russian Library, New York, 1956).

24 For a critical review of the idea of convergence see *Convergence and System Change*, B. Dallago, H. Brezinski and W. Andreff (eds) (Dartmouth, Aldershot, 1992).

25 See for example, J. Tindbergen, 'Do Communist and Free Economies show a converging pattern?', *Soviet Studies*, Vol. XII, No. 4, 1961.

26 See for example M. Ellman's comprehensive critique, 'Against Convergence', in M. Ellman, *Collectivization, Convergence and Capitalism* (Academic Press, London), 1984, pp 291–310. See also G. Roland, 'Tindbergen's convergence thesis: a post-mortem criticism', in Dallago *et al.*, Note 24 above, pp. 39–47.

27 See Anders Aslund, *Gorbachev's Struggle for Economic Reform* (Pinter, London, 1991).

28 See J. Williamson, *The Eastern Transition to a Market Economy*, Centre for Economic Performance, Occasional Paper No. 2, March 1992, p. 3.

29 This phrase comes from Williamson, ibid., p. 2.

30 See Anders Aslund, Note 27 above, pp. 229–233.

31 One influential adviser who has never been backward in coming forward with his advice was the Swedish economist, Anders Aslund. See his *Post-Communist*

Economic Revolutions: How Big a Bang? Center for Strategic and International Studies, Washington DC, 1992.

32   E. Hewett, 'Is Soviet Socialism Reformable?', in *The Soviet System from Crisis to Collapse*, A. Dallin and G. Lapidus (eds) (Westview Press, Boulder, 1995), p. 313.

33   The IMF's view was clearly articulated by the Managing Director of the IMF, Michel Camdessus, in an address to Georgetown University School of Foreign Service, *Economic Transformation in the Fifteen Republics of the Former USSR: A Challenge or an opportunity for the World?*, IMF, 15 April 1992.

34   See for example the conditions attached to the IMF loan to Russia in mid-1995. This involved policy actions prior to disbursements coupled with monthly reviews by the IMF's Executive Board to monitor policy progress, in addition to the normal quarterly reviews. *IMF Survey*, 17 April 1995, p. 116.

35   Williamson, 1992, Note 28 above, p.15 suggests that the origins can be traced to the Erhard Programme of 1948, via the Bolivian policies of 1985 and then through the intermediation of Jeffrey Sachs (who had been an adviser to the losing candidate in the Bolivian elections of 1985) to Poland in the latter half of 1989. He notes that the strategy is attempting to end 'the biggest failed social experiment in history'.

36   See for example, C. Clague, 'The Journey to the Market', in *The Emergence of Market Economies in Eastern Europe*, C. Clague and G. Rausser (eds) (Blackwell, 1992, pp. 1–22).

37   See for example Gur Ofer, 'Stabilizing and restructuring the former Soviet economy: Big-bang or Gradual Sequencing?' in *Trials of Transition*, M. Keren and G. Ofer (eds) (Westview Press, Boulder, 1992), pp. 83–106; R. McKinnon, *The Order of Financial Liberalization: Financial Control in the Transition to a Market Economy* (Johns Hopkins University Press, Baltimore, 1991); and T. Rybczynski, 'The Sequencing of Reform', *Oxford Review of Economic Policy*, Vol. 7, No. 4, 1991.

38   See A. Koves, *Central and East European Economies in Transition* (Westview Press, Boulder, 1992), pp. 17–36.

39   See Williamson, Note 28 above, p. 21.

40   A useful comparison of country performance (1990–1994) with regard to Real GDP and Inflation was provided by the *Financial Times*, 7 March 1995, p. 19.

41   This of course is not the view of the Western advisers nor the IMF. See for example, Ernesto Hernandez-Cata, *Russia and the IMF: The Political Economy of Macro-Stabilization*, IMF Paper on Policy Analysis and Assessment, September 1994, who identifies in Russia 'impressive achievements' in the area of structural reform as opposed to the elusive nature of success in macro-stabilization, or Anders Aslund, 'Russia's Success Story', *Foreign Affairs*, Vol. 73, No. 5, September/October 1994, pp. 58–71.

42   For an account of the early period see Bob Arnot, 'The Continuing Disintegration of the Russian Economy', *Critique*, No. 26, 1994, pp. 11–55.

43   The government had hoped to reduce inflation to 1 per cent per month but by May 1995 it still stood at 7.9 per cent per month, *Izvestiya*, 6 June 1995 and in June and July was only just under 7 per cent, *Interfax*, 28 July 1995. The forecast for October to February 1996 suggested inflation up to 10 per cent per month, *Finansovive Izvestiya*, No. 49, 1995.

44 According to *Interfax*, 17 and 25 January 1995, the decline in GDP, industrial
   output, capital investment and agricultural output was greater in 1994 than in
   1993. Chernomyrdin in a speech to the Duma on 19 July 1995 reported that the
   decline had slowed in 1995 but from September 1994 to March 1995 per capita
   National Income had declined by 25 per cent, *Interfax*, 19 July 1995. Particular
   pessimism was noted in the consumer goods sector but also machine building
   and construction continued to show rapid decline, *Finansovive Izvestiya*, No. 48,
   1995.

45 *Rossiiskaya Gazeta*, 4 July 1995. The total export of capital from Russia for 1994
   alone was estimated at $50 billion, *AFP*, 12 February 1995. A report by Interpol
   suggested that the figure for the period 1991-94 may have exceeded $80
   billion. Reported in *Monitor,* 2 May 1995. For the 1997 figure on capital flight,
   see *The Guardian* (London), 29 May 1998. In 1994 exports of crude oil and oil
   products rose by 11.3 per cent and 10.6 per cent. See *Interfax*, 8 February 1995.
   See also *Finansoviye Izvestiya*, 1995, No. 6 and *Segodnya*, 10 February 1995,
   Analytica Moscow Economica Weekly, Vol. II, No. 6, 11-17 February 1995, and
   Monitor, 27 July 1995.

46 *AFP*, 12 July 1995.

47 In the first half of 1995 inflation rose nearly twice as fast as incomes according
   to an Economics Ministry spokesman. Moscow *Echo Radio* report, in *Monitor*, 29
   June 1995. Furthermore, 20 per cent of Russians could not earn enough to buy
   even basic foodstuffs and 45 per cent spent virtually all their income on
   foodstuffs according to *Interfax*, 30 July 1995.

48 *Trud*, 14 July 1995.

49 Comparative figures suggest that in 1993, 30-35 million were below the poverty
   line. In 1994 the figure had fallen to 24 million. *Segodnya*, 10 September 1995.
   However, a more recent figure suggests 47 million are below the poverty level
   ITAR-TASS, 27 June 1995.

50 See *Interfax*, 28 February 1995. This disparity is what is officially recognized, but
   the reality is probably worse. In part this is because the Ministry of Labour can
   only guess at the very highest incomes as many are illegally obtained outside the
   statistics. What is certain is that the disparities continue to grow.

51 See *Segodnya*, 23 June 1995.

52 *Nezavisimaya Gazeta*, 8 February 1995.

53 *AFP*, 11 July 1995 reported that total population fell by 1.7 million in 1993-94.

54 Infant mortality in 1994 for example reached 19.9 per thousand in comparison
   with rates of between 7 and 9 per thousand in the West, *AFP*, 28 February 1995.
   Furthermore, the number of women who were dying during childbirth had
   risen significantly between 1992 and 1995. See *Interfax*, 24 June 1995.

55 *ITAR-TASS*, 7 February 1995.

56 See ibid. By July 1995 the life expectancy was calculated at 57.3 for men and
   71.1 for women *AFP*, 11 July 1995.

57 For example, through the summer of 1994 a cholera epidemic raged in parts of
   Russia as a result of poor drinking water hygiene and collapsing sewerage
   systems. The incidence of diphtheria increased 30 times in only three years and
   typhoid fever and anthrax made a reappearance. See B. Kagarlitsky, 'Spread of
   cholera mirrors social decay', *KAS-KOR*, Moscow, Summer, 1994. In 1995 the
   diphtheria doubled over that experienced in 1994. *Interfax*, 20 June 1995.

58   R. Clarke, 'Accidents in Russia: the cost to workers and the environment', *KAS-KOR*, Moscow, Summer 1994.

59   *Interfax*, 28 June 1995

60   *TASS*, 7 September 1994.

61   BMA study reported by *AFP*, 10 March 1995.

62   See *Interfax*, 16 July 1995. *ITAR-TASS* reports a 60 per cent increase in drug-related crime in 1994 compared with 1993.

63   For figures on rising suicide in Russia, see *Vechernyava Moskva*, 6 June 1995 and *Komsomolskaya Pravda*, 25 July 1995.

64   Figures on youth crime from *Radio Rossii*, 2 June 1995 reported in *OMRI*, 7 June 1995.

65   *Moskovsky Komsomolets*, 29 June 1995, in *OMRI*, 29 June 1995.

66   See *Interfax*, 11 July 1995.

67   According to the Trade and Industry Chamber of the Russian Federation, in 1995 one business in four paid protection money whilst almost half of all businesses had had contact with the Mafia over the last 12 months. *Moscow Radio*, 12 July 1995 reported in *Monitor*, 13 July 1995.

68   A report on criminal earnings suggested that at least $16 billion 'dirty dollars' were in circulation in Russia by late 1994, and that 40 per cent of the money in circulation had been obtained through criminal operations both within and outside the country. *Interfax*, 4 February 1995.

69   See, in particular, Stephen White and Stephen Cohen.

70   The origins of authoritarian anti-Westernism in Russia is traced by Judith Devlin, 'The Rise of New Russian Nationalism, 1989-90', *Irish Slavonic Studies*, 18, 1997, pp. 25-51.

71   Numerous public opinion surveys suggest a large degree of scepticism with regard to the benefits of the market and democratization. This was reflected in the jaundiced view ordinary people had with regard to the 1996 elections. Surveys suggested that over 800 had not made their minds up whether to vote or not; 50 per cent believed it was not worthwhile; 56 per cent trusted no political leaders. The majority saw the market reforms and democracy as simply opening the way for crime and corruption. *Izvestiya*, 26 July 1995. Furthermore, when asked what they saw as the most important problems, respondents cited soaring prices (76.5 per cent); crime (59.2 per cent); unemployment (49.6 per cent); economic crisis (48.4 per cent); social differentiation (32.2 per cent), *Commersant*, 18 July 1995.

72   See Michael Cox, 'The necessary partnership? The Clinton presidency and post-Soviet Russia', *International Affairs*, Vol. 70, No. 4, October 1994, pp. 635-58.

73   See for example, M. Camdessus, *IMF Survey*, 23 January 1995, pp. 21-4; A. Aslund, 'Russia's Success Story', *Foreign Affairs*, Vol. 73, No. 5, September/October, 1994, pp. 58-71.

74   According to Chernomyrdin, foreign investment in Russia in the first half of 1995 was less than $500 million. *Commersant*, 4 July 1995.

75   The opinion poll was in *Sovetskaya Rossiva*, 8 June 1995, and can be found in *OMRI*, 10 June 95.

76   Interview with Gaidar, in *FNS*, 10 January 1993.

77   See Arnot, Note 42 above, pp. 29-31.

78   In a press conference Gaidar admitted that the second option, under which

most of the privatization had taken place, was forced upon the government and they had reluctantly acceded to it as a way of making sure that the principle of privatization was at least accepted. *FNS*, 2 June 1993.

79   It is difficult to find any of the major capitalist economies that are not experiencing difficulties. The Japanese 'bubble economy' of the late 1980s has burst; the USA continues to decline as an economic superpower; and in Western Europe unemployment remains high.

80   See for example the articles on the possibilities of a 'social partnership' approach to economic development in *Voprosy Ekonomiki*, No. 5, 1994.

81   The conference on economic transition at Moscow State University was held on 13-15 June 1995. The American professors who delivered the report, giving themselves the modest title of the 'American Experts Group', were Alice Amsden (MIT), Michael Intriligator (UCLA), Robert McIntyre (IPS/Bowdoin) and Lance Taylor (New School). The report was entitled *Strategies for a Viable Transition: Lessons from the Political Economy of Renewal*.

82   Ibid., p. 14.

83   Ibid., p. 2.

84   See W. Horsley and R. Buckley, *Nippon–New Superpower: Japan Since 1945* (BBC Books, London, 1990), p. 26.

85   Ibid., p. 29.

86   Ibid., p. 39.

87   Ibid., p. 56.

88   P. Armstrong, A. Glynn and J. Harrison, *Capitalism Since 1945* (Blackwell, Oxford, 1991), pp. 18-19.

89   Ibid., p. 35.

90   See Kirill Buketov, 'Organised Labour in Russia: Trade Unions in the Russian Federation 1995'. Unpublished MS., Moscow, July 1995, p. 7.

91   In January 1995 strikes occurred in 92 enterprises, by February in 249, and by April, in 513, *Vetsi FNPR*, 1995, Nos 2, 3, 4, cited in Buketov, Note 90 above, p. 2. By June, the figure had risen to 829. See *Goskomstat*, 1 August 1995. See also *Trud*, 25 July 1995. It was also estimated that by July 1995 more than 36,000 enterprises owed wages amounting to more than 6.5 trillion roubles. *Trud*, 25 July 1995. For details on the miners' strike see Renfrey Clarke, 'Russian coal strike opens mass political campaign', *KAS-KOR*, 15 February 1995.

92   See Buketov, Note 90 above, p. 17; *Segodnya*, 18 July 1995.

13

Russia: Transition or Tragedy?

STEPHEN F. COHEN

Introduction

This chapter is less concerned with Sovietology than with another issue raised by several contributors to the volume: the extent to which we can speak of a genuine transition to liberal democratic capitalism, or to any kind of decent order, in post-Communist Russia. My special subject here is how my own country, the United States, has impacted on Russia since 1991. And my conclusion is that American policy, including its unwise and unseemly intrusion into Russia's internal affairs, has been little short of disastrous – not the great success trumpeted by Washington but an ill-conceived and failed crusade. The source of this failure can be traced back to the questionable American assumption that Russia must embrace a full-scale Western-style capitalism – an undertaking almost certain to fail because Russia was not ready and probably not suited for such a model. Indeed, the failure and ensuing tragedy were predictable.

Washington has been blind to the extent of the problem and to the role its policies have played in the disaster that has unfolded in Russia. That role has led official America to obscure post-Communist Russian realities so that they seem much brighter than they actually are. This is both morally dubious and politically dangerous. What happens in Russia profoundly affects us all; fairy stories about the 'transition' do no one any good. Nor can such fables form the basis of a wise US policy towards a country whose development will shape prospects for stability and international security in large parts of the world. Getting 'Russia right' is not just an academic matter.

In the first section I will examine some of the false assumptions that have guided American policy towards post-Communist Russia and led to a series of policy decisions that have helped neither country. In the next part, I will look at the nature of the actual 'transition' in Russia, arguing that after nearly a decade of US intervention, Russia is in a worse condition in most respects than it was in 1991. But if so, the question we must then ask is why have so few American analysts and policy-makers focused on this outcome? Why has the scale of the Russian disaster been obscured or even ignored and thus omitted from the American political agenda? In the final section, I will suggest a different approach to Russia and some specific ways in which the USA can help that stricken nation – and ourselves.

False Assumptions

During most of the Cold War, US policy towards the Soviet Union was premised on at least three assumptions: that the USSR's relentless goal was world domination; that its totalitarian nature made real change in the Soviet system virtually impossible; and that Soviet policy posed a huge threat to American interests around the world. Whether these assumptions were ever true is doubtful, but the events of the late 1980s certainly disproved them in modern times. And yet, US policy-makers seem not to have learned from past mistakes. Instead of adopting realistic understandings of post-communist Russia, they have continued to base policy on fundamental misconceptions.

The first and most obvious misconception has been the belief that there was something like a revolution or total collapse of the Soviet system in 1991, and that as a result most if not all major obstacles to liberal democracy and Western-style capitalism had been swept aside. Contrary to the euphoria in Washington (and briefly in post-Communist Moscow), no such complete break with the past occurred. Despite the break up of the Union, crucial aspects of the Soviet system have continued to exist – in enduring elements of the state economy, in the nature and extent of bureaucratic institutions and procedures, in elites and key personnel, and, significantly, in popular attitudes. If there has been no full discontinuity with the past, as other contributors to this volume have also shown, the notion of rapidly creating a new political and economic order on the ashes of the old system was dangerous folly.

The second false assumption is that 1991 witnessed an overwhelming popular rejection of socialism in favour of democratic market capitalism as we understand it. In fact, as opinion polls and elections to the Duma have revealed, there has never been a large constituency in Russia for free market economics. Indeed, as time has passed, what support did exist has sharply declined. To have imposed such policies therefore inevitably led to widespread opposition to economic reform, a clamorous revival of the old despotic Russian question 'Who is to blame?', growing support for authoritarian and reactionary political movements, and a dramatic rise in anti-Americanism. Nor should we be surprised by this turn of events. After all, to American applause, the Yeltsin leadership suddenly and surreptitiously abolished the Soviet Union and its fully integrated economy, with appalling economic consequences, and then attempted to impose a Western-style market economy on Russia by 'shock therapy'. One result of those acts was to undermine the living standards and vaporize the life savings of most Russian families. And as that human calamity has grown, the US-backed International Monetary Fund (IMF) has demanded that Russia remain 'on track' and continue the policies of Western neo-liberal, monetarist orthodoxy.

A third folly has been the American government's virtually uncritical support for Yeltsin himself. Since the fall of the Soviet Union, American policy-makers have been in effect his cheerleader, accomplice and spin doctor – thus implicating America in some of his most ill-advised and even wicked deeds – all the while insisting that Yeltsin remained the best hope for democratic and economic progress in Russia. In truth, the process of democratization begun under Gorbachev has progressed little, if at all, since 1991. In some ways, it has even regressed, due in no small part to President Yeltsin's various assaults on Russia's fledgling parliament and his expansive practice of ruling by decree. American backing for Yeltsin has not merely forced Washington to turn a blind eye to some of the more blatantly anti-democratic measures taken by the Russian President (his tank assault on Parliament in 1993 and genocidal bombing of Chechnaya, in particular) but to adopt the fiction that there are only two meaningful sides in every Russian dispute: the 'good guys' – 'our guys' – the 'democrat reformers' led by Yeltsin, who embody all that is progressive in Russia; and the 'bad guys', usually referred to in the US media as 'Communists and hardline nationalists', or the 'red-brown reactionaries', whose only goal allegedly is to restore the old Soviet system. This is a highly misleading and politically dangerous way of thinking about post-Soviet Russian politics today, one that makes Yeltsin and Yeltsinism seem to be our only hope.

The USA has been equally misguided in assuming that the main struggles under way in Russia are only about democracy and the market. Certainly, they have been important, but they have been secondary to or part of four towering conflicts. First, inflaming all the others, is an acrimonious and as yet unresolved dispute about the desired nature or national identity of Russia. Above all, should it be part of, or apart from, the West? Second, there is an underlying struggle over the distribution of spoils, most often over which members of the old Communist elite will get what, when, where and at what knock-down price. Third, there is a ramifying conflict under way between the Russian centre and its periphery, made all the more potentially explosive by the circumstance that millions of Russians live outside the core Russian federation. Finally, in Moscow itself, there is the ongoing battle between the President and the Parliament and the respective forces grouped around them. None of these conflicts can be easily subsumed under the notion that Russia is in some simple 'transition' from Soviet communism to liberal democratic capitalism.

Nor can cosy American assumptions make much sense of Russia's relations with the outside world. Since 1991, the United States has claimed to have built a constructive relationship with the new Russia, which the Clinton Administration called a 'strategic friendship and partnership' between America and 'Russian reform'. Much was made of this professed achievement, but the likelihood of such a partnership being truly implemented or sustained was negligible.

One reason is that the USA, while insisting loudly on economic policies that have contributed greatly to the Russian tragedy, never delivered on initial promises of large-scale financial aid, private investment, and quick benefits. The result has been to generate an ever-spreading anti-American backlash – even amongst once pro-American Russians. As for those Russians less positively inclined towards the USA, it is widely assumed that America's only interest in their country is to turn it into a Third World outpost supplying cheap raw materials, particularly energy resources to the developed West, a dire view that also has spread across the political spectrum.

Another reason why the fabled 'partnership' was never likely to materialize was the American terms of the relationship. Summit rhetoric aside, since 1991 the USA has in effect, approached Russia as a defeated enemy rather than as a genuine partner. Russian officials have complained repeatedly that US representatives speak to them as though they were 'prodigal children' or supplicants, and that is not even to consider the far harsher reactions of the Russian opposition. America may think it won the Cold War, and Russia may now be governed by self-professed Communists-turned-anti-Communists who according to the United States – lost it. But, Russian leaders are proud inheritors of a great civilization and a twentieth-century superpower; and neither they nor their successors can or will lead – or long be able to govern – Russia as America's servitors.

Finally, though the USA and Russia are no longer avowed ideological foes locked in global conflict, the two countries have strongly divergent views and interests that no amount of American rhetoric about a new special relationship can hide. Thus while Russia might have said 'yes' to almost every American initiative back in 1992, since then it has taken an increasingly independent position on many important international issues, including Serbia, Iran, Iraq, Cuba, the Baltics, India, China, and NATO expansion. Not surprisingly, these have brought Russia into growing conflict with Washington. This should not alarm or even surprise us too much. Nor does it necessarily portend a renewal of the Cold War. It does, however, arouse all those US triumphalists who assumed that post-Communist Russia could and should be turned into America's junior partner in world affairs.

The Silence of the 'Transitionologists'

From flawed assumptions flow flawed policies that have contributed enormously to the terrible tragedy unfolding in Russia since 1991 – though we have heard very little about it in the United States. Instead, we have been told that Russia's 'transition to a free-market economy' and 'democracy' has generally progressed admirably, despite some setbacks and bumps in the road. Pro-Yeltsin apologists point to the extent of privatization, the emergence of new financial markets, the declining rate of inflation, the successful holding of a presidential election and the existence of a free press. All this they argue is clear proof that genuine progress has been made in Russia. What they fail to emphasize, however, is the extent to which Russia's new private sector is dominated by former but still intact Soviet monopolies seized by ex-Communist officials who have become the core of a semi-criminalized business-class. Little is said, moreover, about the collapse in investment and production, the growth of unpaid wages and all the other unkept promises about a better future. And barely anything is made of the fact that President Yeltsin's successful re-election campaign in 1996 was one of the most corrupt in recent European history, and that neither Russia's market nor its national television is truly competitive – let alone free – but is substantially controlled by the same financial oligarchy whose representatives move in and out of the Kremlin as chieftains of the Yeltsin regime and the new order.

In human terms, however, this is not the worst of it. For the great majority of Russian families, their country has not been in 'transition' but in an endless collapse of everything essential to a decent existence – from real wages, welfare provisions and health care to birth-rates and life expectancy; from industrial and agricultural production to higher education, science and traditional culture; from safety in the streets to prosecution of organized crime and thieving bureaucrats; from the still enormous military forces to the safeguarding of nuclear devices and material. Indeed, the general impact of the Western-sponsored and Yeltsin-led economic and social policies since 1991 has been utterly and catastrophically unprecedented: the progressive demodernization of everyday life in what had been a twentieth-century great power – the gradual and not easily retrievable loss of much that is essential for its people's well-being that had been achieved, because of or despite the Soviet experience, in this century. These are the realities – urban and rural, working class and middle class – underlying the 'reforms' that most US officials and commentators continue to extol and insist are the only desirable kind.

Though fragments of this unprecedented, cruel and perilous collapse are reported in the US press, the full extent of the calamity is not conveyed or appreciated. The question is why? After all, we were constantly reminded of the plight of the people under the Soviet regime. Why is so much less made of the appalling situation facing the Russian people under the post-Communist system – especially when the United States and the West now have thousands of so-called specialists actually living and working in Russia? Why have so few journalists and scholars tried to tell the full story about post-Soviet Russia? Indeed, why, despite incomparably greater access to information, do most American reporters, pundits and scholars tell us less that is truly essential about Russia today than they did when it was part of the Soviet Union?

There are, I think, several reasons for the silence – all of them related to American conditions rather than to Russia's. The most important has to do with US foreign policy itself. As during the Cold War, most media and academic commentators think or speak within parameters defined by Washington. Before 1989, our view of the USSR was in large part a negative one, conditioned by the official argument that Moscow was a threat or enemy whose capabilities and intentions we needed to 'know' if we were to contain it effectively. Since 1991, most commentators have more or less followed the White House's line about Russia's successful transition and the US 'strategic' role in its implementation.

But it is not just US officials who have taken this view. American business groups, big foundations and academics have also had a stake in a successful Russian 'transition'. For the business community, it is the prospect of profits; for foundations, another frontier of endowed social engineering; for academia, a new paradigm ('transitionology') for securing new funds, jobs and tenure. But even they cannot fully ignore the situation on the ground – especially if they travel or see beyond Moscow. Confronted with the reality that the results of the 'transition' might have made things worse for most Russians rather than better, defenders of the new order have tried to explain away these consequences in one of three ways: by blaming them on the legacy of the Communist past; by insisting that the problems are merely temporary; or by minimizing them altogether. In the end, though, they continue to deny that the Russian tragedy is in large measure a result of Western prescriptions and their adoption by the post-Soviet leadership.

Finally, and more generally, the tendency to view Russia through rose-coloured glasses has a good deal to do with the belief that the end of the Cold War was bound to make the world a better place. This certitude is tied to a more general American tendency to view Russia (now as in the past) through the prism of its own hopes and expectations. Americans have always seen in Russia (for reasons both ideological and psychological) mainly what they have assumed to be there: the alternative to capitalism in the 1930s; an immutable totalitarian monster after World War II; and now an emerging democratic capitalist system – not exactly like, but becoming like, America's.

Still worse, Americans who hold such views always seem to be highly intolerant of those of us who do not. This was true before 1991, and it has been true since. Indeed, how many of us who doubt that the world may now be less safe because of what has happened in the former Soviet Union, who believe that ordinary Russians (even those much denigrated 'elderly' Communist voters) have been made to suffer unduly and unjustly, who understand that there were less costly and more humane ways to reform Russia – how many of us are willing to say such things publicly, knowing that we will be accused of nostalgia for the USSR or even of pro-Communism? Crude McCarthyism has passed, but not the maligning of those Americans who challenge mainstream orthodoxies about Soviet or post-Soviet Russia. And the presumed 'transition' to a free-market economy and democracy is today's orthodoxy.

Towards a New American Policy

Thus far we have looked at some of the dubious underlying assumptions that have underlaid a misguided American crusade to remake Russia in its own image. The venture was bound to fail – and fail it has. Rather than creating the conditions for future economic development and growth, US-backed policies have kept the Russian economy in near free-fall and prolonged depression since 1991, ravaged by an extraordinary multiple collapse of production, capital investment and consumption. Instead of establishing a stable base for liberal democracy, political forces hostile to individual freedom continue to grow. And far from creating a new partnership with Russia, the USA has ended up alienating a good deal of Russian elite and popular opinion that originally favoured it. In the process, Washington has endorsed undemocratic practices and social injustices, said next to nothing about the concentration of vast public assets in corrupt private hands, and echoed the Yeltsin regime's claim that almost all its opponents are extremists or reactionaries. Nor has any of this resulted in docile Russian support for American initiatives on the international stage.

Failed policies raise the question of alternatives. Most American politicians and opinion-makers say they favour 'helping Russia'; and of course we must help. The main reason is generally well known but worth restating here: If Russia, with all its unprecedented potential for nuclear and ethnic holocaust, lurches into chaos or despotism, no real international security of any kind will be possible. For this reason (there are others), merely allocating $3 to $6 billion annually for aid to Russia for several years, barely 1 to 2 per cent of current US defence spending, would be an excellent and cheap investment in national security. But this alone is not enough. Wiser policies require wiser US principles and guidelines: do's and don'ts that are better informed and more thoughtful about Russian realities and American possibilities.

The first imperative is to create a stable constituency for good US-Russian relations in the United States itself. Formulating its policies, the US government must explain them to the American people realistically, not euphemistically and euphorically (as did Clinton), emphasizing not only their importance for our national interests but also that Russia's journey to a good and stable order will be a long one – and will include along the way developments that do not conform to standard expectations. Without such understanding, even the wisest policies will be quickly undone by disillusionment, impatience and resurgent Cold War attitudes.

The second pre-condition for a successful American policy is to ensure that US policies and programmes designed to help Russia do not assume the missionary form which they have done so far. We lack the right, wisdom and power to convert Russia to America's way of life. Our system cannot be transplanted to Russia where experiences, perceptions and conditions are different. In particular, the United States and its international agencies must desist from trying to design, dictate and supervise Russia's overall reform strategy. Russia must itself decide how and how fast it wants to change. Aid given on condition that it be used only in specifically American ways will invariably cause resentment. US assistance must be informed by Russian realities and possibilities, not by American illusions and conceits.

Nor should any US policy or agency any longer intervene excessively in Russia's internal affairs. Such practices have been counterproductive in the past and they certainly will be so in the future. All they do is inspire a resentful backlash against America. Moreover, while private groups and individuals might have their own agenda, the policy of the American government should be to develop normal relations with as many Russian institutions and movements as possible, including Parliament and parties critical of Yeltsin, as it would do in any 'democratic' country. The USA must, of course, focus on Russia's elected President. But it should also be respectful towards a broad range of Russian political opinion and leaders. Otherwise, America may find that it has few friends, partners, or even acquaintances when Yeltsin finally leaves the scene.

We also need realistic thinking, not illusions, about US-Russian relations in the larger context of world affairs. Predicating the relationship on a fairy tale 'friendship and partnership' as though post-Communist Russia's foreign policy will simply follow that of the United States is certain to breed disillusionment in the USA itself. It also ignores the simple reality that Russia's foreign and defence policies will in the end be based on its own perceived national interests and on positions that can be sustained and defended in Moscow – not Washington. None of this is likely to lead to a new Cold War. Nor is it reason for refusing to help Russia's reforms. But we should be aware that Russia has legitimate interests which do not neatly dovetail with those of the United States.

The USA also has to pay special attention to a particularly problematic issue: post-Communist Russia's relations with other former Soviet republics. The situation here remains unresolved and the future uncertain. The United States evidently assumes that all these new states will and must remain entirely separate and independent from Moscow – and that Russia will treat them accordingly. But powerful factors continue to generate proposals in Russia and several other former republics for a new Union that would naturally revolve around Russia. Those factors include common economic and security problems; the fate of some 25 million Russians living outside Russia; millions of mixed ethnic marriages and families now separated by new borders; disputes over sovereignty, territory and property; and spreading civil violence. Thus far, US policy-makers have given this fateful problem little serious thought, at least publicly. It is time to do so. If the USA really favours economic recovery and stability (as it must), a good case can be made for Washington supporting the restoration of broken economic ties and doing nothing to discourage any voluntary political integration. It must also do what it can to defuse the explosive issue of those 25 million Russians now stranded outside Russia. This means at a minimum unequivocal support for their human rights – especially in Estonia, Latvia and Ukraine – no matter what the political temptation is to do otherwise.

Finally, the USA must take its own rhetoric about supporting democracy more seriously than it has done hitherto. At every turn, it has publicly accepted and even echoed Yeltsin's rationalizations and excuses. It has said virtually nothing about his undemocratic practices and the system he has created, particularly since his cannon assault on Parliament in 1993. But if the savage twentieth century teaches us anything, it is that means and ends are related and that resorting to dubious political methods to achieve some theoretically worthy goal is likely to result in disaster. Yeltsin's American apologists sometimes mindlessly repeat the old Communist excuse 'you can't make an omelette without breaking a few eggs'. But if we are to learn anything from the past, including the years since 1991, there will be no omelette, only a mass of broken eggs in the form of crushed hopes and lives.

Conclusion

A reformed and stable Russia at peace with its neighbours is a crucial American interest. But as I have argued, such a Russia can find its way only within the parameters of its own traditions and possibilities, not our own. If the United States cannot accept this as a first principle of our post-Communist relations with Russia, the sequel to the Cold War is not going to be international stability and order but a cold and insecure peace. To avoid such an outcome we have to start afresh, but to do so we must first recognize that the United States still lacks any well-conceived and workable policies towards Russia - and in practice has had none since the Soviet break-up in 1991. Ceremonial declarations, legions of perhaps well-meaning (but poorly informed) advisers and even burdensome loans are not in themselves a strategy. Nor will we have one worthy of the name until Washington jettisons old assumptions and devises policies based upon a truthful, critical view of what has actually happened in Russia since 1991. Until it does, things will almost certainly get still worse.

But does it even matter what Americans do or say about Russia? Those of us who have opposed the United States' missionary complicity in the 'transition' and the insistence that there is no alternative - that Russia must 'stay the course' - may wish the USA would say and intervene less. Indeed, if it had done so and not embarked on an ill-conceived crusade to transform Russia in ways counter to its historical traditions, present-day realities and actual possibilities, that country would undoubtedly be in much better shape than it now is. Because of this experience, fewer and fewer Russians any longer care what Americans have to say to them.

In one way, however, US commentary does matter greatly. Eventually, today's Russian children will ask what America felt and said during these tragic times for their parents and grandparents, and they will shape their relations with our own children and grandchildren accordingly. For this reason, if no other, it is important that those of us opposed to US policy express our opposition candidly and loudly so that future Russian generations will know that voices here were raised against America's missionary crusade in Russia - the worst and most predictable US foreign policy failure of the late twentieth century, and perhaps the greatest tragedy to be still unfolding in the twenty-first.

14

So What Did Collapse in 1991? Reflections on a Revolution Betrayed

CARL G. JACOBSEN

Introduction

The central concern of this volume has been to explore the intellectual ambitions and pretences of Western Sovietology, and to assess whether or not it failed to anticipate the disintegration of the Soviet Union. My concern is to go behind the scenes so-to-speak and examine a rather different but equally important question: namely, what was it exactly that disintegrated in 1991? Interestingly, this rather important issue has not been addressed by scholars, and I want to do so here by challenging the common-sense assumption that what finally collapsed in that most extraordinary year was a political order known as 'totalitarianism' and an ideological system generally referred to as 'Communism'. That done, I will go on to compare Lenin with Stalin, and then look at the problems that Stalin's successors confronted, but in the end failed to resolve. Finally, I shall draw some historical parallels between the current situation facing Russia reformers and the tasks facing the Bolsheviks after 1917. Though the two might be at different ends of the ideological spectrum – the former after all want to re-create the very capitalism which the latter sought to destroy – there are still useful comparisons that can be made between the two.

Totalitarian? Communism?

Long before Yeltsin pushed the Soviet Union over the political edge, the USSR could in no sense be described as being totalitarian. In fact, it was not Yeltsin at all, but Gorbachev who really changed the nature of Soviet politics by permitting greater pluralism, opening the system up to critical examination, ending the monopoly position of the Communist Party of the Soviet Union (CPSU), introducing free, multiparty elections, securing a 70 per cent referendum approval for a more decentralized Union, and, with Republican leaders, negotiating a confederal constitution to that end, to which all but the three Baltic leaders gave their support.[1] What Sovietologists did not (and probably could not) anticipate was that Boris Yeltsin, issuing edicts in the finest tsarist/commissar tradition even as Gorbachev was addressing Russia's parliament after his return from Crimea detention (by the failed Putschists), would in effect launch his own coup. Boris the 'Democrat' would of course usurp legal authority again, in October 1993, giving him a unique niche in Russian history. Nor, perhaps, did Sovietologists anticipate that Gorbachev, who still commanded sufficient military and paramilitary loyalty to allow other options, which others would surely have chosen, would acquiesce – though he had made the same choice in Eastern Europe, also against the advice and entreaties of some, when faced only with the stark alternatives of force or abdication.[2]

But if totalitarianism did not 'collapse', surely the same cannot be said of 'Communism', which, according to the authorized history of the modern world, persisted in the former USSR until Yeltsin finally delivered the *coup de grâce*? Again, we have to be careful. Certainly, some Soviet leaders continued to use the old language – much as later regimes in France continued and continue to embrace ideals of the French Revolution long after Thermidor devoured its over-zealous vanguard. But this was testimony to the resonance of those ideas in the enduring cultures of their histories and lands, and by no means indicative of revolutionary intent or purpose. Long before the demise of the USSR, in fact, Stalin and Stalinism had long eviscerated the revolution of any true Marxist content. This has been shown most clearly in the work of Barrington Moore and Robert Daniels, whose early studies prove beyond question that under Stalin major readjustments were made in Communist theory to bring it in line with Stalinist practice.[3] Perhaps the best illustration of this process of adaptation was in the area of foreign policy. Here Stalin was a Russian nationalist first and foremost, quite unlike the Bolsheviks who seized power in 1917 and proclaimed that revolutionaries around the world had only one duty: to make revolution. Indeed, even when the early Bolsheviks disagreed about foreign policy – as they did for example over Brest-Litovsk and later over the decision to send the Red Army through Poland to Germany – the differences were never between utopian revolutionaries and 'Russia firsters' but always between different revolutionary options. Neither Trotsky, Lenin nor, of course, the early Bukharin had any nationalist qualms about giving up territory and wealth if it would gain time and resources for the larger task of aiding the world revolution. Fittingly, Lenin's final and total break with Stalin – too late to be effective – was occasioned precisely by the latter's chauvinism. To Lenin, power served other purposes: to Stalin there was no other purpose than power.

In terms of foreign policy, the revolutionary era came to an end when the revolutionary crest waned in West and Central Europe, and Marshal

Tuckachevsky was forced to retreat from Warsaw, after Stalin, Political Commissar for one flank, failed to effect the ordered link-up (his subsequent reprimand would later reverberate in the killings of both Tuckachevsky and Trotsky). The 1922 Rapallo Treaty with Germany then signalled Moscow's prioritizing of state interests. Thereafter, no Soviet foreign policy initiative would again be unambiguously, solely or even predominantly ideological in either purpose or rationale, though Western and Soviet leaders alike habitually found it in their interests to proclaim otherwise.[4] Yet throughout the Soviet era – and especially during the early years of the Cold War – conservative Western politicians routinely and indiscriminately denounced 'Communist aggression' as if it were a self-evident fact.[5] There were even those on what was once the Maoist left who spoke of a rising tide of Soviet 'imperialism' threatening the great globe itself after 1975. Such rhetoric was in one sense perfectly understandable: the American foreign policy elite after all was engaged in a determined struggle on the home front after 1947 to overcome the legacy of isolationism, whilst the Chinese found it a particularly useful device as they moved to cement their new alliance with the United States in the post-Mao era. Yet the gap between such rhetoric and the Soviet record was always great, and became greater the closer we got to Soviet collapse in 1991. But we did not need a Yeltsin, or even a Gorbachev, to inform us that the USSR had abandoned the revolution. Many realists, including the most significant foreign policy figure in the post-war period – George F. Kennan – had come to that conclusion long before new thinking had become a byword.[6] Another noted diplomat and historian of the twentieth century agreed. Indeed, according to Henry Kissinger, Stalin was no red-blooded revolutionary seeking to spread the word of Marxism, or some latter-day version of Leon Trotsky, but the 'supreme realist: patient, shrewd and implacable, the Richelieu of his period', a view endorsed incidentally by other significant scholars of Soviet Russia.[7]

Even after attaining superpower status, Moscow intervened abroad, either with direct military force or 'gunboat' diplomacy, much less frequently than did its main Western rivals.[8] Moreover, when the USSR 'intervened' in Angola and Ethiopia in the 1970s, it was primarily because it had been invited to do so by besieged regimes. Let us not forget either that in Angola, Moscow supported an internationally recognized government against opposition aided by troops from South Africa's apartheid regime; whilst in Ethiopia it defended the regime against Somali incursion intent on border revision.[9] And Moscow's advances were no more immutable than those of the West: notwithstanding the Afghan venture, Moscow's international alliance and allegiance network at the end of Leonid Brezhnev's tenure as Party leader was less extensive than when he first took office. Historically, in fact, no Soviet leader was as adventurous on distant shores as, for example, the early post-Crimean leadership, which briefly established bases in Tsushima and Villefranca, and sent naval vessels to Northern US ports during the American Civil War, when it appeared that Britain would recognize the South. Brzezinzki's highly revisionist claim (one that has been ignored by his mainly conservative admirers) that Stalinism was a blessing in disguise for the West, because amongst other things it impeded rather than encouraged Russian expansion, is one that scholars need to take far more seriously than they have done so far.[10]

Lenin: Stalin: Marx

In many modern accounts of the revolution, notably those by Richard Pipes and Orlando Figes, little effort is made to distinguish between the historical role played by Lenin and that played by Stalin. According to our latest neo-conservative myth-makers, both Lenin and Stalin were cut from the same blood-soaked cloth, and together they fashioned the tools which led to the death of millions in the 1930s.[11]

This crude attempt to rewrite the complex history of Soviet Russia cannot go unchallenged – especially now perhaps when in the wake of 1991 all manner of nonsense is being written about the Soviet Union's past by those less interested in genuine history than in advancing their own political projects.

Lenin created the Bolshevik party under conditions of the severest repression in tsarist Russia. The party was no talking shop but neither was it the monolithic fantasy of right-wing nightmares. Indeed, as many historians of the organization have shown, it changed beyond all recognition in 1917 as literally thousands of new recruits entered its ranks and transformed it into a mass, open party. Lenin, of course, was no saint and he was not squeamish in launching Red Terror against the Whites: but against counter-revolutionaries he was no more ruthless than the Whites had always been against the Reds (recall what happened after the fall of the Paris Commune), and besides Sherman's 'heart-sickening' destruction of Georgia in his long march through that ill-fated southern state in 1864, he was a model of veritable restraint. But the means by which one defended the revolution according to Lenin was not a recipe for the future; they were rather an unfortunate, necessary but temporary way of surviving the bleak odds of civil war and foreign interventions.[12]

Lenin also managed the party and worked with his party comrades very differently to Stalin. Lenin did not even govern as leader of the Party, but as Chairman of the Council of People's Commissars (or Ministers). The fateful 1922 decision to give Stalin the post of Party Secretary General, to vet the flow of opportunists and new recruits, was made because more prominent

Party members considered it marginal; they chose more 'important' positions.[13] Nor did Lenin demand conformity. Lev Kamenev and Grigory Zinoviev, who leaked October plans to force postponement of a coup they thought would fail – the ultimate betrayal – were welcomed into his cabinet. He also encouraged vigorous internal debates, and placed no fetters on the flood of experimentation in literature and arts that marked the early years. Moreover, when a leadership majority opposed his advocacy of peace with Germany, he accepted the decision. And when German troops continued to advance he later secured a one-vote majority for reversal, and acceptance of the peace of Brest-Litovsk; but the threats with which he cajoled were of resignation, not retribution. With the waning of civil war and withdrawal of most (though not all) of the foreign armies that sustained it, he ended the stifling grip of War Communism and introduced NEP, the New Economic Policy, that brought back the market and small-scale private enterprise. He outlawed formal factions, but still insisted on the free flow of inner Party debate.

Only when impaired by a stroke and looked after by Stalin-appointed doctors who limited his movements and intercepted his mail, did he realize that Stalin, by manipulating elections and rival egos, was turning the Party into an instrument of his personal will. Lenin spent his last year smuggling appeals to Trotsky and others to act whilst there was still time; to thwart Stalinist dictatorship.[14] They dallied and lost and within little more than a decade, all members of Lenin's inner circle were dead, in exile, or in the gulag. In the meantime, Stalin had flooded the party with raw new recruits, silenced the opposition (including the hapless Bukharin) and enunciated the novel doctrine of 'Socialism In One Country'. As Carr has noted, the idea that the revolution need no longer depend on the outside world to survive and prosper appealed to many in the party. This is true. But the idea was clearly designed for a new type of ruling (rather than revolutionary) party that would be Russian rather than cosmopolitan and nationalist rather than internationalist.

Indeed, if we are to think of Stalin at all in comparative terms, it would probably be more useful to think of Machiavelli rather than Lenin: certainly he seemed to have learned more from *The Prince* than from *State and Revolution*. His *modus operandi*, moreover, echoed more that of Ivan the Terrible than Lenin. Thus when his rivals threatened to outvote him in 1934, he did not concede or try to convince them through debate and discussion, but launched a pre-emptive attack that finally led to the destruction of the Bolshevik party. Stalin also crushed and then used a now subservient Church. The secret police became his watchdog and enforcer. Law was bent to his will, and his alone. The Red Army's leadership was isolated, then liquidated, whilst tsarist traditions – from epaulettes to ballroom dancing and Kutuzov and Suvorov medals – were reintroduced (only duelling remained illegal!). Stalin also appointed himself Commander-in-Chief, and Generalissimo: while culture that did not glorify the regime became punishable by exile, prison or worse.

Which brings us to Marx: the ultimate source of all these evils according to past and present neo-conservatives. The argument, I would suggest, bears as much resemblance to historical truth as did the Stalinist system to Marx's vision of Communism. Certainly, to blame Marx or to hold him in anyway responsible for what transpired in the Soviet Union seems as logical as blaming the Greek invasion of Cyprus on Plato, the Holocaust on Wagner, and the Inquisition upon Jesus Christ. Indeed, if we hold Christ to be responsible for the death of all those heretics, one could easily imagine the comments of those who finally saw the passing away of that particularly obscene Spanish institution: thank God, the death of Christianity!

Stalin's Successors

Stalin's legacy to Russia was an ambiguous one: under his leadership the nation had industrialized (to a degree), endured the war (just), and had emerged with a level of international support it could only have dreamed of before 1939 or 1941.[15] However, the Soviet Union was by no means the superpower menace it was portrayed as being in Western propaganda. Its agriculture was on the point of collapse in 1953, industry was inefficient to a degree unknown in the West, and the people still traumatized by the experiences they had undergone since the beginning of the 1930s. Furthermore, though the country was no longer isolated, at the global level it confronted a very serious rival indeed in the shape of the United States whose economic prowess, military strength and alliance structure far outweighed anything it had faced before.

Stalin's successors thus faced major problems both internally and internationally. Significantly, however, their first move was not to deal with these, but to secure their own position; and quite literally within weeks of Stalin's death they had reduced the autonomous power of the secret police, and by so doing preventing the emergence of another Stalin. That done, they then moved rather carefully, though over the next three to four years did abandon some of the harsher aspects of Stalinist rule, opened up the camps, and made a belated appeal for Soviet democracy and a return to 'Socialist Legality' and 'Leninist Norms'. Yet there were always very real limits as to how far they were prepared to go. Khrushchev's harsh denunciation of Stalin, his 'crimes' and 'megalomania' (made in his Secret Speech to the 20th Party Congress, in February 1956) remained unpublished in the USSR itself. Very little effort was made to overcome the inequalities and isolation of

Soviet society. The arts were freed, but only to an extent. And though the elite itself became more 'collective' (if not collegial!) it was determined to protect its privileged position against the dangers of 'levelling' from below and the threat of a new Stalin emerging from within the bowels of the CPSU.

Freed from terror, the elite found that it now completely controlled the levers of power; and as time passed – and things settled down in a way that had been impossible under Stalin – it gradually began to resemble what Djilas had earlier called a 'New Class'. And like all ruling groups in history, the Soviet elite was concerned above all with the retention of power and perpetuation of privilege: first for itself, then for its sons and daughters, and finally for their sons and daughters. Party officials and their different allies in the new Soviet upper classes became in effect the modern version of pre-revolutionary boyars, the noblemen of their day. Indeed, the parallels between the post-Stalinist regime and that of the later tsars are quite marked: both were autocracies – though were striving for a benevolent façade; both were extensive and intrusive; both feared spontaneity in any shape or form whether it was political or literary; and both were underpinned by a ubiquitous secret police and the threat of exile, or worse, for dissidents.

Though life in general improved after 1953, it would be plainly absurd to imply that the system even in its less repressive form was evolving towards something higher like Communism. Indeed, when Khrushchev even raised the theoretical possibility in 1961 he was quickly reined in by his comrades. In all truth, Soviet officials only paid lip-service to a vision they did not believe in. But if the USSR was not in transition to Communism, was it still totalitarian after 1953? This is a debate which still rattles on and continues to divide Sovietology – primarily along political lines. The problem, however, with the conservative right is that they consistently confuse intention and outcome. It might well be true, as they insist, that Soviet leaders after Stalin's death aspired to totalitarian power, enforced by overlapping levers of societal control, omnipresent police, informers, and neighbourhood committees. But to aspire to control is one thing: to achieve that end is something else entirely. And if different Western authors agree about anything, it is the overwhelming inability of the Soviet leadership to mould minds or get people to believe in an ideology that bore absolutely no resemblance to Soviet reality. Certainly if Soviet socialization had been as successful as some Western political scientists later claimed, then one has to ask why most of those who actually managed to leave the USSR were so rabidly conservative? But it was not just the émigrés who were so reactionary (with one or two notable exceptions like Zhores Medvedev). Most of the Soviet intelligentsia seemed to be as well – to such an extent that Western Sovietologists used to joke in the 1960s that there were more genuine Marxists at the University of the Sorbonne in Paris than in the whole of the Soviet Union. If it was true then (and it was) it is clearly even more so today. The point is, of course: wishing is not the same thing as reality. A totalitarian state cannot exist merely in the dreams of its masters, or the fears of its enemies. Although neo-Stalinist control was harsh and extensive, it was never total.

From Crisis to Collapse

By the late 1970s this odd hybrid 'bureautocratic' system faced even greater problems than those it had confronted in the years immediately following Stalin's death. Even the Party's ideological Godfather, Mikhail Suslov, acknowledged that old formulas no longer worked. Using Marxist terms, we might even suggest – along with Ronald Reagan in 1982 – that the superstructure no longer corresponded to a rapidly evolving base, whilst the economic base itself was profoundly flawed.[16] Whether we go along with those who argue that the economy was experiencing some difficulties, but could have survived (if left alone) or was facing long-term decline, is a question that has yet to be resolved.[17] What is not in doubt is that the traditional model developed by Stalin and 'perfected' by his successors could no longer deliver what it had been able to deliver before: reasonable growth and a slow but steady improvement in living standards. External factors also contributed to Soviet difficulties, though one of them was not Reagan's much celebrated efforts to spend the USSR into bankruptcy (a myth if ever there was one).[18] Far more important in shaping Soviet options was the sharp decline in world oil prices in the 1980s and the obvious economic success experienced by the countries of the Organization for Economic Cooperation and Development (OECD) and some of the Newly Industrialized Countries of Asia. The Soviet elite might have been able to hide some things from its own people, but it could not ignore basic global indices: and what they showed in raw figures was how far the USSR was falling behind the rest of the capitalist world as it moved towards the twenty-first century.

The story of what followed has been told several times before, so does not need to be restated here. Suffice to note that Gorbachev set out in 1985 to transform the USSR and turn it into what he hoped would one day become an efficient socialist superpower, and ended up helping destroy the country itself. No doubt historians will continue to debate his role in history, and whether or not he caused or accelerated the demise of the USSR. There can be no simple answer to this. Certainly, without Gorbachev the system would have gone on for some time. But for how long remains an open question. What is less open to question is the important role played by Gorbachev in preparing the ground for Yeltsin. Yeltsin in the end dumped Gorbachev – most unceremoniously as it turned out. However, without Gorbachev there would have been no historical role for Yeltsin to play in the first place. Gorbachev might never have needed Yeltsin: Yeltsin, on the other hand, would have remained a minor bit player without Gorbachev. Many now wish that he had.

Historical Parallels

In one sense those who made the 'revolution' in 1991 aimed to destroy an order which they saw as being unjust, exploitative and corrupt. They were similar in that respect at least to the Bolsheviks in 1917. In many ways, both sought profound socioeconomic change, universal rights and opportunities. However, whereas the Bolsheviks aimed to overturn private property, the 'revolutionaries' of 1991 sought to make it legal; and whilst Lenin and the Bolsheviks celebrated the masses, Yeltsin and his entourage were astute enough to know that many of the economic reforms they proposed would fly in the face of popular mass expectation. Moreover, though Yeltsin was no intellectual – and Lenin most certainly was – both in the end faced almost impossible political tasks: in Yeltsin's case to turn Russia into a mature capitalist country and in Lenin's to defend the revolution against its enemies at home and abroad without an army in 1917, or indeed (at first) without a state.

In recognition of the uphill task they both faced, the two regimes initially looked to the outside world for help and support: the Bolsheviks to the revolutionary wave that appeared to sweep Europe after World War I (the Bela Kun government in Hungary; the uprisings in Germany; mutinies in the French Army; the red flag over St. George's Square in Glasgow); Yeltsin and his supporters to massive economic aid from the capitalist world. Both were to be disappointed. The tide of European revolution began to ebb by 1921 – testimony as Lenin admitted at the time of the political resilience of the Western capitalism. And 70 years later the Russian government looked in vain for a new Marshall Plan – testimony as many reformers have argued since, of the West's inability to think strategically about its interest in the post-Cold War era.

Ironically, though, it is not the Bolsheviks but their immediate predecessors who perhaps have greater reason for blaming the West: in much the same way that many Russians today blame the outside world for their current misfortunes. The parallels are not without significance. It was after all the lure of Istanbul and the Bosphorus, promised by London and Paris at the outbreak of World War I, that brought Russian offensives when Germany threatened breakthroughs in the West. These relieved the Allies, but doomed the tsar. The successor Provisional governments acknowledged the need for peace, land redistribution and fair elections. Once again, however, a Western promise over the Straits brought yet another Russian offensive: one which relieved the West but turned the war into a rout for Russia and shredded support for the regime at home. In 1991 and after, of course, the lure was not the Straits but Western aid and investment, in return for adopting harsh Western economic prescriptions. The reforms began but the aid did not flow – and significant numbers of the Russian people revolted, not by turning to the modern equivalent of the Bolshevik party (there is none) but to those organizations opposed to the West and to economic reform: Zhironovsky's Liberal Democrats and Zyuganov's Russian Communist Party.[19] Furthermore, as actual aid lagged ever further behind promises (sometimes addressing donors' needs more than Russia's) a growing number of reformers joined in the regime opponents' refrain, that the reward of aid and investment was a mirage, and that adhering to an 'alien' prescription, was likely to result in aggravating rather than easing the economic crisis.[20]

There are even sharper analogies between then and now. At Brest-Litovsk in 1918, Russia lost one-third of its population and one-fourth of its territory, including most of its iron and steel industries, the food-producing region of the Ukraine, Belorussia, Finland and the Baltic territories. Independence proclamations by Caucasian and Central Asian and other territories followed. Most were reabsorbed, in whole or in part, by 1926, but it was not until World War II that older Russian boundaries were re-established, minus Poland and Finland. The rush to independence by most Republics in late 1991 reflected similar centrifugal dynamics, again fed by the confluence of socioeconomic crisis, the collapse of old and the uncertainty of new central power(s).[21] By 1994, however, Russia was asserting a security sphere or interest throughout the 'near abroad', with particular responsibility for the Russian diaspora. Given its size, economic weight and control over key natural resources, a number of the newly independent republics also began to find that whilst it had been difficult to live with Russia, it was even more difficult living without it. And if Russia could hardly ignore them, they could not ignore Russia, which in spite of the 'new geopolitical environment' still remained 'the most important partner state for the majority of CIS member states'.[22]

The parallels do not end there. In 1918, beset by rapidly spreading civil war, foreign interventions in support of White armies in Ukraine and the Caucasus, the Baltics and Siberia, and a collapsing economy, the Bolsheviks introduced War Communism, and harsh grain (and other) requisition policies. After 1992 also, the ideals of theory were soon buffeted by starker demands of reality and circumstance. Like Gorbachev before him, Boris Yeltsin failed to privatize most agricultural production – their 'greatest failure', according to Vitaly Sobchak. Yet they had little choice; the reform economist and sociologist Tatyana Zaslavskaya's new Sociology Institute's first survey of peasant attitudes showed only 1 per cent ready to accept the uncertain promise and (in)security of private ownership. By 1992 some peasant collectives were again withholding produce and cutting output, in response to a new 'scissors' crisis' that saw the increase in prices for the harvest falling behind those for industrial goods and agricultural implements – deliveries of which also became evermore uncertain. The result was that once more, governments in Kiev and elsewhere felt increasingly compelled to impose and sometimes enforce demands for state-priced requisitions.

There is also the question of personnel. In 1918 Party ranks were swelled by opportunists and careerists. In 1991, some 'democratic' leaders, such as those of Uzbekistan, were erstwhile supporters of the August coup attempt who embraced the new faith only after – and in response to – the coup's failure. In 1991, as in 1917, revolutionaries might proclaim socioeconomic transformation, but the bureaucrats, administrators and managers needed to run the new order were perforce trained by the previous system. In 1918 'old specialists' flooded into the Red Army, new Ministries and organizations. In 1992–4 also, and notwithstanding new names and the exclusion of those most prominently tainted by the old, the corridors of power and influence continued to be staffed by the nomenklatura and their mafia allies of old. Bur[eaut]ocracies are uniquely able to emasculate policies that threaten, and mould the impact of their implementation.

Finally, the military: under commissars and tsars, the Army was always part of, and never apart from, the nation's leadership; the concept of military coup or regime is alien to its culture. A revolutionary context, however, as in 1917–18 and today, is by definition a time of flux, and uncertainty. Then, as now, the Army's conscript base and finance was ravaged; morale suffered under the onslaught of different loyalties; and some defected, to causes old and new. The best (arguably) followed General Alexsey Brusilov's advice, that whilst governments come and go, Russia remains; thus stay aloof from civil strife, but be ready to answer the call when your country needs you. When Poland attacked, in 1920, they followed him into the ranks of the Red Army.

Colonel-General Boris Gromov, Moscow's last commander in Kabul, and perhaps the most interesting of the old 'Afghan cohort' (which includes Alexander Rutskoi, Pavel Grachev and the flamboyant General Alexander Lomov) may turn into the Brusilov of the 1990s.[23] The epitome of the professional soldier, he resigned from the Army in early 1991, apparently forgoing Army leadership and a Marshall's Star, to become Deputy Minister of the Interior, and what soldiers most dislike – a policeman. It was a measure of his concern. He reined in, and reorganized the emergent network of Omon security troops. Yet when his Minister joined the August plotters, surely assuming the network's activation, Gromov gave the contrary signal of no signal; this was not the exigency for which he had prepared. The Moscow Omon's defence of Russia's White House spared him guilt by association. By Fall, in a return to military prominence as unusual as his earlier departure, he was appointed Deputy Commander of the Army. In March 1992, echoing his Afghan finale, he directed the Army's withdrawal from Nagorno-Karabach. The next month he became the First Deputy Minister in Russia's new Ministry of Defence. He might have paraphrased Brusilov: stay aloof from civil strife where Russia's (and the people's) interests are not truly at stake. Conversely, the embrace of Russia's flag by Lomov's ex-Soviet Army in Moldova a few weeks later, in response to Moldovan attacks on breakaway Transdniester's Russian population, suggested that the Army had identified today's Polish analogue: the defence of Russia's diaspora.[24]

There are naturally some major differences between 1917–18 and 1991–8. One, of course, relates to the army itself. The Bolsheviks in the end managed to create an army whose personnel thereafter (and until 1991) enjoyed high prestige in Soviet society. The same can hardly be said of Russian armed forces today, whose numbers are declining and whose position in Russia more generally remains uncertain.[25] Secondly, there are major differences between the two societies. Earlier Soviet society mirrored that of tsarist Russia: overwhelmingly peasant, poor and illiterate; it remained governable by the same, essential formula, entwining authority, faith and discipline. The contemporary nation is fundamentally changed: urban, literate, educated and contemptuous of the homilies and dogmas of the past. Finally, the world of the 1990s is very different to the world turned upside down by the Bolshevik revolution in 1917. At one level, it is a far less threatening world. On the other hand, as a result of globalization it is a far more interdependent world and there can be no escape – as Stalin hoped there might be – to the apparent security of economic isolationism.

Revolutionary Dilemmas and the Future

Premature by definition and acknowledged to be so by both Lenin and Trotsky (who saw revolution in Germany as its only sustaining hope), the revolution in Russia followed the pattern of other revolutions that have sought fundamental socioeconomic change. As Trotsky conceded, all revolutions face a basic and as yet unresolved dilemma: the desperation that fuels revolt is profoundly polarizing, compelling the embrace of visions that are necessarily utopian; but revolutionary governments can rarely if ever fulfil those aspirations. Material circumstances alone make that impossible. Nor can they survive over the longer term without compromising their most cherished ideals. But history does not move in straight lines and the ideals which animated the revolution, though betrayed in practice, have not and in all probability could not be erased from the record. They live on (and will in all certainty be fought for and quite possibly hijacked and perverted again) because they are integral to the yearnings of much of humankind.

Without doubt, the Soviet *apparat* cloaked itself in the rhetoric of Communism. But the rhetoric was Orwellian 'Newspeak'; and to talk of the death of Communism is to adopt that Newspeak. Worse: to assert the death of Communism, with its concepts of equal opportunity and communal responsibility, is to encourage the very kind of rapacious (and narcissistic) capitalism that nurtured early Communist dreams.[26] However, as I have tried to show, what failed in the USSR was not Communism at all - and if it failed (which it obviously did) it was not because it upheld Communist principles, but rather because it betrayed them. Communism, with its aspiration to truer democracy, is as susceptible to perversion as other visions. But it will remain with us because it also embodies some of our highest ideals.

In the meantime the new triumphalists - those who think that history has come to an end and that Communism is dead - should recall that Russian advocates of foreign economic and political prescriptions (like Yeltsin) have always ultimately lost out to more Slavophile sentiments and arguments. This is not to say that democracy is doomed to failure; rather that definitions rooted in other political cultures are likely to be rejected by the body politic of one that is different. Russian political culture has been dominated by authoritarianism. But it also embodies its own notions of democracy, bred by its own historical experiences and aspirations. Today's context of circumstance and hope may be uniquely propitious. But if democracy is truly to evolve, then it must be defined and shaped by - and rest on - these domestic roots. Unless it does so, the longer-term consequence of Soviet disintegration might turn out not to be market democracy at all, but something very different. History has played tricks on the best informed of pundits in the past - as some think it did on so many Sovietologists back in 1991. There is no reason to think it could not do so again.

Notes

1 See Stephen White, *Gorbachev in Power* (Cambridge University Press, 1990), and his *After Gorbachev* (Cambridge University Press, 1993).

2 For a useful discussion of Gorbachev's policy options in Eastern Europe see Jacques Levesque, *The Enigma of 1989: The USSR and the Liberation of Eastern Europe* (University of California Press, 1997).

3 See Barrington Moore Jr, 'Some Readjustments in Communist Theory', *Journal of the History of Ideas*, Volume 6, 1945, pp. 468–82, and Robert Daniels, 'The State

and Revolution: A Case Study in the Genesis and Transformation of Communist Ideology', *The American Slavic and East European Review*, Volume 12, February 1953, pp. 22–43.

4   For an elaboration of this point see Vojtech Mastny, *The Cold War and Soviet Insecurity: the Stalin Year* (New York, Oxford University Press, 1996).

5   On the role of American threat perception in the Cold War and the 'mismatch between Soviet behaviour and US assessments of it', see the chapter by Ken Booth in my edited volume, *Strategic Power: USA/USSR* (London and New York, Macmillan and St. Martin's Press, 1990), pp. 50–71.

6   Kennan wrote in September 1944 that after Lenin's death, Stalin, to his 'credit', began to develop 'a purely nationalist Soviet foreign policy' and to 'lay less stress on the immediate bringing about of revolution in other countries'. See his *Memoirs: 1925–1950* (Boston, Little, Brown and Company, 1967), p. 517.

7   See Henry Kissinger, *Diplomacy* (New York, Simon & Schuster, 1994), p. 333. See also Adam Ulam, *Expansion and Coexistence: Soviet Foreign Policy 1917–73* (Fort Worth, Holt, Rinehart & Winston, Inc., 1974), p. 223, and Nicholas Riasanovsky, *A History of Russia* (Oxford, Oxford University Press, 1993), p. 513.

8   See Barry Blechman, *Force Without War* (Washington DC, Brookings, 1978), and Michael Kidron and Dan Smith (*The War Atlas*, London, Pan Books, 1983).

9   For the most detailed treatment of Soviet foreign policy in the 1970s in the wider context of the Cold War, see Raymond Garthoff, *Détente and Confrontation: American-Soviet Relations from Nixon to Reagan* (Washington DC, The Brookings Institution, 1985). See also my chapter in Alva Myrdal *et al.*, *Dynamics of European Nuclear Disarmament* (Nottingham, Spokesman Books, 1981), pp. 31–56.

10   Zbigniew Brzezinski, *Between Two Ages* (New York, Viking, 1970).

11   Richard Pipes, *The Formation of the Soviet Union*, (Harvard University Press, 1996) and Orlando Figes, *A People's Tragedy: A History of the Russian Revolution* (New York, Viking, 1997).

12   N.N. Sukhanov, *Zapiski o Revolutsii*, Volumes i–vii, (Leningrad, 1925).

13   Isaac Deutscher, *Stalin*, 1949 (Penguin, Harmondsworth, 1966), pp. 232–95.

14   Moshe Lewin, *Lenin's Last Struggle* (New York, Monthly Review Press, 1978).

15   Isaac Deutscher, *Russia after Stalin*, 1953 (London, Jonathan Cape, 1969).

16   Reagan actually spoke to the British parliament in 1982 of a basic conflict between the forces and relations of production in the Soviet Union which would in time consign the Soviet system into the dustbin of history. For a guide to neo-conservative thinking on the USSR in the early 1980s see Richard Pipes, *Survival Is Not Enough: Soviet Realities and Russia's Future* (New York, Simon & Schuster, 1984).

17   See Valdimir G. Treml, 'Debate: Why Did the Soviet Economic System Collapse? Two Schools of Thought', *RFE/RE Research Report*, Volume 2, No. 23, 4 June 1993, pp. 53–5.

18   See my *The Nuclear Era: Its History; Its Implications* (Nottingham, Spokesman Books, 1982), and (ed.), *The Uncertain Course: New Weapons, Strategies, and Mindsets* (Oxford University Press, 1987).

19   On the foreign policy response to the failure of the Western-style reforms see Peter Truscott, *Russia First: Breaking with the West* (London, I.B. Tauris, 1997).

20   According to a September 1992 opinion poll, 80 per cent felt they lived better

before Gorbachev unleashed the first reforms, 67 per cent favoured (past) socialism, and 50 per cent had a positive view of Stalin (up from 29 per cent in a September 1991 poll). Moscow poll reprinted in *The Ottawa Citizen*, 26 September 1992.

21   See Peter J. Stavrakis *et al.*, *Beyond the Monolith: The Emergence of Regionalism in Post-Soviet Russia* (Baltimore, The Johns Hopkins University Press, 1997).

22   Roy Allison and Christopher Bluth (eds), *Security Dilemmas in Russia and Eurasia* (London, The Royal Institute of International Affairs, 1998), p. 1.

23   For background on Gromov, the Afghantsy and Omon networks, see Soviliforni Hypermedia on-disk release *Soviet Military Series 1. 1989–91: Transformation & Transition*, Carleton University Soviet National Security ORU, 1991.

24   For a useful look at the Russian army in the 1990s see Roy Allison, 'The Russian Armed Forces: structures, roles and policies' in Vladimir Baranovsky (ed.), *Russia and Europe: The Emerging Security Agenda* (SIPRI, Oxford University Press, 1997), pp. 165–95.

25   See Alexander A. Konovalov, 'The Changing Role of Military Factors', pp. 196–218.

26   As the most senior American historian recently pointed out about the world we now live in: 'Unbridled capitalism, with its low wages, long hours, and exploited workers, excites social resentment, revives class warfare and infuses Marxism with new life.' See Arthur Schlesinger Jr, 'Has Democracy a Future?', *Foreign Affairs*, September-November 1997.

Bibliography

Abel, L. *The Intellectual Follies*. New York: Norton, 1984.

Adams, Arthur E. 'The Hybrid Art of Sovietology.' *Survey* 50 (1964).

Adams, Arthur E., and Jan Adams. *Men Versus Systems: Agriculture in the USSR, Poland and Czechoslovakia*. New York: Free Press, 1971.

Afanas'ev, V.G. *4-ua vlast'i 4 Genseka*. Moscow: Kedr, 1994.

Agurski, M. *Ideologia Natsional-Bolshevisma*. Paris: YMCA Press, 1980.

Ali, Tariq. *Revolution from Above - Where Is the Soviet Union Going?* London: Hutchinson, 1988.

Allison, Roy, and Christopher Bluth (eds). *Security Dilemmas in Russia and Eurasia*. London: The Royal Institute of International Affairs, 1998.

Almond, Gabriel. *Political Development*. Boston: Little, Brown and Co., 1970.

Almond, Gabriel, and G. Bingham Powell, Jr. *Comparative Politics: A Developmental Approach*. Boston: Little, Brown and Co., 1966.

Amalrik, Andrei. *Will the Soviet Union Survive until 1984?* New York: Harper and Row, 1970.

Amman, R., and J. Cooper. *Industrial Innovation in the Soviet Union*. New Haven: Yale University Press, 1982.

Amman, R., and R.W. Davies. *The Technological Level of Soviet Industry*. New Haven: Yale University Press, 1977.

Andropov, Yuri Vladiminovich. 'Uchenie Karla Marksa i nekotorye voprosy sotsialisti cheskogo stroitellstva v SSSR.' *Kommunist* 3 (1983).

Apter, David E. *The Politics of Modernization*. Chicago: The University of Chicago Press, 1965.

Arendt, Hannah. *The Origins of Totalitarianism*. 5th ed. New York: Harcourt Brace, 1973.

Armstrong, John A. *The Politics of Totalitarianism*. New York: Basic Books, 1961.

—. 'Sources of Administrative Behavior: Some Soviet and Western European Comparisons.' *American Political Science Review* 59 (1965).

— (ed.). *The Soviet Union under Brezhnev and Kosygin*. New York: Van Nostrand-Reinhold Co., 1971.

—. *Ukrainian Nationalism*. New York: Columbia University Press, 1990.

Armstrong, P., A. Glynn and J. Harrison. *Capitalism since 1945*. Oxford: Blackwell, 1991.

Arnot, Bob. 'The Continuing Disintegration of the Russian Economy.' *Critique* 26 (1994).

—. *Controlling Soviet Labour*. London: Macmillan Press, 1988.

Aron, Raymond. *Dix-huit Leçons sur la société industrielle.* Paris: Gallimard, 1962.

Aslund, Anders. *Gorbachev's Struggle for Economic Reform.* London: Pinter, 1989.

—. *Post-Communist Economic Revolutions: How Big a Bang?* Washington, DC: Center for Strategic and International Studies, 1992.

—. 'Russia's Success Story.' *Foreign Affairs* 73 (1994).

Azrael, Jeremy. 'Bringing up the Soviet Man: Dilemmas and Progress.' *Problems of Communism* 17 (1968).

Bahry, Donna. *Outside Moscow: Power, Politics, and Budgetary Policy in the Soviet Republics.* New York: Columbia University Press, 1987.

Balzer, Harley D. (ed.). *Five Years That Shook the World: Gorbachev's Unfinished Revolution.* Boulder, CO: Westview Press, 1991.

Banac, Ivo (ed.). *Eastern Europe in Revolution.* Ithaca, NY: Cornell University Press, 1992.

Baranovsky, Vladimir. (ed.). *Russia and Europe: The Emerging Security Agenda.* Oxford: SIPRI, Oxford University Press, 1997.

Barghoorn, Frederick. 'Changes in Russia: The Need for Perspective.' *Problems of Communism* 15 (1966).

Barnard, F.M. *Pluralism, Socialism and Political Legitimacy.* Cambridge: Cambridge University Press, 1991.

Barringer, Felicity. 'Sovietology Loses Academic Glamour in Cold War Wake.' *New York Herald Tribune,* 1 April 1993.

Batsel, Walter. *Soviet Rule in Russia.* New York: Harvard University Press, 1929.

Bauer, Raymond A., Alex Inkeles and Clyde Kluckholm. *How the Soviet System Works: Cultural, Psychological and Social Themes.* Cambridge, MA: Harvard University Press, 1956.

Bauer, Raymond A. *The New Man in Soviet Psychology.* Cambridge, MA: Harvard University Press, 1952.

Bauman, Zygmunt. 'Social Dissent in East European Politics.' *European Journal of Sociology* 12 (1971).

—. 'Twenty Years After: The Crises of Soviet-Type Systems.' *Problems of Communism* 20 (1971).

Bell, Daniel. *The Coming of Post-Industrial Society.* New York: Basic Books, 1973.

—. *The End of Ideology: On the Exhaustion of Political Ideas in the 1950s.* New York: Glencoe Free Press, 1960.

Benedict, Ruth. *The Chrysanthemum and the Sword.* Boston: Houghton Mifflin, 1946.

Berdiaev, Nicholas. *The Origin of Russian Communism.* London: Saunders, 1937.

—. *The Russian Idea.* London: Macmillan, 1947.

Bergson, Abram. *The Economics of Soviet Planning.* New York: Columbia University Press, 1964.

Bergson, Abram, and H. Levine (eds). *The Soviet Economy: Towards the Year 2000.* London: George Allen & Unwin, 1983.

Berkowitz, Bruce D., and Jeffrey T. Richelson. 'The CIA Vindicated: The Soviet Collapse Was Predicted.' *The National Interest* 41 (1995).

Berliner, Joseph. 'The Voice of American Sovietology.' *NewsNet: The Newsletter of the AAASS* 34 (1994): 11.

Berliner, J.S. *Factory and Manager in the USSR.* Cambridge, MA: Harvard University Press, 1957.

—. *The Innovation Decision in Soviet Industry.* Cambridge, MA: MIT Press, 1976.

Bettelheim, Charles. *The Transition to a Socialist Economy*. Hassocks: Harvester Press, 1975.

Bialer, Seweryn, and Michael Mandelbaum (eds). *Gorbachev's Russia and American Foreign Policy*. Boulder, CO: Westview Press, 1988.

Bialer, Seweryn (ed.). *Politics, Society and Nationality inside Gorbachev's Russia*. Boulder, CO: Westview Press, 1989.

—. *Stalin's Successors*. London: Cambridge University Press, 1980.

—. *The Soviet Paradox*. New York: Knopf, 1986.

—. *The Soviet Union in Transition*. Boulder, CO: Westview Press, 1987.

Birman, Igor. *Secret Incomes of the Soviet State Budget*. Boston: Kluwer, 1981.

Black, Cyril (ed.). *Aspects of Social Changes since 1861*. Cambridge, MA: Harvard University Press, 1960.

Blechman, Barry. *Force Without War*. Washington, DC: The Brookings Institution, 1978.

Bloomfield, Jon. *The Soviet Revolution: Perestroika and the Remaking of Socialism*. London: Lawrence and Wishart, 1989.

Boeva, Irina, and Viacheslav Shironin. *Russians Between State and Market: The Generations Compared*. Glasgow: Centre for the Study of Public Policy, University of Strathclyde, 1992.

Bornstein, M. *Comparative Economic Systems: Models and Cases*. Homewood, IL: R.D. Irwin Inc., 1974.

Bornstein, M., and Daniel R. Fusfeld. *The Soviet Economy: A Book of Readings*. Homewood, IL: R.D. Irwin, 1962.

Brady, Henry E., Sidney Verba and Kay Lehman Schozman. 'Beyond SES: A Resource Model of Political Participation.' *American Political Science Review* 89 (1995).

Breslauer, George. 'In Defense of Sovietology.' *Post-Soviet Affairs* 8 (1992).

—. *Five Images of the Soviet Future*. Berkeley: University of California Press, 1978.

—. *Khrushchev and Brezhnev as Leaders*. London: Allen & Unwin, 1982.

—. 'Reflections on the Anniversary of the August 1991 Coup.' *Soviet Economy* 8 (1992).

Brown, Archie (ed.). *Political Culture and Communist Studies*. Basingstoke: Macmillan, 1984.

—. *Soviet Politics and Political Science*. London: Macmillan, 1974.

Brown, Archie, and J. Gray (eds). *Political Culture and Political Change in Communist States*. London: Macmillan, 1977.

Brym, Robert. 'Anti-Semitism in Moscow: A Re-examination.' *Slavic Review* 53 (1994).

Brzezinski, Zbigniew. *Between Two Ages*. New York: Viking, 1970.

—. (ed.). *Dilemmas of Change in Soviet Politics*. New York: Columbia University Press, 1969.

—. *The Grand Failure: The Birth and Death of Communism in the Twentieth Century*. New York: Collier, 1990.

—. *Ideology and Power in Soviet Politics*. New York: Praeger, 1962.

—. *The Permanent Purge*. Cambridge, MA: Harvard University Press, 1956.

—. 'Reflections on the Soviet System.' *Problems of Communism* 17 (1968).

—. 'The Soviet Political System: Transformation of Degeneration?' *Problems of Communism* 15 (1966).

Brzezinski, Zbigniew, and Samuel P. Huntington. *Political Power: USA/USSR*. New York: Viking Press, 1965.

Buck, T. *Comparative Industrial Systems*. London: Macmillan, 1982.

Bunce, Valerie. *Do New Leaders Make a Difference?* Princeton: Princeton University Press, 1981.

—. 'Eastern Europe: Is the Party Over?' *Political Science & Politics* (1989).

Burks, R.V. 'The Arcane Art of Kremlinology: Faults in the Stars, Faults in Ourselves.' *Encounter* (1983).

—. 'The Coming Crisis in Eastern Europe.' *East European Quarterly* 18 (1984).

Burlatskii, Fedor. 'Politika i nauka.' *Pravda*, 10 January 1965.

Burnham, James. *The Managerial Revolution*. Harmondsworth: Penguin, 1962.

Bush, Keith (ed.). *From the Command Economy to the Market*. Aldershot: Dartmouth, 1991.

Byrnes, Robert F. (ed.). *After Brezhnev*. New York: Pinter, 1983.

Campbell, M. *Capitalism in the UK*. London: Croom Helm, 1981.

Carlo, Antonio. 'The Crisis of Bureaucratic Collectivism.' *Telos* 43 (1980).

—. 'The Socio-economic Nature of the USSR.' *Telos* 21 (1974).

Carnovale, Marco, and William C. Potter (eds). *Continuity and Change in Soviet–East European Relations*. Boulder, CO: Westview, 1989.

Carrol, Malcolm. *Soviet Communism and Western Opinion 1919–1921*. Chapel Hill: The University of North Carolina Press, 1965.

Casals, Felipe Garcia. *The Syncretic Society*. Armonk, NY: M.E. Sharpe, 1980.

Cerny, Philip G. 'Foreign Policy Leadership and National Integration.' *British Journal of International Studies* 5 (1979).

Chamberlin, William. *The Russian Enigma*. New York: Scribner's, 1943.

—. *Soviet Russia: A Living Record and a History*. Boston: Little, Brown and Co., 1930.

Chapman, B. and A.M. Potter (eds). *W. J. M. M. Political Questions: Essays in Honour of W.J.M. Mackenzie*. Manchester: Manchester University Press, 1975.

Churchward, L.G. *The Soviet Intelligentsia: An Essay on the Social Structure and Roles of Soviet Intellectuals During the 1960s*. London: Routledge & Kegan Paul, 1973.

Clague, C., and G. Rausser (eds). *The Emergence of Market Economies in Eastern Europe*. Oxford: Blackwell, 1992.

Clarke, Michael (ed.). *Corruption*. London: Pinter, 1983.

Clarke, R. 'Accidents in Russia: The Cost to Workers and the Environment.' *KAS-KOR* Moscow: Summer 1994.

Clemens, Walter, C. *The USSR and Global Interdependence*. Washington, DC: American Enterprise Institute Press, 1978.

Cliff, Tony. *Russia: A Marxist Analysis*. London: Pluto Press, 1974.

Cocks, Paul *et al.* (eds). *The Dynamics of Soviet Politics*. Cambridge: Harvard University Press, 1976.

Cohen, Stephen. 'American Policy and Russia's Future.' *The Nation*, 12 April 1993.

—. 'America's Failed Crusade in Russia.' *The Nation*, 28 February 1994.

—. *Bukharin and the Bolshevik Revolution: A Political Biography*. New York: Knopf, 1973.

—. 'Clinton's Yeltsin and Yeltsin's Russia.' *The Nation*, 10 October 1994.

—. 'The Election's Missing Issue.' *The Nation*, 22 November 1992.

—. (ed.). *The Soviet Union since Stalin*. Bloomington: Indiana University Press, 1980.

—. *Rethinking the Soviet Experience*. New York: Oxford University Press, 1985.

—. 'Transition or Tragedy?' *The Nation*, 30 December 1996.

Colton, Timothy J. *The Dilemma of Reform in the Soviet Union*. New York: Council on Foreign Affairs, 1987.

Conquest, Robert. 'After Khrushchev: A Conservative Restoration.' *Problems of Communism* (1963).

—. 'Immobilism and Decay.' *Problems of Communism* 15 (1966).

—. (ed.). *The Last Empire*. Palo Alto: Hoover Institution Press, 1986.

—. *Power and Policy in the USSR: The Struggle for Stalin's Succession, 1945–1960*. New York: Harper & Row, 1967.

—. 'Red and Go.' *Times Literary Supplement,* July 1993.

—. *Russia after Khrushchev*. New York: Prager, 1965.

Cook, Linda J. *The Soviet Social Contract and Why it Failed*. Cambridge, MA: Harvard University Press, 1993.

Cornell, Richard (ed.). *The Soviet Political System: A Book of Readings*. Englewood Cliffs, NJ: Prentice Hall Inc., 1970.

Coser, Lewis S. (ed.). *Political Sociology*. New York: Harper & Row, 1966.

Counts, George S. *The Challenge of Soviet Education*. New York: McGraw-Hill, 1957.

Cox, Michael. 'The Cold War and Stalinism in the Age of Capitalist Decline.' *Critique* 17 (1986).

—. 'The End of the USSR and the Collapse of Soviet Studies.' *Coexistence* 31 (1994).

—. 'The Necessary Partnership? The Clinton Presidency and Post-Soviet Russia.' *International Affairs* 70 (1994).

—. 'The Politics of the Dissenting Intellectual.' *Critique* 5 (1975).

Crankshaw, Edward. *Russia and the Russians*. New York: Viking, 1948.

Crick, Bernard. *Basic Forms of Government: A Sketch and a Model*. London: Macmillan, 1973.

Crummey, Robert (ed.). *Reform in Russia and the USSR*. Urbana: University of Illinois Press, 1989.

Curtis, John Shelton. *The Russian Church and the Soviet State*. Boston: Little, Brown and Co., 1953.

Dahl, Robert. 'A Critique of the Ruling Elite Model.' *American Political Science Review* 52 (1958).

—. *Polyarchy: Participation and Opposition*. New Haven: Yale University Press, 1971.

Dallago, B., H. Brezinski and W. Andreff (eds). *Convergence and System Change*. Aldershot: Dartmouth, 1992.

Dallin, Alexander. 'Biases and Blunders in American Studies on the USSR.' *Slavic Review* 32 (1973).

—. 'Causes of Collapse of the USSR.' *Post-Soviet Affairs* 8 (1992).

—. 'Osteuropaforschung in den Vereinigten Staaten.' *Osteuropa* 32 (1982).

—. *The Soviet System from Crisis to Collapse*. Boulder, CO: Westview Press, 1995.

Dallin, Alexander, and Gail W. Lapidus (eds). *The Soviet System in Crisis*. Boulder, CO: Westview, 1991.

Dallin, David. *The Real Soviet Russia*. New Haven: Yale University Press, 1944.

Daniels, Robert. 'The Bolshevik Gamble.' *Russian Review* 26 (1967).

—. *Il procietto Gorbaciov*. Rome: Rinascita, 1987.

—. *Is Russia Reformable? Change and Resistance from Stalin to Gorbachev*. Boulder, CO: Westview Press, 1988.

—. 'Moscow's Rubber Marx.' *New Leader* 28 December 1987.

—. 'The Riddle of Russian Reform.' *Dissent* Autumn 1993.

—. *Russia: The Roots of Confrontation*. Cambridge, MA: Harvard University Press, 1985.

—. 'Russian Political Culture and the Post-Revolutionary Impasse.' *Russian Review* 46 (1987).

—. (ed.). *Soviet Communism: From Reform to Collapse.* Lexington, MA: D.C. Heath, 1995.

—. 'The State of the Field and Its Future.' *Newsnet: The Newsletter of the AAASS* (1995).

—. 'The State and Revolution: A Case Study in the Genesis and Transformation of Communist Ideology.' *American Slavic and East European Review* 12 (1953).

Davies, Joseph E. *Mission to Moscow.* Sydney and London: Angus and Robertson, 1942.

D'Encausse, Helene Carrere. *Confused Power.* New York: Harper and Row, 1982.

—. *Decline of an Empire: The Soviet Socialist Republics in Revolt.* New York: Newsweek Books, 1979.

Deutscher, Isaac. *Russia after Stalin.* London: Jonathan Cape, 1969.

—. *Russia, What Next?* London: Hamilton, 1953.

—. *Stalin: A Political Biography.* New York: Oxford University Press, 1949.

—. *The Unfinished Revolution: Russia 1917-1967.* New York: Oxford University Press, 1967.

Devlin, Judith. 'The Rise of New Russian Nationalism, 1989-90.' *Irish Slavonic Studies* 18 (1997).

Di Leo, Rita. *L'economia sovietica tra crisi e riforme (1965-1982).* Naples: Liguori, 1983.

Di Palma, Giuseppe. 'Legitimation from the Top to Civil Society: Politico-Cultural Change in Eastern Europe.' *World Politics* 44 (1991).

Djilas, Milovan. *The New Class.* London: Unwin Books, 1966.

Dobb, Maurice. *Soviet Economic Development Since 1917.* London: Routledge and Kegan Paul, 1948.

—. *Soviet Russia and the World.* London: Sidgwick and Jackson, 1932.

Dobrokhotov, L. N. *et al. Krasnoe ili beloe? Drama avgusta-91.* Moscow: Terra, 1992.

Drachkovich, M. *The Appeals and Paradoxes of Contemporary Communism.* New York: Praeger, 1966.

Draper, Theodore. 'Is the CIA Necessary?' *New York Review of Books* 14 August 1997.

Drewnowski, Jan (ed.). *Crisis in the East European Economies.* London: Croom Helm, 1982.

Dunham, Vera. *In Stalin's Time: Middle Class Values in Soviet Fiction.* Cambridge: Cambridge University Press, 1976.

Duranty, Walter. *I Write as I Please.* New York: Simon and Schuster, 1935.

—. *USSR: The Story of Soviet Russia.* Philadelphia & New York: J.B. Lippincott, 1944.

Eckstein, Harry, and David E. Apter. *Comparative Politics: A Reader.* New York: The Free Press, 1963.

Elliot, J. *Comparative Economic Systems.* Belmont, CA: Wadsworth, 1985.

Ellman, Michael. *Collectivisation, Convergence and Capitalism.* London: Academic Press, 1984.

Ellman, Michael, and Vladimir Kontorovich (eds). *The Disintegration of the Soviet Economic System.* London: Routledge, 1992.

Ellman, Michael. 'The Many Causes of the Collapse.' *RFE/RL Research Report* 2 (1993).

Enteen, George, Lewis H. Siegelbaum and Robert V. Daniels. 'The Dynamics of Revolution in Soviet History: A Discussion.' *Russian Review* 54 (1995).

Etzioni, A. *Social Change: Sources, Patterns and Consequences.* New York: Basic Books, 1964.

Fainsod, Merle. *How Russia Is Ruled.* 2nd ed. Cambridge, MA: Harvard University Press, 1963.

—. 'Whither Russia? Roads to the Future.' *Problems of Communism* 16 (1967).

—. *Smolensk under Soviet Rule.* Cambridge, MA: Harvard University Press, 1958.

Fairbanks Jr., Charles H. 'The Suicide of Soviet Communism.' *Journal of Democracy* Spring 1990.

Feher, Ferenc, and Andrew Arato (eds). *Gorbachev: The Debate.* Atlantic Highlands, NJ: Humanities Press, 1989.

Feher, Ferenc, Agnes Heller and Gyorgy Markus. *Dictatorship over Needs.* London: Basil Blackwell, 1983.

Ferguson, Niall (ed.). *Virtual History: Alternatives and Counterfactuals.* London: Papermac, 1997.

Field, Mark G. *Doctor and Patient in Soviet Russia.* Cambridge, MA: Harvard University Press, 1957.

Figes, Orlando. *A People's Tragedy: A History of the Russian Revolution.* New York: Viking, 1997.

Finer, S.E. *Comparative Government.* London: Allen Lane, 1970.

Fisher, Louis. *Men and Politics.* New York: Duell, Sloan and Pearce, 1941.

Fisher, Ralph T. *Pattern for Soviet Youth.* New York: Columbia University Press, 1959.

Fitzpatrick, Sheila. *Education and Social Mobility in the Soviet Union, 1921–34.* Cambridge: Cambridge University Press, 1979.

Fleron, Frederic (ed.). *Communist Studies and the Social Sciences: Essays on Methodology and Empirical Theory.* Chicago: Rand McNally, 1969.

—. 'Soviet Area Studies and the Social Sciences: Some Methodological Problems in Communist Studies.' *Soviet Studies* 19 (1968).

—. 'Sovietology and Perestroika: Methodology and Lessons from the Past.' Paper given at Harriman Institute Forum. September 1991.

Fleron, Frederic, and Erik P. Hoffman (eds). *Post-Communist Studies and Political Science: Methodology and Empirical Theory in Sovietology.* Boulder, CO: Westview, 1993.

Foucault, Michel. *Discipline and Punish.* New York: Pantheon, 1977.

Freund, H.A. *Russia from A to Z.* Sydney: Angus and Robertson, 1945.

Friedgut, Theodore H. *Political Participation in the USSR.* Princeton: Princeton University Press, 1979.

Friedgut, Theodore H., and Jeffrey W. Hahn (eds). *Local Power and Post-Soviet Politics.* Armonk, NJ: M.E. Sharpe, 1994.

Friedrich, Carl J., and Zbigniew K. Brzezinski. *Totalitarian Dictatorship and Autocracy.* 2nd ed. Cambridge, MA: Harvard University Press, 1965.

Friedrich, Carl J., Michael Curtis and Benjamin R. Barber (eds). *Totalitarianism in Perspective: Three Views.* New York: Praeger Publishers, 1969.

Friedrich, Carl J. 'Whither Russia? Totalitarianism: Recent Trends.' *Problems of Communism* 17 (1968).

Fukuyama, Francis. *The End of History and the Last Man.* New York: Free Press, 1992.

—. 'The End of History.' *The National Interest,* Summer 1989.

Gaddis, John Lewis. 'International Relations Theory and the End of the Cold War.' *International Security* 17 (1992/93).

—. *The United States and the End of the Cold War.* New York: Oxford University Press, 1992.

Galbraith, J.K. BBC Reith Lectures, *The Listener*, 15 December 1966.

—. *The New Industrial State*. Boston: Houghton Mifflin, 1967.

Garthoff, Raymond. *Detente and Confrontation: American-Soviet Relations from Nixon to Reagan*. Washington, DC: The Brookings Institution, 1985.

—. *Soviet Military Policy: A Historical Analysis*. London: Faber, 1966.

Gates, Robert M. *From the Shadows: The Ultimate Insider's Story of Five Presidents and How They Won the Cold War*. New York: Touchstone, 1996.

Gati, Charles. 'Gorbachev and Eastern Europe.' *Foreign Affairs* 67 (1987).

Gehlen, Michael P. *The Communist Party of the Soviet Union*. Bloomington: Indiana University Press, 1969.

Gellner, Ernest. *The Conditions of Liberty: Civil Society and Its Rivals*. London: Hamish Hamilton, 1994.

Gerschenkron, Alexander. 'The Study of the Soviet Economy in the USA.' *Survey* 50 (1964).

Getty, J.A. *Origins of the Great Purges: The Soviet Communist Party Reconsidered: 1933–1938*. New York: Cambridge University Press, 1985.

Getty, J.A., and Roberta T. Manning (eds). *Stalinist Terror: New Perspectives*. Cambridge: Cambridge University Press, 1993.

Gibson, James L. 'Perceived Political Freedom in the Soviet Union.' *Journal of Politics* 55 (1993).

Giddens, A. *The Class Structure of the Advanced Societies*. London: Hutchinson University Library, 1973.

Gilison, J. 'Misunderstandings of Anti-Semitism in Russia: An Analysis of the Politics of Anti-Jewish Attitudes.' *Slavic Review* 53 (1994).

—. 'Understanding Anti-Semitism in Russia: An Analysis of the Politics of Anti-Jewish Attitudes.' *Slavic Review* 53 (1994).

Gilison, Jerome M. 'Soviet Elections as a Measure of Dissent: The Missing One Percent.' *American Political Science Review* 62 (1968).

Gill, Graeme. *The Collapse of a Single Party System: The Disintegration of the Communist Party of the Soviet Union*. Cambridge: Cambridge University Press, 1994.

Gills, Barry, Joel Rocamora and Richard Wilson (eds). *Low Intensity Democracy: Political Power in the New World Order*. London: Pluto Press, 1993.

Glazer, Nathan. 'New York Intellectuals: Up from Revolution.' *New York Times Review of Books*, 26 February 1984.

Gleason, Abbott. *Totalitarianism: The Inner History of the Cold War*. New York: Oxford University Press, 1995.

Godet, Martine (ed.). *De Russie et d'ailleurs: feux croises sur l'histoire, pour Marc Ferro*. Paris: Insitut d'Etudes Slaves, 1995.

Goldman, Marshall I. *Gorbachev's Challenge: Economic Reform in the Age of High Technology*. New York: W.W. Norton, 1987.

—. *The USSR in Crisis: The Failure of an Economic System*. New York: Norton, 1983.

Goodman, Melvin. 'Ending the CIA's Cold War Legacy.' *Foreign Policy* 106 (1997).

Grachev, Andrei. *Dallshe bez menya . . . Ukhod Prezidenta*. Moscow: Progress-Kultora, 1994.

Graham, Stephen. *The Dividing Line of Europe*. New York: Appleton, 1925.

Granick, David. *Management of the Industrial Firm in the USSR*. New York: Columbia University Press, 1954.

—. *The Red Executive*. London: Macmillan, 1960.

Gray, John. *Post-Communist Societies in Transition: A Social Market Perspective.* London: The Social Market Foundation, 1994.

–. *Post-Liberalism: Studies in Political Thought.* London: Routledge, 1993.

Gregory, Paul, and Robert Stuart. *Comparative Economic Systems.* 4th ed. Boston: Houghton Mifflin, 1992.

–. *Soviet Economic Structure and Performance.* New York: Harper, 1974.

Greider, William. *One World, Ready or Not: The Manic Logic of One World Capitalism.* Harmondsworth: Penguin Books, 1997.

Griffiths, F. 'Images, Politics and Learning in Soviet Behavior Toward the United States.' PhD dissertation. New York: Columbia University, 1972.

Gustafson, Thane. *Reform in Soviet Politics.* Cambridge: Cambridge University Press, 1981.

Hahn, Jeffrey W. 'Continuity and Change in Russian Political Culture.' *British Journal of Political Science* 21 (1991).

–. *Soviet Grassroots: Citizen Participation in Local Soviet Government.* Princeton: Princeton University Press, 1988.

Hajda, Lubomyr, and Mark Beissinger (eds). *The Nationalities Factor in Soviet Politics and Society.* Boulder, CO: Westview Press, 1990.

–. *Nationalities and Reform in Soviet Politics.* Boulder, CO: Westview Press, 1990.

Hankiss, Elemer. *East European Alternatives.* Oxford: Clarendon Press, 1990.

Hanson, Phillip. *The Consumer Sector in the Soviet Economy.* Evanston, IL: Northwestern University Press, 1969.

The Soviet Economy: A New Course? Brussels: NATO, 1-3 April 1987.

Harding, Neil (ed.). *The State in Socialist Society.* New York: Macmillan, 1984.

Harper, Samuel. *Civic Training in Soviet Russia.* Chicago: The University of Chicago Press, 1929.

–. *The Government of the Soviet Union.* New York: Nostrand, 1938.

–. *Making Bolsheviks.* Chicago: The University of Chicago Press, 1931.

Haynes, Mike. 'Understanding the Soviet Crisis.' *International Socialism* 34 (1987).

Hedlund, Stefan. *Crisis in Soviet Agriculture.* New York: St. Martin's Press, 1990.

Hegenbotham, Stanely J. 'Rethinking International Scholarship: The Challenge of Transition from the Cold War Era.' *Items* June/September 1994.

Hernandez-Cata, Ernesto. *Russia and the IMF: The Political Economy of Macro-Stabilisation.* IMF Paper on Policy Analysis and Assessment, September 1994.

Hesli, Vicki, Arthur Miller and William Reisinger. 'Comment on Brym and Degtyarev's Discussion of Anti-Semitism in Moscow.' *Slavic Review* 53 (1994).

Hesli, Vicki, Arthur Miller, William Reisinger and Kevin Morgan. 'Social Distance from Jews in Russia and Ukraine.' *Slavic Review* 53 (1994).

Hewett, Ed. A. 'An Idle US Debate about Gorbachev.' *New York Times* 30 March 1989.

–. *Reforming the Soviet Economy: Equality vs Efficiency.* Washington, DC: The Brookings Institution, 1988.

Hazard, John N. *The Soviet System of Government.* Chicago: University of Chicago Press, 1961.

Hilferding, Rudolf. 'A 1940 Social Democratic View of Stalin's Russia.' *Modern Review* (1947).

Hill, Ronald J. *Soviet Political Elites: The Case of Tiraspol.* London: Martin Robertson, 1977.

Hindus, Maurice. *The Great Offensive.* London: H. Smith and R. Haas, 1933.

—. *Humanity Uprooted.* New York: J. Cape and H. Smith, 1929.

—. *Red Bread.* New York: J. Cape and H. Smith, 1931.

Hoffmann, Erik P., and Robbin F. Laird (eds). *The Soviet Polity in the Modern Era.* New York: Aldine Publishing, 1984.

Holmes, Leslie. *Politics in the Communist World.* Oxford: Clarendon Press, 1986.

Hook, Sidney. 'Whither Russia? Fifty Years After.' *Problems of Communism* 16 (1967).

Hoover, J. Edgar. *Masters of Deceit.* New York: Holt, 1958.

Horkheimer, Max. *Eclipse of Reason.* New York: Oxford University Press, 1947.

Horsley, W., and R. Buckley. *Nippon-New Superpower: Japan Since 1945.* London: BBC Books, 1990.

Hough, Jerry. *How the Soviet Union Is Governed.* Cambridge, MA: Harvard University Press, 1979.

—. 'The Man and the System.' *Problems of Communism* 25 (1976).

—. *Russia and the West.* New York: Simon and Schuster, 1988.

—. *Soviet Leadership in Transition.* Washington, DC: The Brookings Institution, 1980.

—. *The Soviet Prefects.* Cambridge, MA: Harvard University Press, 1969.

—. 'The Soviet System: Petrification or Pluralism?' *Problems of Communism* 21 (1972).

—. *The Soviet Union and Social Science Theory.* Cambridge, MA: Harvard University Press, 1977.

Howe, I. *A Margin of Hope: An Intellectual Biography.* San Diego, CA: Harcourt, 1982.

Hubbard, Leonard. *Soviet Trade and Distribution.* London: Macmillan, 1938.

Huber, Robert T., and Susan Bronson. 'The August Revolution and Soviet Studies.' *Items* 45 (1991).

Huber, Robert T., Blair A. Ruble and Peter J. Stavrakis. 'Post-Cold War "International" Scholarship: A Brave New World or the Triumph of Form over Substance.' *Items* March 1995.

Hudelson, Johann. *The Future That Failed: Origins and Destinies of the Soviet Model.* London: Routledge, 1993.

Hughes, Colin. 'CIA Is Accused of Crying Wolf on Soviet Economy.' *Independent,* 25 July 1990.

Hunt, R.N. Carew. *The Theory and Practice of Communism.* New York: Macmillan, 1951.

Huntington, Samuel P. *Order in Changing Societies.* New Haven: Yale University Press, 1968.

—. 'The Clash of Civilizations?' *Foreign Affairs* 72 (1993).

—. *The Third Wave: Democratization in the Late Twentieth Century.* Norman: University of Oklahoma Press, 1991.

—. 'Will More Countries Be Democratic?' *Political Science Quarterly* 99 (1984).

Humphrey, Caroline. *Karl Marx Collective: Economy, Society and Religion in a Siberian Collective Farm.* Cambridge: Cambridge University Press, 1933.

Inkeles, Alex. *Public Opinion in Soviet Russia: A Study in Mass Persuasion.* Cambridge, MA: Harvard University Press, 1950.

—. (ed.). *Social Changes in Soviet Russia.* Cambridge, MA: Harvard University Press, 1968.

Inkeles, Alex, and R.A. Bauer. *The Soviet Citizen.* Cambridge, MA: Harvard University Press, 1959.

Inkeles, Alex, and Kent Geiger (eds). *Soviet Society: A Book of Readings.* London: Constable and Company Ltd, 1961.

International Encyclopedia of the Social Sciences, vol. 16. London: Macmillan, 1968.

Jacobson, Carl G. *The Nuclear Era: Its History; Its Implications*. Nottingham: Spokesman Books, 1982.

—. (ed.). *Strategic Power: USA/USSR*. New York: St. Martin's Press, 1990.

—. (ed.). *The Uncertain Course: New Weapons, Strategies, and Mindsets*. Oxford: Oxford University Press, 1987.

Jervis, Robert. 'The Future of World Politics: Will It Resemble the Past?' *International Security* 16 (1991/92).

Johnson, Chalmers A. (ed.). *Change in Communist Systems*. Stanford: Stanford University Press, 1970.

Joravsky, David. 'Communism in Historical Perspective.' *American Historical Review* 99 (1994).

Jowitt, Ken. *New World Disorder: The Leninist Extinction*. Berkeley: University of California Press, 1968.

—. 'Weber, Trotsky, and Holmes on the Study of Leninist Regimes.' *Journal of International Affairs* 45 (1991).

Kagarlitsky, Boris. 'The Importance of Being Marxist.' *New Left Review* 178 (1989).

Kanet, Roger. *The Behavioral Revolution and Communist Studies*. New York: Free Press, 1971.

Kassof, Alan. 'The Administered Society: Totalitarianism Without Terror.' *World Politics* 16 (1964).

Katouzian, Homa. *Ideology and Method in Economics*. London: Macmillan, 1980.

Katsenelinboigen, Aron. *The Soviet Union: Empire, Nation and System*. New Brunswick, NJ: Transaction, 1990.

Kautsky, John. *Communism and the Politics of Development*. New York: John Wiley and Sons, 1968.

Keenan, Edward. 'What Have We Learned?' *NewsNet: The Newsletter of the AAASS* 35 (1995).

Kelley, Donald R. *The Politics of Developed Socialism*. Westport, CT: Greenwood Press, 1986.

Kelson, Hans. *The Political Theory of Bolshevism: A Critical Analysis*. Berkeley: University of California Press, 1948.

Kennan, George. *Memoirs: 1925-1950*. Boston: Little, Brown and Co., 1967.

—. *Russia and the West under Lenin and Stalin*. Boston: Little, Brown and co., 1961.

—. 'The Sources of Soviet Conduct.' *Foreign Affairs* July (1947).

Kennedy, Paul. *The Rise and Fall of the Great Powers: Economic Change and Military Conflict from 1500 to 2000*. London: Fontana Press, 1989.

Keren, M., and G. Ofer (eds). *Trials of Transition*. Boulder, CO: Westview Press, 1992.

Kerr, C. *et al*. *Industrialism and Industrial Man: The Problem of Labour and Management in Economic Growth*. London: Heinemann, 1962.

Kerr, Richard J. Letter. 'C.I.A.'s Track Record Stands up to Scrutiny.' *New York Times*, 24 October 1991.

Kidron, Michael, and Dan Smith. *The War Atlas*. London: Pan Books, 1983.

Kirkpatrick, Jeane J. *The Withering Away of the Soviet State*. Washington, DC: American Enterprise Institute Press, 1990.

Kissinger, Henry. *Diplomacy*. New York: Simon & Schuster, 1994.

Koenker, Diane. *Moscow Workers and the 1917 Revolution*. Princeton: Princeton University Press, 1981.

Kohler, Phyllis (ed.). *Journey for Our Time: The Journals of Marquis de Custine.* New York: Pellegrini and Cudahy, 1951.

Kolakowski, Leszek. *Main Currents of Marxism: Its Rise, Growth and Dissolution.* Oxford: Clarendon Press, 1978.

Komarov, Boris. *The Destruction of Nature in the Soviet Union.* London: Pluto, 1980.

Koves, A. *Central and East European Economies in Transition.* Boulder, CO: Westview Press, 1992.

Krause, Michael, and Ronald Liebowitz (eds). *Russia and East Europe after Communism.* Boulder, CO: Westview Press, 1995.

Kryshtanovskaya, Olga. 'Transformatsiya staroi nomenklatury v novuyu rossiiskuya elitu.' *Obshchestvennye nauki i sovremennost* 1 (1995).

Kukathas, C., D.W. Lovell and W. Malley (eds). *The Transition from Socialism.* Melbourne: Longman Cheshire, 1991.

Kusin, Vladimir. 'Gorbachev and Eastern Europe.' *Problems of Communism* 35 (1986).

Labedz, Leopold. 'False Dilemmas, Real Alternatives.' *Encounter* LV (1980).

Laird, Robin A. *The Soviet Paradigm: An Experiment in Creating a Monohierarchical Polity.* New York: The Free Press, 1970.

Lambert, Richard D. *et al. Beyond Growth: The Next Stage in Language Area Studies.* Washington, DC: Association of American Universities, 1984.

Lane, David. *The End of Inequality? Stratification under State Socialism.* Harmondsworth: Penguin Books, 1971.

—. *Leninism: A Sociological Interpretation.* Cambridge: Cambridge University Press, 1981.

—. *Politics and Society in the USSR.* London: Weidenfeld and Nicholson, 1970.

—. *Politics and Society in the USSR,* 2nd ed. Oxford: Martin Robertson & Co. Ltd, 1978.

—. (ed.). *Russia in Transition.* London: Longman, 1995.

—. *The Socialist Industrial State: Towards a Political Sociology of State Socialism.* London: George Allen & Unwin, 1976.

—. *Society under Perestroika.* London: Routledge, 1992.

Lange, Oskar. *On the Economic Theory of Socialism.* Minneapolis: University of Minnesota Press, 1938.

Lapidus, Gail. 'Ethnonationalism and Political Stability: The Soviet Case.' *World Politics* 36 (1984).

—. 'Political Mobilization, Participation, and Leadership.' *Comparative Politics* 8 (1975).

—. 'USSR Women at Work: Changing Patterns.' *Industrial Relations* 14 (1975).

—. *Women in Soviet Society.* Berkeley: University of California Press, 1978.

Laqueur, Walter. *The Dream That Failed: Reflections on the Soviet Union.* Oxford: Oxford University Press, 1995.

—. *The Long Road to Freedom: Russia and Glasnost.* London: Unwin Hyman, 1989.

Lash, Christopher. *American Liberals and the Russian Revolution.* New York: Columbia University Press, 1962.

Leites, Nathan. *The Operational Code of the Politburo.* New York: McGraw-Hill, 1951.

Lepeshkin, A.I. 'Nazrevshie voprosy razvitiya nauki Sovetskogo gosudarstvennogo prava.' *Sovetskoe gosudantvo ipravo* 2 (1965).

Lerner, Lawrence W., and Donald Treadgold (eds). *Gorbachev and the Soviet Future.* Boulder, CO: Westview Press, 1988.

Levada, Yuri. ' "Chelo'vek sovetskii" pyat" let spustya.' *Ekonomicheskie i sotsial'nye peremeny: monitoring obshchestvennogo mneniya* 1 (1995).

Levesque, Jaques. *The Enigma of 1989: The USSR and the Liberation of Eastern Europe.* Berkeley: University of California Press, 1997.

Levi, Arrigo. 'The Evolution of the Soviet System.' *Problems of Communism* 16 (1967).

Levine, Herbert. 'An American View of Economic Relations with the USSR.' *Annals of the American Academy* 414 (1974).

Lewin, Moshe. *The Drive and the Drift of a Superstate: Russia, USSR, Russia.* New York: The Free Press, 1995.

—. *The Gorbachev Phenomenon: A Historical Interpretation.* Berkeley: University of California Press, 1988.

—. *Lenin's Last Struggle.* New York: Monthly Review Press, 1978.

—. *Russian Peasants and Soviet Power: A Study of Collectivization.* New York: Norton, 1975.

Lichtheim, George. *Marxism: An Historical and Critical Study.* New York: Praeger, 1961.

Linden, Carl A. *Khrushchev and the Soviet Leadership, 1957–1964.* Baltimore: Johns Hopkins University Press, 1966.

—. *The Soviet Party-State: The Politics of Ideocratic Despotism.* New York: Praeger Publishers, 1983.

Lipset, Seymour Martin. *Class Status and Power.* London: Routledge, 1966.

—. 'Social Stratification and Sociology in the Soviet Union.' *Survey* 19 (1973).

Lipset, Seymour Martin, and Richard B. Dobson. 'The Intellectuals as Critics and Rebels: With Special Reference to the United States and the Soviet Union.' *Daedalus* 101 (1973).

Lipset, Seymour Martin, and Everett Ladd. 'The Politics of American Sociologists.' *American Review of Sociology* (1972).

Lowenthal, Richard. 'The Permanent Revolution Is on Again.' *Commentary* 24 (1957).

Lubrano, Linda, and Susan Solomon (eds). *The Social Context of Soviet Sciences.* Boulder, CO: Westview Press, 1980.

Lyons, Eugene. 'The Realities of a Vision.' *Problems of Communism* 15 (1966).

—. 'Russia Postpones Utopia.' *Scribner's Magazine* 98 (1935).

—. *Stalin: Czar of All the Russias.* New York: J.B. Lippincott, 1940.

Mainwaring, Scott, Guillermo O'Donnell and J. Samuel Valenzula (eds). *Issues in Democratic Consolidation: The New South American Democracies in Comparative Perspective.* Notre Dame, IN: University of Notre Dame Press, 1992.

Malia, Martin. 'A Fatal Logic.' *National Interest* 31 (1993).

—. 'The Hunt for the True October.' *Commentary* 92 (1991).

—. 'The Nomenclature Capitalists.' *New Republic,* 22 May 1995.

—. *The Soviet Tragedy: A History of Socialism in Russia, 1917–1991.* New York: Free Press, 1994.

—. 'To the Stalin Mausoleum.' *Daedalus* 119 (1990).

Mandel, David. *Perestroika and the Soviet People.* Montreal: Black Rose Books, 1991.

Mandel, Ernest. *Beyond Perestroika: The Future of Gorbachev's USSR.* London: Verso, 1989.

—. 'Ten Theses on the Social and Economic Laws Governing the Society Transitional Between Capitalism.' *Critique* 3 (1974).

Mannheim, Karl. *Ideology and Utopia.* New York: Harcourt Brace & World, 1965.

Manson, P. 'The Owl of Minerva and the Fall of the USSR.' *Sociologisk Forskning* 31 (1994).

Marcuse, Herbert. *One-Dimensional Man, The Ideology of Industrial Society.* London: Routledge & Kegan Paul, 1964.

Mason, David S. 'Glasnost, Perestroika and Eastern Europe.' *International Affairs* 64 (1988).

Mastny, Vojtech. *The Cold War and Soviet Insecurity: The Stalin Year.* New York: Oxford University Press, 1996.

Matthews, Mervyn. *Poverty in the Soviet Union.* Cambridge: Cambridge University Press, 1986.

—. *Privilege in the Soviet Union.* London: Allen and Unwin, 1978.

—. 'Top Incomes in the USSR: Towards a Definition of the Soviet Elite.' *Survey* 21 (1975).

Maynard, John. *Russia in Flux.* New York: Macmillan, 1948.

Maximov, Vladimir (ed.). *Kontinent 1: The Alternative Voice of Russia and Eastern Europe.* London: André Deutsch, 1976.

McAdams, James. 'New Deal for Eastern Europe.' *The Nation,* 13 June 1987.

McAuley, Mary. 'In Search of Nationalism in the USSR.' Paper presented to the National Association of Soviet and East European Studies, Cambridge, March 1982.

—. *Politics and the Soviet Union.* Harmondsworth: Penguin Books, 1977.

—. *Soviet Politics: 1917-1991.* New York: Oxford University Press, 1992.

McCagg, William. *Stalin Embattled.* Detroit: Wayne State University Press, 1978.

McClure, Timothy. 'The Politics of Soviet Culture 1964-1967.' *Problems of Communism* 16 (1967).

McCormick, Anne O'Hare. *The Hammer and the Scythe: Russia Enters the Second Decade.* New York: Knopf, 1929.

McKinnon, R. *The Order of Financial Liberalisation: Financial Control in the Transition to a Market Economy.* Baltimore: Johns Hopkins University Press, 1991.

Medvedev, Roy. 'What Lies Ahead for Us?' *New Left Review* nos. 87-8, 1974.

Meissner, Boris. 'Whither Russia? Totalitarian Rule and Social Change.' *Problems of Communism* 15 (1966).

Merton, R.K. *Sociology Today.* New York: Free Press, 1959.

Meyer, Alfred G. 'The Functions of Ideology in the Soviet Political System.' *Soviet Studies* 15 (1966).

—. *Leninism.* Cambridge, MA: Harvard University Press, 1957.

—. *Marxism: The Unity of Theory and Practice.* Cambridge, MA: Harvard University Press, 1953.

—. *The Soviet Political System: An Interpretation.* New York: Random House, 1965.

Mihajilov, Mihajio. *Underground Notes.* London: Routledge & Kegan Paul, 1977.

Millar, James R. *The ABCs of Soviet Socialism.* New York: Cambridge University Press, 1982.

—. 'The Little Deal: Brezhnev's Contribution to Acquisitive Socialism.' *Slavic Review* 44 (1985).

—. (ed.). *Politics, Work and Daily Life in the Soviet Union.* New York: Cambridge University Press, 1987.

—. 'Rethinking Soviet Economic Studies.' Ford Foundation Workshop Series. 'Rethinking Soviet Studies,' Kennan Institute, Washington, DC, 23 October 1992.

Millar, James R., and Sharon Wolchick (eds). *The Social Legacy of Communism.* Cambridge: Cambridge University Press, 1994.

Miller, Jack. *Life in Russia Today*. London: Batsford, 1969.

Mills, C. Wright. *The Causes of World War Three*. Armonk, NY: M.E. Sharpe, 1958.

—. *The Power Elite*. London: Oxford University Press, 1956.

Misiunas, Romuald J., and Rein Taagepera. *The Baltic States: Years of Dependence, 1940–1980*. Berkeley: University of California Press, 1983.

Moore, Barrington Jr. *Political Power and Social Theory*. New York: Harper & Row, 1965.

—. 'Some Readjustments in Communist Theory.' *Journal of Ideas* 6 (1945).

—. *Soviet Politics: The Dilemma of Power*. Cambridge, MA: Harvard University Press, 1950.

—. *Terror and Progress: USSR*. Cambridge, MA: Harvard University Press, 1987.

Morgenthau, Hans J. 'Alternatives for Change.' *Problems of Communism* 15 (1966).

Morris, Aldon D., and Carol McClurg Mueller (eds). *Frontiers in Social Movement Theory*. New Haven: Yale University Press, 1992.

Mosca, Gaetano. *The Ruling Class*. New York: McGraw-Hill, 1939.

Motyl, Alexander. *Sovietology, Rationality, Nationality: Coming to Grips with Nationalism in the USSR*. New York: Columbia University Press, 1990.

—. *Thinking Theoretically about Soviet Nationalities*. New York: Columbia University Press, 1992.

—. *Will the Non-Russians Rebel?* Ithaca, NY: Cornell University Press, 1987.

Murray, John. *The Russian Press from Brezhnev to Yeltsin*. Aldershot: Edward Elgar, 1994.

Mydral, Alva *et al. Dynamics of European Nuclear Disarmament*. Nottingham: Spokesman Books, 1981.

Nahaylo, Bohdan, and Victor Swoboda. *Soviet Disunion: A History of the Nationalities Problem in the USSR*. New York: The Free Press, 1990.

Naim, Moises. 'Editor's Note.' *Foreign Policy* 110 (1998).

Nesterov, F. *Sviaz' Vremen*, 2nd ed. Moscow: Molodaia Gvardia, 1984.

Neumann, Sigmund. *Permanent Revolution: Totalitarianism in the Age of Civil War*, 2nd ed. New York: Frederick A. Praeger, 1965.

The New World Order: An Analysis and Document Collection. London: United States Information Service, July 1991.

Nossiter, T. (ed.). *Imagination and Precision in the Social Sciences*. London: Faber, 1972.

Nove, Alec. *An Economic History of the USSR*. Harmondsworth: Penguin, 1972.

—. *The Economics of Feasible Socialism*. London: Unwin Hyman, 1983.

—. *The Economics of Feasible Socialism Revisited*. London: Harper Collins, 1991.

—. *Glasnost in Action: Cultural Renaissance in Russia*. London & Boston: Unwin Hyman, 1989.

—. 'Is There a Ruling Class in the USSR?' *Soviet Studies* 27 (1975).

—. *Political Economy and Soviet Socialism*. London: Allen & Unwin, 1979.

—. *The Soviet Economic System*. London: Allen & Unwin, 1986.

—. *The Soviet Economy: An Introduction*. London: Allen & Unwin, 1962.

—. *Stalinism and After*. London: Allen & Unwin, 1975.

—. *Was Stalin Really Necessary? Some Problems of Political Economy*. London: Allen & Unwin, 1964.

Nove, Alec, and I. Thatcher (eds). *Market Socialism*. London: Blackwell, 1995.

O'Connell, Charles. 'Social Structure and Science: Soviet Studies at Harvard.' PhD dissertation. UCLA: Los Angeles, 1990.

Odom, William E. 'Soviet Politics and After.' *World Politics* 45 (1992).

Offe, Claus. 'Capitalism by Democratic Design? Democratic Theory Facing the Triple Transition in East Central Europe.' *Social Research* 58 (1991).

Olcott, Martha Brill. *The Kazakhs*. Stanford: Hoover Institution Press, 1987.

'The Once and Future C.I.A.' Editorial. *New York Times*, 18 October 1990.

Orwell, George. *1984*. New York: New American Library, 1961.

Pareto, Vilfredo. *Systemes Socialistes*, 2nd ed. Paris, 1926.

Parkin, Frank. 'System Contradiction and Political Transformation.' *European Journal of Sociology* 13 (1972).

Parry, Albert. *The New Class Divided: Science and Technology Versus Communism*. London: Macmillan Press, 1966.

Parsons, Talcott. 'Evolutionary Universals.' *American Sociological Review* 39 (1964).

—. *Societies: Evolutionary and Comparative Perspectives*. Englewood Cliffs, NJ: Prentice Hall, 1966.

—. *The System of Modern Societies*. Englewood Cliffs, NJ: Prentice Hall, 1971.

Pipes, Richard. 'Can the Soviet Union Reform?' *Foreign Affairs* 63 (1984).

—. *The Formation of the Soviet Union*. Cambridge, MA: Harvard University Press, 1997.

—. *Russia under the Bolshevik Regime*. New York: Knopf, 1990.

—. *The Russian Revolution*. New York: Knopf, 1990.

—. 'The Soviet Impact on Central Asia.' *Problems of Communism* 6 (1957).

—. *Survival Is Not Enough: Soviet Realities and Russia's Future*. New York: Simon and Schuster, 1984.

Podhoretz, N. *Breaking Ranks: A Political Memoir*. New York: Harper and Row, 1979.

Polan, A.J. *Lenin and the End of Politics*. London: Methuen, 1984.

Polanyi, Karl. *The Great Transformations: The Political and Economic Origins of Our Time*. London: Gollancz, 1945.

Popper, Karl. *The Open Society and Its Enemies*, 4th ed. Princeton: Princeton University Press, 1963.

Possony, Stefan. *A Century of Conflict: Communist Techniques of World Revolution*. Chicago: Regnery, 1953.

Pozdnyakov, Elgiz. 'The Problems of Returning the Soviet Union to European Civilization.' *Paradigms: The Kent Journal of International Relations* 5 (1991).

Pye, Lucian. 'Political Science and the Crisis of Authoritarianism.' *American Political Science Review* 84 (1990).

Rakovski, Marc. *Towards an East European Marxism*. London: Alison Busby, 1978.

Read, Conyers. 'The Social Responsibilities of the Historian.' *American Historical Review* January 1950.

Realism, Strength, Negotiation: Key Foreign Policy Statements of the Reagan Administration. Washington, DC: United States Department of State, 1984.

Rabinowitch, Alexander. *The Bolsheviks Come to Power: The Revolution of 1917 in Petrodgrad*. New York: W.W. Norton, 1976.

Reiss Jr, A.J. (ed.). *On Cities and Social Life*. Chicago: University of Chicago Press, 1964.

Remington, Thomas F. 'Common Knowledge: Soviet Political Studies and the Problem of System Stability.' Paper delivered at Kennan Institute, October 1992.

Remnick, David. 'Getting Russia Right.' *New York Review of Books,* September 1994.

Riasanovsky, Nicholas. *A History of Russia*. Oxford: Oxford University Press, 1993.

Rigby, T.H. *The Changing Soviet System: Mono-Organizational Socialism from Its Origins to Gorbachev's Restructuring*. Aldershot: Edward Elgar, 1990.

—. 'Traditional, Market and Organisational Societies in the USSR.' *World Politics* 16 (1964).

Rizzi, Bruno. *La Bureaucratisation du monde*. Paris: Edite pour l'auteur en depot aux messageries Hachette, 1939.

Rocher, G. *Talcott Parsons and American Sociology*. London: Nelson, 1974.

Rose, Richard, and Christian Haerpfer. *New Russia Barometer III: The Results*. Glasgow: Centre for the Study of Public Policy, University of Strathclyde, 1994.

Ross, Cameron. *Local Government in the Soviet Union: Problems of Implementation and Control*. London: Croom Helm, 1987.

Ross, Edward. *Russia in Upheaval*. New York: The Century Co., 1918.

Rostow, Walt Whitman. *The Dynamics of Soviet Society*. Cambridge, MA: MIT Press, 1967.

Rothstein, Andrew. *Soviet Foreign Policy During the Patriotic War: Documents and Materials*. London: Hutchison, 1946.

—. *Wreckers on Trial: A Record of the Industrial Party Trial Held in Moscow Nov.–Dec. 1930*. London: Modern Books, 1931.

Rowen, Henry S., and Charles Wolf (eds). *The Future of the Soviet Empire*. New York: St. Martin's, 1987.

Rush, Myron. *Political Succession in the USSR*. New York: Columbia University Press, 1965.

Rustow, Dankwart A. 'Transitions to Democracy: Toward a Dynamic Model.' *Comparative Politics* 2 (1970).

Rutland, Peter. 'Labour Movements and Unrest 1989–91.' *Soviet Economy*, Winter 1990.

—. 'Nationalism and the Soviet State: A Functionalist Account.' Paper presented to the Annual Conference of the National Association of Soviet and East European Studies, Cambridge, March 1982.

—. 'Sovietology: From Stagnation to Perestroika? A Decade of Doctoral Research in Soviet Politics.' Kennan Institute, Occasional Paper no 241. October 1990.

Ryavec, Karl W. (ed.). *Soviet Society and the Communist Party*. Amherst: University of Massachusetts Press, 1978.

Rybczynski, T. 'The Sequencing of Reform.' *Oxford Review of Economic Policy* 7 (1991).

Rywkin, Michael. *Moscow's Muslim Challenge*. Armonk, NY: M.E. Sharpe, 1990.

Sachs, Jeffrey. *Understanding 'Shock Therapy'*. London: The Social Market Foundation, 1994.

Sarnoff, David. *Looking Ahead: The Papers of David Sarnoff*. New York: McGraw-Hill, 1968.

Schapiro, Leonard. *The Communist Party of the Soviet Union*. New York: Random House, 1960.

—. (ed.). *Political Opposition in One Party States*. London: Macmillan, 1972.

—. *Totalitarianism*. London: Macmillan, 1972.

Schlesinger, Arthur. 'Has Democracy a Future?' *Foreign Affairs* (1997).

—. 'A Mudding Evolution.' *Problems of Communism* 15 (1966).

Schmitter, Philippe C., and Terry Lynn Karl. 'The Conceptual Travels of Transitologists and Consolidologists: How Far to the East Should They Attempt to Go?' *Slavic Review* 53 (1994).

Schneider, David. *American Kinship: A Cultural Account.* Chicago: University of Chicago Press, 1968.

Schopflin, G. 'The End of Communism in Eastern Europe.' *International Affairs* 66 (1990).

Schumann, Frederick. *Russia Since 1917: Four Decades of Soviet Politics.* New York: Knopf, 1957.

Schutz, Alfred. 'Concepts and Theory Formation in the Social Science.' *Journal of Philosophy* 51 (1954).

—. 'Some Leading Concepts in Phenomenology.' *Social Research* 12 (1945).

Schwartz, Joel J., and William R. Keech. 'Group Influence and the Policy Process in the Soviet Union.' *American Political Science Review* 62 (1968).

Scott, Derek J.R. *Russian Political Institutions,* 4th ed. London: Allen & Unwin, 1969.

Sedov, L.A. 'Mezhdu putchem i vyborami.' *Ekonomicheskie i sotsial'nye peremeny: monitoring obshchestvennogo mneniya* 1 (1994).

Serge, Victor. *Destiny of a Revolution.* London: Jarrolds, 1937.

Seton-Watson, Hugh. 'The Soviet Ruling Class.' *Problems of Communism* 5 (1956).

—. 'Totalitarianism Reconsidered.' *Problems of Communism* 16 (1967).

Shachtman, Max. *The Bureaucratic Revolution.* New York: Donald Press, 1962.

Shaikh, Anwar. *Crisis Theories in Economic Thought.* Thames Papers in Political Economy, Thames Polytechnic, 1977.

Sharlet, Robert S. 'Concept Formation in Political Science and Communist Studies: Conceptualizing Political Participation.' *Canadian Slavic Studies* 1 (1967).

Shea, Christopher. 'New Faces and New Methodologies Invigorate Russian Studies.' *Chronicle of Higher Education,* 20 February 1998.

Shlapentokh, Alexander. 'The American Vision of the World: The Tendency to Find Nice Things.' *NewsNet: The Newsletter of the AAASS* 33 (1993).

—. *Soviet Ideologies in the Period of Glasnost.* New York: Prager, 1988.

—. *Soviet Intellectuals and Political Power.* Princeton: Princeton University Press, 1990.

—. *Soviet Public Opinion and Ideology: Pragmatism in Interaction.* New York: Praeger, 1986.

Shtromas, Alexander, and Morton A. Kaplan (eds). *The Soviet Union and the Challenge of the Future.* New York: Paragon House Publishers, 1987.

Shuligin, Vasili. *Gody: Dni 1920.* Moscow: Novosti, 1990.

—. *Tri Stolitisy.* Moscow: Sovremennik, 1991.

Silver, Brian. 'Social Mobilization and the Russification of Soviet Nationalities.' *American Political Science Review* 68 (1974).

Simis, Konstantin. *Secrets of a Corrupt Society.* London: Dent, 1982.

Simmonds, George W. (ed.). *Nationalism in the USSR and Eastern Europe in the Era of Brezhnev and Kosygin.* Detroit: University of Detroit, 1977.

Skilling, H. Gordon. 'Interest Groups and Communist Politics.' *World Politics* 18 (1966).

Skilling, H. Gordon, and Franklyn Griffiths (eds). *Interest Groups in Soviet Politics.* Princeton: Princeton University Press, 1971.

Skocpol, Theda. *States and Social Revolutions: A Comparative Study of France, Russia, and China.* Cambridge: Cambridge University Press, 1979.

Solomon, Susan G. *Beyond Sovietology: Essays in Politics and History.* Armonk, NY: M.E. Sharpe, 1993.

—. (ed.). *Pluralism in the Soviet Union.* New York: Macmillan, 1983.

Solzhenitsyn, Alexander. *The Gulag Archipelago.* London: Collins and Harvill, 1974.
—. *Lenin in Zurich.* New York: Farrar Strauss and Giroux, 1976.
—. *Letters to Soviet Leaders.* London: Index on Censorship, 1974.
—. *Under the Rubble.* London: Fontana, 1975.
Sorokin, Pitrim. *The Basic Trends of Our Times.* New Haven: Yale University Press, 1964.
—. *Russia and the West.* New York: Dutton, 1944.
Stalin, Joseph. *Vorposy Leninisma.* Moscow: Politizdat, 1952.
Stavrakis, Peter J. et al. *Beyond the Monolith: The Emergence of Regionalism in Post-Soviet Russia.* Baltimore: John Hopkins University Press, 1997.
Steffens, Lincoln. *The Letters of Lincoln Steffens.* New York: Harcourt Brace, 1938.
Stewart, Philip D. *Political Power in the Soviet Union: A Study of Decision-Making in Stalingrad.* New York: Bobbs-Merrill, 1968.
Strakhovsky, Leonid. *American Opinion about Russia: 1917–1920.* Toronto: University of Toronto Press, 1961.
Strausz-Hupe, Robert. 'Some Historical Parallels.' *Problems of Communism* 15 (1966).
Stubbs, R., and G.R.D. Underhill (eds). *Political Economy and the Changing Global Order.* London: Macmillan, 1994.
Suny, Ronald Grigor (ed.). *Transcaucasia: Nationalism and Social Change: Essays in the History of Armenia, Azerbaijhan, and Georgia.* Ann Arbor: Michigan Slavic Publications, 1983.
Sweezy, Paul, and Leo Huberman. 'The Split in the Socialist World.' *Monthly Review* 15 (1963).
Szakolczai, Arpad. 'Types of Mayors, Types of Subjectivity.' Florence: EUI Working Papers SPS No. 93/5, 1993.
Szamuely, Tibor. *The Russian Tradition.* London: Fontana, 1974.
Taracousio, T. *War and Peace in Soviet Diplomacy.* New York: Macmillan, 1940.
Tarrow, Sidney. *Power in Movement: Social Movements, Collective Action and Politics.* Cambridge: Cambridge University Press, 1994.
Tatu, Michael. 'The Beginning of the End?' *Problems of Communism* 15 (1966): 45.
Taubman, William. *Governing Soviet Cities: Bureaucratic Politics and Urban Development in the USSR.* New York: Praeger, 1973.
Thompson, Terry L. *Soviet Ideology from Khrushchev to Gorbachev: Developed Socialism under Brezhnev.* Denver: Westview Press, 1988.
Thurston, Robert W. *Liberal City, Conservative State.* Oxford: Oxford University Press, 1987.
Ticktin, Hillel. 'Towards a Political Economy of the USSR.' *Critique* 1 (1973).
—. 'The Contradictions of Soviet Society and Professor Bettelheim.' *Critique* 6 (1976).
—. 'The USSR: The Beginning of the End.' *Critique* 7 (1976).
—. 'Is Market-Socialism Possible or Necessary?' *Critique* 14 (1981).
—. 'Andropov: Disintegration and Discipline.' *Critique* 16 (1984).
—. *Origins of the Crisis in USSR: Essays on the Political Economy of a Disintegrating System.* Armonk, NY: Myron Sharpe, 1992.
Timasheff, Nicholas. *The Great Retreat.* New York: Dutton, 1946.
Tindbergan, J. 'Do Communist and Free Economies Show a Convergence Pattern?' *Soviet Studies* 12 (1961).
Tocqueville, Alexis De. *Democracy in America.* New York: Random House, 1981.
Treml, Vladimir. 'Debate: Why Did the Soviet Economic System Collapse?: Two Schools of Thought.' *RFE/RL Research Report* 2 (1993).

Trotsky, Leon. *The Class Nature of the Soviet State*. London: New Park Publications, 1968.
—. *The Revolution Betrayed: What Is the Soviet Union and Where Is It Going?* Garden City: Doubleday, Doran & Co., 1937.
—. *The Revolution Betrayed: What Is the Soviet Union and Where Is It Going?* New York: Pioneer Publishers, 1957.
Truscott, Peter. *Russia First: Breaking with the West*. London: I.B. Tauris, 1997.
Tsebelis, George. *Nested Games: Rational Choice in Comparative Politics*. Berkeley: University of California Press, 1990.
Tucker, Robert. 'Communism and Russia.' *Foreign Affairs* (1980).
—. 'Communist Revolutions, National Cultures, and Divided Nations.' *Studies in Comparative Communism* 3 (1961).
—. 'Czars and Commiczars.' *New Republic*, 21 January 1991.
—. 'Giving up the Ghost.' *New Republic*, 17 October 1988.
—. 'The Question of Totalitarianism.' *Slavic Review* 20 (1961).
—. 'Sovietology and Russian History.' *Post-Soviet Affairs* 8 (1992).
—. 'The Stalin Period as an Historical Problem.' *Russian Review* 46 (1987).
—. *Stalinism: Essays in Historical Interpretation*. New York: Norton, 1977.
—. 'Swollen State, Spent Society: Stalin's Legacy to Brezhnev's Russia.' *Foreign Affairs* 60 (1982).
Ulam, Adam. *The Bolsheviks*. New York: Macmillan, 1968.
—. *Expansion and Coexistence: Soviet Foreign Policy 1917–73*. Fort Worth: Holt, Rinehart & Winston, Inc., 1974.
—. *The New Face of Soviet Totalitarianism*. Cambridge, MA: MIT Press, 1963.
United States Congress, Joint Economic Committee. *Soviet Economic Prospects for the Seventies*. Washington, DC: Government Printing Office, 1973.
—. *The Soviet Economy in a New Perspective*. Washington, DC: Government Printing Office, 1976.
—. *The Soviet Economy in a Time of Change*. Washington, DC: Government Printing Office, 1979.
—. *The Soviet Economy in the 1980s: Problems and Prospects*. Washington, DC: Government Printing Office, 1982.
Urban, George (ed.). *Can the Soviet System Survive Reform?* New York: Pinter, 1989.
Von Hayek, F.A. (ed.). *Collectivist Economic Planning*. London: Routledge, 1935.
—. *The Road to Serfdom*. Chicago: University of Chicago Press, 1944.
Von Mises, Ludwig. *Socialism: An Economic and Sociological Analysis*. New Haven: Yale University Press, 1951.
Von Wright, George H. *Explanation and Understanding*. Ithaca, NY: Cornell University Press, 1971.
Webb, Sidney, and Beatrice Webb. *Soviet Communism: A New Civilization*. London: Longmans, Green, 1937.
Welch, Stephen. *The Concept of Political Culture*. London: Macmillan, 1993.
—. 'Issues in the Study of Political Culture: The Example of Communist Party States.' *British Journal of Political Science* 17 (1987).
Wells, H.G. *Interviews with J.V. Stalin*. Sydney: Current Book Distributors, 1950.
Werth, Alexander. *Moscow 1941*. London: Hamish Hamilton, 1942.
White, Stephen. *After Gorbachev*. Cambridge: Cambridge University Press, 1993.
—. 'Communist Systems and the "Iron Law of Pluralism."' *British Journal of Political Science* 8 (1978).

—. 'Contradiction and Change in State Socialism.' *Soviet Studies* 26 (1974).

—. *Gorbachev in Power*. Cambridge: Cambridge University Press, 1990.

—. *Political Culture and Soviet Politics*. London: Macmillan, 1979.

Wieczynski, Joseph L. *The Gorbachev Reader*. Salt Lake City: Charles Schlacks Publisher, 1993.

Wittfogel, Karl. *Oriental Despotism*. New Haven: Yale University Press, 1963.

Williamson, J. *The Eastern Transition to a Market Economy*. Center for Economic Performance, Occasional Paper No. 2, March 1992.

Willkie, Wendell. *One World*. New York: Simon and Schuster, 1943.

Wines, Michael. 'C.I.A. Accused of Overestimating Soviet Economy.' *New York Times*, 23 July 1990.

Wolfe, Bertram D. *Communist Totalitarianism*. Boston: Beacon Press, 1956.

—. 'The Durability of Soviet Despotism.' *Commentary* 24 (1957).

Wyman, Matthew. 'Russian Political Culture: Evidence from Public Opinion Surveys.' *Journal of Communist Studies* 10 (1994).

Yanov. A. *The Russian New Right: Right Wing Ideologies in the Contemporary USSR*. Berkeley: Institute of International Studies, 1978.

Yasmann, Victor. 'Petr Romanov Named Leader of Irreconcilable Opposition.' *RFE/RL Daily Report*, 26 October 1994.

—. 'Sergei Mavrodi Is Elected to the Duma.' *RFE/RL Daily Report* 2 Nov. 1994.

Zamyatin, Eugene. *We*. New York: Dutton & Co., 1924.

Zaslavskaya, Tatiana. 'The Novosibirsk Report.' *Survey* 28 (1984).

Zaslavsky, Victor. *The Neo-Stalinist State*. Brighton: Harvester, 1982.

Zinoviev, Alexander. *Homo Soviecticus*. Paris: L'Age d'Homme, 1982.

—. 'Ne vse my dissidenty. O sotsial'noi oppositssii v Sovietskom obshschestve.' *Kontinent* 44 (1985).

—. *The Reality of Communism*. London: Paladin Books, 1984.

—. *Svetloie Budushheie*. Lausanne: L'Age d'Homme, 1978.

—. *Ziauscheie Vysoty*. Lausanne: L'Age d'Homme, 1976.

Index